LINDLEY J. STILES
Dean of the School of Education, University of Wisconsin
ADVISORY EDITOR TO DODD, MEAD & COMPANY

FORMATIVE IDEAS IN
AMERICAN EDUCATION:
From the Colonial Period
to the Present

FORMATIVE IDEAS IN AMERICAN EDUCATION

FROM THE COLONIAL PERIOD TO THE PRESENT

V. T. THAYER

DODD, MEAD & COMPANY, INC.
NEW YORK   TORONTO   1970

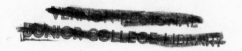

Sixth Printing

Copyright © 1965 by Dodd, Mead & Company, Inc.

Library of Congress catalog card number: 65-12348

Printed in the United States of America

EDITOR'S INTRODUCTION

TO understand American education is to know the ideas that shape its form and substance. From colonial times to the present schools have mirrored the changes, the conflicts, the torments, as well as the hopes and aspirations, of a pioneer people in search of a new way of life. Out of established old-world orthodoxies, rival theories about nature, man, and social institutions have played upon conceptions about the role and character of the educational enterprise. Many contemporary concepts and conflicts, as this book so skillfully documents, have grown from roots as old or older than our nation itself. Other ideas that have shaped American education are young and vibrant, indigenous to local, sectional, and national conditions as well as to social, economic, and political forces. One word, "plurality," perhaps best describes the character of American education. But out of diversity has come a unique type of unity—the concept of public education.

That all people should be educated is a revolutionary idea, but one that is embracing practically all the world today. It rests on the premise, so ably championed by Horace Mann and others, that to learn is a natural right of mankind. As matured and expanded in the United States over three centuries, this right to know, to think, to speak, to act on convictions has become the quest of free men everywhere. Freedom is its banner, and education is its guardian strength.

The extension of national boundary lines, the expansion of commerce and industry, the advent of an age of science and technology, the objective examination of the nature of man, and the refinement of democratic, social, economic, and political philosophy—all found reflection in rapidly expanding programs of education in American communities. The conflicts such forces created produced an array of distinguished spokesmen whose ideas still mark present-day educational debates—although modern-day advocates are often uninformed about the origins of the arguments. Significantly it is ideas more so than people that have shaped American education. Thus it is ideas that must be examined if education is to be understood.

The responsiveness of American public education to the ideas that gave it birth and sustained its expansion has marked a new conception of interdependence between school and society. Represented is an intertwining reciprocal relationship best expressed by the words, "of and for," with each influenced by the other. In a heterogeneous nation, however, such a partnership is subject to the cross-currents inherent in the absence of an orthodoxy—in religion, social customs, economic habits, political partnership, and cultural tastes. As a result, controversy has characterized American public education from its inception and promises to mark its further progress. But controversy can be constructive only if it is informed.

For the professional educator, and the informed citizen as well, *Formative Ideas in American Education* is a valuable and authentic source of information. It brings together in one concise, readable volume the historical development of the significant ideas that are pertinent to understanding public education today and its promise and perils of tomorrow. It deals with the real philosophies of education, described in clear, concise concepts that form the threads of educational policy, programs, and practices. Significantly, it makes real the relationships that exist between ideas and commitments, between goals and procedures, and between values and appraisals in public education.

Dr. V. T. Thayer, author of this book, is a scholar of rare talent, scholarship, and wisdom. Recognized as one of America's most distinguished educational philosophers, he combines an unusual background of practical teaching and administration in both public and private schools and universities. Dr. Thayer possesses unique ability to identify the ideas that shape American Education. His classic analysis, *The Passing of the Recitation*, forecast a revolution in teaching practice that has moved through elementary and secondary schools and is now challenging higher education. *The Role of the School in American Society* (Dodd, Mead & Co.), which is in reality a companion volume to the present one, has become a standard textbook for prospective teachers in hundreds of colleges and universities. *Formative Ideas in American Education* is a fresh and dynamic approach to the study of educational philosophy. In this work, Dr.

Thayer skillfully links theory to practice, educational movements to social events, and advocated directions to value judgments. His objective is to help the educators and citizens of the United States to know better their most precious heritage—public education.

LINDLEY J. STILES

PREFACE

EACH conscious moment in the ongoing life of an individual is a unique combination of past experience and intimations of an impending future. Much the same may be said of an institution that retains its vitality in an ever changing society. Consequently, for those who would influence an institution such as the American school to function in a manner relevant to tomorrow as well as today, two things are essential: an analysis of factors of change in contemporary society and the history of that institution. The needed history is not one with fullness of detail, as the historian would write it; it is the history of ideas—of conceptions of nature, of man, and of the world in which man lives that have come into being under conditions, in this instance uniquely American, and which, through the school, have exercised a formative influence upon the American way of life.

It is hoped that this book may serve as an introduction to this history of ideas. Its major purpose is to direct attention to the origin and development of ideas in American education (chiefly elementary and secondary) from the early seventeenth century to the present. Not all of these ideas and influences have originated in American soil, but all reflect cultural factors which have been distinctively American and, in turn, have helped to shape the American mind.

Part I is concerned with developments in seventeenth- and eighteenth-century America. This was a period in which theological and philosophical presuppositions were dominant in education. But it was also a period in which an open country with its seemingly inexhaustible natural resources contributed to the transformation of a closed society into one more nearly open, with revolutionary effects upon conceptions of the Deity, of nature, and of man and society—conceptions that have not ceased to give direction to men's lives. The section concludes with a chapter on John Locke, whose influence upon the minds of educators until well into the nineteenth century was as potent as was his influence upon the political philosophy of the Founding Fathers of the Republic.

Part II deals with the nineteenth century and the reciprocal influence of revolutionary changes in the economic, social, and political development of the United States and the "knowledge explosion" of that century, particularly the ramifying effects of the Darwinian conception of evolution upon philosophy, religion, science, and the formative ideas inherited from the eighteenth century. The nineteenth century witnessed the emergence and evolution of the American public school from an essentially Protestant sectarian institution into one more genuinely public. Parallel with this development and as a dominating influence in education, theology yielded to philosophy, and philosophy gave birth to the sciences concerned with nature, man, and society which sought to become free of both theological and philosophical presuppositions.

Finally, in Part III are described the major trends in education since the turn of the twentieth century, with emphasis again upon the interplay between cultural factors and educational practice. The section concludes with an analysis of conditions today which are bringing about an agonizing reappraisal of public education.

The author hopes that this survey will assist not only the student in the history and philosophy of American education but the school administrator, the curriculum specialist, and the classroom teacher (not to exclude the interested layman) who wish to relate their special fields to those of others and to envisage the school as a functioning whole.

Grateful acknowledgment is given to the many publishers who have granted permission to quote from publications cited in the text.

V. T. THAYER

CONTENTS

PART I

FORMATIVE IDEAS
IN AMERICAN EDUCATION
TAKE SHAPE

CHAPTER 1

SEVENTEENTH-CENTURY NEW ENGLAND'S CONTRIBUTIONS TO EDUCATION

TEXTBOOKS in the history and philosophy of education tend to give but meager attention to the contributions of the colonial period to American education. Several considerations seemingly justify this neglect. One was the tardy influence of the wilderness upon the institutions—religious, educational, and civil—which the colonists brought with them. Emphasis was given rather to perpetuation of those institutions than to adaptation to novel conditions. As John Norton of the Massachusetts Bay Colony put it, "... we have only changed our Climate, not our minds."

CONSERVATIVE INFLUENCES IN EARLY NEW ENGLAND

Take New England, for example, which, of all the early settlements, manifested the keenest concern for education, as evidenced by acts of the General Court in 1642 and 1647. Suggestive as this legislation was for the later assumption of public responsibility for education, the first of these two acts was primarily an apprenticeship law, similar in design to English law and intended to remedy "the great neglect in many parents and masters in training up their children in learning and labor and other employments which may be profitable to the commonwealth." As Bernard Bailyn has pointed out,[1] a major purpose was to shore up "the weak-

---

[1] See Bernard Bailyn, *Education in the Forming of American Society* (Chapel Hill, N.C.: University of North Carolina Press, 1960), pp. 15-49, for a discussion of changes in the educational role of the family in the colonial period.

ening structure of family discipline" and to offset the disintegrating influences that early began to manifest themselves under the novel conditions of living in a new country—influences that were destined to revolutionize traditional relations between members of the family and to transfer many of its functions to other institutions. Similarly, the Act of 1647 required (1) that towns of fifty householders appoint a master "to teach all children as shall resort to him to write and read," and (2) that towns of one hundred householders set up a grammar school to prepare youth for the university. Thus it reflected more the determination of colonial officials to insure orthodoxy in religion than the stirrings of a democratic conscience.

A second reason for an abbreviated discussion of education in seventeenth-century America was the limited character of instruction (as judged by later standards) on all levels of education—elementary, secondary, and higher. Elementary instruction, for example, attempted no more than to develop "an ability to read and to understand the principles of religion and the capital laws of the country." And the grammar schools did well if they imparted to their students the ability to read, write, and speak Latin plus the rudiments of Greek, in preparation for the predominantly classical and literary education in college.[2]

Finally, the forms of government that prevailed in the early colonial period were alien to later democratic developments. Particularly was this true of Massachusetts, despite Cotton Mather's assertion that God had chosen the Puritans to establish a Holy Commonwealth "upon the designs of a glorious transformation." Viewed from the perspective of today, it would seem that the fruits of their labors in government are more to be avoided than imitated.

Not only was the ideal of government a theocracy, in which the interests of church and state were intermingled, but an oligarchy within the theocracy—an oligarchy composed of the "visible saints," or the "elect," who alone might select minister and magistrate! As John Cotton insisted, in justifying this union of spiritual and temporal power, "it is better that the commonwealth be fashioned to the setting forth of God's

[2] This description of grammar school and college omits the intimate connection between education in school and college and dominant cultural trends of the period, trends less alien to subsequent developments in American life than a first glance at the curriculum suggests. We shall return to this point later in the chapter.

house, which is his church, than to accommodate the church frame to the civil state."

To those who objected to the exclusion of the people from participation in decisions that intimately affected their lives, Cotton was able to quote chapter and verse from the Bible in support of the declaration: "Democracy I do not conceyve that ever God did ordeyne as a fit government either for church or commonwealth. If the people be governors, who shall be governed?"

It is frequently asserted that the function of the minister in "God's house" was to interpret; of the magistrate, to execute; of other people, to obey the laws. This was more accurate in theory than in practice. John Winthrop, for example, as the first magistrate of Massachusetts Bay Colony, insisted that the selection of a magistrate by the visible saints constituted not only a covenant between the people and their elected representative but a contract between the latter and God as well. As Winthrop explained on one occasion when the freemen of Hingham attempted to impeach him for exceeding his authority by intervening in a disputed election of militia, "the covenant between you and us is the oath you have taken, which is to this purpose, that we shall govern you and judge your causes by the rules of God's laws and our own, according to our best skill."

The rules of God's laws were stated in the Bible, but who in the Holy Commonwealth was best qualified to interpret and apply them to specific situations? The answer was not the people in general or even the "elect," according to Winthrop. Rather were the magistrates "by their church covenant and by their oath, and by the dutye of their places to square all their proceedings by the rule of God's word, and for the advancement of the gospell and the whole public." That is to say, little was permitted those endowed with legislative authority, beyond the selection of leaders who were thereafter to interpret and administer the laws.

Nor is the common assumption accurate that devotion to the principles of religious liberty prompted the Puritan to abandon home and occupation in England and to establish communities in America of more generous pattern than those of the homeland. Liberty in the sense of a generous toleration of differences and the assured right of each individual to speak and to write as his conscience might dictate, or to accept conclusions responsibly as they emerge from the weighing, comparing, and contrasting of competing theories, was quite the opposite of the Massachusetts ideal. Rather was the New England Puritan obsessed by the conviction that God had entrusted him not only with the truth but with the responsibility as well of organizing and perpetuating a society exclusively in its image. Parrington's remarks about John Cotton ("The desire for liberty he regarded as the sinful promptings of the natural man, a denial of the righteous authority of God's chosen rulers") in no way applied to Cotton alone.[3]

In this respect the Puritan in America differed significantly from his English brother. Thus John Milton, writing in his *Second Defense of the English People* (1654), could urge Oliver Cromwell in the latter's hour of victory:

> ... it is my earnest wish that you would give permission to those who are inclined to freedom of inquiry, to publish what they have to communicate at their own peril, without the private inquisition of any magisterial censor: for nothing could contribute so much to the growth of truth; nor would all science be forever measured out to us in a bushel, and be bestowed at the pleasure of the half-learned.... Lastly, it is my fervent wish, that you should not be afraid to listen either to truth or falsehood, of whatever description that may be: but that you should listen the least of all to those, who never fancy that they themselves are free, unless they deprive others of their freedom; who labor at nothing with so much zeal and earnestness, as to enchain not the bodies only, but the consciences of their brethren; and to introduce into the church and state the worst of all tyrannies, the tyranny of their own misshapen customs and opinions. May you ever take part with those who think it just that not their own sect or faction alone, but all the citizens alike should have an equal right to be free.

In England Puritans of many sects—Presbyterians, Independents, Separatists, Levelers, Millenarians, to mention but a few—lived side by side, each determined to convince his rivals of the errors in their beliefs. Moreover, in England there was an awareness, on occasion, of the potential contributions of free expression to the emergence of final truth. For example, the author of an English pamphlet on liberty of conscience (1645) contended "... better many errors of some kind suffered than one useful truth be obstructed or destroyed."

[3] Vernon Louis Parrington, *Main Currents in American Thought*, Vol. I, *The Colonial Mind* (New York: Harcourt, Brace & Co., 1927), p. 31.

Contrast this attitude with that of Nathaniel Ward's *Simple Cobbler of Aggawam* (1647): "I dare take upon me, to be the Herauld of New England so farre, as to proclaim to the world, in the name of our Colony, that all Familists, Antinomians, Anabaptists, and other Enthusiasts, shall have free liberty to keep away from us, and such as will come to be gone as fast as they can, the sooner the better." Or consider the order of the General Court of Massachusetts in 1637 which prohibited anyone from settling within the colony without prior approval by the magistrates of his orthodoxy!

Rigid insistence upon orthodoxy necessarily influenced the character of education in New England, as, indeed, it did in all of the colonies. Modern emphasis upon the tentative nature of facts and principles was, of course, altogether unknown. Rather was it assumed that all essential facts and principles bearing upon the world of nature and of man, together with the logic and the methods of thinking relevant to the applications of truth, were long established. The task of the student, accordingly, was to master these facts and truths, together with the principles of "right reason" necessary to apply them correctly.

BUT THE OLD ORDER CHANGETH

Were these the sole contributions of Puritan experience to American life and education we might use seventeenth-century New England as an illustration of the narrowing and stunting influence of a pioneer environment upon intellectual life. Or we might use it to illustrate the manner in which a theory devised originally in England as one means of undermining the divine right of kings to rule arbitrarily evolved in America into an equally repressive theory of the divine right of the "saints" to dominate the lives of the unregenerate.

But this is only half the story. As the Puritans strove to preserve their ideas of the relations of God to man and, by implication, of man to man in the face of popular resentment to disenfranchisement, they encountered early opposition from equally devoted servants of the Lord—from the Pilgrims of Plymouth, Thomas Hooker of Hartford, the unfortunate Anne Hutchinson, and the irrepressible Roger Williams. Moreover, two significant economic factors—the system of freehold tenure of land, with its encouragement of rugged individualism, and the rise of a well-to-do merchant class tempted by secular interests—quickly generated formidable opposition to government by the "saints." To this should be added certain germs within Puritan theology itself that militated against government by an aristocracy, be it based on birth, or election, or education.

THE COVENANT GIVES SUPPORT TO THE PEOPLE

One Puritan conviction held that the state and its government derive from a covenant, or a contract, voluntarily entered into, between those who govern and the governed. This concept prompted English Puritans to repudiate the declaration of James I to the effect that kings are "the authors and makers of the Lawes, not the Lawes of the kings" and, ultimately, to bring Charles I to the bar of justice, not merely for specific violations of the compact of government but also for impiety in claiming the right to rule arbitrarily, a right that in their view God alone possessed. According to the Puritan, the social compact, or compact of government, derived logically from a prior Covenant of Grace between God and man. In this an all-powerful Deity absolved man of Adam's sin and assured him of certain rights, provided that man believed in Him and agreed to serve Him faithfully and honestly.

It is significant that the *Mayflower Compact* (1620) not only antedated by a decade the founding of the Massachusetts Bay Colony but was written by the Pilgrims who were more democratically disposed than their Boston neighbors. In contrast with the latter's concept of the magistrate as a steward of the Lord, endowed with divine authority to rule, the Pilgrims inclined toward the democratic theory of a priesthood of all believers. Faced, as they were, both with the practical necessity of establishing the rule of law over themselves and of controlling an unruly group of "strangers" who had shared ship's passage with them, they prudently resolved to draw up a compact that would bind all members of the new community to abide by laws "just and equal."

The theory of a priesthood of all believers implied more responsible participation of the average "saint" in the affairs of state and less autonomy on the part of minister and magistrate than the Cottons, the Winthrops, and the Wards were willing to concede. And it was the former theory that eventually established itself as the wave of the future. One of its most persuasive advocates was Thomas Hooker, of whom it was said, "after Mr. Hooker's coming over, it was observed that many of the freemen grew to be very jealous of their liberties." [4]

[4] Parrington, *op. cit.*, p. 57.

Dissatisfaction with the policies of the oligarchy led Hooker and his congregation in 1639 to move from Newton, Massachusetts, to Hartford, Connecticut. Prior to this action, however, in a sermon delivered before the General Court in 1638, Hooker had defined the relations between the people and their magistrates as follows: ". . . the foundation of authority is laid, firstly, in the free consent of the people," and, therefore, "the choice of public magistrates belongs unto the people by God's own allowance"; and "they who have the power to appoint officers and magistrates, it is in their power also, to set the bonds and limitations of the power and pace unto which they call them."

The privileges and responsibilities in government which Hooker strove to establish for all church members, Roger Williams boldly claimed for the unchurched as well. Cotton Mather was doubtless correct in describing Williams as the *"first rebel* against the divine church order established in the wilderness," since Williams clearly should be credited with the most devastating attack of the period upon theocratic government and its underlying assumptions. Grounding his arguments in the same undisputed authority (the Holy Bible) as his opposition, Williams deduced from this source not only the concept of government by the consent of the governed but the far more radical doctrines of freedom for the religious conscience and separation of church and state.

Williams agreed with his antagonist, John Cotton, that the state is divine in origin. He insisted, however, that the purpose of an ordinance of God, is "to conserve the Civill peace of the people, so farre as concerns their Bodies and Goods," but not their spiritual and intellectual activities. "Render, therefore, unto Caesar the things which are Caesar's, and unto God the things that are God's." Government, he contended, in harmony with Thomas Hobbes and John Locke, arises out of social necessity. Without it, "the World, otherwise, would be a sea, wherein Men, like Fishes, would hunt and devoure each other, and the greater devoure the lesse." The church, on the other hand, is best conceived as a corporation within the state, and endowed by the state with authority to govern itself.[5]

From this distinction in functions Williams concluded that the state cannot properly interfere with the religious conscience. Nor can it aid

[5] The quotations from Roger Williams in these paragraphs are taken from two tracts: *The Bloody Tenent of Persecution for the Cause of Conscience* (1644), and *The Bloody Tenent Yet More Bloody: By Mr. Cotton's Endeavor to Wash It White in the Blood of the Lamb* (1652).

or give preference to one religion as against another. It is the will of God that "permission" of conscience and worship "be granted to *all* men in all *Nations* and *Countries:* and they are onely to bee *fought* against with that *Sword* which is onely (in Soule matters) *able* to *conquer,* to wit, the *Sword* of *God's* Spirit, the *Word* of *God."*

Thus, in contrast with the theocrats, Roger Williams deduced the idea of government as a compact from the concept of an original state of nature, rather than from the Covenant of Grace. In contrast, also, to the autocratic notion that "the powers that be are ordained of God," as stated by the Apostle Paul, Williams argued: "the Sovereign power of all civill Authority is founded in the consent of the People that every Commonwealth hath radically and fundamentally." The people "have fundamentally in themselves and the Root of Power to set up what Government and Governor they shall agree upon." A people may thus "erect and establish what *forme* of *Government* seemes to them most meete for their *civill condition."* Moreover, "it is evident that such *Governments* as are by them erected and established, have no more *power,* nor for no longer time, than the *civill power* or people consenting and agreeing shall entrust them with." Finally, in striking contrast with the prevailing insistence upon orthodoxy and conformity in matters both spiritual and civil, Williams emphasized the utmost freedom of thought and expression as a condition of the health of church and state.

RIVAL CONCEPTIONS OF
GOVERNMENT ARE FORMULATED

It appears, then, that in seventeenth-century America, as well as in England, the concept of constitutional government as opposed to the divine right of kings (and magistrates!) to rule arbitrarily received clear formulation. Government by compact meant to the Puritan—conservative and radical alike—that obedience to law and to government, properly conceived, implies an act of free will on the part of "subjects," that since God alone is privileged to rule arbitrarily, a violation of the conditions of the compact on the part of those who govern on earth frees the governed from obligation to obey. "That magistrates were limited by compact," writes Perry Miller, "that government shall be by laws and not by men, that the covenant was annulled by any serious violation of the terms, and that people possessed a right to resist all such infringements—these principles were declared no less emphatically in Puritan theory than in the Declaration of Independence." [6]

Agreement upon these two basic principles, however, in no way precluded serious disagreement with respect to their application. To seventeenth-century New England, indeed, we are indebted for clear enunciation of two rival conceptions of the role of the people and their representatives in government—two conceptions which still divide political thinkers into what may roughly be termed republicans and democrats (spelled, however, with a small "r" and a small "d"). The first group favor government of the people, for the people, by the elite (variously interpreted as the wise, the good, the wealthy, the racially superior, or the educated). The second, less impressed by the ideal of efficiency than by the educational possibilities of participation in government by the many, strive to realize Lincoln's vision of a government of the people and for the people, but by the people.

A second item of disagreement within Puritan circles took the form of Presbyterianism versus Congregationalism. Congregationalists favored local autonomy in matters of church government and creed. Presbyterians, fearful of deviation from orthodoxy, saw in an assembly of representatives of ministers and carefully selected laymen one means of resisting change and the undermining of the Holy Commonwealth.

Presbyterianism succeeded for a period in enforcing conformity in matters both spiritual and civil. Under the theocracy, the General Court of Massachusetts was for all practical purposes a presbytery with authority to enforce conformity in belief and in action—with the result that deviation from orthodoxy contributed generously to the founding of new communities outside the jurisdiction of Massachusetts rather than to richness and variety of points of view within the colony!

Congregationalism, with its emphasis upon local self-government, was aided eventually by practical conditions of living. Difficulties of transportation and communication tend to isolate communities intellectually as well as geographically. The necessity of adapting old habits and ideas to novel conditions, together with the spirit of independence, stimulated and nourished by life on the frontier, of necessity tipped the scales in favor of local self-determination and opposition to remote control, not only in New England but in the Middle and Southern Colonies as well.

[6] Perry Miller, *The New England Mind: The Seventeenth Century* (Cambridge, Mass.: Harvard University Press, 1954), p. 409.

THE PRINCIPLE OF LOCAL AUTONOMY
IN EDUCATION IS ESTABLISHED

Particularly did this emphasis on self-determination hold true of schools and schooling. Congregationalism in New England, together with religious variation in the colonies farther south, led to the establishment of schools by individual communities well in advance of legislation on the part of central governments (by Boston, for example, in 1635, by Ipswich and Salem in 1641). Moreover, with the passage of legislation requiring communities to provide schools, responsibility for the enforcement of these laws and for the manner of their compliance was left quite largely to local authorities. Thus, early in our educational history, was established as principle the concept of local initiative and autonomy. Even when the state as final authority undertook to legislate in matters educational, the tendency was to require all localities to follow the example of pioneer communities.

THE MOVING SPIRIT IN EDUCATION IS PRACTICAL

Few statements are quoted more frequently than the following from the Preamble to the Act of the Massachusetts General Court in 1647 requiring towns to provide for the education of their young: "that learning may not be buried in the graves of our fathers in the Church and Commonwealth, the Lord assisting our endeavors." The purpose in repeating this once again is to emphasize the scholarly concerns of the first settlers of New England. Observe, however, that the learning so eagerly desired was not viewed as an end in itself. Rather was it valued as a means or an instrument for clarifying the ways of God to man and thus rendering certain the conditions of eternal salvation. That is to say, to the Puritans are we indebted for establishing early the practical role of education in American history and the subordinate position assigned to scholarship for the sake of scholarship.

On the primary level, for example, practical motives—social, religious, economic—reinforced each other. In Puritan theology the Bible was the source of all law, civil as well as religious. Consequently, the ability of each child to read and to understand its injunctions assumed social as well as individual importance and was so recognized in legislation. But economic self-direction also ranked high. Accordingly, legislation was enacted to insure the ability of each child to read, write, perform the simple operations of arithmetic, and master the elements of some lawful calling, labor, or employment. As Bernard Bailyn has emphasized, the failure of the family to exercise its onetime educational functions effectively in the New World, with respect to the religious and vocational training of the young, constituted a primary reason for the establishment of schools under the Act of 1647. Thus early did Americans come to conceive of the school as a supplementary institution, one designed to achieve through associated action what individuals alone are unable to realize.

The purpose of education on the secondary and college levels, on the other hand, was to insure an adequate supply of competent leaders in church and state—that is, an intellectual and spiritual elite. As a means to this end, the classics, grammar, rhetoric, and logic were deemed essential, both as intellectual capital and as tools for disciplining the reason. As Increase Mather remarked, the classics were important for the reason "that the Interest of Religion and good literature hath risen and fallen together." Accordingly, the preparation which the Puritan considered a prerequisite for preaching the Christian gospel "included Plato, Seneca, and Plutarch, as well as Augustine and William Ames." [7]

Considered similarly important were grammar, rhetoric, and logic. Within the Bible were to be found the major premises of correct thought and right conduct. But these premises required elucidation and skillful application to the practical problems of living. Logic properly understood and applied held forth this promise. So important, indeed, was logic for this purpose that John Eliot, the evangelist to the Indians, translated a short treatise into the Algonquin language, in order, as he said, "to initiate the Indians in the knowledge of the Rule of Reason."

This pragmatic emphasis in education in no way excluded a burning concern for scholarship on the part of our Puritan forebears. But it impelled them to emphasize its practical value in much the same manner that the scientist of today urges support of pure research as an essential condition of advancement in the applied sciences. The dictates of faith and the authority of the Gospel were primary—the starting and the end points of theological discussion. The function of reason was, therefore, not to modify these premises but to render clear and understandable their meaning through their applications. Thus it was said of John Preston that he "proved his points first by authority and then by reason."

[7] Miller, *op. cit.*, p. 98.

ANTI-INTELLECTUALISM FOSTERS DEMOCRACY

Emphasis upon learning and the importance of an educated clergy as interpreters of God's will led to the establishment of schools and to the founding of Harvard College (1636) in early New England—but not without growing opposition. Despite Nathaniel Ward's earnest invitation for dissenters from orthodoxy to keep clear of Massachusetts, Antinomians and Anabaptists from within and Quakers from without (ardent followers of the inner voice) persistently appeared as dragons' teeth of old to challenge those in control. According to these heretics no intermediary was necessary in order to determine the ways of God to man. Nor was it essential to wait upon the training of the mind in order to follow the straight and narrow path to salvation. God, they insisted, spoke directly and immediately to all who believed in Him. From Divine Grace, therefore, rather than from books and scholarly dissertations, came instinctive knowledge and a galvanizing of the will sufficient for the good life.

Anti-intellectualism in America, as in England, took the form of opposition to an educated clergy and, with the diminishing influence of the latter, an undermining of the theocratic form of government. It was one factor leading eventually to the neglect of schools and schooling and an unwillingness of the general public to support institutions devoted to the preparation of an intellectual elite. Thus did it contribute unwittingly to a realization of the fear of the early Puritans that learning might eventually be buried in the graves of their fathers.

On the other hand, anti-intellectualism gave aid and comfort to democratic trends that gained in momentum with each advance on the western frontier—trends such as an increasing participation of the people in government, a leveling of class lines, and a diminishing influence of the aristocracy in both social and political life—and to a growing conviction "that all men are created equal." Moreover, when schools once again assumed importance, as they did with the emergence of the middle classes and the rise of the academy in the eighteenth century, their justification was more practical and utilitarian than theological and religious.

MAN'S NATURE AND EDUCATION

Finally we come to the influence of seventeenth-century conceptions of man and his moral nature upon subsequent education. This was Protestant and Calvinistic in origin, rather than Catholic, and grounded in the conviction that with Adam's sin man's originally pure nature was corrupted for all time. It followed that each individual is "born in sin" and endowed with a will and a disposition to choose evil rather than good.

REASON AS A SOURCE OF MORAL PRINCIPLES

Obviously it could not be expected that God would entrust man so constituted with the responsibility for originating the principles of ethics and morality. Their source was rather the mind and will of the Deity himself. Nevertheless, as the Puritan saw it, God has given to man the faculty of reason by means of which he can recognize a priori moral principles and, with the help of logic, deduce from these axioms and principles appropriate applications to the problems of living. Reason, thus conceived, and the methods of its operation are the natural endowments of all men, not merely of those blessed with a privileged relationship to the Deity. Moreover, from this fact follows an identity between what God commands and what reason reveals as fit and proper. That is to say, the principles of morality, as other truths, may be established either by reference to the Scriptures or by an appeal to nature and to reason.

To the Puritan it was inconceivable that these two sources of wisdom and authority should conflict. As Thomas Shepard explained, "Law natural is part of the law moral." And again, "it is his will and good pleasure to make all laws that are moral to be first good in themselves for all men, before he will impose them upon all men."

The attempt to establish an identity of moral injunction as revealed alike in the Scriptures and by reason and logic provided ample grist for sermon and learned dissertation. In recognizing, however, that reason and nature as well as revelation constitute an appropriate source of moral principles, a basis was laid for developments in a later century—an appeal to the "laws of nature"—that would assuredly have shocked the seventeenth-century mind.

MORAL DISCIPLINE AS REPRESSION

Of unusual significance for education has been the assumption of man's nature as originally corrupt and the principles of law and morality as formulated for men rather than by them out of the fruits of their own experience. The assumption of man's originally corrupt nature bore heavily upon children since it implied that they came into the world as "little vipers," to employ Cotton Mather's words. It seemed to imply further that their one opportunity for transformation turned upon the use of repressive discipline. Thus John Wesley, more than a century after the founding of New England, could advise parents to "break their child's will" in order that it may not perish. "Break its will as soon as it can speak plainly—or even before it can speak at all. It should be forced to do as it is told, even if you have to whip it ten times running. Break its will, in order that its soul may live."

Wesley's method of discipline involved a generous use of the whip. Supplementing this has been an appeal to fear, vivid portrayal of the consequences of transgression—as in James Whitcomb Riley's poem "Little Orphant Annie." The reader will recall the concluding advice of Annie to her young listeners, following a lurid recital of the consequences of disobedience:

> An' one time a little girl ud allus laugh an' grin,
> An' make fun of ever'one, an' all her blood an' kin;
> An' onc't, when they was "company," an' ole folks was there,
> She mocked 'em an' shocked 'em, an' said she didn't care!
> An' thist as she kicked her heels, an' turn't to run an' hide,
> They was great big Black Things a-standin' by her side,
> An' they snatched her through the ceilin' for she knowed
>   what she's about!
> An' the Gobble-uns'll git you
> Ef you Don't Watch Out!

This conception of the nature of children and its implications for discipline has still not given ground entirely to the modern view that assurance of being loved, a sense of security, and a conviction of inner worth are essential conditions for health of personality. Witness, for example, the frequent advice to parents of a wayward child that they resort more frequently than is common today to the woodshed method of moulding the will of the child.

THE VERBAL ROUTE TO MORAL EDUCATION

The assumption that the principles of morals originate outside the experience of human beings but are identifiable and demonstrable by reason also rendered imperative moral education by means of verbal instruction. If, as was assumed, God has implanted in man's reason in the form of innate ideas the major premises of right conduct, it follows that one purpose of instruction is to bring these original axioms to conscious expression and, by means of logic, to train the individual in their proper use. Moreover, since it was also assumed that man's will is subordinate in influence to reason, instruction in a moral dialectic became an essential ingredient in moral education—with the result, as Perry Miller remarks, that "in the complete body of New England divinity as many tenets were entered on the authority of the syllogism as of revelation." [8] To illustrate the lasting influence of this formal approach to moral education, Miller quotes the following remarks of a character in the novel *Oldtown Folks* (1867) by Harriet Beecher Stowe:

> If there is a golden calf worshipped in our sanctified New England, its name is Logic; and my good friend the parson burns incense before it with a most sacred innocence of intention. He believes that sinners can be converted by logic, and that, if he could once get me into one of these neat little traps aforesaid, the salvation of my soul would be assured. He has caught numbers of the shrewdest infidel foes among the farmers around, and I must say that there is no trap for the Yankee like the logic trap.

The intellectual and verbal approach to moral education has not lost its influence in educational circles. It thrives still as an assumption in the educational philosophy of a vigorous group which seeks today to stem the tide of what it considers an "anti-intellectual trend" in modern education. Efforts of educators to "relate the school to the community" and to provide an experimental basis for the understanding of intellectual concepts are condemned as misguided and wasteful. "Today as yesterday," insists Robert M. Hutchins, "we may leave experience to other institutions and influences and emphasize in education the contribution that it is supremely fitted to make, the intellectual training of the mind." [9] The assumption here is that men share a "common human nature," a faculty of the mind or a reason that contains within itself ideas and principles which one and only one subject matter and discipline are competent to develop.

[8] *Ibid.*, p. 115.
[9] Robert M. Hutchins, *The Higher Learning in America* (New Haven, Conn.: Yale University Press, 1936), p. 69. See also the criticism of contemporary education in Arthur E. Bestor, *Educational Wastelands: The Retreat From Learning in Our Public Schools* (Urbana, Ill.: University of Illinois Press, 1953); John Keats, *Schools Without Scholars* (Boston: Houghton Mifflin Co., 1958); H. G. Rickover, *Education and Freedom* (New York: E. P. Dutton & Co., 1959); and the publications of the Council for Basic Education, Washington, D.C., to mention but a few representative expressions of exclusive emphasis upon verbal instruction as a means of educating the "mind."

Hutchins' voice is not as one crying in the wilderness. The reappraisal of American education—which has been under way since the launching of Sputnik I by the Russians in 1957 and the resulting emphasis upon bettering the quality of education—has added fuel to the conflict in theory between the advocates of education vitalized by immediate experience and those who espouse an education conceived as a "training of the mind" through exclusively verbal means. With respect to moral education this second view represents a reaffirmation of the early assumption that right conduct is conditioned upon the possession of right ideas. Or, as Hutchins has put it, since "character is the result of choice, it is difficult to see how you can develop it unless you train the mind to make intelligent choices."

We shall have occasion to refer again to these two opposing theories of moral education. It may be relevant at this time, however, to point out that each in practice neglects an important aspect of the other. Verbal instruction as a clarification and interpretation of firsthand experience can be vital, whereas concepts not so related to the stream of life activities are likely to take on a pale and hollow look. On the other hand, to assume literally that allegiance to the principles of morality is something "caught" rather than "taught" and thus requires no conscious interpretation of experience can result in equally disappointing outcomes.

IN SUMMARY

From this brief description of intellectual concerns in seventeenth-century New England it is hoped the reader will conclude the period is related more intimately to later American life and education than is commonly assumed. As we have seen, the form of government was theocratic; the media for exchange of ideas, largely the sermon and theological tract; and the undisputed authority to which disputants referred, the word of God. From these facts it is easy to conclude that questions at issue were exclusively religious and theological. But this is to confuse outer form with inner reality, since preoccupation with a theological problem involved as well the mutual responsibilities of rulers and ruled, relationships between classes in society, and orthodoxy in matters religious and civil versus freedom of thought and expression.

Out of these conflicts came not so much final agreement as a clear formulation of rival theories respecting the nature of man and his institutions. These theories have profoundly influenced American life and education throughout our history.

1. Consider, for example, the nature of government at issue in the vigorous debates between John Cotton and Roger Williams. Both contestants accepted the compact theory of government, a forerunner of government under a written constitution. Both opposed the concept of the divine right of kings to rule. But here agreement ended—Cotton supporting Winthrop in his theory of government by the elect for the many, in contrast with Williams exhibiting revolutionary faith in the common man and the right of the latter to participate directly in his government.

2. Second, there was the conflict between the Congregational and Presbyterian forms of church government. In a theocracy, however, this concerned the merits of local autonomy versus centralized authority, a conflict between the democratic and republican forms of government and a problem that still divides Americans under the captions of "states' rights" versus a "bureaucracy in Washington." Out of the original debate came, eventually, the unique solution of direct representation of the people on all levels—local, state, and federal. In the field of education, emphasis upon local autonomy in education has been of first importance in setting the pattern early for local initiative and local control under general state supervision in the administration of schools.

3. The dominant rule in the Massachusetts Bay Colony, as, indeed, in other colonies, was insistence upon orthodoxy and rigid conformity in thought as well as action. The assumption was that dissent weakened the health—moral and civil—of a community, an assumption that has in no way lost its vigor with age, as acts of Congress, state legislative bodies, and school boards amply demonstrate today. Nevertheless, we find clearly expressed in the colonial period the theory of dissent and the importance of freedom of thought and expression to the well-being of the state. Admittedly, school and college were slow in translating the implications of freedom in the content and the method of education, but the origins of academic freedom are traceable to this early period.

4. Again, the emphasis in the colonial period on all levels of education was practical. Even the lovers of scholarship were careful to emphasize its practical advantages. At no time have Americans established schools and colleges or organized curricula within these institutions purely

out of respect for learning or scholarship. Rather has the justification been consistently pragmatic and the curriculum—whether in the liberal arts or in frankly vocational education—been envisaged as an instrument of utilitarian value.

5. Attention has also been called to the concept of the priesthood of all believers and the difficulties this engendered for the religiously aristocratic. Although this concept encountered more friendly reception outside New England than within, its influence was general. Implicit in the conviction that God speaks directly to the individual without the necessity of learned interpreters of his word was a concept of equality which life in a new country was to extend beyond the field of religion. In the political sphere it quickly undermined the concept of stewardship (of the elect, the wellborn, or the educated) and eventuated in the well-known declaration that "all men are created equal, that they are endowed by their Creator with certain inalienable rights. . . ." In religion and education this tended to downgrade the position of an educated clergy and, in so doing, contributed directly to a weakened conviction of the importance of schools and schooling. But, as we shall see in more detail later, this downgrading of schooling was furthered by an obvious lack of correspondence between the methods of thinking emphasized in school and college and those essential for success in life under conditions ever new and novel. Life required the ability to substitute new ways for old in coping with variations in soil and climate, ingenuity in developing trade and commerce, and inventiveness in the applications of science to industry—all of which put a premium upon an intellectual discipline (ways of defining a problem, searching for its solution, and validating conclusions) strikingly different from the logic of the schools.

6. Finally, with respect to law and morality, we have established early the external nature of the principles which are to govern man's relation to man. This followed from both the generally accepted concepts of the Deity, as the ultimate source of all law and an absolute monarch, and of man as hopelessly corrupt in nature. Consequently it was inconceivable that human beings could formulate out of their own experience the criteria with which to enrich and to ennoble human relationships. Indeed, the idea that moral principles are designed to ease and free and enrich relationships, that they are positive and creative rather than negative and restrictive in essence, ran counter not only to assumptions as to their origins but to those of their function as well. That is to say, moral in-

junctions were thought to restrict and confine men's actions rather than to release and expand their energies. From this it followed that moral and religious education were inseparable and the methods employed primarily didactic and formal—characteristics, incidentally, in no way confined to yesterday.

SUGGESTED READING

Bailyn, Bernard, *Education in the Forming of American Society* (Chapel Hill, N.C.: University of North Carolina Press, 1960), pp. 3-47.

Boorstin, Daniel J., *The Americans: The Colonial Experience* (New York: Random House, 1958), Chapters 1-5.

Butts, R. Freeman, and Cremin, Lawrence A., *A History of Education in American Culture* (New York: Holt, Rinehart & Winston, 1953), Chapters 1-2.

Hofstadter, Richard, *Anti-intellectualism in American Life* (New York: Alfred A. Knopf, 1963), Chapter III.

Miller, Perry, *The New England Mind: The Seventeenth Century* (Cambridge, Mass.: Harvard University Press, 1954), Chapters III, V, VII, IX, XIV.

Parrington, Vernon Louis, *Main Currents in American Thought*, Vol. I, *The Colonial Mind* (New York: Harcourt, Brace & Co., 1927), Chapters I-V.

CHAPTER 2
THE EIGHTEENTH-CENTURY MIND

ECONOMIC AND SOCIAL CHANGES IN EIGHTEENTH-CENTURY AMERICA

As we have seen, the dictates of religion loomed large in seventeenth-century New England. Rigorous obedience to the will of God and the critical importance of obedience for life after death determined what was relevant and appropriate for thought and action in this world. The interests of church and state were closely interknit, and government by the religiously orthodox comprised the dominant form of community organization.

It was not long, however, before economic changes and material well-being brought aspirations of a secular nature which began to dilute religious interests. Thus in the affairs of state the influence of the clergy was weakened, and the authority of the "saints" was undermined. The rewards of trade and commerce on land and sea, together with speculation in undeveloped lands, gave rise to a class of merchants and capitalists and large landowners of upper-middle-class status, hungry for the goods and services available to the economically fortunate in this world, and increasingly restive under a theocratic government. Moreover, the children of the "saints" were not slow in discovering that the exercise of the Puritan virtues of temperance, order, frugality, industry, and honesty yielded material as well as spiritual returns. By 1680 the monopoly of

22

the spiritually elect in government was broken and the franchise broadened to include all males possessed of property qualifications.

Equally significant was the growing recognition in town meetings accorded small farmers, tradesmen, and artisans, even the everyday laborer. In Europe members of the lower classes had little to look forward to in the way of change of status; born as social underlings they tended to remain as such, with little or no political influence. But the outlook was different in the liberating atmosphere of America. Here they gradually improved their economic status both as individuals and as groups, and as a result their political influence grew. With the substitution of a property qualification for religious orthodoxy as a condition of responsible participation in government, their voices in town meeting and colonial legislature became ever more decisive, thus adding to the discomfort of the king's representatives and his upper-class supporters. Moreover, from these humble origins came, eventually and in sizable numbers, lawyers, doctors, judges, even colonial representatives of the king—in other words, leaders in all walks of life.

Similar developments occurred in the Middle Colonies, where the religious motive from the beginning was less dominant than in New England. Diverse as was the population in religion and nationality, in social origin and social outlook, class and economic divisions resembled roughly those of New England: an aristocracy of landed gentry and merchants; a middle class of small farmers and tenants, tradesmen, and artisans; and a lower class of laborers, bonded servants, and slaves. Here, too, conditions favored the evolution of a more democratic society and the gradual erosion of rigid distinctions of class and status.

Of the Middle Colonies, New York most closely resembled the mother country in class structure. More tardy was it also in bridging the gap that separated landed gentry and large merchant from the tradesman, artisan, and farmer. There was little resemblance, for example, between the patroon with his huge estate on the Hudson and the gentleman farmer of New Jersey, Pennsylvania, and Delaware. Many of the latter, devoted followers of William Penn, experienced little stress or pain in identifying their interests with those of the small freeholder and merchant. There, too, the Quaker spirit tempered the treatment of bonded servant and slave.

Significantly different also from that of the New York aristocrat was the attitude of the upper and middle classes generally toward the world's work. Work was nowhere considered degrading—in the field, behind the desk or counter, in the shop, or at the workbench—a fact that rendered easier the task of ambitious members of the middle and lower classes to better their stations in life.

It is not surprising, therefore, that the privileges of direct participation in government and the exercise of religious freedom were more easily acquired south of the Hudson than north. Only after an uprising of farmers and tradesmen in 1689, under the leadership of Jacob Leisler, was the base of suffrage broadened in New York (1691) to include males possessed of personal estates of forty or more pounds. In New Jersey, Pennsylvania, and Delaware, on the other hand, relatively liberal provisions for the exercise of the suffrage were made by the Quakers from the beginning.

To these developments the Southern Colonies constituted an exception. Indeed, with the advent of the large plantation and its reliance upon a single crop and slave labor, a trend in the opposite direction characterized Maryland, Virginia, and the Carolinas. Throughout the seventeenth century the population of these colonies consisted primarily of independent farmers, dependent for their hired labor upon indentured servants who envisaged for themselves a future in which they, too, would be free and independent landowners. The introduction of slave labor and the rapid development of the plantation system undermined this situation, and large landowners came to dominate the political, economic, and social scene. The number of Negroes in Maryland increased from about 17 percent of the population in 1715 to 29 percent by 1755. The proportion grew in Virginia, where, by 1715, one-fourth of a total population of 95,000 were Negroes. Slaves eventually replaced indentured servants, and the small independent farmer with meager capital soon found it necessary either to accept a subordinate status in the tideland area or to seek new opportunities in the West.

Radically different as were the economic and social systems in which were born and reared a John Adams and a Benjamin Franklin on the one hand and a Thomas Jefferson and a George Washington on the other, it was still possible in the eighteenth century for these leaders and their associates to unite in common opposition to the external control of English commercial and political interests and to ground this opposition in the philosophical assumptions of the Enlightenment. Not until the American Revolution had been fought and won and a new government established under the Federal Constitution did differences between the sections become acute.

Finally should be mentioned the western frontier which has functioned as a democratic influence throughout American history, persistently and consistently promoting change and challenging the validity of static conceptions of the nature of man and his institutions. As we have seen, it was to the frontier in New England that the dissidents in religion and politics migrated originally in order to establish new communities in harmony with their sacred convictions. In the Middle Colonies a variety of motives —religious, economic, and social—induced the Scotch-Irish, Swiss, Germans, French Huguenots, and many others, in the late seventeenth and early eighteenth centuries, to seek a new life in America. Finding the coastal areas largely preempted by earlier arrivals, these newcomers proceeded first to occupy the western sections of the Middle Colonies and then to follow the valleys into the back counties of Virginia and the Carolinas. But they did not rest there. By 1800 over 1,000,000 persons had moved beyond the mountains. Heterogeneous in religion—Presbyterian and Baptist, Lutheran and German Reformed, Methodist and others—and national origin, ruggedly individualistic and independent in character, indifferent, if not hostile, to the authority of King and Parliament alike, and firmly opposed to the union of church and state, they constituted a significant addition to middle-class groups in the colonies.

The contrast between the seventeenth- and eighteenth-century American is well illustrated in the *Letters* (1782) of Crèvecoeur, a Norman-French gentleman who entered the English colonies from Canada about 1760 and later traveled extensively through them, including their frontiers. The following is his description of the transformation of a European into an American.

An European, when he first arrives, seems limited in his intentions, as well as in his views; but he very suddenly alters his scale. . . . He begins to feel the effects of a sort of resurrection; hitherto he had not lived, but simply vegetated; he now feels himself a man, because he is treated as such; the laws of his own country had overlooked him in his insignificancy; the laws of this cover him with their mantle. Judge what an alteration there must arise in the mind and thoughts of this man; he begins to forget his former servitude and dependence, his heart involuntarily swells and glows; this first swell inspires him with those new thoughts which constitute an American. . . . From nothing to start into being, to become a free man, invested with lands, to which every municipal blessing is annexed!

What a change indeed! It is in consequence of that change that he becomes an American.

MAN'S CONCEPT OF HIMSELF ALSO CHANGES

These changes were accompanied by equally significant transformations in people's conceptions of the Deity, of nature, and of themselves. Daniel J. Boorstin contrasts the logic by means of which ideas of the Enlightenment were validated in Europe and America.[1] In Europe, advocates of progress and the continuous perfectibility of man, of natural rights, of the original equality of men, of the supremacy of reason and its function in revealing the laws of nature both physical and human, grounded these assumptions and the methods of their verification in philosophy. In Europe, also, these views were advocated by a relatively small group of intellectuals. The American, in contrast, saw them validated by experience and "the common sense of mankind." Consequently, when a Thomas Jefferson or a Benjamin Franklin sought to justify American policy in opposition to English interests by an appeal to "self-evident truths," he had in mind no philosophic theorizing but rather the firsthand experience of countless individuals. As Jefferson put it (in the preamble to his draft of the Virginia Bill for Establishing Religious Freedom), "the opinions and beliefs of men depend not on their own will, but follow involuntarily the evidence proposed to their minds."

GOD BECOMES A BENEVOLENT
ARCHITECT OF THE UNIVERSE

The "evidence proposed to their minds" by the transforming experiences of a century resulted in significant revisions in conceptions of God, of his purposes, and of the values which govern men's activities. As we saw in Chapter 1, for the seventeenth-century mind, God resembled an oriental despot, a Being infinite in wisdom and power, whose will had brought about the creation of the universe and the laws governing its operations. On this view all law—physical as well as that governing human behavior—derived from God. This Being was also a jealous God, one easily stirred to wrath, although his mercy was also infinite. Moreover,

---

[1] Daniel J. Boorstin, *The Americans: The Colonial Experience* (New York: Random House, 1958), Part V, on "An American Frame of Mind."

as Jonathan Edwards, the last influential proponent of Puritanism in the eighteenth century argued, since God is an Infinite Being, infinitely perfect, and sin represents a violation of his decrees, transgression merits infinite punishment.

Add the Calvinistic doctrine of election—the assumption that God has decided prior to birth and experience which of his children are to be saved and which to be damned—and little was left to man in the way of originality and creative initiative! To be sure, there were dissenters who insisted upon picturing the Deity in more generous terms. But in this challenge to orthodox Calvinism there was no questioning the basic conception of a God, infinite and all powerful in nature, who ruled by arbitrary decree.

Repeated experience of individuals in easing and freeing conditions of living rendered difficult any consistent adherence to this conception of a Deity. Similarly, steady progress of the middle classes toward democracy in government weakened, for many, adherence to theological dogmatism. "When the common man," writes Parrington, "has freed himself from political absolutism, he will become dissatisfied with theological absolutism. The right to achieve salvation is a natural corollary to the right to win social distinction; that one's future status lay wholly beyond the reach of one's will, that it rested in the hands of an arbitrary God who gave or withheld salvation at pleasure was a conception that ill accorded with the nascent ideal of democracy." [2]

More consistent with experience in the New World, as with the conclusions of science in Europe under the influence of Newton and his followers, was the concept of God as a wise and benevolent architect, the Designer of an intricately organized and complicated machine, nature, which operates in accordance with consistent and unchanging laws. An analogy commonly employed to explain the nature of God and his handiwork was that of a watchmaker and his watch. Once manufactured, a watch functions in accordance with the principles of physics utilized by its designer. It is the same with the universe, except for this difference: the author of nature is also the author of the unchanging laws which govern his creation. Under the influence of this world view, Alexander Pope wrote:

[2] Vernon Louis Parrington, *Main Currents in American Thought*, Vol. I, *The Colonial Mind* (New York: Harcourt, Brace & Co., 1927), p. 151.

All are but parts of one stupendous whole,
Whose body Nature is, and God the soul; ...
All Nature is but Art, unknown to thee;
All chance, direction, which thou canst not see;
All discord, harmony, not understood;
All partial evil, universal good;
And, spite of pride, in erring reason's spite,
One truth is clear, whatever is, is right.

Obviously, these revised conceptions of the Deity and of nature were not universally accepted. It requires time for minds "edged by theology," as one historian describes the early colonists, "still under the spell of medieval science: 'moon-signs, zodiac-signs, horoscopes, ominous eclipses followed by devastating fires and comets presaging disaster and the death of princes,' and the active meddling of grotesque evil spirits and house-haunting demons" [3] to emancipate themselves. But this many succeeded in doing by the late seventeenth century and increasingly so in the eighteenth century.

Evidence of this emancipation was the spread of Deism with its substitution of a natural theology for a theology based exclusively upon the Bible. Deists substituted the concept of "Nature's God" and a mechanistic view of the universe for the God of the Old Testament and a cosmology that assumed the intervention of supernatural beings in the affairs of men and the operations of nature. They also questioned the divinity of Christ. The Constitutional Convention of 1787 included a considerable number of Deists and Unitarians. In the words of the Beards, "It was not Cotton Mather's God to whom the authors of the Declaration of Independence appealed; it was to Nature's God." [4]

MAN ALSO ADDS TO HIS STATURE

Significant changes likewise followed in man's view of himself. Reference has been made to a "sort of resurrection" that Crèvecoeur observed in the lowly and oppressed immigrant from Europe as he improved his status in America. This mutual transformation in outer circumstance and inner vision of countless individuals challenged traditional

[3] Edgar W. Knight, *Education in the United States* (Boston: Ginn & Co., 1929), p. 91.
[4] Charles and Mary Beard, *The Rise of American Civilization*, Vol. I (New York: The Macmillan Co., 1929), p. 449.

notions of man as innately worthless and naturally prone to evil. Even in New England, where theological doctrine was most persistent in survival, the actual relationships of people in towns and villages as well as in new communities on the frontier tended to undermine theological doctrine and to foster instead a growing sense of man's dignity and worth and his creative potentialities. To quote Parrington:

> In the corrupt worlds of Augustine and John Calvin such a doctrine [total depravity] must have seemed a reasonable explanation of the common brutality; an evil society must spring from the evil heart of man. But in the village world of New England the doctrine had lost its social sanction. . . . The everyday life of the New England village was animated by rugged virtues—by kindliness toward neighbors and faithfulness to a strict ethical code, rather than by hatred to God and man, or brutal wallowing in sin. In short, these villagers knew they were very far from a bad lot. . . . Although they repeated the familiar creed, the sanction for that creed was gone; it was the voice of dogma that spoke, and not the voice of reason and experience.[5]

"The voice of reason and experience" in America eventually reversed earlier conceptions of man and nature. As against the traditional notion of original sin, reason indicated that men in their original state were free of evil tendencies, that the evil they do derives from corrupt institutions. Elihu Palmer, a militant Deist, contended in his *Principles of Nature* (1797): [6]

> It is neither in the upper nor lower regions, it is not in heaven or hell, that the moral evil will be discovered; it is found only among those intelligent beings who exist upon the earth. Man has created it, and man must destroy it. Let reason, righteous and immortal reason, with the argument of the printing types in one hand, and the keen argument of the sword in the other . . . attack the thrones and the hierarchies of the world, and level them with the dust; then the emancipated slave must be raised by the power of science into the character of an enlightened citizen; thus possessing a knowledge of his rights, a knowledge of his duties will consequently follow,

5 Parrington, *op. cit.*, p. 150.
6 The views of Elihu Palmer are discussed extensively by G. Adolph Koch in *Republican Religion: The American Revolution and the Cult of Reason* (New York: Henry Holt & Co., 1933), Chapter II.

and he will discover the intimate and essential union between the highest interests of existence and the practice of an exalted virtue.

REASON REVEALS LAW IN NATURE AND MORALS

It was thus assumed that a "natural order of morals" governs "right relations" for the individual and society much as natural law regulates the behavior of objects and events in the physical realm. In each instance it was reason that identified law and, with the aid of science and experiment, deduced from it applications of benefit to mankind. Natural laws (properly envisaged as commands of God) were of necessity universal, uniform, and, when uncorrupted by custom and tradition, analogous to the axioms that serve as major premises in syllogisms. For example, Samuel Clarke (1675-1729), an English moralist, theologian, and friend of Isaac Newton, could argue in his *Discourse on Natural Religion* (1706) that just as the "necessary and eternal" relationships (fit or unfit) that obtain between things in the material world are consistent with "what is agreeable to justice, Goodness and Truth in order to promote the Welfare of the whole Universe," so, with respect to creatures, the "eternal and necessary differences of Things" make it "fit and reasonable" for them to act for the good of the whole without regard to "personal Advantage or Disadvantage, Reward or Punishment." Moreover, since for Clarke what is "fit and reasonable" coincides with "the obligation of Duty," he that "refuses to deal with all men equitably is [as] guilty of the same contradiction" as he who refuses to affirm that things equal to the same thing are equal to each other. "In a word: all wilful wickedness and perversion of Right, is the same Insolence and Absurdity in Moral Matters, as it would be in Natural Things for a man to pretend to alter the certain Proportions of Numbers, to take away the Demonstrable Relations and Properties of Mathematical Figures." [7]

Observe that natural laws and the universal principles of morality were derived from "reason," but the term was used in two senses: (1) to indicate a faculty of the mind competent to identify intuitively the laws of nature and of morality precisely as it is compelled to accept the principle that an object at one and the same time cannot both possess and not possess the same properties or that a proposition cannot be both true and

---

[7] For an excellent discussion of "The Morality of Reasonableness," see John Herman Randall, Jr., *The Making of the Modern Mind* (Boston: Houghton Mifflin Co., 1940), Chapter XV.

false at one and the same time; and (2) as an obvious and rationally supported inference from "science and experience" or from the "common sense of mankind." In each instance, however, natural laws thus identified were accorded a status superior to laws that issue from men, be they the edicts of king or acts of parliament! Thus Du Pont de Nemours, the French economist, boldly asserted in his *Origines et Progrès d'une Science nouvelle*, "If the ordinances of sovereigns were contradictory to the laws of the social order . . . they would not be laws, they would be insane acts obligatory upon no one. Thus there is a natural judge, a court of final appeal, for the ordinances of sovereigns themselves, and this judge is the evidence of their conformity or their opposition to the natural laws of the social order."

On similar grounds James Otis of Massachusetts in 1761 opposed Writs of Assistance, as did John Adams, later, the validity of the Stamp Act. Said Adams of the latter, it is "of no binding force upon us; for it is against our rights as men and our privileges as Englishmen. . . . There are certain principles fixed unalterably in Nature."

Perhaps the classic expression of "the common sense of the matter," as Jefferson termed the doctrine of natural rights, is found in the Declaration of Independence, to which Americans have appealed repeatedly in order to justify reform (advocates of the Bill of Rights in the Constitution of the United States, abolitionists seeking to free the slave, William H. Seward in his appeal to a law "higher" than the Constitution). And the doctrine is undoubtedly the original source of the judgment of those members of the United States Supreme Court today who insist that the rights to freedom of thought, expression, and religion, as provided for in the First Amendment, are "absolute" rights and thus not subject to infringement by act of Congress.

REVOLUTIONARY IDEAS GENERATED BY REASON AND EXPERIENCE

Chapter 1 drew attention to the manner in which the Puritan derived his concept of a social compact from the Covenant of Grace and interpreted the compact so as to substitute the "stewardship of the elect" in government for the divine right of kings to rule. We also saw that with the development of trade and commerce worldly interests came to compete with all-absorbing religious concerns. Similarly, in New England as in the colonies farther south, with firsthand experience in creating new communities and devising new institutions in response to common needs, a secular conception of the origin and purpose of government came into being.

In the back counties and on the remote frontier, individuals of plural origins and diverse backgrounds found it necessary to cooperate in order to provide for defense and to satisfy other needs that could be met only through associated action. Thus, from direct participation in the development of their own institutions and the selection of their own representatives, the common people came to accept as "natural" democratic conceptions of government and its proper relations to the individual. Parallel with these changes, indeed, aiding and abetting them, were transformations in popular notions of the Deity and his designs for men. These fundamental changes in experience and resulting theory gave substance to a number of ideas of later significance for American life and education.

1. First was the concept of progress, of faith in the continuous perfectibility of man and his institutions. As so often happens, the repudiation of one conviction of long standing was followed by an equally vigorous assertion of its opposite. Not satisfied merely to reject the traditional theological notion of inherited sin, many now proclaimed the innate worth, dignity, and goodness of the individual.

It is difficult for Americans of today, confused and frustrated as they are by complex problems, domestic and international, to appreciate the wave of optimism that surged upward in the late eighteenth and early nineteenth centuries. The conviction of the early Puritan that the establishment of the Holy Commonwealth in Massachusetts was in accordance with "the designs of a glorious transformation" was now extended to the "manifest destiny" of the American Republic. All that was necessary, it seemed, to insure uninterrupted progress for the individual and his society was to free and to educate his native powers.

Typical of the thought of the time were the writings of William Godwin, an Englishman with a substantial following in both England and America. In common with others of this period, Godwin "conceived of man as creative unless repressed by obsolete and fixed institutions," and "he believed education to be the only instrument for creating a flexible social organization that would respect the creative genius of man...." [8] In *An Inquiry Concerning Political Justice* (1793), Godwin

---

[8] Allen Oscar Hansen, *Liberalism and American Education* (New York: The Macmillan Co., 1926), p. 2.

posed the question: "Is it possible for us to contemplate what he [man] has already done without being impressed with a strong presentiment of the improvements he has yet to accomplish? There is no science that is not capable of additions; there is no art that may not be carried to a still higher perfection. . . . If this be true of all other sciences, why not of morals? If this be true of all other arts, why not of social institutions?" Furthermore, it was not considered essential, in order to insure continued progress, to do more than remove the impediments of ignorance and superstition and the disabilities which the institutions of society imposed upon people. Such a task seemed relatively simple in a virgin country of unlimited resources and boundless opportunities.

2. Second was the concept of equality: "We hold these truths to be self-evident, that all men are created equal . . ." proclaimed the Declaration of Independence. Much has been written to explain or to justify this radical assertion. Was it written for progaganda effect only? Or did Jefferson and the signers of the Declaration of Independence actually believe in the doctrine of original and native equality?

The answer is not altogether clear. Uppermost in the minds of members of the Continental Congress was undoubtedly the principle that all men are, or should be, equal before the law; that government should play no favorites and should aid no individual or class at the expense of another. That it may have meant little more than this at the time explains the willingness of those hardheaded realists John Adams and Benjamin Franklin, who were members of the drafting committee with Thomas Jefferson, to affix their names to the Declaration. It is probably also true that members of the Congress were concerned less at the time with philosophic theory and more with the effects of the economic and political policies of the English government upon the colonies.

Granted these reservations with respect to the Declaration's assertions that "all men are created equal," both philosophic thought and life in America were in process of undermining traditional notions of inherited characteristics. For example, John Locke (1632-1704), the intellectual father of American political leaders, had written, many years before, in *The Conduct of the Understanding* (1697):

We are born with faculties and powers capable almost of anything, such at least as would carry us further than can easily be imagined: but it is only the exercise of those powers which gives us ability and skill in anything and leads us toward perfection. I do not deny that natural disposition may often give the rise to it [excellence] but that never carries a man far without use and exercise, and it is practice alone that brings the powers of the mind, as well as those of the body, to their perfection. (Section 4.)

In short, a man's worth is measured by what he does with his talents, rather than by the accidents of birth or position.

Locke's emphasis upon use and exercise, together with the influence of environment was soon transformed by many of his followers into a doctrine of innate equality. Thus we find Helvetius, in eighteenth-century France, expounding the doctrine that all intellects in their original state are equal and the differences which do in fact distinguish men result from education.

In America the idea of innate equality fell upon fertile soil. Here, a constantly expanding economy—with its invitation to individuals on all levels of society to carve out an attractive future for themselves by means of their own efforts—seemed to confirm with each generation the principle that by their works ye shall know them. Consequently, the assertion that all men are created equal went much farther in its popular appeal than many of the signers of the Declaration of Independence intended. It laid the basis for an impending revolution in social and economic as well as in political relationships. Once it is assumed that all men are created equal and that governments are established to insure the enjoyments of rights that derive from equality, the future is indeed malleable!

3. Third was the principle of self-interest and its implications for moral, economic, and political relationships. Self-interest as a normal and justifiable expression of human behavior thus replaced the earlier conviction of man's normal and natural proneness toward evil. But this was not self-interest in its raw and brutal state. An inherent aspect of self-interest, in the minds of its advocates, was its affinity with benevolence when uncorrupted and intelligently pursued. Men were thought to be endowed with an allied instinct of sympathy and a concern for the welfare of others.

It was this conception of a preestablished harmony between self-interest and benevolence that induced the English Bishop Joseph Butler to state in the Preface to his *Sermons* I and II (1726) that "Self-love and benevolence, virtue and interest, are not opposed, but only to be distinguished from each other. . . . There are as real indications in human nature, that we were made for society and to do good to our fellow creatures, as that we were intended to take care of our own life and health and private good."

If we interpret the theory of self-interest to mean, in the realm of politics and economics, that individuals contribute to the welfare of others in the process of wisely promoting their own well-being, there was much in American life to support the doctrine. American merchants and tradesmen had become restive under the restraints imposed by Parliament and King. Consequently, Franklin, who had met Adam Smith in England and shared the latter's views on the doctrine of laissez-faire, could argue convincingly that the general welfare would be served best if government gave free play to individual initiative. "Perhaps in general it would be better," wrote Franklin in his pamphlet on "Principles of Trade," "if government meddled no farther with trade than to protect it and let it take its course."

This was a period, too, when towns and cities and rural communities in America seemed to prosper from the activities of individuals seeking to better their own circumstances. Speculators in real estate and undeveloped land obviously prospered, but they found it easy to convince themselves and others that their activities contributed equally to the growth and prosperity of the country. In short, in a country hungry for the material goods that trade and commerce might bring, and favored with natural resources awaiting only exploitation and development at the hands of ambitious and courageous individuals, it was not difficult to conclude that the beneficent Author of nature had ordained a preestablished harmony between the pursuit of self-interest and the public good.

Nor was this conclusion weakened by the further observation that the virtues emphasized by the Puritans were the stepping stones to material success in this world as well as the means of spiritual reward in the next. Writing in his *Autobiography*, Franklin states: "Revelation had no weight with me, as such; but I entertained an opinion, that though certain actions might not be bad, *because* they were forbidden by it, or good, *because* it commanded them; yet probably these actions might be forbidden *because* they were bad for us, or commanded *because* they were beneficial to us, in their own natures all the circumstances considered."

Few statements illustrate better the transformation of the Puritan virtues into the instruments of worldly success. The good life was conceived of as health, wealth, and wisdom and these were the rewards of self-interest *intelligently* pursued. ("Early to bed, and early to rise, makes a man healthy, wealthy, and wise.") But not to be forgotten in Franklin's conception of self-interest, as in that of others, were its implications for a secular humanitarianism and the genuine satisfaction that comes from promoting the happiness of others.

The concept of self-interest as a law of nature was a convenient instrument to use in opposing government control and the regulation of trade, commerce, and manufacture. Particularly was this true of Americans in their opposition to attempts of Parliament and King to levy taxes upon their commercial operations. Grounding their economic interests in natural law and identifying this law with the injunction of the Deity, they had no reason to question the justice of their cause!

Similarly, in the political field it seemed to follow, as Jefferson put it, that the best government is one that governs least, thus limiting its authority to the protection of natural rights and not neglecting property, contracts, and other essentials for "the pursuit of happiness." American experience with the creating of new communities and the development of new institutions tended to agree with John Locke's description of the "Social Contract" in his *Treatise on Civil Government* (1690):

> Men being by nature all free, equal and independent, no one can be put out of this estate and subjected to the political power of another without his own consent, which is done by agreeing with other men, to join and unite in a community for their comfortable, safe, and peaceable living, one amongst another, in a secure enjoyment of their properties, and a greater security against any that are not of it. . . . When any number of men have so consented to make one community or government, they are thereby presently incorporated, and make one body politic, wherein a majority have a right to act and include the rest.—Chapter VIII.

4. Two conflicting conceptions of government emerge, reflecting two attitudes toward government that have long characterized American thought. The first is fearful and suspicious of central authority and external control. It was this conception that immigrants, in process of fleeing from oppressive governments abroad, brought with them to this country; and it is this they have tended to express toward proposed extensions of powers on the part of the national government and, to a lesser degree, state governments. In theory this attitude would limit government to

minimum essentials, such as common defense, protection of property, insuring the rights of contract and other indispensables in the conduct of trade and commerce, and to the dispensing of justice. In a world in which the legitimate interests of men and groups normally conflict, one major function of the government so conceived is to serve as an umpire and, when necessary, as a disinterested policeman. From this theory with its fear of uncontrolled power emerged the American system of checks and balances in which each division of government (executive, legislative, judicial) is empowered to exercise restraint upon the other two.

The second attitude has evolved out of the practical necessities of cooperative action on the part of people who face common dangers and imperative needs that can be met less effectively, if at all, by individuals and groups acting alone. It views government not as an external agency but as an expression of the people, a mutual insurance association. On the frontier this conception resulted in the cooperative meeting of common needs such as the protection of life, limb, and property and the building of roads. Eventually, as communities became more complex, the attitude resulted in the creation of public agencies and institutions to achieve a variety of common purposes. Thus there appeared schools, libraries, health departments, fire and water departments, and the like— in short, whatever changing conditions demanded and for which the people by majority vote were willing to tax themselves. On this view government has no assignable limits so long as it functions effectively and, by common consent, contributes to the general welfare.

It is this second theory that has given vitality to local government in the United States. From the beginning it has encouraged local initiative in the solution of local problems, in contrast with the dependence upon a central authority that often results when localities are viewed as mere departments of a larger organization. And it is this second attitude that has come to modify the first as governments on all levels, federal as well as state and local, have tended to lose their insulated character and their interests have become intertwined with those of others.

Conflict between these two theories explains in part contemporary divisions of opinion with respect to the creation and maintenance of government services in novel areas. Shall schools, for example, provide health and recreation services, free textbooks, school lunches, an enriched curriculum? Or shall they refuse to substitute for the home? Shall the community provide public housing, health centers, low-priced medical care, and hospital services? Or shall it refrain from "pauperizing" and "collectivizing" its inhabitants? Should the federal government grant federal aid to schools? Or should it consider education strictly a state and local responsibility? Should our country follow in the path of Theodore Roosevelt, armed with the big stick in pursuit of its own interests? Or should it heed the pioneer example of Franklin Roosevelt and extend the principles of a good neighbor policy to the impoverished and undernourished peoples of the free world?

5. It will be recalled that separation of church and state was advocated by Roger Williams in the seventeenth century and applied by him as a principle in this Rhode Island settlement. Nevertheless, it remained a novel and revolutionary idea until well into the eighteenth century, when a number of factors contributed to its gradual adoption: the continued growth of the secular spirit and of tolerance in matters of religion, together with opposition to political control by the religiously orthodox; the influence of Deism with its concept of a natural religion; and a steady influx of immigrants of diverse religious faiths for whom separation of church and state was an article of faith.

These changes eventually undermined the original assumption that orthodoxy in religion is an essential condition of individual morality and community health. First came the acknowledged right of dissenters to reside in a colony without molestation. Second came the privilege of nonattendance upon the established church and the right to maintain the church of one's choice (while continuing, of course, to pay taxes in support of the established church). Third came the prohibition of an established church. And finally came legal recognition of the principle, as Jefferson phrased it, that it is "sinful and tyrannical" for the state to force contributions from an individual in support of *any religious belief*, be this his own or that of another.

To be sure, the evolution of religious freedom in the colonies was far from even, and the causes were not similar in all instances. In Virginia, for example, freedom of worship came about as a defense measure. Baptists, Methodists, Presbyterians, and others were welcomed in the back counties as buffer settlements against Indian attacks. In Massachusetts, on the other hand, it required the same courage and indifference to danger on the part of a dissenter to establish residence as it did for a frontiersman to clear his land and build his lonely cabin in hostile Indian territory. Not until it became a royal colony in 1691 were Protestant sects other than Congregationalists accorded right of residence. And not until some years following the adoption of the First Amendment might a Catholic priest enter Massachusetts without fear of imprisonment. In contrast with both Virginia and Massachusetts, religious toleration in the Middle Colonies received early recognition.

That a majority of the original thirteen states had arrived at the more advanced stage of religious freedom by the time of the Revolution is evidenced by provisions in the state constitutions adopted between the years 1776 and 1791. Nine of the thirteen states in this period (including Rhode Island, which retained its original charter) wrote into their constitutions unmistakable prohibitions against establishments of religion, plural as well as singular. Only four continued to sanction the levying of taxes in support of religious organizations: Maryland until 1810, Connecticut until 1818, New Hampshire until 1819, and Massachusetts until 1833.

The reasons for this change in the attitude of the people toward state-supported religion can be summarized quickly. Most obvious was the objection of an ardent adherent of one sect to assessments in support of a religion he believed to be heretical. A second motive was well stated in a resolution adopted in 1785 by the Virginia Baptists, in opposition to a proposed "Bill Establishing a Provision for Teachers of the Christian Religion." This resolution declared:

> [that] no human laws ought to be established for this purpose; but that every person ought to be left entirely free in respect to matters of religion; that the holy Author of our religion needs no such compulsive measures for the promotion of his cause; that the Gospel wants not the feeble arm of man for its support; that it has made and will again through divine power make its way against all opposition; and that should the Legislature assume the right of taxing the people for the support of the Gospel, it will be destructive to religious liberty.

Finally should be mentioned the Deists and other liberals in religion who conceived of the exercise of religion as a "natural right" and thus not properly subject to the control, support, or interference of government. Religious organizations, as they envisaged them, were private corporations, free to operate within the state but dependent for their support upon the voluntary contributions of their members and friends.

To men of this frame of mind, Thomas Paine's statement in *Common Sense* (1776) seemed most sound. "As to religion, I hold it to be the indispensable duty of government to protect all conscientious professions thereof; and I know of no other business which government hath to do therewith."

There is difference of opinion today among historians as to the original intentions of the authors of the religious clause in the First Amendment to the federal Constitution. Some hold that the statement "Congress shall make no law respecting an Establishment of religion, or prohibiting the free exercise thereof . . ." forbids no more than government assistance to one religion in preference to all others (that is, the prohibition of a single establishment). Others maintain that it applies not merely to one establishment—that is, to one favored church—but to religions in the plural. In this they are at one with Judge Jeremiah S. Black, whom Justice Felix Frankfurter, in his concurring opinion in *McCollum* v. *Board of Education,* 333 U.S. 203 (1948), characterized as "one of the most distinguished of American judges." In 1856 Judge Black stated:

> The manifest object of the men who framed the institutions of this country, was to have a State *without religion* and a Church *without politics*—that is to say, they meant that one should never be used as an engine for any purpose of the other. . . . Our fathers seem to have been perfectly sincere in their belief that the members of the Church would be more patriotic, and the citizens of the State more religious by keeping their respective functions separate. For that reason they built up a wall of complete and perfect partition between the two.

It was Madison's original intention to apply the principle of separation of church and state to the states as well as to the federal government. But in this he was not successful. In *Pierce* v. *Society of Sisters,* 268 U.S. 510 (1925), Madison's objective found realization, however. This decision of the United States Supreme Court ruled that with the adoption of the Fourteenth Amendment the civil liberties guaranteed to the people by the federal Constitution, but not necessarily by the constitutions of the states, were made binding upon both state and federal governments.

Moreover, since education under the Constitution was made a state rather than a federal concern, the application of the principle of separation to education was not envisaged in 1791. Not until the first quarter of the nineteenth century did state governments assume direct responsibility for the development of state school systems. One of the first of these was Connecticut, fortunate in the possession of public lands, the sale of which yielded monies that could be made available to education. In 1818, Connecticut revised its constitution so as to prohibit multiple establishment and also to insure that all public funds which might be appropriated for education should be used exclusively for public education. Connecticut's example was followed by other states in the East, and by new states upon their admission to the Union. The pattern followed was that laid down in the Bill of Rights and, in particular, the First Amendment of the federal Constitution. With respect to education these provisions carried a twofold purpose: to ban the teaching of sectarian doctrines in public schools and to restrict the use of public funds exclusively for public education.

6. Attention was directed to the importance of education by the assumption that all men are endowed with the faculty of reason and that environment more than heredity determines the use they make of it. This assumption prompted Thomas Jefferson, for example, to propose public support of schools in Virginia in order that the state might avail itself "of those talents which nature has sown as liberally among the poor as the rich, but which perish without use, if not sought for and cultivated." It was this conviction also that induced the Congresses of 1785 and 1787 to grant public lands in support of education, acts which insured the eventual development of public education in the western territories.

Education, as liberals in the eighteenth century envisaged it, was all-important in order that the individual and his society might exploit fully the gifts of nature. But education so conceived bore little resemblance to the schooling of the day. Schools emphasized orthodoxy in religion and politics; Jefferson and others of like mind, freedom of thought and an intellectual discipline competent to cope with novelty and a changing society.

CONSERVATIVES DISSENT

Despite the tendency of liberals in the eighteenth century to ground their sacred convictions in the "common sense of mankind" and the principle of "self-evidence," we should not conclude that these premises were shared by all. Indeed, they were vigorously opposed by the colonial aristocracy—royal governors, numerous merchants, capitalists, and others

—whose interests as well as honest convictions bound them to the English Crown. Members of this group were disposed to ascribe the difficulties of the period to the excesses of democracy rather than to the mistakes of the Crown and of Parliament. As Daniel Leonard, a prominent lawyer, contended, the colonial legislatures were excessively represented by the people (the rising middle classes) and lacked the restraining influence of a peerage such as that in England. Leonard adopted Hobbes's view that men in a state of nature live in a condition of anarchy and strife, the hand of all against all. Thus he concluded that security of person and property requires a coercive state, a sovereign "who can do no wrong" and subjects who are "bound to believe" their king "is not inclined to do any." [9] Obviously, to subjects of this caste of mind, the advocacy of freedom of thought and expression as natural rights, and thus above and beyond the control of the state, constituted heresy of the rankest sort.

The American Revolution and the banishment of large numbers of Tories severely weakened the influence of conservatives who had been loyal to the Crown. The second group, typified by John Dickinson, John Adams, and Alexander Hamilton, probably constituted a majority of the members of the Constitutional Convention of 1787. These men accepted the doctrines of natural law and natural rights and the principles of representative government, but they looked upon themselves as "realists." As they saw it, the pre-Revolutionary alliance of merchants, investors, large landowners, and the professional classes with small farmers, tradesmen, debtors, and squatters had led to "excesses of democracy." Consequently they proposed to devise ways and means of limiting the principles they had employed so successfully against England.

Of this group, Richard Hofstadter has written: "The men who drew up the Constitution in Philadelphia during the summer of 1787 had a vivid Calvinistic sense of human evil and damnation and believed with Hobbes that men are selfish and contentious. . . . To them a human being was an atom of self-interest. They did not believe in man, but they did believe in the power of a good political constitution to control him." [10]

Unlike the philosophers who were convinced of a preestablished harmony between self-interest and benevolence, Adams and his colleagues looked to a system of checks and balances in government and society as

[9] See Parrington, *op. cit.*, Part II, Chapter II, for an excellent description of "The Mind of the American Tory."

[10] Richard Hofstadter, *The American Political Tradition* (New York: Random House, 1961), p. 3.

a practical device for controlling the excesses of self-interests and love of power. "There never was a democracy yet," wrote John Adams to John Taylor of Caroline, "that did not commit suicide." And again: "If you give more than a share in the sovereignty to the democrats, that is, if you give them the command or preponderance in the . . . legislature, they will vote all property out of the hands of you aristocrats, and if they let you escape with your lives, it will be more humanity, consideration, and generosity than any triumphant democracy ever displayed since the creation. And what will follow? The aristocracy among the democrats will take your place and treat their fellows as severely as you treated them." On the other hand, Adams was willing to grant with Gouverneur Morris that "Wealth tends to corrupt the mind and to nourish its love of power, and to stimulate it to oppression. History proves this to be the spirit of the opulent."

The adoption of the Constitution in 1789 thus represented a victory for the conservatives. But it was temporary only. The future was to favor the liberals. The westward movement of population, the organization of new territories, and the eventual admission of new states to the Union led consistently to a broadening of the base of suffrage and to a government, in theory at least, ever more responsive to the voice of the people. The American mind came to be characterized by faith in progress, in the infinite perfectibility of man's nature, and in the improvement of his lot in life through the creation and use of institutions of his own creation; opposition to rigid class lines, and acceptance of the ideal of social mobility; together with generous provisions for equality of opportunity.

High on the list of conditions and priorities favorable to these ends was education. "Enlighten the people generally," promised Jefferson, "and tyranny and oppression of the body and mind will vanish like evil spirits at the dawn of day."

The full results of this confidence in man and the potentialities of education were not realized in the eighteenth century. Schooling, other than that provided in charity schools, was largely private. Not until the nineteenth century did free schools, established and fully maintained by the public, come into existence. The mission of the eighteenth century was largely to formulate clearly the ideas and ideals to which educators and public-spirited citizens later were to give concrete form and substance.

Before we turn to the nineteenth century, we should consider the influence of John Locke's philosophy upon the theory and practice of education in the eighteenth and nineteenth centuries—an influence as formative in the minds of educators as were his views on government and society upon the Revolutionary fathers and the framers of the Constitution. Accordingly, it is to Locke that we now turn.

SUGGESTED READING

Bailyn, Bernard, *Education in the Forming of American Society* (Chapel Hill, N.C.: University of North Carolina Press, 1960), pp. 84-112.

Boorstin, Daniel, *The Americans: The Colonial Experience* (New York: Random House, 1958), Chapters 24-26.

Butts, R. Freeman, and Cremin, Lawrence A., *A History of Education in American Culture* (New York: Holt, Rinehart & Winston, 1953), Chapters 5-7.

Cash, W. J., *The Mind of the South* (New York: Random House, Vintage Books, 1961), Book I.

Gross, Carl H., and Chandler, Charles C., *The History of American Education Through Readings* (Boston: D. C. Heath & Co., 1964), Part II.

Hansen, Allen Oscar, *Liberalism and American Education* (New York: The Macmillan Co., 1926), Chapter I.

Hofstadter, Richard, *The American Political Tradition* (New York: Random House, 1961), Chapter I.

Parrington, Vernon Louis, *Main Currents in American Thought*, Vol. I, *The Colonial Mind* (New York: Harcourt, Brace & Co., 1927), Part II, Chapters II, III.

Randall, John Herman, Jr., *The Career of Philosophy: From the Middle Ages to the Enlightenment* (New York: Columbia University Press, 1962), Chapters 7, 8.

CHAPTER 3
THE INFLUENCE OF JOHN LOCKE

SOME years ago at a meeting of the National Association of Manufacturers in New York City, an executive vice-president of that organization extolled the spirit of free enterprise in America, in part, as follows: "That's the nice thing about our social and economic setup here in America. Everyone concentrates on getting what he wants for himself, but finds that the only way he can do it is by providing others with things they want enough to be willing to buy or pay for it. We don't have to be philanthropists. We can be selfish as all hell and still find that, unless we can fool the police, we can't get something without giving something in return."

The historian will recognize in these remarks an atavistic and inverted expression of a philosophy which seemed validated by American experience two centuries ago. There was a period when this country welcomed the weary and the oppressed of all lands and invited them here to contribute to the general welfare by serving their own ends. Indeed, European philosophers who contended that the Deity had willed a preestablished harmony between expressions of self-interest and the good of others might have cited life in America as evidence, for it seemed that neither time nor custom had as yet interfered with the original designs of the Architect of nature for a state of peaceful coexistence between rugged individualism and the public welfare!

To be sure, life was often hard, and individuals were frequently trod upon and mutilated in the competitive struggle for success; but defeat was seldom final. New opportunities consistently waited "just around the corner," as evidenced by the multiple careers of countless individuals— men like Sam Houston and Edward Livingston for whom disappoint- ment, even ruin, in one location or vocation served merely as an invita- tion to win distinction in another.

Common experience thus encouraged an optimistic attitude toward life in America and a conviction, shared by a majority, that the future is malleable, that men can make of themselves what they will. Consequently, neither heredity nor status at birth defined a man adequately. Rather was it opportunity and the use he made of it that measured his worth.

THE TIMES AND LOCKE'S PSYCHOLOGY REINFORCE EACH OTHER

Eventually a national mood is reflected in education and a psychology of learning. Just as in Chapter 2 we found leaders in American political life drawing upon the writings of John Locke for inspiration and guidance, so, with the advent of the academy in the eighteenth century and the decline of the colonial grammar school, Locke's description of the mind and its operations influenced both curriculum and method.

While typically American in its development, the American academy had its origin in what might be termed an English bootleg institution that came into being during the reign of Charles II. With the exclusion of Nonconformists from the public schools and universities, Noncon- formist ministers were moved to provide the best substitute they could for their fellow sectarians.[1] The provisions of the Act of Conformity and the Five Mile Act were only partially modified by the Toleration Act of 1689, with the result that these schools continued to lead a "half-out- lawed" existence under the guidance of the ejected ministers. Of signifi- cance for our purpose was their attempt to liberalize the curriculum of the secondary school with instruction in such subjects as natural philoso- phy, mathematics, geography, anatomy, and shorthand, in addition to the traditional subjects of Greek, Latin, and Hebrew.

Significant also was the influence of Locke. To quote Brown, "Aside

---

[1] Few writers have provided a better description of English and American academies than did Elmer Ellsworth Brown in *The Making of Our Middle Schools* (New York: Longmans, Green & Co., 1914). See particularly Chapters VIII-XI.

from theological doctrine, the real intellectual stimulus of the eighteenth-century academies seems to have come largely from John Locke and Sir Isaac Newton; and while the thought of these master minds oftenest reached the schools through the writings of Watts and other popularizers, there are other instances in which we find the original masterpieces freely studied in the academies." [2]

A similar situation existed when the academy developed in America. In his *Sketch of an English School*, prepared as a suggestive course of study for the Philadelphia Academy, opened in 1751, Benjamin Franklin included Locke among the authors to be read in the sixth class. As Brown states, however, it was largely through Isaac Watts's *Improvement of the Mind* that Locke came to influence successive generations of teachers and students in American schools for well over a century.

Watts made no claim to originality but frankly popularized and gave detailed application to ideas in Locke's *The Conduct of the Understanding* (1697). When we consider that the academy served the dual purpose of secondary school and teacher-training institution until well into the nineteenth century, we can appreciate how Locke's common-sense psychology gave character to both curriculum and method from elementary school through college.

INNATE IDEAS DENIED—ALL IDEAS COME FROM EXPERIENCE

Locke began his monumental work, *An Essay Concerning Human Understanding* (1690), with a lengthy denial of the existence of innate ideas, or "primary notions ... characters, as it were, stamped upon the mind of man, which the soul receives in its very first being, and brings into the world with it." (Book I, Chapter 2, Section 1.) His purpose was to refute the rationalists in philosophy who assumed that the mind is so constituted that it accepts without proof or prior experience the truth of certain logical principles or axioms as well as those practical and moral principles that constitute the foundation of universally accepted moral values. As evidence of his position, Locke argued that the recognition and acceptance of "innate ideas" come not at birth but with experience and maturity. He contended also that moral principles, far from being universally accepted, vary with time and place or, as we would say today,

[2] *Ibid.*, p. 166.

with cultures. In modern terms what Locke denied is the existence of inborn tendencies to think, feel, and act in ways predetermined and unrelated to the experience of individuals; his concept of human nature was admirably designed to validate American ideas of innate equality already in process of winning popular acceptance.

Having demonstrated to his satisfaction the nonexistence of innate ideas, Locke attempted to describe the nature of the mind at birth and the manner in which it comes to be furnished. All that the rationalists attributed to mind in its native state, he contended, derives from experience, from ideas of sensation in the first instance, and from ideas of reflection (operations of the mind upon the original sources of experience) in the second. For his detailed and repetitive argument in this connection, see *An Essay Concerning Human Understanding*, Book I. In the same work, he wrote: "Let us suppose the mind to be, as we say, white paper, void of all characters, without any ideas; how comes it to be furnished? Whence comes it by that vast store which the busy and boundless fancy of man has painted on it with an almost endless variety? Whence has it all the materials of reason and knowledge? To this I answer in one word, from experience; in that all our knowledge is founded, and from that it ultimately derives itself." (Book II, Chapter 1, Section 2.)

SOME IMPLICATIONS FOR LOGIC AND EDUCATION

This is a simple and common-sense explanation of the origins of experience. But its implications for education, if taken literally, are far-reaching:

1. For example, the explanation limits man's knowledge of the external world to what his senses convey. Let one sense be injured, and accuracy of reception is destroyed. Increase the number of senses, or intakes from without, or improve their functioning, and the validity of knowledge increases.

Locke used these seemingly obvious facts to stress the importance not only of using all possible sources of information in seeking a solution to problems but of modesty with respect to the validity of conclusions one may draw from data no matter how conscientiously arrived at these conclusions may be. For example, in *The Conduct of the Understanding*, after explaining in some detail the common faults which lead to "miscarriages" of reason (thinking "according to the example of others" and putting "passion in the place of reason"), he wrote:

The third sort is of those who readily and sincerely follow reason, but for want of having that which we may call large, sound, round-about sense, have not a full view of all that relates to the question, and may be of moment to decide it. We are all shortsighted, and very often see but one side of a matter.... Here we may imagine a vast and almost infinite advantage that angels and separate spirits may have over us, who, in their several degrees of elevation above us may be endowed with more comprehensive faculties; and some of them perhaps, having perfect and exact views of all finite beings that come under their consideration, can, as it were, in the twinkling of an eye, collect together all their scattered and almost boundless relations. A mind so furnished, what reason has it to acquiesce in the certainty of its conclusions! (Section 3.)

And, conversely, for a mind not so endowed, what reason has it to exercise restraint and tolerance with respect to conclusions in religion, politics, and other important areas while searching earnestly for ever new data! Again Locke wrote in the same work:

In this we may see the reason why some men of study and thought, that reason right and are lovers of truth, do make no great advances in their discoveries of it. Error and truth are uncertainly blended in their minds; their decisions are lame and defective, and they are very often mistaken in their judgments: the reason whereof is, they converse with but one sort of men, they read but one sort of books, they will not come in the hearing but of one sort of notions; the truth is, they canton out to themselves a little Goshen in the intellectual world, where light shines, and as they conclude, day blesses them; but the rest of that vast expansium they give up to night and darkness, and so avoid coming near it. They have a pretty traffic with known correspondents, in some little creek; within that they confine themselves, but will not venture out into the great ocean of knowledge, to survey the riches that nature hath stored other parts with, no less genuine, no less solid, no less useful than what has fallen to their lot, in the admired plenty and sufficiency of their own little spot which to them contains whatsoever is good in the universe. (Section 3.)

2. A second factor of significance for learning in Locke's psychology was his assumption that knowledge begins with the logically simple. Hence the first step for the beginner in learning is analysis. In reading

this was interpreted to mean starting with the letters of the alphabet. Similarly in other subjects the obvious approach was first to identify the simplest elements and thereafter gradually to build complex concepts. In practice, however, the simple parts thus identified were the simple and primary as viewed by the mind of the master or the adult, not by the mind of the beginner or the child. That is to say, the logically simple and the psychologically simple were identified as one and the same until new developments in psychology in the late nineteenth century, with the advent of child psychology, prompted educators to distinguish (as did Rousseau in his *Émile* as early as 1762) between a logical and a psychological analysis of materials put before children.

3. Our minds, according to Locke, are our *conscious minds,* an assumption basic to his contention that all knowledge originates from experience: from sensation in the first instance; from reflection in the second. This not only ruled out the unconscious as known today; it also subordinated the emotional nature to the understanding on the assumption that ideas give direction to a man's will. In *The Conduct of the Understanding* Locke put it as follows: "The last resort a man has recourse to, in the conduct of himself, is his understanding; for though we distinguish the faculties of the mind, and give the supreme command to the will, as to an agent, yet the truth is, the man, who is the agent, determines himself to this or that voluntary action, upon some precedent knowledge, or appearance of knowledge, in the Understanding." (Introduction, Section 1.)

4. Ideas are easily equated with words. The moral that educators less worldly-wise than Locke drew from this assumption of mind as the conscious mind only was to identify character training and moral education with verbal instruction, to the neglect, often, of emotional and social factors in character development. Hence the emphasis in textbook and other materials prepared for children was frequently upon the moral the reader should draw. Locke, on the other hand, conceived of ideas as including more than verbal experience alone and emphasized constantly the importance of relating principles to actual experience in the development of personality.

Such a method is not ineffective when the moral expressed interprets firsthand experience, as was often the case when life was simpler than today and the moral, as stated, was relatively close to the daily experience of the reader; it is less effective when divorced or unrelated to direct experience. Consider, for example, the effect of Poor Richard's observation, "Early to bed and early to rise, makes a man healthy, wealthy, and wise," upon a country boy in Benjamin Franklin's day with that upon a city boy of today. The latter may play with the children of a family whose hour of retirement differs from that his parents seek to impose upon him. Is he not prone to reply to his mother, when she quotes Poor Richard as a means of inducing him to retire early, "Mother, John does not have to go to bed when I do, and his parents stay up later than you do. How come they have more money than we and they are just as wise too?" Locke's own common-sense approach to the bearing of words upon conduct is exemplified in the following statement from *The Conduct of the Understanding:* "Nobody is made anything by hearing of rules or laying them up in his memory; practice must settle the habit of doing without reflecting on the rule; and you may as well hope to make a good painter or musician extempore, by a lecture or instruction in the arts of music and painting, as a coherent thinker or a strict reasoner by a set of rules showing him wherein right reasoning consists." (Section 4 on Practice and Habits.)

Sensation was the original and primary source of experience for Locke. A second was reflection. Sensation presents the mind with simple ideas. It is reflection that brings these simple ideas together in the form of percepts, or ideas of objects (as, for example, the simple ideas of color, size, shape, and odor to construct the idea of "apple"); and it is reflection (such as memory, discerning, comparing, compounding, naming, abstracting, and reasoning) that utimately furnishes the mind with ideas ("roundabout knowledge," seasoned principles, for example) and renders the individual competent to direct his life.

SOME AMBIGUITIES AND "MISCARRIAGES"

From this brief description of Locke's psychology we can see how important it was, in his view, to recognize the limits of the human understanding as well as its potentialities. Tolerance of other men's opinions, tentative judgments with respect to the results of one's own investigations, and the necessity of acquiring "roundabout" knowledge before venturing a conclusion—in short, disciplined methods of thinking—were constantly stressed. On the other hand, there was the vagueness in the use of terms that of necessity accompanies pioneer thinking in a novel field. Locke is frequently called the father of modern psychology, which is another way of saying that he has served much the same function as a "generalized type" serves in biology. Formulations that doubtless seemed clean-cut to him have been for others vague and ambiguous and often the starting points for conclusions quite different from what the master would have drawn.

Take, for example, what Locke termed ideas of reflection. Evidently for him these were no more than functions of the mind, or characteristic ways in which the latter operates upon the materials furnished by the senses. It was only a matter of time, however, before ideas (functions) of perception, memory, reason, and the like acquired the status of faculties, analogous to the organs of the body, faculties that lent themselves to general training and discipline once they were exercised by the appropriate subject matter. Thus it was assumed that the faculty of memory, when trained by one set of materials (let us say memorizing a Latin vocabulary), would function better thereafter in any and all situations involving the use of memory or that the faculty of reason, if disciplined by mathematics or logic, would enable its possessor to reason effectively on any and all occasions calling for the use of reason.

Or take Locke's naïve assumption of the mind as an immaterial substance, different in all respects from the body or a material substance. This distinction (first clearly drawn by Descartes, and accepted by Locke) persisted well into the nineteenth century, until developments in physiology and the insight these afforded of interactions between "mind and body" forced psychologists to reexamine initial assumptions. Locke's ambition had been to formulate clearly the laws governing the operations of the mind much as Newton had succeeded in doing for matter. He accomplished quite the opposite by stimulating research and investigation into problems that defied solution on the basis of his original definitions.[3]

LOCKE'S IDEAS AND SOME TRENDS OF THE TIMES

In his biography of Thomas Jefferson, Dumas Malone cites an interesting request which Jefferson made of his friend Trumbull in France. It was to procure life-sized busts of Bacon, Newton, and Locke, "the three greatest men that ever lived, without any exception, and as having

[3] We return to this problem in Chapter 7.

laid the foundations of those superstructures which have been raised in the physical and moral sciences." [4]

Certain it is that Locke's psychology, as interpreted and used by his followers, provided the "foundations of a superstructure" of a new society far more democratic and equalitarian than he himself would have ventured to contemplate. Take, for example, his conception of the mind at birth as a white sheet of paper upon which no innate knowledge has been written. In the revolutionary atmosphere of France and America this was used to support a literal interpretation of the principle that all men are born equal. From this it is but a step to conclude that an individual is to be judged solely in terms of what he is, what he has made of himself, rather than in terms of birth and inheritance. From this it also follows as a corollary that fluidity of class lines and social mobility, if not the total elimination of class distinctions, is the normal and natural condition of a healthy society.

Locke's emphasis upon the partial nature of truth, as human beings with a limited number of senses (or avenues of information) are privileged to ascertain the truth, likewise carried a moral for a society in which change and novelty were dominant characteristics. It validated not only freedom of thought and inquiry and expression as a governmental policy but an open-minded attitude toward the opinions of others as an essential condition for arriving at truth. With respect to formal education it suggested also the acquisition of a "roundabout knowledge," information of a many-sided character, together with a disciplined method of arriving at conclusions.

But such knowledge was not suggested as a privilege for one class alone, or for individuals of one type of mind! As property qualifications for voting and the holding of public office gave way to manhood suffrage, education in preparation for citizenship began to loom large in importance. Liberals favored it because they shared Jefferson's optimistic belief that with education "tyranny and oppression of the body and mind will vanish like evil spirits at the dawn of day"; conservatives, in increasing numbers, in the hope that schools would impress upon the minds of future citizens convictions regarding the sacred rights of property and the values of a stable society.

[4] Dumas Malone, *Jefferson and His Times,* Vol. II (Boston: Little, Brown & Co., 1951), p. 211.

Not until the nineteenth century, however, did these views find expression in schools open and free to all children at public expense. As we have seen, the seeds of public education had been sown in New England as early as 1642 and 1647 with acts of the General Court of Massachusetts requiring towns of fifty householders to provide elementary instruction and towns of one hundred householders to establish secondary schools. Ground was also broken in the Middle Colonies by legislation providing for the establishment of charity schools. Thus Pennsylvania, in 1790, stated in its constitution that "the legislature shall, as soon as conveniently may be, provide for the establishment of schools throughout the state in such a manner that the poor may be taught gratis." All too often, however, legislation mandatory in form was only hortatory in fact and dependent for enforcement upon the enlightened will of each locality. In Virginia and the South, despite the efforts of Thomas Jefferson and others, only transient and isolated schools were to be found, sustained by private initiative and serving private interests. Not until 1796 was legislative provision made in Virginia for a compulsory system of elementary schools, and not until 1810 was assistance from the state extended to counties in support of public education.

Although efforts prior to 1800 got little farther than state assistance to localities willing to provide elementary education for the poor and state subsidies to private schools of a secondary character, theory pointed the way to future developments that many consider relevant to the needs of today. For example, Benjamin Rush and other members of the American Philosophical Society in the late 1780's formulated plans on a national scale for all youth of both sexes to have an education that would emphasize the principles of democracy and insure an understanding of the machinery of democratic government.[5]

Practical applications of Locke's theories found more immediate expression in the curriculum of the academies. As suggested earlier, these came into being in order to provide an education more in tune with the times than that of the colonial grammar school. For example, in discussing his plans for the Philadelphia Academy in 1749, Franklin expressed very well a conception of education that was to characterize both the Academy and its eventual successor, the public high school. Said he, "it would be well if they could be taught everything that is useful, and everything that

[5] For an excellent discussion of these plans, see Allen Oscar Hansen, *Liberalism and American Education* (New York: The Macmillan Co., 1926), pp. 48-63.

is ornamental," but since "art is long and their time is short ... it is therefore proposed that they learn those things that are useful and most ornamental; regard being had for the several professions for which they are intended."

We are not suggesting that Locke's philosophy was alone in bringing about changes in educational theory and practice. Rather was it a case of liberals finding in him philosophical and psychological justification for a type of education rich and varied in its offerings, practical in its emphasis.

It will be recalled that Locke recognized two sources of knowledge: sensation, or the reception of impressions from without by means of the senses, and reflection, or the operations of the mind upon the materials of sensation. By emphasizing one of these sources to the disadvantage of the other, two rival schools of education developed. The first stressed the originally passive and receptive nature of the learner; the second, the original powers of the mind or faculties and the possibilities of general training through their proper exercise. Not until the nineteenth century, however, did the second assume prominence, whereas the first received from the beginning encouragement from cultural factors in the American environment.

These factors explain the central position of the textbook in American schools in contrast with European classrooms. In rural and small-town America access to books was difficult. Libraries were the private possession of the few and seldom accessible to the run-of-the-mill individual. Teachers were ill-prepared and commonly as dependent as their pupils upon external sources of information. Consequently, teaching easily became identified with the absorption of the material in the textbook, in the first instance by the teacher, in the second by the pupil.

An incident early in the career of the writer will illustrate the persistence of this conception of teaching. When he decided, as a young man, to take up teaching as a life work and informed a relative of his decision, he was told: "Well, you will find that much easier than studying. Now you can keep your book open before you and let the pupils do the work!"

The conception of schooling as a means of bettering the individual's future status in life was a further factor in giving to education an external, if not an alien, character. Few attended school out of a passion for learning or for gaining a liberal understanding of life. The out-of-school environment was far richer than it is today, in town as well as country, in educational experiences, but not in facilities for "book larnin." Consequently, education was designed more to supplement life outside the school than to interpret and enrich the here and now. Verbal instruction loomed large in importance and easily became identified with education—the three R's in the elementary school and subjects of study in the academy of a practical nature that might enable young people to play a responsible role in a rapidly expanding commercial and industrial economy.

And we should not omit the influence of mobility and change which have characterized American life from the beginning. As cities grew in importance, young people flocked to them in increasing numbers from the country. Similarly, for immigrants from abroad, accustomed often to rural life and, in all instances, unfamiliar with American ways, the school served as an instrument of assimilation, again, largely through verbal media. But verbal or nonverbal, the education offered consisted largely of what William Heard Kilpatrick has termed "pre-digested subject matter" —information, ideas, habits, and skills to be absorbed passively by the pupil rather than an original and creative working over of experiences encountered.

Accordingly, Locke's psychology, as interpreted and applied, furthered a conception of culture as an external acquisition, something one procures more or less as he purchases a suit of clothes to better his appearance, rather than as a genuine *cultivation* of worthy interests in their many possible ramifications.

To these facts may be traced, in part, the subordinate role of the arts in American education, a status not unlike that of poor relatives in a wealthy family. Life on the frontier was hard, and schools were difficult to support. At their best, art expressions were appropriate for hours of leisure, for women, and for men of not quite manly stature. That they should play a significant role in the development of the normal personality was long unappreciated, as was the significance of emotional and social factors in development.

Indeed, an appreciation of emotional and social development and its bearing upon the intellectual life is relatively recent and related to conceptions of human development far more complex in nature than eighteenth- and early nineteenth-century theories envisaged. While Locke and his followers stressed the influence of environment in learning, it was the environment as experienced by a mind in isolation. That is to say, learning was considered to be exclusively an individual enterprise, and the conditions that made for success in learning were those that fostered the self-sustained individual. Here again we find a one-to-one relationship between the qualities of personality that make for success in a virgin country, rich in resources, and a psychology that attempts to explain human behavior. What man became depended upon the use he made of the opportunities furnished by the environment. The failure had only himself to blame!

The same considerations applied to school and schooling. Education available for children was analogous to free land open to settlement and cultivation by adults. Consequently, it was expected that the child should adjust himself to the school, not the school to the child. As the saying ran, it was not the task of the school to make a silk purse out of a sow's ear.

This individualistic conception of learning was reflected in methods of instruction. Prior to 1800 instruction was predominantly individual. The master's chief occupation seems to have been that of maintaining order and of whittling goose quills. And while school legislation usually provided that at twelve or thirteen years of age the pupil should whittle his own pens, these regulations, like so many laws of today, were not always enforced. The results of this procedure were, of course, wasteful in the extreme. Not only was the master unable to give attention to the pupil's study habits, but the practice of individual recitation severely limited the amount and character of attention devoted to each pupil. For example, a pupil in the Boston reading school of 1800 recorded that he received about twenty minutes of instruction each half day out of a total of three hundred and sixty minutes daily. And as late as 1855 Grimshaw, writing in *Barnard's Journal*, deplored the time wasted "by the old-fashioned and false method of teaching individuals instead of classes. I notice," he wrote, "in my visits to the schools many pupils sitting idle; sometimes part of the school is asleep, or what is worse, making a noise and disturbing the remainder who desire to be industrious."

We mentioned earlier that Locke's psychology gave aid and comfort to democratic trends in excess of what Locke himself would have sanctioned. In the realm of morals and moral education, however, his influence aided the conservative. As Richard D. Mosier has so well documented, textbook writers following the Revolution, and especially during the reign of the McGuffey readers, served as a medium for transmitting conservative values to the young. Particularly did they emphasize the rights of property which conservatives feared the democratic trends of the times were undermining.

Viewed in retrospect, this should not surprise us, since the virtues prized by people seeking to climb are identical in many respects with those valued by the upper classes. Thomas Jefferson might consider too limited Locke's statement in his *Second Treatise on Civil Government* (1690) that "The great and chief end, therefore, of men uniting into commonwealths and putting themselves under government is the preservation of property." Instead, Jefferson might prefer to emphasize, as a purpose of government, insuring the rights of life, liberty, and the pursuit of happiness (more broadly speaking, the general welfare). But he would have agreed with Benjamin Franklin's effort to validate the Puritan virtues on secular rather than religious grounds. And he would have done so for the very good reason that such virtues as temperance, silence, order, resolution, frugality, and industry, as Herbert Schneider points out, are not the original virtues of Christianity. Rather are they the Puritan substitutes for such traditional Christian virtues as humility, charity, penitence, poverty, and self-denial—qualities, all, with less appeal than the former in communities where virtually everyone aspires to an independent economic existence. "The clergy," writes Schneider, "were careful that God should command whatever needed doing and prohibit whatever proved an obstacle." [6]

Finally should be mentioned Locke's assumption that all minds are essentially alike—an assumption, incidentally, that persisted in psychology and gave character to educational procedure, roughly speaking, until Thorndike and others near the end of the nineteenth century began to call attention to the significance of individual differences in learning. As late as 1890 William James could write, "Until very recent years it was supposed by all that there was a typical human mind which all individual minds were like, and that propositions of universal validity could be laid down about such faculties as 'the Imagination.'" [7] This encouraged educators to oversimplify the task of the classroom and to assume that one type of educational material and one method were appropriate for all.

The assumption of a typical mind gave plausibility to faculty psychol-

6 Herbert W. Schneider, *A History of American Philosophy* (New York: Columbia University Press, 1946), p. 41.

7 William James, *Principles of Psychology*, Vol. II (New York: Henry Holt & Co., 1890), p. 49.

ogy and survives today as an unexpressed premise in the thinking of the advocates of a "basic education" or a curriculum uniform for all students in secondary education.

It is doubtful that John Locke would have been altogether happy with this educational philosophy. As indicated earlier, what he meant when he spoke of the "faculties" of the mind might better be termed "functions" or "operations," or processes, rather than "organs," which, when exercised by one sort of material and in one situation, will function with equal effectiveness in all other situations. The latter view, termed the "doctrine of formal discipline," tends to come to the fore when traditional subjects of study or traditional methods are challenged by new subjects and new methods (as, for example, the classics and formal grammar by the sciences and "practical" subjects). Locke was too shrewd an observer not to realize that what he called the faculties of reason, memory, imagination, and the like are in fact but names for a plurality of potential responses to plural situations; that the ability of a mechanic to exercise his imagination with respect to things mechanical differs significantly from his ability to exercise imagination in areas other than the mechanical. In *The Conduct of the Understanding*, Locke wrote of reason as follows: "It is true that he that reasons well in any one thing has a mind naturally capable of reasoning well in others, and to the same degree of strength and clearness, had his understanding been employed. But it is as true that he who can reason well today about one sort of matters, cannot at all reason today about others, although perhaps a year hence he may." (Section 6.)

Not only has the assumption of a typical mind been used to justify a narrow curriculum; it has also restricted and narrowed the conception of the teacher's role in instruction. Did one wish to understand how the mind of a student works, or the difficulties a learner might experience in mastering a subject, or the procedures best to follow, the answer was simple. Review one's own experience as a student. Moreover, since educators, by and large, have been verbally inclined, it has seemed natural and normal to them to equate intelligence in general with verbal intelligence. Cultural factors previously mentioned contributed to this tendency well into the late nineteenth century.

OUR OBLIGATION TO LOCKE

Despite severe limitations in Locke's psychology—limitations for which his followers must assume a large measure of responsibility—Americans owe a heavy obligation to this founder of modern psychology. His was an interpretation of the nature of the mind and its operations that played havoc with absolutes and all forms of dogmatism. The very nature of knowledge, as humans are privileged to acquire knowledge, emphasized its tentative and partial character. Only the angels, he reminded us, and they only "perhaps," are privileged to envisage the truth with completeness. Consequently, of greatest importance are tentative judgments, tolerance for the opinions of others, and freedom of inquiry in all areas of experience. Here was drawn an educational moral of profound import in a new country busily engaged in the process of creating new institutions. It was a moral also that insured an eventual correction, modification, and revision of Locke's psychology in the light of new and changing circumstances.

SUGGESTED READING

Butts, R. Freeman, and Cremin, Lawrence A., *A History of Education in American Culture* (New York: Holt, Rinehart & Winston, 1953), Chapter 6.

Curti, Merle, *The Social Ideas of American Educators* (New York: Charles Scribner's Sons, 1935), Chapter I.

Drake, William E., *The American School in Transition* (Englewood Cliffs, N.J.: Prentice-Hall, 1955), Chapters III, IV.

Hansen, Allen Oscar, *Liberalism and American Education* (New York: The Macmillan Co., 1926), Chapters II, III.

Locke, John, *The Conduct of the Understanding* (1697); and *An Essay Concerning Human Understanding* (1690), Books I, II.

PART II

PHILOSOPHY AND SCIENCE GIVE CHARACTER TO EDUCATION

CHAPTER 4
ECONOMIC AND SOCIAL CHANGES IN THE NINETEENTH CENTURY

SIGNIFICANT as were the contributions of eighteenth-century thought for education, they remained more in the realm of theory than of practical application. Benjamin Rush, Thomas Jefferson, and other representatives of the Enlightenment formulated ambitious plans—local, state, and national—far in advance of their day. Indeed, in this respect, the eighteenth century may be viewed as sowing seeds which only the fertile soil and more favorable climate of a later period would permit to germinate.

The nineteenth century was such a period, with its revolutionary developments in economic and social relationships and its steady progress from a society predominantly agricultural and rural into one increasingly industrial and urban. As a background for conceptions of education that were later to win acceptance, it may be well to review the most important of these transformations.

Eighteenth-century America, as we have said, was predominantly small-town and rural. As late as 1789 only six cities in the entire country could boast a population of more than 8,000. Philadelphia, the largest, registered about 60,000. Trade and commerce flourished in the Middle Colonies and in New England, but not in the corporate form it was later to assume, with the result that relationships between employer and employee, customer and owner, were still of a person-to-person character. Manufacturing was in its infancy, and few either anticipated or desired that it would one day acquire a dominating influence in the economy. Thus

Benjamin Franklin could write in 1760 that "no man, who can have a piece of land of his own, sufficient by his labor to subsist his family in plenty, is poor enough to be a manufacturer, and work for a master. Hence while there is land enough in America for our people, there can never be manufactures to any amount or value."

Further, Franklin and other influential thinkers of his day did not question that land would cease to exist in abundance for many generations to come. Indeed, as late as 1827, the Secretary of the Treasury stated as his view that "it would take five hundred years to settle the public domain."

In this period, also, the philosopher's ideal individual was one who harmonized the two basic impulses of the human being—self-interest and benevolence. Personal experience supplemented by the observations of others had convinced him that the beneficent Author of the universe had endowed man with two primary instincts, the one to serve oneself, the other to promote the well-being of others.

It is not suggested that this optimistic appraisal of human nature had replaced altogether the more conservative concept of man's innately evil and selfish nature. Alexander Hamilton, for example, is said to have repeated frequently David Hume's admonition: "In contriving any system of government... *every man* ought to be supposed a knave; and to have no other end in all his actions, but *private interest*. By this interest, we must govern him, and by means of it, *make him cooperate to public good,* notwithstanding his unsatiable avarice and ambition." Nevertheless, it can be said that in no period of our history have the average American and the intellectual agreed more in their appraisal of man and his fruitful potentialities.

Probably no one exemplified this theory better than that self-made and practical-minded individual, Benjamin Franklin, of whom Vernon Parrington could write: "All his life his sympathy went out to whoever suffered in person or fortune from the injustice of society: to the debtor who found himself pinched by the shrinking supply of currancy; to the black slave who suffered the most elementary of wrongs; to the impressed seaman; to the weak and wretched of earth. He was a part of that emerging humanitarian movement which, during the last half of the eighteenth century, was creating a new sense of social responsibility."[1]

[1] Vernon Louis Parrington, *Main Currents in American Thought,* Vol. I, *The Colonial Mind* (New York: Harcourt, Brace & Co., 1927), p. 178.

We now turn to a period in our history which seemed to validate a quite different concept of human nature. This later concept was to emphasize man's "struggle for existence," the "survival of the fittest," and, the virtues of "rugged individualism."

THE NATION EXPANDS, AND ITS PEOPLE CHANGE

Victory in the American Revolution had removed legal barriers to settlements west of the mountains, with the result that from the seaboard states as well as from abroad there began a westward movement of population that neither prosperity nor adversity could stop. By 1800 over 1,000,000 persons had moved beyond the mountains. By 1820 this number had increased to some 2,500,000, or to one-fourth of the total population of the entire country and 1,000,000 in excess of that of all New England. The mid-1820's also saw the original thirteen states increased in number to twenty-four. By 1830 Ohio (admitted to the Union in 1803) had become more populous than Massachusetts; Indiana (admitted in 1816), more populous than Connecticut. In the same year Kentucky and Tennessee, settled largely by people from Virginia, outnumbered the Old Dominion, as did Alabama, Mississippi, and Louisiana outnumber their major sources of population, the Carolinas. The years 1812 and 1821 witnessed the admission of two states, Louisiana and Missouri, from west of the Mississippi River, to be followed by five more (including California and Oregon on the western coast) prior to the election of Lincoln in 1860. By 1893 the Land Office was required to announce the exhaustion of arable land on the frontier. With this announcement a phenomenal era of exploitation and development of natural resources appeared to have come to an end, and a nation of forty-five states prepared to face changes in the twentieth century no less novel and surprising than those of the nineteenth.

This rapid expansion in population and territory was rendered possible by the combination of a high birthrate in the native population and a steadily mounting stream of immigrants from abroad. Between 1789 and the 1829 inauguration of Jackson as President some 400,000 immigrants entered the United States. By 1840 this number increased to 1,713,251; and by 1850, to 2,598,214. Industrial development following the Civil War, together with the rapid exploitations of the matchless resources of the West, further encouraged Europeans to respond to the invitation engraved on the Statue of Liberty and erected in New York Harbor in 1884:

... Give me your tired, your poor,
Your huddled masses yearning to breathe free,
The wretched refuse of your teeming shore.
Send these, the homeless, tempest-tost to me,
I lift my lamp beside the golden door!

The high-water mark of immigration was reached in the first decade of 1900 with an influx of 5,246,613, two and one-half times that of the 1870's and one and one-half times larger than in the depression decade of the 1890's. And the tide was not stemmed until the restrictive legislation of the 1920's. For example, between 1901 and 1910 nearly 9,000,000 immigrants entered the United States; between 1911 and 1920, almost 6,000,000.

Significant also were the sources of immigration during this period. Prior to 1880 a majority were similar in nationality to the original settlers —English, Irish, Scotch, German, and Scandinavian. With the rapid industrial development and growth of cities from 1880 on, southern and eastern Europe became the primary sources, supplying 1,000,000 between 1881 and 1890, 2,000,000 between 1891 and 1900, and 6,000,000 in the first decade of the twentieth century.

It was of significance to education that many of these immigrants encountered radically different conditions of living in the United States from those they were accustomed to in their original homes. In Europe they had lived primarily in rural villages and had earned their living principally as farm laborers, an occupation from which they hoped to escape upon coming to America. Once in the United States, they flocked to the cities or to mining towns, there to share in slum conditions of living with relatives and friends, and there, too, to create complicated patterns of diversity in what had once been relatively homogeneous communities.

WE BECOME AN INDUSTRIAL NATION

In 1793 Eli Whitney invented the cotton gin, a device which was to increase tremendously the production of cotton. To this he added, shortly thereafter, the equally revolutionary invention of interchangeable parts in the manufacture of machines. In New England factories were beginning to use steam as a source of power, thus multiplying the productive capacity of human hands.

The full effects of these changes were not felt, however, until after the War of 1812. Then a number of factors contributed to stimulate manufacturing and with it a phenomenal growth of cities: rapid increase in cotton production as a source of raw material for northern factories; tariff legislation designed to protect domestic industries from foreign competition; improved means of transportation and communication resulting from the construction of canals and, later, railroads; and the expansion of the western market for manufactured goods following settlement upon public lands and the exploitation of western mineral resources.

By 1830 Lowell in Massachusetts, Rochester on the Erie Canal, Buffalo and Cleveland on Lake Erie, Pittsburgh and Cincinnati on the Ohio River, and St. Louis on the Mississippi River were developing rapidly. Between 1830 and 1840 the population of Chicago multiplied eight times (from 500 to 4,000); by 1860 it totaled some 110,000. In the same year New York registered more than 1,000,000; St. Louis and Cincinnati, more than 160,000. By 1860 one-fifth of all Americans were living in places of 2,500 or more, and of these one-half lived in cities of over 50,000 in population.

And these developments were not checked by the Civil War. On the contrary, they were accelerated by what the Beards termed "the furious years of the commercial development that followed the Civil War." Particularly significant was the application of science and technology to mining and manufacture and of "Yankee ingenuity" to more efficient and profitable methods of business organizations in trade and commerce. By the 1880's the once rural Midwest and the "Wild West" were outstripping the East in rapidity of growth.

Immigration and the growth of cities were, of course, but the outward and visible signs of fundamental changes in the character of American life. These changes were, however, far from identical in all sections.

THE SOUTH DEVELOPS ITS OWN "PECULIAR" INSTITUTIONS

Mention was made in Chapter 2 of the manner in which the plantation system gradually replaced small farms in the South, discouraging the immigration of free labor and the evolution of a vigorous middle class. In the nineteenth century, King Cotton insisted ever more urgently upon recognition of his superior status. Small landowners continued to retreat westward in the face of the advancing large plantation. Within one generation, the cotton kingdom spread from South Carolina to Texas. Like tobacco, cotton production quickly exhausted the soil. Since its production also thrived better on slave labor than on free, there resulted both a consolidation of holdings and a hungry demand for ever new land for plantation owners to exploit. "As late as 1860," writes William Miller, "hardly 350,000 Southerners owned any slaves at all. Fewer than 8,000 owned as many as 50 slaves. But these men, heading less than 1 per cent of southern families, probably owned a fourth of all hands. Their purchases were chiefly responsible for pushing the slave population from 1,500,000 in 1820 to nearly 4,000,000 in 1860, despite a death rate that claimed every second Negro infant." [2] Slavery was also responsible for pushing cotton production "from 335,000 bales in 1820, virtually all of it in South Carolina and Georgia, to a record 5,387,000 bales in 1859, two-thirds of it in the rich Gulf states." [3]

These changes wrought havoc with the ideals of equality and the rights of men as once expressed by George Mason, Thomas Jefferson, and other eighteenth-century southerners. Voices in favor of the emancipation and manumission of slaves became weaker and weaker as legal restrictions upon the freeing of slaves became more common. According to a southern historian, "the sale of slaves became the source of the largest profit of nearly all the slaveholders of the upper South," [4] where sentiment in favor of manumission had once been most keen. And Thomas Jefferson Randolph could tell the State Legislature of Virginia in 1832, "It is the practice, and an increasing practice, in parts of Virginia, to rear slaves ... The exportation [from Virginia] has averaged 8,500 for the last twenty years." [5]

As the abolition movement in the North gained momentum, science and religion were appealed to in order to justify slavery; science, to establish the biological inferiority of the Negro; religion and the Bible, to picture slavery as ordained by God. As one southerner put it, it is "God's law that fetters on black skins don't chap." [6]

2 William Miller, A New History of the United States (New York: George Braziller, 1958), p. 190.
3 Ibid., p. 190.
4 Quoted in Miller, ibid., p. 164.
5 Ibid., p. 164.
6 Ibid., p. 190.

AND EDUCATION SUFFERED

The economic and social system in the South, consisting of an aristocratic upper class, a relatively weak middle class, "poor whites," free Negroes, and, on the lowest level, slaves, was unfavorable to the development of publicly supported free schools. Such development is more characteristic of a society composed of free labor and a vigorous middle class. Nevertheless, prior to the Civil War, in Virginia, North and South Carolina, and Georgia, valiant efforts were made to establish free schools. Following the American Revolution, a number of the southern states had incorporated in their constitutions provisions for the establishment of schools. These were, however, vague in formulation and only partially realized in practice. Virginia and other states in the North and South early in the nineteenth century established Literary Funds, the proceeds of which were to be used in support of schools. Quite generally, however, the schools thus established were intended for the poor. Property owners of substance tended to object to the imposition of taxes in support of schools open and free to all. When John Randolph of Virginia stated in the Constitutional Convention of that state in 1829, "It is the very essence of property that none shall tax it but the owner himself, or one who has a common feeling and interest with him," he expressed a sentiment common to the southern upper class. This group favored private schools for those who could afford to pay for their education and free public education, if at all, for the poor only.

During the 1840's and the 1850's, in Virginia, the Carolinas, and Georgia, educators and other interested citizens strove manfully to realize through state action the ideal of public support and control of free schools, but with all too little success. The nearest approaches to tangible results were legislation in North Carolina in 1852 and the appointment of Calvin H. Wiley as superintendent of schools in 1853. Wiley served courageously and effectively in this capacity until 1861. Not until the conclusion of the Civil War and the period of Reconstruction did public schools, publicly supported, become general in the South.

By that time, however, the South lacked the resources with which to support education in a manner equal to free education in the North and West. The Reconstruction period, with its disastrous effects upon the planter class, was followed by the sharecropper and crop-lien system which chained plantation owners to northern creditors and sharecroppers to merchants for food, seed, and fertilizers. Moreover, freedom did not prove an unmixed blessing for the Negro, once the carpetbagger and federal troops had withdrawn from the region. Decisions of the United States Supreme Court, ending with the Civil Rights Cases of 1883, virtually withdrew federal protection from the Negro and remanded him to the mercy of states embittered by Reconstruction. "After that," concludes Miller, "the white southern farmer became the avenging spirit of the 'Old Time South'; he in particular made freedom a nightmare for the descendants of the old-time slave." [7]

Had manufacturing and education been available for poor white and Negro the situation might have been eased for both. Unfortunately, manufacturing in textiles, for which the South was adapted, developed slowly, largely for want of capital. As late as 1900, for example, southern manufacturing accounted for a smaller proportion of manufacturing in the country as a whole than it did in 1860. [8]

Without economic resources it was impossible to provide schooling appropriate to the needs of the times or the section. Under Reconstruction and as a condition for the readmission of states to the Union, systems of free schools came into being in the South. But the resources available for their development were meager, and their effectiveness was lessened by the decision to maintain a dual system of schools, one for white children and one for Negroes.

CHANGES IN THE NORTH AND WEST

In contrast with its disastrous effects upon the South, the Civil War, if anything, in the North and West accentuated economic and social developments that were well on their way prior to the outbreak of hostilities. These began, in fact, with the conclusion of the War of 1812, as the above data on population, immigration, and the growth of cities suggest.

"Mr. Madison's War" in 1812 closed American markets to English trade and encouraged Americans to manufacture goods previously produced in English factories. "Infant industries," once started, were generously aided by a series of protective tariffs, beginning with the Act of 1816.

To protection against external competition were added the rewards of

[7] *Ibid.*, p. 237.
[8] *Ibid.*, p. 235.

Yankee inventiveness. A pioneer in this respect was a Waltham factory that opened in 1815. Unlike its predecessors in the manufacturing of textiles, it introduced power machines and the techniques of mass production. So successful were the Boston Associates, as the owners came to be called, in perfecting the manufacture of cheap textiles demanded by the West and South that, in spite of the years of depression from 1819 to 1821, dividends repaid the initial investment within six years. This success set a pattern for others to follow not only in textiles but in other articles as well, with the result that "The profits of Massachusetts textile mills were thus transformed into railroad tracks in Michigan, Illinois, and Iowa, into buildings in Cleveland and Chicago, and into hundreds of other new American enterprises." [9]

One ingenious means used by New England factory owners in order to reduce the costs of production was to employ "well-brought-up farm girls." These girls lived in boarding houses owned and operated by the company, carefully supervised by responsible matrons. To the advantages of wages that yielded savings of a dollar or two a week above expenses were added, at the end of a long day in the factory, the educational advantages of lectures and library facilities! Later, with the continued expansion of industry in New England and the West, immigrants from Europe constituted a generous source of cheap labor for whose living conditions few employers assumed an obligation similar to that accorded New England girls.

Heavy investments of European capital in American railroad construction and canals constituted a further advantage for American business enterprise, opening up both southern and western markets to eastern manufactures and enabling the latter to plow back profits into further expansion of their factories. Between 1820 and 1837 investments in plant and machinery showed a fivefold increase (from $50,000,000 to some $250,000,000), of which most derived from profits.[10]

Finally should be mentioned the abundance of cheap land and the inducements this afforded for speculation as well as settlement by individuals from home and abroad who saw in the ownership and exploitation of the soil, with its untapped resources (agricultural and mineral), a golden opportunity. Chicago affords an excellent example of the effects

[9] Thomas C. Cochran, "The Factory Comes to New England," in Earl Schenck Miers (ed.), *The American Story* (New York: Channel Press, 1956), p. 126.
[10] Miller, *op. cit.*, p. 173.

of the speculative fever upon land values. In the 1820's land in Chicago, as elsewhere in the unoccupied public domain, could be purchased for $1.25 per acre. By 1832 the price had risen to $100; by 1836, to $3,500 per acre. When, in 1836, the Illinois legislature approved the construction of a canal to link the city with the Mississippi River and began the sale of bonds with which to finance this construction, the price of one lot along the proposed route rose to $21,400.

The white man's hunger for land bore heavily upon the American Indian. Tens of millions of acres in the Southwest were opened to speculation in the 1830's by the forcible removal of Indian tribes from their lands; millions more acres were added when Texas achieved its independence from Mexico in 1836. And in the Northwest the Black Hawk War of 1831 resulted in the acquisition of over 100,000,000 acres of fertile soil.

In speaking of the relations of the white man to the Negro in the South, Lillian Smith remarks, "Our grandfathers' conscience compelled them to justify slavery, and they did by making the black man different; setting him outside God's law, reducing him to less than human." [11] Much the same may be said of the treatment of the Indian from the early colonial period to the present, suggesting that American ideals of equality and of freedom have too often applied only to what the sociologists term the "ingroup"!

BUSINESS ENTERPRISE ACQUIRES ECONOMIC AND POLITICAL POWER

The conquest of the West both stimulated and was assisted by expansion in business enterprise. At no time in history had business developed on a scale equal to that in the United States following the Civil War. "With a stride that astounded statisticians," wrote Charles and Mary Beard, "the conquering hosts of business enterprise swept over the continent; twenty-five years after the death of Lincoln, America had become, in the quantity and the value of her products, the first manufacturing nation of the world. What England had once accomplished in a hundred years, the United States had achieved in half the time." [12]

Perhaps we should add that seldom in history have equally favorable factors cooperated more generously with business enterprise. Yankee

[11] Lillian Smith, *Killers of the Dream* (New York: W. W. Norton & Co., 1961), p. 61.
[12] Charles Beard and Mary Beard, *The Rise of American Civilization*, Vol. II (New York: The Macmillan Co., 1930), p. 176.

ingenuity had already solved the mechanical problems of mass production. It now created the corporation, a plan of organization that made possible the merging of financial resources for productive purposes while limiting the liability of individual investors to their own holdings. The corporate plan also both encouraged risk-taking adventures in fields that might otherwise have remained fallow and strengthened the hands of management in meeting competition.

To these advantages should be added the friendly assistance of the Supreme Court and Congress in the 1870's and 1880's. By interpreting the Fourteenth Amendment so as to identify corporations as "persons" the Court rendered them virtually free from regulation on the part of both state and federal governments. At the same time, Congress, heavily represented in its membership by representatives of business, combined both to "protect" American business from foreign competition and to enact legislation designed to stimulate the exploitation and development of the nation's natural resources.

Thus encouraged, business organizations grew by leaps and bounds. Corporation combined with corporation to form trusts, pools, and holding companies in order to control output, manipulate prices, and monopolize markets. For example, the Standard Oil Trust was organized in 1882. Within ten years of that date, the Cottonseed Oil Trust, the Sugar Trust, the Salt Trust, the Feather Trust, the Cordage Trust, and others were formed. Of the Sugar Trust, a judge of the Supreme Court of New York wrote, "It can close every refinery at will, close some and open others, limit the purchase of raw material, artificially limit the production of refined sugar, enhance the price to enrich themselves and their associates at the public expense, and depress the price when necessary to crush out and impoverish a foolhardy rival." [13]

There was no great moral uprising on the part of the public to methods thus employed or to the philosophy used to justify the activities of the "robber barons." On the contrary, economic theory and the philosophy of Social Darwinism pointed to these developments as an illustration of the inevitable manifestation of the "struggle for existence" that eventuates, ultimately, in the "survival of the fittest." Opposition centered more upon attempts to equalize conditions of competition than upon its elimination. Farmers and small businessmen organized with a view to the outlawing of unfair practices—tariffs too high for adequate protection, railroad re-

[13] Quoted in Miller, op. cit., p. 275.

bates to favored shippers, discriminatory fares, and the like—with only minor success because of the ease with which large financial interests maintained control over Congress and state legislatures and the tendency of the courts to identify the philosophy of Social Darwinism with a strict interpretation of the Constitution.

The effects of these changes were widespread. The earlier direct and intimate relationships between employer and employee, seller and buyer, tended to disappear, and, with them, the workman's pride in craftsmanship and excellence of product. Separation of ownership and management became a common characteristic of large-scale enterprise. And management—in its rush for profits—was often as concerned with the manipulation of stocks and the suppression of competition as with the quality of product and the cheapest and most effective methods of production.

It was not that efficiency of production ceased to be important. On the contrary, the applications of science and technology to industry stimulated widespread interest in education and the reorganization of curricula of school and college with an eye not only to more generous provision for science and its applications but to the establishment of separate vocational and professional schools.

LABOR COMES OF AGE

Historians of the labor movement in the United States commonly date its beginnings with the organization of the Mechanics' Union of Trade Associations in Philadelphia in 1827. Authorities tell us that this was the first central organization of trades in the world. Prior to this event, however, workers in a number of trades in the cities of Philadelphia, Boston, New York, and Baltimore had combined for the purpose of bettering wages and improving working conditions. Indeed, the first recorded strike in the United States in support of a demand for higher wages was that of printers in Philadelphia in 1786. Other strikes by printers and shoemakers occurred in the 1790's. Prior to 1830 workingmen's organizations of hatters, tailors, weavers, nailers, cabinetmakers, carpenters, and, in one instance, female factory workers were formed in efforts to better wages and working conditions. These organizations were temporary only and limited to a specific purpose. One result, however, was to stimulate the formation of associations of masters, who, with the help of the courts, succeeded in checking the growth of organizations of labor on the ground that their members were engaged in an unlawful conspiracy.

As defined by the courts, conspiracy consisted in efforts of persons to combine "together by direct means to impoverish or prejudice a third person, or to do acts prejudicial to the community." Perlman points out that the decisions of the courts turned less on the attempt of labor to secure higher wages than on its efforts to achieve this object by means of the closed shop.[14]

In 1828 the Mechanics' Union of Trade Associations entered the political field in order to achieve "equality of citizenship." Like farmers and liberals, they saw in the democratic upheaval led by Andrew Jackson an opportunity to realize through the exercise of the recently acquired suffrage the ideals of equality as expressed in the Declaration of Independence. (In 1790 all but three states had property qualifications for the exercise of the franchise. By 1830 eight states had adopted universal manhood suffrage; and nine, a taxpaying qualification. Only South and North Carolina, Virginia, New Jersey, and Rhode Island continued to require a heavy property qualification.) The alliance with the followers of Andrew Jackson led workers and farmers to unite in opposition to the Bank of the United States and to oppose bankers and capitalists generally on the ground that the latter's power was used to restrict credit and thus to place the workingman at a disadvantage.

Labor also joined liberal and humanitarian groups in an effort to eliminate the system of imprisonment for debt. The Boston Prison Discipline Society, an organization devoted to the abolition of imprisonment for debt, estimated in 1829 that some 75,000 persons in the United States were imprisoned annually for debt. In many instances the sums involved were small, as in the case of a widow whose husband, as Perlman records it, lost his life in a fire while attempting to save the property of an individual who later had the woman imprisoned for a debt of 68 cents! [15]

Other measures supported by labor prior to the Civil War were Mechanic Lien Laws, acts designed to safeguard the wages of laborers from liens in the event of bankruptcy on the part of their employer; legislation in Congress that would grant each would-be settler upon the

[14] Selig Perlman, A History of Trade Unionism in the United States (New York: The Macmillan Co., 1922), Chapter 7, on "Trade Unionism and the Courts," pp. 146 ff.
[15] Ibid., p. 12.

public lands a homestead free of charge; laws assuring workers the right to organize and bargain with their employers; and federal legislation limiting the workday of federal employees to ten hours. This last was supported in the hope that federal example would render easier the acceptance of a ten-hour day by private industry. In the factories of New England, for example, the average working day for women and children was nearly thirteen hours. Little success attended efforts on the part of workers to achieve a ten-hour day prior to the 1830's, when strikes for this purpose enlisted the support not only of labor but of professional groups as well. Victory on the federal level was finally won when President Van Buren, on March 31, 1840, issued an executive order establishing the ten-hour day on government work without a corresponding reduction in wages. By and large, the ten-hour day persisted even in the most favored trades until the end of the century. In occupations dependent upon woman and child labor, improved conditions of work in the form of wages and hours of work came still more slowly.

From the standpoint of education this development was most important. Edwards and Richey estimate that two-fifths of all laborers in factories in 1832 were children, few of whom had an opportunity to learn to read or write. Factories served as a magnet, especially in New England, with which to attract both children and adults away from the farm. These factories, and the towns and cities that grew up around them, expanded more rapidly than the social vision with which to solve the problems generated. Edwards and Richey describe the situation as follows:

> It was in the rapidly growing urban centers that the inadequacies of institutions which had served the old order first became apparent. ... Intemperance, poverty, sickness, disease, crime, and moral decay thrived in the new urban centers. Illiterate and unruly children roamed the streets uncared for and considered only as potential workers in factories which took them at a tender age. Employers of young workers were looked upon as public benefactors because they kept small boys and girls from idleness and from succumbing to criminal tendencies during the ten to thirteen working hours of the day.[16]

Mother, father, and children were commonly employed, but the wages of all provided only a bare subsistence.

[16] Newton Edwards and Herman G. Richey, *The School in the American Social Order* (Boston: Houghton Mifflin Co., 1947), p. 328.

LABOR ORGANIZATION ON A NATIONAL SCALE

The period following the Civil War marked the growth of national organizations of labor. In 1869, the Noble Order of the Knights of Labor was organized in Philadelphia as a secret organization. To its ranks were invited all laborers, skilled and unskilled, white and Negro, male and female, without distinction of trade, race, sex, or nationality, in the hope that thus united both the economic and political interests of the common people might be realized. The Knights contended that, as a secret organization, "we but imitate the example of capital, for in all the multifarious branches of trade, capital has its combinations and, whether intended or not, it crushes the manly hopes of labor and tramples poor humanity into the dust." [17]

In the economic field the Knights were fairly successful in securing higher wages and in preventing severe cuts in wages that so frequently accompanied periods of economic depression in the 1870's and 1880's. In the political field they strove for the passage of Chinese Exclusion Acts, the eight-hour day in government and on government projects, the establishment of both state and federal labor bureaus, and the elimination of contract labor. The worst form of contract labor was the "padrone system," in which a padrone contracted for the labor of men for a stated period while they were still in Europe, farmed them out to employers in this country, received their wages, and paid them only a minimum sum at the conclusion of the agreed-upon period.

For a brief time the Knights of Labor developed considerable influence in both the economic and political fields. Eventually, however, the organization lost its influence and gave way to the more tightly organized American Federation of Labor.[18]

Several factors contributed to this demise of the Knights. One was the organization's identification with revolutionary changes in society, such as the public ownership of public utilities, the establishment of pro-

[17] Quoted by Beard and Beard, op. cit., p. 220.
[18] The American Federation of Labor was organized under the leadership of Samuel Gompers and Adolph Strasser in 1886. Unlike the Knights of Labor, it constituted a federation of national craft unions in the skilled trades. Each union was represented in the national organization but exercised autonomy in the conduct of its own affairs. The central organization was assigned specific functions such as assisting in the organization of new unions, helping in the conduct of labor disputes, and seeking legislation of concern to all. From the beginning it was careful to center upon the economic interests of labor and to avoid identification with political parties.

ducers' cooperatives with the idea of eliminating conventional capitalism; another, its friendly associations with the Socialist, Populist, and Green-back parties. A second factor was the organized opposition to labor that developed in connection with bitterly fought strikes on a nationwide scale, such as the railroad strike in 1877; the bloody contests in Home-stead, Pennsylvania, involving the Carnegie plants; and the Pullman strike in Chicago in 1894, which resulted in the famous Haymarket riots. During this period the employing groups were successful in enlisting the help of both state and federal governments and of the courts through the issuing of injunctions which severely crippled union activity in the con-duct of strikes.

Under these circumstances the more limited and conservative policies of the American Federation of Labor seemed to serve better the interests of organized labor. It refused consistently to affiliate with radical political movements or to act as an independent political party. It did, however, exert pressure upon Congress and state legislatures in favor of specific measures of concern to labor and, by rewarding its friends and punishing its enemies without respect to party affiliation, succeeded in accomplish-ing many of its objects.

Late in the century, also, economic thought under the pioneer influence of Richard T. Ely and his students tended to veer more favorably in the direction of labor and to offset the dominance of conservative economic thought of Social Darwinists. Authoritative voices outside the ranks of labor were now heard in favor of the organization of labor as a normal phase of economic development and the right of labor to bargain collec-tively with employers under conditions more nearly equal than formerly. The year 1900 likewise witnessed the organization of the American Civic Federation (an association of businessmen and professional people), de-voted to the task of promoting friendly relations between capital and labor, assisting in the settlement of labor disputes, and creating generally a better understanding on the part of the public of the role of labor in a democratic society.

THE "COMMON SCHOOL" COMES INTO EXISTENCE

Of special significance for public education was the demand of labor for schooling free from the taint of public charity. In this, labor received support from members of the rapidly increasing middle class (who saw in education an indispensable means for the advancement of their children), from humanitarians, political leaders, educators, and forward-looking businessmen. To reconcile businessmen generally to the principle of taxation of one man for the education of another man's child, Horace Mann and others stressed the market value of education. To this argument of practical advantage was added by some an appeal to fear. "Anxious to wring support for public schools from propertied interest, then opposed to taxation for this purpose," writes Merle Curti, "educational spokesmen warned them of the dangers to property rights from universal suffrage, Jacksonian democracy, and even possible revolution—any of which might result if the masses were left undisciplined by education." [19]

Intellectuals and statesmen of the caliber of Edward Everett also warned eastern capitalists of dangers threatening the status quo from the use of the ballot by frontier folk as well as by labor. Thus, in an address to a group of Boston capitalists in 1833, Everett used the following argument in support of contributions to education in the far-off state of Ohio: "We can from our surplus, contribute toward the establishment and endowment of the seminaries where the mind of the west shall be trained and enlightened . . . [in order] to give security to our property, by diffusing the means of light and truth throughout the region where so much of the power to preserve or to shake it resides." [20]

These united efforts brought about the establishment of free schools in a manner characteristically American—by means of state authorization for individual communities to levy taxes upon the local population in support of public schools. Typical of this legislation was the passage of a law in Missouri in 1824 that permitted school districts to levy taxes in support of public schools with the consent of two-thirds of the voters of each district. A second step was the establishment of state funds, frequently termed "literary funds," the proceeds of which were to be used in support of the "common schools." To funds provided by the states were added, from time to time, substantial assistance to education on the part of the federal government—grants of public land to states upon their admission to the Union, outright appropriations in support of both general and special education, the distribution of surplus revenues, and the like. So acceptable, indeed, had the principle of public education become by the third quarter of the nineteenth century that every state admitted to

[19] Merle Curti, The Social Ideas of American Educators (New York: Charles Scribner's Sons, 1935), p. 81.

[20] Edward Everett, The Importance of Practical Education and Useful Knowledge (New York: Harper & Bros., 1856), pp. 169-170.

the Union since 1876 has been required by congressional resolution to provide in its constitution "for the establishment and maintenance of a system of public schools which shall be open to all children of the State and free from sectarian control."

As we shall see later, when we deal more specifically with conflicting concepts in education, the establishment of public schools did not come without stubborn resistance. Nevertheless, the nineteenth century witnessed not only the beginnings of publicly supported schools, open and free to all without the taint of charity, but, by the end of the century, pioneered by Massachusetts in 1865 and New York in 1866, the adoption of compulsory school attendance laws in some thirty-two states.

THE STATUS OF THE FARMER ALSO CHANGES

Labor was but one segment of the American economy vitally affected by industrial growth and urban development in the period under review. The independent farmer also experienced the growing pains of revolutionary change.

Traditionally Americans have considered agriculture the most important factor in the economy and farmers by nature as their best citizens. From his observations in Europe, for example, Jefferson concluded that manufacturing tended to produce the worst citizens and warned against its development in America. "I consider the class of artificers as the panders of vice," he wrote in a letter to John Jay, "and the instrument by which the liberties of a country are generally overturned."

Few in Jefferson's day realized how short a period was to elapse before an inevitable conflict of interests between farmers and capitalists was to develop. Indeed, within three years of Jefferson's death "a son of the soil" was to enter the lists in opposition to "the moneyed classes" and the banking interests whom he accused of controlling credit, manipulating the tariffs upon manufactured articles with an eye to the maintenance of high prices, and opposing legislation favorable to settlement upon the public lands (lest this cut too deeply into the supply of cheap labor).

Land speculation and generous governmental policies with respect to the sale and disposition of public lands served as a magnet with which to attract prospective settlers from the East and immigrants from abroad. The Land Act of 1820, for example, permitted settlers to buy tracts as small as eighty acres at $1.25 per acre, despite the opposition of John Quincy Adams and his followers, who wished to hold the public lands for a better price and to use the proceeds for internal improvements and education. For the westerners, however, eager both to further settlement and to assist speculators in land, the terms of this act were too restrictive. They wished the government to grant land free to all genuine settlers. Grants of land to railroads both prior to and following the Civil War and the passage of the Homestead Act in 1862 further encouraged rapid development of the West. Railroads, land companies, and western states sent agents abroad to drum up prospective settlers. Between 1862 and 1900 some 80,000,000 acres were registered by homesteaders. In the same period, writes Miller, railroads, land companies, and states which had received grants of public land from the federal government for educational purposes sold more than 520,000,000 acres to prospective settlers.[21]

As indicated earlier, this rapid expansion of western settlement, together with the exploitation of resources in minerals as well as land, stimulated an equally phenomenal development of American industry and business. Up to the close of the century the domestic market was able to absorb practically all of the products of mill and mine. By the turn of the century, however, the period of rapid expansion was obviously drawing to a close, with the exhaustion of arable land for settlement—a fact of revolutionary significance for the future.

Revolutionary changes in methods of farming were also evident by 1900. At the beginning of the century ownership of a farm constituted good insurance for an independent existence. Relatively small as were farms, worked as they were by hand, they nevertheless provided the owner with the basic essentials of food, clothing, and shelter. And the information and skill required for the successful operation of a farm were none other than those which parents could transmit to their children, father to son, mother to daughter. By the end of the century, in contrast, the large farm—with its expensive machinery for planting, fertilizing, and harvesting—was making it increasingly difficult for the small farmer with limited capital and dependence upon hand labor to earn a substantial income.

The science of agriculture had likewise come into being with its requirement for scientific and technical training. With the applications of science and technology to farming came also changes in the farmer's household—plumbing, electric lights, modern heating, books and magazines—erasing in many respects earlier distinctions between urban and

[21] Miller, *op. cit.*, p. 254.

rural conditions of living for those blessed with the capital essential for successful existence under these new conditions. Others, less successful, were reduced to tenancy or forced to abandon farming for work in town and city.

In 1880, state the Beards, 25 percent of all farms in the United States were tilled by renters. By 1900, the proportion had risen to 35 percent and was on the increase. "No longer beckoned westward by free land, the ambitious farm laborer, bent on winning a homestead for himself, had no choice except to plod on through tenancy and debts to his goal; if ill-health or crop failures fell to his lot, he remained all his days in the tenant class." [22]

At no time, however, has the American farmer been disposed to surrender his independence without a struggle. Early in the nineteenth century he united with labor to oppose high tariffs and trends toward monopoly in business and in order to secure legislation favorable for easy settlement upon the public domain. So, too, in the period following the Civil War, he organized politically in order to wage a two-front battle: on one front, to secure legislation that would eliminate discrimination in railroad rates, prohibit unjust warehouse charges, and abolish trusts and monopolies; on the other, to bring about the establishment of departments in government that would concern themselves specifically with problems confronting agriculture. While only partially successful in eliminating the first group of factors, success attended efforts to establish bureaus of research designed to better the lot of the farmer. In 1862 a Bureau of Agriculture was established in Washington; in 1884, a Bureau of Animal Husbandry. In 1889 the Bureau of Agriculture was raised to the status of a Department, and its secretary was made a member of the President's Cabinet. Significant also was legislation in 1887 providing for the establishment of an agriculture experiment station in each state of the Union.

SCHOOLING BECOMES FOR YOUNG PEOPLE WHAT FREE LAND HAS BEEN FOR ADULTS

Finally, of relevance to our discussion, was the farmer's realization of his dependence upon education. The year 1862 marked the passage of the Morrill Act with its generous grants of public land to the states in support of higher education in "agriculture and the mechanic arts."

[22] Beard and Beard, *op. cit.*, pp. 275-276.

The Morrill Act, as Allan Nevins has shown,[23] was plural in its intentions. It represented, in part, a reaction against the overly classical emphasis in higher education;[24] in part, a realization that the national welfare now required generous provision for scientific and technical education on school and college levels; and, in part (Nevins states, "primarily"), an expression of "a fundamental emotion that gave force to the principle that every child should have free opportunity for as complete an education as his tastes and abilities warranted."[25] For a nation rapidly becoming industrial and urban, generous grants of land to its citizens from the public domain no longer sufficed to insure equality of opportunity. Rather was education, particularly education in science and technology, envisaged as a prime essential for keeping open the doors of opportunity in farming, business, industry, and the professions. Accordingly, far-seeing and socially minded individuals began to demand of government that precisely as it once used the public domain as *material capital* with which to insure liberty and equality for adults it now provide future generations of young people with free access to the *intellectual capital* without which the blessings of liberty and equality were in danger of disappearing with the frontier. It is not surprising, on this assumption, that education in secondary school, college and university, as well as in institutions of a specialized vocational character, entered upon a period of phenomenal expansion.

All too hurried as this review of changes in the nineteenth century has been, it will have served its purpose if it has highlighted the revolutionary character of developments in the United States in the course of

[23] Allan Nevins, *The State Universities and Democracy* (Urbana, Ill.: University of Illinois Press, 1962), Chapter I.

[24] Nevins mentions an address delivered by James A. Garfield at Hiram College in Ohio in June, 1867. In preparation for this address Garfield examined the catalogs of some twenty colleges in the East, West, and South, finding them all alike in their emphasis upon Greek and Latin and in their neglect of science and mathematics, literature, political economy, and social science. To earn a bachelor's degree at Harvard, for example, the student had to devote four-fifths of his time to Greece and Rome. "No wonder," said Garfield, "that men are demanding with an earnestness that will not be repressed, to know how it happens, that, placing in one end of the balance all of the mathematical studies, all the physical sciences in their recent rapid developments, all the political economy and social science which underlie the commerce and industry, and shape the legislation of nations, the history of our own nation, the constitution of government, and its great industrial interests, all the literature and history of modern civilization—placing all this, I say, in one end of the balance, they kick the beam when Greece and Rome are placed in the other."—*Ibid.*, p. 6.

[25] *Ibid.*, p. 16.

one century. A population of slightly more than 4,000,000 in 1800 had increased to nearly 76,000,000 by 1900. A Union of thirteen states scattered along the Atlantic seaboard at the time of the adoption of the Constitution had become one of forty-five states with a territory extending not only from the Atlantic to the Pacific, but, with the inclusion of the Hawaiian Islands in 1900, still farther toward the point where West becomes East.

No less revolutionary were the economic and social transformations. Primarily rural and agricultural at the beginning of the century, and with manufacturing and trade in their infancy, the United States, by the end of the century, had become one of the leading industrial nations of the world. And even though in the first decade of the twentieth century over 50,000,000 of its people were living on farms or in villages sustained by agriculture, its population was predominantly urban and industrial in character.

Phenomenal as were these changes in American life, of equal significance was the emergence of public schools, publicly supported, in response to the ideals and aspirations of educational reformers. Accordingly, it is to the development of a philosophy of public education that we now turn.

SUGGESTED READING

Beard, Charles, and Beard, Mary, *The Rise of American Civilization,* Vol. II (New York: The Macmillan Co., 1930), Chapters XX-XXII.

Butts, R. Freeman, and Cremin, Lawrence A., *A History of Education in American Culture* (New York: Holt, Rinehart & Winston, 1953), Chapters 9, 10.

Cremin, Lawrence A., *The Transformation of the School* (New York: Alfred A. Knopf, 1961), Chapter 2.

Miller, William, *A New History of the United States* (New York: George Braziller, 1958), Chapters 6-10.

Nevins, Allan, *The State Universities and Democracy* (Urbana, Ill.: University of Illinois Press, 1962), Chapters I, II.

CHAPTER 5
A PHILOSOPHY OF
PUBLIC EDUCATION EMERGES

CHAPTER 4 briefly summarized significant transformations in American life with respect to business, industry, labor, and agriculture. No less impressive were developments in educational opportunities for American youth. Of all the colonies prior to the Revolution, New England was probably most conscious of the importance of education and most conscientious in providing opportunities for its realization. But even in New England, according to an estimate of Horace Mann's, no more than one youngster out of ten at the time of the Revolution had attended school—and this only intermittently and for short periods of time. By 1840, however, approximately "one-half of the children of New England were given a free education, one-seventh of those of the middle states, and one-sixth of those of the west." [1] By 1850 some 2,000 academies were serving over 250,000 students and the 9 colleges of the colonial period had increased in number to some 200 colleges and universities. By 1850, also, secondary education was no longer a monopoly of privately supported academies. Public high schools as well as public elementary schools were rapidly becoming an inherent part of state school systems.

These developments were most conspicuous in the West, where private education was less firmly established than in the East, and where public support, in the form of grants of land from state and federal govern-

[1] Quoted from the historian Carl Russell Fish, in Charles Beard and Mary Beard, *The American Spirit* (New York: The Macmillan Co., 1942), pp. 251-252.

ments, served to stimulate local initiative. On the other hand, in the South, despite the efforts of such pioneers as Calvin Wiley of North Carolina and Charles Fenton Mercer of Virginia, education remained primarily a private enterprise and served chiefly members of the upper and upper-middle classes. It can be said, however, that elsewhere in the country by 1865, despite uneven developments, the principle of public support of common schools had taken root and the American people were definitely committed to their support.

How do we explain this rapid acceptance of the principle of free education? The answer is found in a unique blend of eighteenth-century ideals and conclusions derived from the American experience following the Revolution and prior to the Civil War.

TO INSURE THESE RIGHTS, GOVERNMENTS ARE INSTITUTED AMONG MEN

Of the rights guaranteed by the Constitution none was more important than that of equality, for this was a period in which the optimist had reason to believe that in America, at least, the "times" were validating the proposition of the Declaration of Independence "that all men are created equal, that they are endowed by their Creator with certain inalienable Rights, that among these are Life, Liberty, and the pursuit of Happiness." Of equal importance was the assumption that governments are instituted among men to insure the realization of their rights!

Mention was made in Chapter 3 of the manner in which the concept of equality, as stated in the Declaration of Independence, had evolved, under conditions of frontier living and in the early stages of industrial development, into a principle that would have horrified many of the Founding Fathers who had appended their names to the Declaration. What began as little more than an affirmation of equality before the law soon became a revolutionary conception of the nature of the individual and of rights which governments are obliged to safeguard and promote.

It was this widened conception of equality, nourished by the fluid conditions of frontier living, that brought about a gradual elimination of property qualifications for voting and the extension of manhood suffrage. Underlying these changes was the assumption that all (barring Negroes and Indians) who are subject to law are entitled to a voice in its formulation. This assumption Jacksonian democracy undertook to validate, and it was to this principle that labor appealed in its attempt to establish the right of workers to unite, to bargain collectively with their employers, and in other ways to remove traditional impediments upon individuals who were striving to improve their economic status. Moreover, it was but a step from the obligation of government to remove artificial obstacles blocking the workingman to the insuring of positive conditions favorable to his progress. Accordingly, we find both state and national governments, early in the nineteenth century, concerned with legislation designed to provide an open road to the economic and social advancement of its citizens. This disposition of government to assist in the material advancement of the individual is illustrated both by tariff legislation designed to protect infant industries from foreign competition and by generous grants of land from the public domain.

Humanitarian movements and the spirit of reform characteristic of the period prior to the Civil War testified further to widespread efforts to give reality to the ideal of equality. These included prison reform; attempts to dignify the position of women through education and the bettering of their legal status; education of the deaf and the blind; social experiments, such as those of Brook Farm, the Owenites at New Harmony in Indiana, and other religious and communal settlements; and, of course, the abolition movement.

THE DEITY ASSUMES MORE HUMANE QUALITIES

Nowhere was the humanitarian and democratic spirit more manifest than in religion and philosophy. For the arbitrary and authoritarian God of Calvin, as we have seen, Deism had substituted the concept of a God of nature—a Cosmic Architect—as the Creator of the universe, a God who operates in accordance with unvarying principles of natural laws, laws that man's reason can discover and use for his own benefit.

Despite the appeal of a God of reason to many, the concept lacked an essential warmth and immediacy for large numbers of men and women who hungered for an emotional as well as an intellectual assurance of a friend behind phenomena. Consequently, the early nineteenth century witnessed a multiplication of Evangelical sects and the establishment of numerous religious communities in which a meagerly educated clergy and the converted layman played a conspicuous role. This was the period of the circuit rider, camp meetings on the frontier, and religious revival with its conversions and public confessions of sin in the more heavily settled and established communities. Common to the many sects that proliferated generously was the conception of a Deity altogether human in nature and intimately concerned with the minute details of each individual's life. Here was a Deity of contradictory qualities—at once a kind and loving Father to all who believed in Him and obeyed His commandments and a God of wrath and vengeance, threatening hellfire and eternal damnation for all who ignored His words and violated His commandments.

W. J. Cash writes of the South as he might well have written of the West and other sections: "What our Southerner required...was a faith as simple and emotional as himself. A faith to draw men together in hordes, to terrify them with Apocalyptic rhetoric, to cast them into the pit, rescue them, and at last bring them shouting into the fold of Grace. A faith, not of liturgy and prayer book, but of primitive frenzy and the blood sacrifice—often of fits and jerks and barks. The God demanded was an anthropomorphic God—the Jehovah of the Old Testament; a God who might be seen, a God who *had* been seen. A passionate, whimsical tyrant, to be trembled before, but whose favor was the sweeter for that. A personal God, a God for the individualist, a God whose representatives were not silken priests but preachers risen from the people themselves." [2]

On a somewhat loftier intellectual plane were the contributions of New England thought to the concepts of democracy, equality, and the brotherhood of man. Unable, philosophically, to accept Calvinistic theology, and profoundly disturbed by the ugly fruits of early industrialism with its exploitation of women and children and the deplorable conditions of living in factory towns and cities, philosophic idealism introduced into American thought new conceptions of man, nature, and the Deity. These have served as an inspiration for reform from the days of William Ellery Channing (1780-1842) and Ralph Waldo Emerson (1803-1882) to the present.

In contrast with the Calvinistic God of wrath, and the Deist's Master Mechanic, New England liberals affirmed the imminent existence of a "loving Father in the human heart of love" (an expression used frequently by Channing). In opposition to the traditional notion of man as one born in sin and naturally disposed to evil was asserted the essential goodness of human nature, together with the uniqueness and worth of each individual soul—an assumption that carried with it the right of each individual to creative self-development and the duty of society to insure the utmost possible realization of this right.

[2] W. J. Cash, *The Mind of the South* (New York: Random House, 1961), p. 58.

Channing, in opposing slavery, summed up these convictions as follows (*Introductory Remarks,* 1841):

> It is because I have learned the essential equality of men before the common Father, that I cannot endure to see one man establishing his arbitrary will over another by fraud, or force, or wealth, or rank, or superstitious claims. It is because the human being has moral powers, because he carries a law in his own breast and was made to govern himself, that I cannot endure to see him taken out of his own hands and fashioned into a tool by another's avarice or pride. It is because I see in him a great nature, the divine image, and vast capacities, that I demand for him means of self-development, spheres for free-action—that I call society not to fetter, but to aid his growth.

EMERSON AND TRANSCENDENTALISM

The philosophic expression of this democratic conception of man and society flowered in Transcendentalism, particularly in the writings of Ralph Waldo Emerson. Not all who drew inspiration from his words understood—nor would they have accepted fully, had they understood—the philosophic concepts from which he derived his vision of man and nature. Nor was it necessary for them to agree literally with his description of the Over-Soul in order to welcome his assertion that "within man is the soul of the whole; the wise silence; the universal beauty, to which every part and particle is equally related; the Eternal One"—in contrast with the Puritans' conviction that man is but a worm.

Consider also the appeal of the following passages from Emerson to a generation of men and women who had firsthand experience of the manner in which man, in cooperation with the bounties of nature, can transform his environment in harmony with inner will and purpose:

> The book of nature is the book of fate. She turns the gigantic pages leaf after leaf, never re-turning one. One leaf she lays down, a floor of granite; a thousand ages, and a measure of coal; a thousand ages, and a layer of marl and mud; vegetable forms appear; her first misshapen animals, zoophyte, trilobium, fish; then saurians, rude forms, in which she has only blocked her future statue, concealing under these unwieldly monsters the finer type of her coming king. The face of the planet cools and dries; the races meliorate, and man is born. . . . (*Essay on Fate*)

We call these millions men; but they are not yet men. Half engaged in the soil, pawing to get free, man needs all the music that can be brought to disengage him. If love, real love, with tears and joy; if want with its scourge, if war with its cannonade, if Christianity with its charity, if trade with its money, if art with its portfolios, if science with her telegraphs through the deeps of space and time, can set his dull nerves throbbing and by loud taps on the tough chrysalis can break its walls and let the new creature emerge erect and free, make way and sing paeon. The age of the quadruped is to go out, the age of the brain and of the heart is to come in. . . . And if one shall read the future of the race hinted in the organic effort of nature to mount and meliorate, and the corresponding impulse to the better in the human being, we shall dare to affirm that there is nothing he will not overcome and convert, until at last culture shall absorb the chaos and gehenna. He will convert the furies into muses, and the hells into benefit. (*Essay on Culture*)

From Emerson's assumption that each individual is a unique expression of the Eternal One follows as a corollary the uniqueness, integrity, and worth of each person—an equality of differences, if you will. And with this goes the moral obligation for each individual to develop and give play to his unique talents. For example, in his lecture on *The American Scholar*, Emerson referred to one of those fables "which, out of unknown antiquity, convey an unlooked-for wisdom, that the gods, in the beginning, divided Man into men, that he might be more helpful to himself; just as the hand was divided into fingers, the better to answer its end."

Self-expression and the inner confidence or "self-reliance" which gives genuineness and value to self-expression were for Emerson the highest form of morality. "Whoso would be a man must be a non-conformist. He who would gather immortal palms must not be hindered by the name of goodness, but must explore if it be goodness. Nothing is at last sacred but the integrity of your own mind." (*Essay on Self-Reliance*)

Emerson was not indifferent to the penalty one must pay, often, in opposing popular opinion, but he valued more the conviction that to intuition "a perfect faith is due," for the reason that "We lie in the lap of an immense intelligence, which makes us receivers of truth and organs of its activity. When we discern justice, when we discern truth, we do nothing of ourselves, but allow a passage to its beams."

The moral for education that Emerson drew from his affirmation of the divine in man was quite the opposite of that provided by the schools of his day. Education for conformity and the passive acceptance of pre-digested ideas were, in his view, inadequate for young people whose essential natures were unique expressions of the divine spirit. Originality in thought and action, originality to the point of nonconformity alone met his prescription. Anticipating the child-centered emphasis in progressive education by several generations, he stated in his address on *The American Scholar*, "Of course there is a portion of reading quite indispensable to a wise man. History and science he must learn by laborious reading. Colleges, in like manner, have their indispensable office—to teach elements. But they can only highly serve us, when they aim not to drill, but to create; when they gather from far every ray of various genius to their hospitable halls, and, by the concentrated fires, set the hearts of youth on fire."

And, again, in his poem "Culture," he wrote:

> Can rulers or tutors educate
> The semigod whom we await?
> He must be musical,
> Tremulous, impressional,
> Alive to gentle influence
> Of landscape and of sky,
> And tender to the spirit-touch
> Of man's or maiden's eye:
> But, to his native centre fast,
> Shall into Future fuse the Past,
> And the world's flowing fates in his own mould recast.

PSYCHOLOGY ALSO AIDS AND ABETS THE CONCEPT OF EQUALITY

Contributing also to the widespread conviction that "all men are created equal" was the psychology of the period. This was still dominantly Lockian in its basic assumptions, except that Locke's "powers of the mind" were now commonly conceived as faculties which await only the stimulation of appropriate content and methods of procedure from without in order to realize their potentialities. These potentialities, however, in common with Locke's basic premise, were not specific, either in the earlier sense of innate ideas or the twentieth-century assumption of specific tendencies to respond in specific ways to specific stimuli. That is to say, the mind, as viewed by materialists, realists, and idealists alike, was unformed at birth, but receptive to the writings of experience upon it.

Take, for example, the materialists, as represented by Benjamin Rush, Thomas Cooper, and Joseph Buchanan, who either subordinated the mind to bodily functions or conceived of mental phenomena as no more than physiological activities of an extremely complex and sensitive nature.[3] All agreed that environment was primarily responsible in determining what the individual becomes and were active in urging the state through education to provide the conditions that would inaugurate a more perfect society. Buchanan saw in the Pestalozzian method the possibility of producing genius at will. Writing in *The Kentucky Gazette* of February 2, 1812, he asserted,

> In human nature, sentiment is the only spring of action—the sole power which puts the whole man in motion, and determines in a great degree the measure of his abilities. There is nothing more essential to genius itself, than strength and durability of intellectual feeling. The success of the educator in cultivating the understanding itself must depend very much on the plastic influence and rational control which he is able to exercise over the sentiments of his pupils. By instituting an ardent perseverance of temper he may generate capacity, talents, genius.

Later, in 1820, he outlined a treatise on "The Art of Popularity" in which he hoped to demonstrate how to raise up political leaders through education.[4]

---

[3] Benjamin Rush (1745-1813) is recognized today as a pioneer in physiological psychology and in studies of abnormal behavior. In his *Influence of Physical Causes upon the Moral Faculty* (1786) and other published studies, he demonstrated from specific cases the manner in which physical conditions playing upon the individual influence moral behavior and other intellectual functions. Thomas Cooper came to the United States in 1794; taught at Dickinson College, the University of Pennsylvania, and the University of Virginia; and was president of South Carolina College (later the University of South Carolina) from 1820 to 1834. He was a friend of Thomas Jefferson, wrote numerous political pamphlets, and was both imprisoned and fined for his opposition to the Alien and Sedition Acts. Among his more scholarly works were *The Memoirs of Dr. Joseph Priestley* (1806), *Lectures on the Elements of Political Economy* (1826), and a *Treatise on the Law of Libel* (1830). Joseph Buchanan was a Kentucky journalist and educator and an ardent follower of Thomas Jefferson. His major work, *Philosophy of Human Nature* (1812), was based upon medical psychology and treated the mind as an integral part of the human organism.

[4] Herbert W. Schneider, *A History of American Philosophy* (New York: Columbia University Press, 1946), p. 229.

Horrified as were the realists with the implications of materialism for religious orthodoxy (particularly belief in the existence of an immaterial soul and of immortality after death), they were nevertheless equally convinced of the innate equality of men and the possibilities of education for the improvement of the individual and the bettering of society.[5] Furthermore, since it was the realists with their belief in faculty psychology who exercised the dominant influence in the United States through their representatives in church and college,[6] it was highly significant that their leaders should insist that differences commonly attributed to race and sex result from environmental influences such as climate, custom, and culture rather than from native endowment. These views remained minority views in their effects upon the status of Negroes and Indians, but at the same time they gave body and substance to the efforts of labor, liberals, and humanitarians to equalize opportunities for members of the rising middle classes.

Not only did faculty psychology give validity to the argument in favor of the establishment of schools open and free to all who wished to profit from them; it provided as well theoretical justification for a one-track

[5] Realism represented a reaction in this country, as well as abroad, both to Bishop Berkeley and David Hume. Realists rejected the theory that objects become known through the mediation of ideas or occasional causes, insisting instead, in accordance with common sense, that objects are known directly and intuitively. In this view the mind knows immediately and directly three kinds of reality: (1) matter in the form of external objects and the body; (2) the perceiving self as a thinking, feeling, and willing substance; and (3) objects perceived by conscience or the moral faculty, that is, the knowledge of right and wrong.

[6] The center of realism and the doctrine of common sense was Princeton University, from whence, according to Woodbridge Riley, "it over-ran the country, and had an exclusive and preponderant influence well beyond the centennial of the country's independence." Riley ascribes the dominance of realism to several factors: (1) Not only "was the common sense philosophy of Reid, Stewart, Brown, and Hamilton in harmony with the practical note of the country, but it was also an aid to faith, a safeguard to morality as against the skepticism of Hume and the atheism of the Voltairians"; (2) as such it appealed to the Protestant clergy and the faculties of denominational colleges, thus constituting a formidable influence in a country in which most colleges were church-affiliated; (3) the influence of Scotch-Irish immigrants who, entering the country "by way of the ports of the Middle States, carried along with their Presbyterian connections their philosophy of common sense" into the Allegheny Mountains and down the valleys of Virginia and the Cumberland. "This glacial age in American thought," continues Riley, "was of greatest significance. Because of it Deism disappeared, save in the tide-water counties where planters of English blood still remained, and materialism was wiped out, save in the Gallicized portions of the country, such as the Carolinas, and the Bourbon sectors of Kentucky."—Woodbridge Riley, *American Thought: From Puritanism to Pragmatism and Beyond* (Gloucester, Mass.: Peter Smith, 1959), pp. 119-121.

curriculum and methods of teaching common to all. This it did with its assumption of a typical mind (the operations of which might be identified by introspection) possessed of general powers that lend themselves to formal training. On the level of the elementary school, or the common school as it was called, this conception of the faculties of the mind and methods of instruction consistent with it were given widespread application through the Pestalozzian movement.[7]

In the elementary school this conception of the mind found application in object teaching, an effort to educate the child first through the senses, since these were thought to develop and require discipline prior to such faculties as imagination, memory, and reason. As a result of this concern for the needs of development, the curriculum of the school was enriched by the addition of materials in science, geography, arithmetic, oral language, and the like. But the assumption of general faculties, or general potentialities of the mind, that evolve in a serial order and are assisted in so doing by (if not dependent upon) the stimulation of outside material also lent itself to a concept of formal discipline. Here was the notion that once such faculties as memory and reason are trained and disciplined by appropriate material of one kind they will function efficiently in all other situations calling for their exercise. For a considerable period of time the doctrine of formal discipline was used by conservatives in secondary school and college to oppose the introduction of science and practical subjects of study and to maintain the supremacy of the classics, mathematics, and literature. It was also a theory which prompted labor leaders to oppose, for a time, in the "interests of democracy" the introduction of vocational courses in the schools.

A CONCERN FOR CITIZENSHIP ALSO LENDS SUPPORT TO PUBLIC EDUCATION

The democratic principle of equality constituted a primary motive in the establishment of public school systems. Allied with this principle was a growing concern for citizenship education, which, too, received sup-

---

[7] It is true that there was no general adoption or, we might say, no well-conceived professional application of Pestalozzian methods in the United States prior to 1860 and the establishment of the Oswego training school in Oswego, New York, under the direction of Superintendent Edward A. Sheldon. Educators were, however, influenced by Pestalozzi and his work from 1820 on, through the writings of Henry Barnard, William Russell, W. C. Woodbridge, Horace Mann, and others in American educational journals. Warren Colburn's *First Lessons in Arithmetic on the Plan of Pestalozzi* was published in 1821 and received widespread adoption in American schools.

port from individuals and groups of varying complexion. Liberal-minded people from all classes joined with labor in emphasizing the intimate connection between education and the responsibilities of a citizen in a government in which the people are both governors and governed. When, for example, the workingmen of Philadelphia, in 1820, demanded of each candidate for the state legislature that he state his attitude toward an equal and general system of education for the state, and the Association of Workingmen of New Castle, Delaware, declared in their constitution, "Let us unite at the polls and give our vote to no candidate who is not pledged to support a national system of education to be paid for out of public funds," they did so on the assumption that the right of suffrage is an empty right unless those who participate in government are properly prepared through education to exercise it.

Not to be ignored in this connection was the conviction of many that with schooling as a weapon the common people might wrest control of society from the upper classes—from the financially advantaged and the learned, who often served the former. Consequently, as pointed out by Richard Hofstadter, the campaign on behalf of free schools on the elementary level paralleled, often, opposition to genuine intellectual values as these might be developed in secondary school and college. "As the demand for the rights of the common man took form in nineteenth-century America," writes Hofstadter, "it included a program of free elementary education, but it also carried with it a dark and sullen suspicion of high culture, as a creation of the enemy." [8]

Furthermore, according to Hofstadter, the strictly utilitarian and down-to-earth motive in American education has not played itself out. Only thus can we explain today, as yesterday, the contrast between the American's much-heralded "faith in education" and his failure to dignify the profession of teaching with both status and salary or to insure the obvious essentials of a good education in the way of materials of learning, class size, physical facilities, and other primary conditions for carrying on the educational enterprise.

No one stated the argument in behalf of public education more forcefully than did Horace Mann (1796-1859) in his annual reports as Secretary to the State Board of Education of Massachusetts. Of the relation of

[8] See, in this connection, Richard Hofstadter, *Anti-Intellectualism in American Life* (New York: Alfred A. Knopf, 1963), Chapters VI and XII, on "The Decline of the Gentleman" and "The School and the Teacher."

education to the exercise of citizenship he wrote: "Now, as a republican government represents almost all interests, whether social or military, the necessity of a degree of intelligence adequate to the due administration of them all, is so self-evident, that a bare statement is the best argument. ... In a republican government, legislators are a mirror reflecting the moral countenance of their constituents. And hence it is, that the establishment of a republican government, without well-appointed and efficient means for the universal education of the people, is the most rash and foolhardy experiment ever tried by man." [9]

Of the political leaders favoring the establishment of state school systems, Thaddeus Stevens (1792-1868) merits special mention for the part he played in the Pennsylvania legislature of 1835. There, the opponents of free schools had sought to appeal an act of the previous year which permitted school districts to levy taxes in support of public schools. The address delivered by Stevens on this occasion, in the face of strong public opinion to the contrary, not only persuaded the legislature to retain the permissive legislation but, when printed and distributed throughout the country, served for many years to further the cause of free public education. In this address, Stevens answered virtually all the common objections to public education and demonstrated as well the positive values that would derive from it. On the importance of education for the exercise of citizenship, Stevens said, in part: "If an elective republic is to endure for any length of time, every elector must have sufficient information, not only to accumulate wealth and take care of his primary concerns, but to direct wisely the Legislature, the Ambassadors, and the Executive of the Nation; for some part of all these things, some agency in approving or disapproving of them, falls to every free man."

The impending danger to unity in a republic with a population as diverse in religion and national origins as the United States, a diversity obviously on the increase with immigration mounting daily, likewise impressed educators and laymen. Horace Mann and Henry Barnard (1811-1900) in particular stressed the importance of schools, publicly supported and attended by all children, as a means for developing values that all might share in common despite differences of class, creed, and national origin.

[9] Lawrence A. Cremin (ed.), *The Republic and the School: Horace Mann on the Education of Free Men*, Classics in Education, No. 1 (New York: Bureau of Publications, Teachers College, Columbia University, 1957), p. 91.

A speaker before the Middlesex County Association for the Improvement of Schools stated in 1839, as recorded in the *Common School Journal* of the time: "I want to see the rich and the poor sit down side by side on equal terms, as members of one family—a great brotherhood—deeming no one distinguished above the rest but the best scholar and the best boy—giving free and natural play to their affections, at a time of life when lasting friendships are often formed, and worldliness and pride, and envy have not alienated heart from heart." He thus expressed a point of view that was leading many forward-looking people throughout the country to see in public education an essential for the preservation and development of republican institutions. Thus, Charles Fenton Mercer, a Federalist from Virginia, pointed out in 1826 that

> Intellectual and moral worth constitute in America our only nobility; and this high distinction is placed by the laws, and should be brought in fact, within the reach of every citizen.
>
> Where distinct ranks exist in a society, it may be plausibly objected to the intellectual improvement of the lower classes of the community, that it will invert the public sentiment, or impose on the privileged orders the necessity of proportional exertion to protect themselves from the scorn of their inferiors. But the equality on which our institutions are founded, cannot be too intimately interwoven in the habits of thinking among our youth; and it is obvious that it would be greatly promoted by their continuance together, for the longest possible period, in the same schools of juvenile instruction; to sit upon the same forms; engage in the same competitions; partake of the same recreations and amusements, and pursue the same studies, in connexion with each other; under the same discipline, and in obedience to the same authority.[10]

ECONOMIC AND MORAL CONSIDERATIONS
LIKEWISE FAVOR PUBLIC EDUCATION

The reader will have observed in the quotation from Thaddeus Stevens that he stressed the economic as well as the civic advantages of education. In this he was not alone. Indeed, as one examines the educational literature of the period, it becomes obvious that economic independence

---

[10] Quoted in Lawrence A. Cremin, *The American Common School* (New York: Bureau of Publications, Teachers College, Columbia University, 1951), p. 57. See Part II, "The Common School as an Educational Ideal," for an excellent discussion of the common school movement.

was commonly viewed as an essential characteristic of good citizenship. Implicit in the demands of labor for schools, open and free to all without the taint of charity, was the assumption that education would keep open the road to economic independence. As Horace Mann put it, "Knowledge and abundance sustain to each other the relation of cause and effect." Thus it was possible to argue that a government which protects its infant industries from foreign competition by means of a protective tariff, assists private corporations engaged in the construction of canals and the building of railroads, and opens up the public domain for settlement by individuals on easy terms is equally obligated to provide an education for its young that will insure for them a fair start in life.

Horace Mann employed the economic argument for public education in a manner to appeal to liberals and conservatives, to labor and capital alike. For example, in his *Fifth Annual Report* (1841),[11] Mann put this question to businessmen: "Finally, in regard to those who possess the largest shares in the stock of worldly goods, could there, in your opinion, be any police so vigilant and effective, for the protection of all the rights of person, property and character, as such a sound and comprehensive education and training, as our system of Common Schools could be made to impart; and would not the payment of a sufficient tax to make such education and training universal, be the cheapest means of self-protection and insurance?"

On the other hand, with a view to allaying the fears of the many who were becoming increasingly concerned with the rapid accumulation of wealth in the hands of a few and the dangers which follow "when all the capital," as in England, "is in the hands of one class, and all the labor is thrown upon another," Mann pointed to Universal Education as a remedy. In his *Twelfth Annual Report* (1848), he wrote:

> If education be equally diffused, it will draw property after it, by the strongest of all attractions; for such a thing never did happen, and never can happen, as that an intelligent and practical body of men should be permanently poor... Education, then, beyond all other devices of human origin, is the great equalizer of the condi-

[11] Curti informs us that this report was circulated to the number of 18,000 by the New York Legislature, quoted repeatedly in educational journals and addresses by educational leaders throughout the country, and endorsed by a large number of well-to-do citizens of Massachusetts. See Merle Curti, *The Social Ideas of American Educators* (New York: Charles Scribner's Sons, 1935), p. 113.

tions of men—the balance-wheel of the social machinery. I do not here mean that it so elevates the moral nature as to make men disdain and abhor the oppression of their fellow-men. This idea pertains to another of its attributes. But I mean it gives each man the independence and the means, by which he can resist the selfishness of other men. It does better than to disarm the poor of their hostility towards the rich; it prevents being poor.[12]

A story, dating from frontier days, describes the manner in which a hunter shot his bear. "The first time," he is recorded as saying, "I missed him; but the second time I hit him just where I missed him before!"

Much the same may be said of arguments in support of the establishment and maintenance of public schools in the formative period. The citizenship argument, as we have seen, glided easily into one which stressed the economic values of an education for the individual and his society. In a similar manner, advocates of the economic importance of universal education frequently identified the economic and the moral. That is to say, the virtues which, in their minds, universal education would instill in all were those prized by a middle-class structure as essential alike for material success and a sound character—the virtues of honesty, frugality, industry, temperance, generosity, responsibility, and the like. As such, they were designed to appeal not only to conservative men of wealth, concerned to safeguard the status quo, but to the man seeking to climb and eager for his children to achieve material success.

Benjamin Franklin, it will be recalled, drew attention in his *Autobiography* (1771-1789) to the manner in which the Puritan virtues served the dual purpose of salvation in the next world and economic success in this. Similarly, Henry Barnard sought to popularize in his *American Journal of Education* (1855-1882) the maxims of Poor Richard, which, as he stated, "by household and schoolbook repetition, have become inwrought into the texture of every American mind." [13] "Anxious to wring support for public schools from propertied interests then opposed to taxation for this purpose," writes Merle Curti, "educational statesmen warned them of the dangers to property rights from universal suffrage, Jack-

[12] Cremin (ed.), *op. cit.*, pp. 86-87.
[13] Curti, *op. cit.*, p. 154. Curti develops at some length the arguments employed by American educators to convince men of wealth of the wisdom of supporting public schools as one way of safeguarding their property from the excesses of mob rule—an ever present danger in a popular government!

sonian democracy, and, even, revolution—any of which might result if the masses were left undisciplined by education." [14]

For example, in addressing the Indiana Legislature in 1847, Caleb Mills dwelt heavily upon the primacy of character training in the schools. "Can the manufacturer invest his capital with equal security," he asked rhetorically, "among an ignorant and vicious people, that he would in an intelligent and virtuous community?" And the Secretary of the State Board of Education of Maine, in his report of 1847, put the question, "What surer guarantee can the capitalist find for the security of his investments, than is found in the sense of a community morally and intellectually enlightened?"

A similar emphasis upon the practical value of the virtues which public schools would impart to their charges is found in the address of Thaddeus Stevens, to which we referred above. To the argument that it is unjust to tax people in order to provide an education from which they can observe no direct return to themselves, Stevens replied:

> It is for their own benefit, inasmuch as it perpetuates the government and ensures the due administration of the laws under which they live, and by which their lives and property are protected. Why do they not urge the same objection against all other taxes? The industrious, thrifty, rich farmer pays a heavy county tax to support criminal courts, build jails, and pay sheriffs and jail keepers, and yet probably he never had and probably never will have any direct personal use for them. . . . He cheerfully pays the burdensome taxes which are necessarily levied to support and punish convicts, but loudly complains of that which goes to prevent his fellow-being from becoming a criminal and to obviate the necessity of those humiliating institutions.

EDUCATION AS A NATURAL RIGHT

It was Horace Mann, however, who most effectively challenged the right of men of wealth *not* to support education! [15] This he did by assert-

[14] *Ibid.*, pp. 80-81. How faithfully the schools undertook to perform the task of instilling the virtues of responsible citizenship as seen through the eyes of men of property and Protestant Christianity is amply documented in Richard D. Mosier, *Making the American Mind, Social and Moral Ideas in the McGuffey Readers* (New York: King's Crown Press, 1947).

[15] See his *Tenth Annual Report* (1846). The following quotations are taken from this report as published in Cremin (ed.), *op. cit.*, pp. 59-78.

ing the right of each child to an education as "absolute" and of "divine origin . . . legible in the order of nature and in the history of the race . . . which proves the correlative duty of government to see that the means of education are provided for all."

To the query "How far does this obligation of government extend?" Mann answered that this

> can never be less than such as is sufficient to qualify each citizen for the civil and social duties he will be called to discharge;—such an education as teaches the individual the great laws of bodily health; as qualifies for the fulfillment of parental duties; as is indispensable for the civil function of a witness or a juror; as is necessary for the voter in municipal affairs; and finally, for the faithful and conscientious discharge of all those duties which devolve upon the inheritor of a portion of the sovereignty of this great republic.

Mann was aware that many would press the question, Why, if the right to an education is a natural right, "is there not at the present time, with the exception of New England and a few small localities elsewhere, a State or a community in Christendom, which maintains a system of Free Schools for the education of its children?" The answer he found "for this amazing dereliction of duty, especially in our own country . . . more in the false notions which men entertain respecting the nature of their right to property, than to anything else."

Mann then embarked upon an elaborate discussion to establish the principle that ownership of property is more in the nature of a trusteeship than an absolute right. This he detailed as follows:

1. " . . . the primary and natural elements or ingredients of all property consist in the riches of the soil, in the treasures of the sea, in the light and warmth of the sun, in the clouds and streams and dews, in the winds, and in the chemical and vegetative agencies of nature," which man receives "without cost and without recompense from the all-bountiful giver." These gifts of nature are not limited but enter into all activities of men—agriculture, manufacturing, commerce, and the like. Nor were they "created for Adam alone, nor for Noah alone, nor for the first discoverers or colonists who may have found or have peopled any part of the earth's ample domain. No! They were created for the race collectively. . . . If we consider the earth and fulness thereof, as one great

habitation or domain, then each generation, subject to certain modifications for the encouragement of industry and frugality . . . has only a life-lease on them."

2. "The *present* wealth of the world has an additional element in it. Much of all that is capable of being earned by man, has been earned by our predecessors. . . . We have not reclaimed from the wilderness all the fields whose harvests we now reap; and if we had no precious metals, or stones, or pearls, but such as we ourselves had dug from the mines, or brought up from the bottom of the ocean, our coffers and our caskets would be empty indeed." The situation is similar with respect to the arts, the sciences, and technology. "Most of all this was found out by those who have gone before us, and some of it has come down to us from remote antiquity," and thus belongs as much to posterity as to us.

3. Finally, there are the institutions of society and our relations with our contemporaries which condition the use and enjoyment of our possessions. These, too, constitute an inheritance and a trust which each generation receives and is obligated to hand on to the next. But "at what point, are the latter to take possession of, or to derive benefit from it, or at what time, are the former to surrender it in their behalf?" The answer, upon which Mann again expands, varies with need. "The claim of a child . . . to a portion of pre-existent property begins with the first breath he draws." Here he speaks of the child's claim to sustenance, shelter, care, and, later, an education that develops his mind and forms his character.

Thus did Horace Mann endeavor to establish the right of a child to an education and the obligation of property owners to contribute of their property to its realization. Again, he wrote:

> The will of God, as conspicuously manifested in the order of nature, and in the relations which he has established among men, places the *right* of every child that is born into the world to such a degree of education as will enable him, and, as far as possible, will predispose him, to perform all domestic, social, civic, and moral duties, upon the same clear ground of natural law and equity, as it places a child's *right*, upon his first coming into the world, to distend his lungs with a portion of the common air, or to open his eyes to the common light, or to receive that shelter, protection, and nourishment which are necessary to the continuance of his bodily existence. And so far it is from being a wrong or a hardship, to demand of the possessors

of property their respective shares for the prosecution of their divinely-ordained work, that they themselves are guilty of the most far-reaching injustice, who seek to resist or to evade the contribution. The complainers are the wrong doers. The cry, "Stop thief," comes from the thief himself.

Mann's contention that education is a natural right for the individual and an obligation for the state to insure undoubtedly encouraged not only Massachusetts but other states as well to match conviction with performance. Within six years of the *Tenth Annual Report* (1846), Massachusetts adopted a compulsory school attendance act. Other states followed at a rate that varied roughly with their advance in industrialization and urbanization. Not until 1918 was the circle complete when Mississippi, the last of the southern states, finally adopted its compulsory school attendance law.

We should not underestimate the stubborn resistance encountered by the friends of public schools in their efforts to convince state legislatures to enact not only compulsory school attendance laws but legislation which did no more than permit localities to exercise initiative in the establishment of public schools. Education was still associated in the minds of many with class status and the enjoyment of leisure. Only a minority saw in it an essential condition for the effective performance of one's life work. Some even viewed it as a positive handicap for the poor in that it fostered discontent and stimulated false notions of their importance. In rural areas, particularly, agreement would be found with the sentiments expressed in a letter addressed to a Raleigh newspaper in 1828:"Would it not redound as much, to the advantage of young persons and to the honor of the state, if they should pass their days in the cotton patch, or at the plow, or in the cornfield, instead of being mewed up in a schoolhouse where they are earning nothing?" [16] In Rhode Island an irate farmer threatened to do violence to Henry Barnard for "preaching such a horrible 'heresy' as the partial confiscation of one man's property to educate another man's child."

Finally, there was formidable opposition to public education from religious organizations that saw in the public school both a dangerous rival for financial support and a secular influence threatening to undermine

[16] Quoted in Edgar W. Knight, *Education in the United States* (Boston: Ginn & Co., 1934), p. 244.

orthodoxy in religion. Butts and Cremin, for example, quote from a *Report to the Synod of New Jersey on the Subject of Parochial Schools* (1845) which expressed alarm that the "race of irreligious and infidel youth, such as may be expected to issue from public schools, *deteriorating more* and more, with revolving years will not be fit to sustain our free institutions." [17]

THE PRINCIPLE OF SEPARATION OF CHURCH AND STATE IS MADE APPLICABLE TO EDUCATION

The fear of the Synod of New Jersey that irreligious and infidel youth would emerge from public schools was based upon the assumption that morality and the "one true religion" were inseparably connected. This fear was shared by other denominations, each assuming, however, that it alone represented the one true religion! Still, despite a general conviction that a union between education and sectarian religion was essential, an increasing number of individuals and groups came to see in the nonsectarian school a logical extension of the principle of separation of church and state.

As we observed in Chapter 2, separation of church and state as a political principle was incorporated in the constitutions of state and federal governments during and following the American Revolution. A number of factors contributed to this end: the influence of Deism and natural theology, with its emphasis upon reason in contrast with revelation as a source of morality; dissatisfaction of liberals in religion on the one hand with the political domination of the clergy and of Evangelical groups, on the other, with state interference and control in matters of religion; and, finally, the unsatisfactory experiences of the states with establishments of religion both single and plural, experiences which led them to incorporate in their constitutions explicit provisions forbidding public assistance to religious establishments.

The range of agreements between liberals and conservatives in religion with respect to separation of church and state is well illustrated by contrasting two statements, one by Thomas Paine and the other by the General Committee of the Virginia Baptists. Writing in his pamphlet on *Common Sense* (1776), Paine declared: "As to religion, I hold it to be the indispensable duty of government to protect all conscientious pro-

[17] R. Freeman Butts and Lawrence A. Cremin, *A History of Education in American Culture* (New York: Holt, Rinehart & Winston, 1953), p. 196.

fessions thereof; and I know of no other business which government hath to do therewith."

In a similar vein, the Virginia Baptists, in a 1784 resolution, voiced their opposition to a bill in the Virginia Assembly that was designed to subsidize the teachers of the Christian religion:

> Resolved, That it be recommended to those counties which have not yet prepared petitions to be presented to the General Assembly against the engrossed bill for a general assessment for the support of the teachers of the Christian religion, to proceed thereon as soon as possible; that it is believed to be repugnant to the spirit of the Gospel for the Legislature thus to proceed in matters of religion; that no human laws ought to be established for this purpose; but that every person ought to be left entirely free in respect to matters of religion; that the holy author of our religion needs no such compulsive measures for the promotion of his cause; that the Gospel wants not the feeble arm of man for its support; that it has made, and will again through divine power make its way against all opposition; and that should the Legislature assume the right of taxing the people for the support of the Gospel, it will be destructive to religious liberty.

By 1791 nine of the original thirteen states had adopted constitutional provisions forbidding public assistance to religious establishments. Of the four remaining states Maryland did likewise in 1810, Connecticut in 1818, Massachusetts in 1833, and New Hampshire by statute in 1819. With the admission of new states to the Union in the early nineteenth century, constitutional prohibitions not only of state support for religious establishments but of religious tests as a condition for the exercise of the franchise or for holding public office became common, together with general guarantees of freedom of conscience and of religion.

It was natural, therefore, for the friends of public education to extend the principle of nonsectarianism to instruction given in the schools. In this, the constitution adopted by Connecticut in 1818 served as a precedent for other states to follow. This instrument provided, first, that the support and maintenance of church buildings and ministers should be "by a tax of the members of any such society only, to be laid by a majority vote of the legal voters assembled at any society meeting" and, second, that "the fund, called the School Fund, shall remain a perpetual fund, the interest of which shall be *inviolably* appropriated to the support and

encouragement of the public, or common schools, throughout the State
... and no law shall be made, authorizing said fund to be diverted to
any other use than the encouragement and support of public or common
schools...."

The facts of diversity of religious organizations and the understandable
objections of the adherents of one sect to the indoctrination of their children by partisans of another likewise encouraged the development of
nonsectarianism in education. Charles and Mary Beard have stated: "The
strife among religious sects, the struggle of each denomination to subdue
all the pupils in its schools to its theological bias, and the resistance of
parents all combined to augment the demand for general public schools
supported by taxes and freed from clerical control. America had not become irreligious but no one sect was strong enough to dominate the whole
terrain. And secular instruction was the only thing on which all the sects
could agree." [18]

It is not strictly accurate, however, for the Beards to say that "secular
instruction was the only thing on which all the sects could agree." Rather
was it "nonsectarian" instruction of a Protestant hue. In the West, for
example, sectarian private schools were less of a vested interest than in
the East, and church denominations were less able financially to establish
sectarian schools. Consequently, there the concept of religious instruction in public schools that embodied common elements of belief and
eliminated tenets of disagreements as between the various sects seemed
both logical and sensible. Nor were there influential voices to be raised
in objection to the religious emphasis in these schools of a predominantly
Protestant orientation under the caption of "nonsectarian" instruction.

In the East, also, both religious and secular influences were favorable
to nonsectarian education and thus to the establishment of public schools.
In New England, for example, Unitarianism, in common with Deism
(which, incidentally, was giving ground to Transcendentalism) emphasized the native goodness of man and human reason as the source of
morality without necessary dependence upon sectarian dogma. It thus
gave support to the efforts of Horace Mann and others to restrict religious
instruction in the schools to the "common elements" of Christianity.
Of similar influence were the Transcendentalists, with their conception of God as a divine immanence, or an Over-Soul, and their convic-

[18] Charles Beard and Mary Beard, *The Rise of American Civilization*, Vol. I (New
York: The Macmillan Co., 1929), p. 813.

tions, as Emerson stated, that "the moral lies at the center of nature and radiates to the circumference"; that "all things with which we deal preach to us"; and that the "axioms of physics translate the laws of ethics." They were in no way disposed to accept the thesis that moral education derives from the Scriptures alone, or from the sectarian tenets of religious sects—unless, indeed, one were willing to grant that the laws of nature are sectarian in character, since, according to Emerson in his *Essay on Nature* (1836), "the laws of moral nature answer to those of matter as face to face in a glass!"

Moreover, realism, which, as we have seen, was a major philosophic influence in the denominational colleges as well as the churches of the country, did not raise fundamental objections to nonsectarian education. On the contrary, its conception of the faculties of the mind, of which the moral sense was one (a faculty which, it was thought, enables men either to distinguish right from wrong, in specific instances by means of intuition, or to identify the general principles from which the right or wrong of individual acts might be deduced), lent itself to a religious instruction acceptable only to all denominations.

It was Horace Mann's basic assumption both that the school can develop allegiance to moral principles common to all religions without dependence upon sectarian interpretation and that the state has the duty so to educate which prompted him to devote his energies to the development of public education in Massachusetts. His *Twelfth Annual Report* (1848), his last to the State Board of Education, developed in detail his views on the relations of church, state, and public education. One extract is relevant here:

> The very terms, *Public School*, and *Common School*, bear upon their face, that they are schools which the children of the entire community may attend. Every man, not on the pauper list, is taxed for their support.... But he is not taxed to support them as special religious institutions; if he were, it would satisfy, at once, the largest definition of a Religious Establishment. But he is taxed to support them, as a preventive means against dishonesty, against fraud, and against violence; on the same principle that he is taxed to support criminal courts as a punitive means against the same offenses.... The elements of a political education are not bestowed upon any school child, for the purpose of making him vote with this or that political party, when he becomes of age; but for the purpose of enabling him

to choose for himself, with which party he will vote. So the religious education which a child receives at school, is not imparted to him, for the purpose of making him join this or that denomination, when he arrives at years of discretion, but for the purpose of enabling him to judge for himself, according to the dictates of his own reason and conscience, what his religious obligations are, and whither they lead. But if a man is taxed to support a school, where religious doctrines are inculcated which he believes to be false, and which he believes that God condemns; then he is excluded from the school by the Divine law, at the same time that he is compelled to support it by the human law.[19]

THE PRINCIPLE OF NONSECTARIAN INSTRUCTION APPLIED TO AREAS OTHER THAN RELIGION

It is obvious that Mann's thesis with respect to religious instruction applied as well to questions other than religion upon which the community was not of one mind. Take the field of politics, for example. In Mann's words, quoted earlier, the "establishment of a republican government, without well-appointed and sufficient means for the universal education of the people, is the most rash and fool-hardy experiment ever tried by man." But how could this be done without indoctrination certain to arouse controversy? Would not the school be faced with an unhappy dilemma—should it provide partisan instruction in matters political or no instruction at all? Mann answered as follows:

Surely, between these extremes, there must be a medium not difficult to be found. And is not this the middle course, which all sensible
and judicious men, all patriots, and all genuine republicans, must
approve?—namely, that these articles in the creed of republicanism,
which are accepted by all, and which form the common basis of our
political faith, shall be taught to all. But when the teacher, in the
course of his lessons or lectures on the fundamental law, arrives at
a controverted text, he is either to read it without comment or remark; or, at most, he is only to say that the passage is the subject
of disputation, and that the schoolroom is neither the tribunal to
adjudicate, nor the forum to discuss it.

Despite the opposition of some religious groups to nonsectarian education and the efforts of the friends of church-related schools to secure

[19] Cremin (ed.), *op. cit.*, pp. 103-104.

government support for their programs in preference to the establishment of public schools, the latter gained preeminence in the North and the West. Not until the period following the Civil War did public schools gain widespread adoption in the South. For this victory in the North much credit must go to the united efforts of labor and farm groups and to heavy immigration with the obvious need that foreign-born children receive instruction in the ways of American life and American institutions. As Charles and Mary Beard have said,

> For a nation of farmers and mechanics, bent on self-government and possessed of the ballot, there was only one kind of an educational program in keeping with self-respect, namely, a free and open public school system supported by taxation and non-sectarian in its control. . . . Moreover, the increasing flood of Irish and Continental immigrants, likely to fall under Catholic direction if educated at all in charity schools, frightened Protestants of every proclivity, making them willing to accept secularism rather than papal authority.[20]

THE LIMITATIONS OF NONSECTARIAN INSTRUCTION BECOME EVIDENT

It was the presence of the immigrant non-Protestant background together with the continued development of the secular mind in American life that quickly demonstrated the limitations of "nonsectarian" education as Horace Mann and other educators of the period conceived it. In 1848, in Protestant Massachusetts,[21] for example, it was possible for Horace Mann to note with pride that the Bible (the King James Version), "the acknowledged expositor of Christianity," was being used in the common schools by common consent at one and the same time that he emphasized the importance of nonsectarian instruction.

The rapid influx of non-Protestant immigrants into Massachusetts and other states of the Union soon cast doubt upon the assumption that the Protestant Bible and instruction in religious tenets common to Protestants constituted genuine nonsectarian instruction. Between 1845 and 1850 alone, for example, more than 1,250,000 Irish immigrants (predominantly Catholic) entered the United States, and some 4,250,000 crowded into the eastern cities during the nineteenth century. As this Catholic immigra-

[20] Beard and Beard, *The Rise of American Civilization, op. cit.,* pp. 810-811.
[21] Until well into the nineteenth century, Catholic priests were forbidden to enter the state of Massachusetts on pain of life imprisonment.

tion increased, liberal-minded educators and religious leaders came to realize that what constitutes nonsectarian instruction under one set of conditions becomes sectarian under other circumstances. Consequently, reading from the King James Version of the Bible, singing Protestant hymns, engaging in Protestant prayers, and performing other rites and ceremonies that long seemed normal and natural and *nonsectarian,* eventually took on a sectarian hue and were objected to vigorously as an infringement upon freedom of conscience.

This decision was arrived at, however, only after many a bitterly fought battle. The first reaction to Catholic demands that Catholic children be exempted from the law requiring them to read from the Protestant edition of the Bible was to compel compliance, often on pain of physical punishment. On occasion, when Catholics ventured to express publicly their opposition to violations of freedom of conscience, mobs rose up to demonstrate in mob fashion the superiority of the Protestant faith! In Philadelphia, for example, Catholic schools were burned in answer to a Catholic bishop's suggestion that the public schools exempt Catholic children from the necessity of reading the Protestant Bible.

In time a more charitable spirit came to assert itself both in law and in practice, and the principle of the Golden Rule was seen to apply to Catholics and Jews, even to atheists, as well as to Protestants. This was made possible by the eventual realization that just as the principles of morality common to Protestants might be imparted without reference to doctrines which divided Protestants, so principles common to still wider groupings—Protestants and Catholics, Jews and others—might be imparted to the young without necessary reference to the theological tenets peculiar to but one of these groups. In the early experiments with nonsectarian schools men had come to see that the children of Quakers, Baptists, Methodists, Presbyterians, Congregationalists, Episcopalians, and other sects could be educated together without emphasis upon divisive theological doctrines, and that children so educated could possess themselves of the common virtues of honesty, truthfulness, fair dealing, and the like. So now, with the further exclusion of articles of faith and of religious ceremony, which set Protestant apart from Catholic, and Christian from Jew, people came to conclude that these selfsame principles of morality might be developed in schools without resorting to religious indoctrination of any kind.

An incident in New York State in 1853 testifies to progress in this respect. A teacher had punished a Catholic child for refusing to memorize passages from the Bible. In disciplining the teacher the state superintendent wrote in part:

> The government not relying on the ability or the willingness of every part of the State to maintain efficient schools for the education of the young, by voluntary contributions, and recognizing the imperative necessity of universal education for the maintenance of our civil and political institutions, organized a general common school system.... The common schools were thus clearly made a government institution. To introduce into them, or permit to be introduced into them, a course of religious instruction conformable to the views of any religious denomination, would be tantamount to the adoption of a government religion—a step contrary to the constitution, and equally at variance with the policy of a free government and the wishes of the people. *To form for the schools a course of instruction which could bear the name of a religious one, and which would meet the views of all, was manifestly impossible. To give to every sect a pro rata share of the school moneys to enable it to support its own schools and to teach its own system of religious faith in them, would be ... to divide the children ... into a dozen or more schools.* Indeed, under this arrangement a single indigent family would often be required to support its own school, to go without any, or to violate its conscience by joining with others in one in which a religious system was taught wholly at variance with its own....

"In view of the above facts," writes R. Freeman Butts, "the position was early, distinctly, and almost universally taken by our statesmen, legislators, and prominent friends of education—men of the warmest religious zeal and belonging to every sect—that *religious education must be banished from the common school and consigned to the family and church.*" [22] With this general realization, the nonsectarian school graduated into the secular public school.

Were it not for this evolution of moral education from sectarianism into nonsectarianism and from nonsectarianism into secularism, without loss of interest in the moral training of the young, it is doubtful that a people as religious, and at the same time as practical, as the American

[22] R. Freeman Butts, *The American Tradition in Religion and Education* (Boston: Beacon Press, 1950), p. 136.

people could have envisaged the development of a public or a common school. In short, the discovery that nonsectarian instruction is consistent with moral education enabled educational administrators and legislative bodies to set about the business of excluding sectarian interests of all types from public education.

While the principle of secular public education was clearly established prior to the Civil War, its general adoption belongs more particularly to the period following the War. In this the courts served both to reflect and to influence public opinion. In 1872, to take one conspicuous example, the Supreme Court of Ohio sustained the Cincinnati Board of Education in prohibiting on constitutional grounds "religious instruction and the reading of religious books, including the Bible," in the common schools of that city.

Although court decisions were by no means consistent, the court of one state interpreting the Bible as a sectarian document and that of another holding it to be above sectarianism, the general trend in the latter part of the nineteenth century was toward a broadening of the base of tolerance and a growing conception of the public school as one charged with a secular responsibility. For example, in 1890 the Wisconsin Supreme Court ruled that the reading of the Bible in the schools of that state was unconstitutional; and in 1902, 1910, and 1915 the supreme courts of Nebraska, Illinois, and Louisiana, respectively, rendered similar decisions. These courts held that both the reading of the Bible and the singing of denominational hymns constituted sectarian instruction and acts of worship within the meaning of the state constitutions. By 1913 only two states continued to retain mandatory provisions of this character.

THE STATUS TODAY OF SEPARATION OF CHURCH AND STATE IN EDUCATION

To bring the story up to date, it should be pointed out that the first half of the twentieth century witnessed a retreat from strict adherence to the principle of separation of church and state, with respect both to religious instruction conducted directly or indirectly under the auspices of public schools and to government assistance to church-related schools. For example, religious instruction in cooperation with public schools on a released-time basis, first begun in 1913, was reaching approximately 2,000,000 pupils in some 2,500 communities by 1948, the year in which, in *McCollum* v. *Board of Education,* 333 U.S. 203, the United States

Supreme Court declared the practice unconstitutional when conducted inside school buildings and on school time. Despite this ruling, released-time programs continued to thrive, in some instances inside school buildings in open defiance of the Court's ruling, in other instances off the school grounds in a manner approved in 1952 by the Court in *Zorach* v. *Clauson*, 343 U.S. 306. (In this decision, written by Justice William O. Douglas, the Court stated, "The government must be neutral when it comes to competition between sects. It may not thrust any sect on any person. It may not make a religious observance compulsory. It may not coerce anyone to attend church, to observe a religious holiday, or to take religious instruction. But it can close its doors or suspend its operations as to those who want to repair to their religious sanctuary for worship or instruction. No more than that is undertaken here.")

Bible reading and the use of prayers at opening exercises likewise increased as a practice in public schools after 1913. By midcentury thirteen states were requiring the reading of the Bible in public schools, and twenty-four specifically permitted the practice. In only eight states was the Bible not in use. By 1963, the *New York Times* concluded from a countrywide survey of religious practices current in public schools that 42 percent of all school systems in the nation were observing a daily routine of Bible reading.[23]

The United States Supreme Court in 1963 rendered its momentous decision, in *School District of Abington Township* v. *Schempp*, outlawing both Bible reading and school prayers on the ground that these practices violate both the Free Exercise and Establishment clauses of the Constitution. What the effects of this decision will be, it is too early to state at the present writing. Although numerous localities have announced their intention to ignore the Court's injunctions, influential organizations, including the National Council of the Churches of Christ in the United States of America and the General Assembly of the United Presbyterian Church, have indicated their wholehearted support of the decision and the grounds upon which it is based.

The decision is significant for the reason that Justice Thomas C. Clark, speaking for the Court, clearly undertook to clarify with copious references to prior decisions of the Court what is now its firm position with respect to the meaning of the Free Exercise and Establishment clauses of the First Amendment. Significant also is the long concurring opinion of

[23] *The New York Times*, June 18, 1963, p. 27.

Justice William J. Brennan, Jr. This consists of an exhaustive review of the history of the First Amendment and the court decisions devoted to its interpretation. Together with Justice Wiley B. Rutledge's dissent in *Everson* v. *Board of Education,* 330 U.S. 1 (1947), and Justice Felix Frankfurter's concurring opinion in *McCollum* v. *Board of Education,* it may well stand as a classic statement on relations between government and religion.

Briefly summarized, Justice Clark affirmed that:

1. The First Amendment, with its "mandate that 'Congress shall make no law respecting an establishment of religion, or prohibiting the free exercise thereof,' has been made wholly applicable to the states by the Fourteenth Amendment." That is to say, "The Fourteenth Amendment has rendered the legislatures of the states as incompetent as Congress to enact such laws. . . ."

2. The Supreme Court "has rejected unequivocally the contention that the Establishment Clause forbids only governmental preference of one religion over another." The prohibitions of the First Amendment thus apply to establishments in the plural as well as in the singular. Consequently, people are engaged only in "academic exercises" when they continue to dispute the accuracy of Justice Hugo L. Black's words in *Everson* v. *Board of Education,* and repeated in *McCollum* v. *Board,* to the effect that "Neither a state nor the Federal Government . . . can pass laws which aid one religion, aid all religions, or prefer one religion over another. . . ."

3. The Establishment Clause "withdraws from the sphere of legitimate legislative concern and competence a specific, but comprehensive, area of human conduct: man's belief or disbelief in the verity of some transcendental idea and man's expression of that belief or disbelief." Therefore, in matters of religion, a policy of "wholesome neutrality" is imposed upon government. This means that government and its agencies must "abstain from fusing functions of government and religious sects" and must avoid "those official involvements of religion which would tend to foster or discourage religious worship or belief."

Finally, with an eye upon those who contend that to deny the majority in a community the right to engage in religious exercise in public schools is in itself a denial of religious freedom, Justice Clark states, "While the Free Exercise Clause prohibits the use of state action to deny the rights of free exercise to *anyone*, it has never meant that a majority could use the machinery of the State to practice its beliefs."

While it is true that the words of the majority decision in *School District of Abington Township* v. *Schempp*, further amplified by Justice Brennan's detailed explication of the Free Exercise and Establishment clauses of the First Amendment, have clarified the relations of religious instruction and religious practices to public education, ambiguity persists with respect to government assistance to church-related institutions. This follows from (a) failure of the courts to distinguish between aid to the individual and aid to an institution, as in the case of the state providing parochial as well as public school children with free textbooks,[24] loans and grants to students, and the like; and (b) the present uncertainty as to whether the interdiction of support for "any religious activities or institutions" by government precludes such assistance to the nonreligious and secular activities of church-related institutions.

That aid of this character is not forbidden by the First Amendment is the conclusion of a study conducted by the Legal Department of the National Catholic Welfare Conference and published in December, 1961 under the title, "The Constitutionality of the Inclusion of Church-Related Schools in Federal Aid to Education." [25] It is also the assumption of a 1963 act of Congress which provides direct grants to church-controlled colleges for the construction of buildings, on condition these buildings be used exclusively for secular instruction. In passing this act, Congress rejected an amendment which would require a prompt test of its constitutionality in the courts. That such a test is inevitable, however, seems most probable, carrying with it the most serious implications for the future of both public and private education.

Ambiguity relates also to the public financing of the transportation of parochial school children to and from school, despite the favorable decision of the United States Supreme Court in *Everson* v. *Board of Education* in 1947. For example, the courts of the states of Washington

---

[24] A practice sanctioned by the United States Supreme Court in 1930 (*Cochran* v. *Louisiana State Board of Education*, 281 U.S. 370) on the ground that the child and not the institution was being assisted, and that "the taxing power of the State is exerted for a public purpose" when the books distributed are identical with those used in the public schools and are nonreligious and nonsectarian in content.

[25] Published in full in the *Georgetown Law Journal*, Winter, 1961, pp. 399-455. For a brief summary, see *NEA Journal*, May, 1962, pp. 26-28.

(1949), New Mexico (1951), Missouri (1953), Alaska (1955), and Wisconsin (1962) have ruled against the practice, while those of Maine (1959) and Connecticut (1960) have approved it. At present some twenty-two states sanction public transportation of parochial school children by bus. Appeals to the United States Supreme Court for a rehearing of the constitutional question involved have thus far been denied (the last being that of Alaska in 1962). That the Court will eventually face the problem once again seems certain.

For the present, then, it would seem that the words Justice Rutledge was moved to utter in his dissenting opinion in *Everson* v. *Board of Education* are still relevant: "Neither so high nor so impregnable today as yesterday is the wall raised between Church and State by Virginia's great statute of religious freedom and the First Amendment, now made applicable to all States by the Fourteenth. New Jersey's statute sustained is the first, if indeed it is not the second, breach to be made by the Court's action. That a third and a fourth, and still others may be attempted we may be sure."

ENCOURAGEMENT OF EDUCATION BECOMES ONE FUNCTION OF GOVERNMENT

Finally should be mentioned—in this enumeration of factors leading to the establishment of free public schools—the conception of government and its relation to the individual favorable to the development of such schools. Earlier, in Chapter 2, attention was called to two theories of government that have operated throughout American experience. The one is fearful of centralized authority, viewing the state as external to the individual and disposed, unless restrained from so doing, to interfere with and to regulate its subjects without respect to their essential interests. The best government, so conceived, is one that governs least. The second theory is that of a compact entered into by individuals and groups in order to insure for themselves through associated action the realization of needs they cannot obtain singly and alone. We also saw that the first conception of government was brought to this country by people seeking to free themselves from oppression at the hands of a state firmly in the control of a small group who were using the state to further their own interests and with only minimal concern for the welfare of the common people. The second was nearer to the soil, representing the experience of repeated generations in the establishment of new communities, new territories, and new states. It was a conception that became ever more general as the common people came to participate actively in their government—local, state, national—and to use it to improve their lot.

It was this second theory of government that led to the reform and humanitarian movements characteristic of the first half of the nineteenth century (the abolition of imprisonment for debt, the confirmation of labor's right to organize for the improvement of working conditions, the passage of mechanics' lien laws, the attempts to improve the status of women, and, of course, the abolition movement, to mention but a few). It was also this conception of government as an instrument of the people with which to promote the general welfare that sanctioned tariff legislation favorable to infant industries, state and national legislation in support of agriculture, opening up the public domain for easy settlement, and, finally, the creation of state funds in support of education (beginning with the establishment of "literary funds" early in the century) and grants of land by both state and national governments for the specific purpose of furthering public education.

The passage of the Northwest Ordinance by the Continental Congress in 1785 with its provision for setting aside the sixteenth section of each township for the maintenance of schools served as a precedent for later action by both state and federal governments. Substantial assistance to state efforts on behalf of education was rendered by the federal government in 1837 by a grant of $28,000,000 under the Surplus Revenue Act, and, in 1841 and 1850, respectively, by the Federal Internal Improvement Act and Swamp Land Grant Act. In 1862, even though engaged in the Civil War, the national government passed the Morrill Act, which assigned to each state a share of the public lands in proportion to its representation in Congress, for the support of agriculture and mechanical education.

Horace Greeley put it as follows: "We believe that the government like every other intelligent agency is bound to do good to the extent of its ability—that it ought actively to promote and increase the general well-being—that it should encourage and foster Industry, Science, Invention, Social and Physical Progress. . . . Such is our idea of the sphere of government." Not until the period following the Civil War and the advent of Social Darwinism in economic and political theory did this conception of the purposes of government encounter a formidable rival in the resurgence of the earlier theory of the least possible intervention of government in the affairs of men.

IN SUMMARY

In the preceding pages we have emphasized frequently the diversity in customs, ideas, and institutions that has characterized the various sections of the United States—the South, the North, the East, the West. Moreover, since education, under the Constitution, has been state and locally administered, the evolution of public school systems has varied not only with sections of the country but within one and the same state. Nevertheless, it can be said with a fair degree of accuracy that by 1860 the American people were committed to the establishment of free schools, publicly supported and publicly controlled. In this they were institutionalizing ideas of the eighteenth century that experience seemed to have validated. From the conviction that all men are created equal and that governments are created among men to insure to all the rights of equality, several conclusions with respect to education were drawn: (1) that each child is possessed of a *natural right* to an education at the hands of the state sufficient to insure economic independence and the performance of his duties as a citizen; (2) that the state, in its own interests, must prepare each oncoming generation for intelligent participation in government both as citizens and as good servants of the people; (3) that moral and intellectual training is essential, but that this training, in a population as diverse in origin, religion, and political conviction as the traditional coat of many colors, must not be sectarian in any sense. Rather should the school strive to develop disciplined ways of thinking, feeling, and acting, that is, a common morality to function as a unifying influence in change.

These principles, at times, have been explicitly stated; at times, implied only, in the arguments of educators and laymen seeking the establishment of public schools. It is needless to add that they have been vigorously opposed by many who could not accept the idea that one man should be taxed for the education of another man's child or, indeed, the concept of universal education as such. By 1860, however, it had become clear that the opponents of public schools could do no more than delay their establishment here and there. Ultimate adoption by the states was inevitable. Fortunate it was, from the standpoint of the friends of public education, that this was so, since the period following the Civil War, to which we now turn, was one in which the ideas of equality, of natural rights, of progress through government intervention in the operations of man and of nature, even the idea of democracy, were to be severely challenged by new developments in science and the philosophy of Social Darwinism based on "science."

SUGGESTED READING

Cremin, Lawrence A. (ed.), *The Republic and the School: Horace Mann on the Education of Free Men*, Classics in Education, No. 1 (New York: Teachers College, Columbia University, 1957).

Curti, Merle, *The Growth of American Thought*, 2nd ed. (New York: Harper & Brothers, 1951), Chapters XII-XVI.

———, *The Social Ideas of American Educators* (New York: Charles Scribner's Sons, 1935), Chapters III, IV.

McCluskey, Neal Gerard, S.J., *Public Schools and Moral Education* (New York: Columbia University Press, 1958), Chapters II, III.

Thayer, V. T., *The Role of the School in American Society* (New York: Dodd, Mead & Co., 1960), Chapters I-V.

United States Supreme Court, *School District of Abington Township* v. *Schempp*, 374 U.S. 203 (1963).

CHAPTER 6
EVOLUTION AND MAN'S
PLACE IN NATURE

IN our rapid survey of changes in American life during the nineteenth century (Chapter 4), little more than passing reference was made to the influence of science. So important, however, were the applications of science to all aspects of life during this period that they require an additional word.

In his description of the Americans during the period of Jacksonian democracy, Alexis de Tocqueville (*Democracy in America,* 1835) remarked:

> Those very Americans who have not discovered one of the general laws of mechanics have introduced into navigation an engine that changes the aspect of the world. . . . If the democratic principle does not on the one hand induce men to cultivate science for its own sake, on the other, it does enormously increase the number of those who do cultivate it. . . . Permanent inequality of conditions leads men to confine themselves to the arrogant and sterile researches of abstract truths, whilst the social conditions and institutions of democracy prepare them to seek the immediate and useful practical results of the sciences. The tendency is natural and inevitable.

Suggestive as this observation may be of an intimate relationship between the applications of knowledge and an open society, it should be pointed out that the practical motive has characterized American intellectual life from the beginning. Indeed, Daniel J. Boorstin considers the American's emphasis upon the relationship of knowledge to experience as a distinctive contribution to logic:

> The most fertile novelty of the New World was not its climate, its plants, its animals, or its minerals, but its concept of knowledge. . . . Men here were more interested in the elaboration of experience than in the elaboration of "truth"; the novelties of a New World led them to suspect that elaborate verification might itself mislead. As William James explained at the close of the nineteenth century, technically completed verifications are seldom needed in experience. In America, he said, "the possession of truth, so far from being . . . an end in itself, is only a preliminary means toward other vital satisfactions." [1]

It was this pragmatic spirit that prompted Benjamin Franklin to explain, in the same letter which described to a friend his proposed experiment on the relationship of lightning to electricity, that the lightning rod, if his theory were correct, would be useful "in preserving houses, churches, ships, etc., from the stroke of lightning." And Franklin was not alone in his eagerness to apply the results of scientific investigation to material conditions of living. But for advancements in geology, physics, chemistry, biology, and the like, together with their applications to agriculture, maritime commerce, mining, manufacturing, oil refining, transportation, and communication, as well as to the problems of health and hygiene in urban centers—to mention but a few examples—the transformation of a rural America into an industrial nation in less than a century would have been impossible.

Specialization in science necessarily accompanied these developments. Early in the century, for example, the physical sciences were grouped under the single heading "natural philosophy" and the biological sciences under that of "natural history." But by 1850 each of these fields had become so rich that it required subdivision (natural philosophy into chemistry, physics, and geology; natural history into botany and zoology) with separate textbooks for each. In 1818 Benjamin Silliman of Yale launched

---

[1] Daniel J. Boorstin, *The Americans: The Colonial Experience* (New York: Random House, 1958), p. 150. Richard Hofstadter relates this preoccupation with the practical to the opposition of many Americans, until recently, to education of the masses above the common school. See his *Anti-intellectualism in American Life* (New York: Alfred A. Knopf, 1963), Chapters 9, 10.

his *American Journal of Science and Arts.* Between that date and the Civil War, other journals appeared, and geologists, geographers, ethnologists, and statisticians each established national associations. In 1846, the Smithsonian Institution was established in Washington, D.C. In 1847, the American Association for the Advancement of Science was founded to "promote intercourse between American scientists, to give a strong and more systematic impulse to research, and to procure for the labors of scientific men increased facilities and wider usefulness."

Widespread interest in science and technology encouraged not only the introduction of science and practical subjects in both secondary schools and colleges but the establishment of separate institutes and schools devoted to technical and vocational subjects. The decade of the Civil War alone witnessed the founding of twenty-five institutions for the training of engineers and technicians. From both state and national governments came support for research in science; and science, like a grateful child, returned the principal with generous interest.

SCIENCE INFLUENCES PHILOSOPHY AND RELIGION

We must not assume, however, that the applications of science were limited to the material aspects of life. No less important for the investigators and the public at large were the implications of research in physics, chemistry, biology, geology, paleontology, and the like for philosophy and religion. Here, in the light shed by the new knowledge, problems were raised with respect to man, his origins, his nature, and his destiny. Indeed, one of the major issues in each of these fields throughout the century was the manner and the extent to which new knowledge confirmed or suggested modifications in contemporary conceptions of the Deity and his relations to nature and to man.

The dominant conception of God was still either that of an anthropomorphic being as pictured by the Calvinists (an arbitrary God who created all things by an act of his will and who intervenes in the order of nature from time to time as He alone determines) or that of the Deists (a beneficent Author of the universe who in one act of creation brought into being both the world of nature and the invariable laws according to which this world operates without need or occasion for his later intervention in the form of creative acts, miracles, or the like).

Interpretation thus went hand in hand with new discoveries in the sciences, as textbooks of the period amply illustrate. Steele's *Fourteen Weeks of Chemistry* (1873), for example, informed the student that "Every tiny atom is watched by the Eternal Eye and guided by the Eternal Hand." And Colton's *Geography* drew attention to the peculiarities of animals as evidence of God's superior wisdom and benevolence rather than as a natural result of variations in climate and other environmental influences. Similarly, Cruikshank's *Primary Geography* was careful to impress upon its readers the fact that "God made the world for man to live in and has fitted it for man's convenience and comfort." [2]

Moreover, the merging of theology and science was not confined to elementary and secondary school instruction. Eventually, studies of the earth's surface brought forth evidence of geological periods in the planet's existence that seemed to conflict with the biblical account of creation. Paleontology likewise confronted scientists with data suggesting the appearance and disappearance of forms of life that failed to accord with inferences drawn from the biblical account.

Consequently, authorities in geology and paleontology considered it necessary to relate their findings to the principles of theology as well as to contemporary science. As late as 1886, for instance, Alexander Winchell, professor of geology and paleontology at Yale, published his *Walks and Talks in the Geological Field* in order to validate the theory of pattern, design, and plan in the world. And the famous botanist, Louis Agassiz, in his *Contributions to the Natural History of the United States of North America* (1857), emphasized that classes, orders, families, and the like are evidences of the work of God in nature. In discovering these natural divisions, he asserted man is privileged to "think God's thoughts after him. In one word all these facts in their natural connection proclaim aloud the One God, whom man may know, adore, alone; and Natural History must, in good time, become the analysis of the thoughts of the Creator of the Universe, as manifested in the animal and vegetable kingdoms."

Similar assumptions of intervention on the part of Providence in the affairs of man were common in the writings of historians, economists, and political scientists. It was not surprising, therefore, that the publica-

[2] For an excellent description of relations between science and supernaturalistic views of the period, see Merle Curti, *The Growth of American Thought*, 2nd ed. (New York: Harper & Brothers, 1951), Chapter XXI, from which these illustrations are taken.

tion of Charles Darwin's *The Origin of Species* in 1859, followed by *The Descent of Man* in 1871, attracted the attention not only of scientists and theologians but of thoughtful people in general.

THE CHALLENGE OF "NATURAL SELECTION"

The concept of evolution in itself was not unfamiliar, of course. Geology and paleontology, as we have seen, had already drawn attention to transformations in the structure of plants and animals in response to differences and changes in environmental conditions. Familiar also was the Lamarckian explanation of changes of this character in terms of the inheritance of acquired characteristics. The giraffe, for example, was supposed by Lamarck to have increased its neck length gradually through many successive generations of stretching in order to reach high foliage. Not only had paleontologists discovered fossil remains which suggested adaptations in the physical structure of existing species of plants and animals; they had also found specimens that indicated the apparent "creation," transformation, and ultimate elimination of species no longer in existence. Moreover, a number of orthodox religionists had found it possible to explain these facts without doing violence to the concept of God as a divine Creator who intervenes from time to time in natural events and the affairs of men.

Why, then, did Darwin's *The Origin of Species* and *The Descent of Man* create consternation not ony in scientific and religious circles but in the mind of the general public as well? Historian John Fiske provided one answer in *The Destiny of Man Viewed in the Light of His Origin* (1884). Fiske equated the influence of Darwin's theory of evolution by means of natural selection with the Copernican theory in astronomy. Prior to the acceptance of the latter, he wrote, men assumed that "this earth, the fair home of man, was placed in the centre of a universe wherein all things were ordained for his sole behoof: the sun to give him light and warmth, the stars in their courses to preside over his strangely checkered destinies, the winds to blow, the floods to rise, or the fiend of pestilence to stalk abroad over the land,—all for the blessing, or the warning, or the chiding, of the chief among God's creatures, Man." The Copernican theory, continued Fiske, rudely unseated man from his position "in the centre of a universe" and revealed him instead as "the denizen of an obscure and tiny speck of cosmical matter quite invisible amid the innumerable throng of flaming suns that make up our galaxy." Severe as was this blow to man's exalted conception of his place in nature, we have found it possible "to smile" at the "quaint conceit" that man must occupy a central position, physically, in the stellar universe in order "to be the central object of God's care."

Now, what Darwin has done, said Fiske, is to bring about a second revolution in man's conception of himself by questioning the assumption that the latter is a "creature apart by himself," the object of an act of "special creation." Rather is he "descended from a common stock of primates back to which we may trace the converging pedigrees of monkeys and lemurs, until their ancestry becomes indistinguishable from that of rabbits and squirrels," and, he might have added, still farther back to a simple one-celled structure.

It was thus Darwin's identification of man as a mammal among other mammals that most shocked religious leaders of his day. Impious also was his explanation of the origin and later adaptations of species to their environments as the result of the "natural selection" of minute and "accidental variations" rather than as a result of the intervention of transcendent purpose in the operations of nature. He, himself, was neutral and noncommittal on the question of the origin of life itself. But the concept of evolution through natural selection contradicted the theories of scientists and theologians who had contended that species are the physical expressions of archetypes in the mind of God (and are therefore "fixed") and that variations within species, as well as the emergence of new species in nature, result from the intervention, or "providential" acts of the Deity.

Violence was also done to the traditional notion of the operations of nature by the concepts of "struggle for existence" and "survival of the fittest." Science and theology, prior to this period in American thought, had stressed design in nature as evidence of the presence of a wise and beneficent purpose. As against this, there now emerged a picture of nature as wasteful in the extreme, cruel, and indifferent: wasteful in its excessive and prolific reproduction of candidates for existence, cruel in the methods employed for reducing their numbers, impersonal in the selection of the "fit" for survival. Reactions to the theory of evolution by means of natural selection, particularly in its applications to man, were widespread, affecting deeply the general public as well as individuals more professionally concerned with its implications for science (physical and natural), the social studies, arts, and humanities.

In Fundamentalist and Evangelical circles, the concept of evolution was promptly rejected as antireligious and atheistic—with the result that in many sections of the country its consideration in school and college classrooms was prohibited, except for purposes of refutation. Teachers who ventured to suggest that the theory contained some grains of truth were often subject to immediate dismissal. One of the first to receive this treatment was the Reverend James Woodrow, an uncle of Woodrow Wilson, at the time professor of natural science and president of the University of South Carolina. In an address delivered to the Alumni Association of the Presbyterian Theological Seminary of Columbia, South Carolina (where he also occupied the chair of "Perkins Professor of Natural Science in connection with Revelation"), Woodrow put forth the view that the Bible was not intended to teach science and that evolution might be true as "mediate creation." He was promptly removed from the faculty of the Seminary.

The famous trial of John Thomas Scopes in Tennessee in 1925, a trial in which William Jennings Bryan and Clarence Darrow played conspicuous roles, testified to the persistence of popular resistance to the theory of evolution well into the twentieth century. Scopes, a high school teacher of science, was judged guilty of violating a Tennessee state law which prohibited the teaching of evolution in the public schools of that state. Even as late as today a number of states forbid the teaching of evolution as a fact in their public schools.

A second group attempted to meet the challenge of Darwinism to traditional theology in a more scholarly manner. This it did by identifying the "accidental variations" of species in Darwin's theory with the "special providences" or arbitrary interventions of the Deity in nature as recognized by traditional theology. Prominent in this effort was James McCosh of Princeton University. Indeed, McCosh had faced the problem of the appearance of new species in nature and their adaptations to change of environment as early as 1850, in his volume on *The Method of Divine Government*. His solution was to identify natural selection with the beneficent interventions of the Deity in nature ("special providences"), a solution he reaffirmed in *The Religious Aspect of Evolution* (1888), contending that "Supernatural design produces natural selection." As Herbert Schneider remarks, McCosh merely "reasserted the Calvinist faith in special providences, in spontaneous or unpredictable acts of God whereby some are elected and others rejected, and restated the argument from design, which was the commonplace of natural theology, to include the gradual achievement of fitness or adaptation in nature by means of numerous 'accidental' interferences with the normal course of events." [3] This was obviously an explanation unlikely to satisfy long either scientist, theologian, or thoughtful layman eager to reconcile the concept of a beneficent Deity with an orderly system of nature.

Of the scientists who attempted to reconcile theism and Darwin's theory of natural selection, Asa Gray, the famous botanist, merits special mention, for it was he who first reviewed favorably *The Origin of Species* and, in numerous articles thereafter, effectively refuted Louis Agassiz and other opponents of Darwinism.

JOHN FISKE AND PHILOSOPHICAL THEISM

Few writers were more widely read on the subject of evolution and religion than John Fiske (1842-1901). As historian, lecturer, and author, Fiske was in a position to influence the thoughts of scientist, theologian, and layman alike. And gifted as he was with an attractive style in writing, he succeeded in formulating for thousands an interpretation of evolution that erased for them the conflict between science and religion. Fiske's most ambitious work in philosophy was his four-volume *Outlines of Cosmic Philosophy* (1874), of which Charles Darwin wrote in a letter to the author, "I never in my life read so lucid an expositor (and therefore thinker) as you are." For well over a half-century, Fiske's three popular lectures, *The Destiny of Man* (1884), *The Idea of God* (1885), and *Through Nature to God* (1889) enabled the liberal-minded in religion to reconcile the data of science and the tenets of Protestant religion. This he made plausible in *The Idea of God* by drawing a contrast between the "primitive" conception of God as "a Being actuated by human passions and purposes, localized in space and utterly remote from that inert machine, the universe in which we live, and upon which He acts intermittently through the suspension of what are called natural laws" and the conception of an immanent God, a cosmic consciousness that pervades the universe and gives direction to it.

The primitive and conventional theory, wrote Fiske in the same work, assumes the universe to have been created by "a Being possessed of intelligence and volition essentially similar to the intelligence and volition

[3] Herbert W. Schneider, *A History of American Philosophy* (New York: Columbia University Press, 1946), p. 370.

of Man. This Being is actuated by a desire for the good of his creatures, and in pursuance thereof entertains purposes and adapts means to ends with consummate ingenuity."

By analogy then, the world is conceived as the creation of an Intelligent Artist, a "Divine Architect," or a "Divine Designer" who is responsible for the marvelous adaptations everywhere evident in nature. But this conception, continued Fiske, involves difficulties when we consider the other side of the picture. How reconcile, for example, the assumption of a Creator, "omnipotent and absolutely benevolent," with the cruelty and maladaptations found in nature? "In every part of the animal world we find implements of torture surpassing in devilish ingenuity anything that was ever seen in the dungeons of the Inquisition."

This, of course, involves us in the problem of evil, a problem that Fiske attempted to solve in *Through Nature to God* by means both of his concept of an immanent God and the stern facts of psychology. In a chapter entitled "Simile of the Watch Replaced by Simile of the Flower," Fiske stated frankly that the problem of evil is impossible of solution on Paley's assumption of a Divine Creator who stands outside the universe. "In the twinkling of an eye," he wrote, the Darwinian theory of natural selection succeeded in knocking out all support from under the argument that adaptations between living creatures and their environments testify to design, that is, to the creative planning of a Divine Designer. "It is not that the organism and its environment have been adapted to each other by an exercise of creative intelligence," he continued, "but it is that the organism is necessarily fitted to the environment because in the perennial slaughter that has gone on from the beginning only the fittest have survived."

Fiske's psychological argument turned upon the nature of consciousness. Our awareness of events and objects (consciousness) is possible only by virtue of incessant change and contrast, "a fact deeply rooted in the innermost structure of the human mind." Consequently, to know good, we must also know evil. In a world without sin and pain "the moral element would be lacking." Therefore, he continued in *Through Nature to God*, "In a happy world there must be sorrow and pain, and in a moral world the knowledge of evil is indispensable." (We ask the reader to judge whether the contention that evil is justified because it is necessary satisfactorily solves the "problem of evil"!)

All of this constitutes a revolution in conventional notions of God and the operations of nature. But, Fiske continued in the same work, it undermines not at all the conception of man as the central object of God's care. The argument for design assumed the world to be a machine, and thus external to the Deity. But the universe, as Fiske viewed it, is not a machine; rather is it "an organism with an indwelling principle of life. It was not made, but it grows."

Evolution, so conceived, applies to the entire physical universe, even to the laws of nature which Deists and Calvinists alike had assumed to have sprung full-blown from the mind of God. Moreover, with the emergence of man, cosmic evolution took a new turn. Prior to this significant event, organic survival had been dependent upon the "natural" selection of physical variations. In man, however, psychical variations take priority over the physical, with the result that the "last act in the great drama of creation" is now under way; or, to change the simile, "an entirely new chapter in the history of the universe" has opened.

The significance of this change was developed by Fiske in *The Destiny of Man*. Here he sketched the evolution of consciousness from its first crude beginnings in lower forms of life to its final expressions in man, where, in contrast with other animals, it enables him to adjust flexibly to his environment, even to adapt environmental conditions to human needs; to lengthen the period of infancy and to prolong the dependence of the young upon adults (with all the advantages that learning affords, in contrast with the dependence of other animals upon instinct); and to develop family life and other institutions of an evolving civilization to the point at which, ultimately, factors of moral growth and intellectual activity acquire a dominating influence over the desires and activities of men. Once this point is reached, "the wholesale destruction of life which has heretofore characterized evolution ever since life began," will come to an end in its application to "the chief of God's creatures. It means that the universal struggle for existence, having succeeded in bringing forth that consummate product of creative energy, the Human Soul, has done its work and will presently cease. In the lower regions of organic life it must go on, but as a determining factor in the highest work of evolution it will disappear."

Fiske's theory of evolution, in its applications to concepts of God, man, and nature appealed alike to Transcendentalists and other liberals in religion, lay and clerical, as well as to many men of science. In the religious field Henry Ward Beecher in New York, Washington Gladden of

Columbus, Ohio, Phillips Brooks of Boston, and Lyman Abbott, Beecher's successor and for many years editor of *The Outlook,* did much to reconcile the popular mind to the concept of evolution. Furthermore, many colleges, previously denominational, became nonsectarian in this period, thus removing obstacles to the introduction of evolution in the curriculum. Not only in science but in history, economics, political science, and the arts, the concept of evolution soon brought significant changes in content and organization. To its influence on psychology and the philosophy of education we shall return in Chapter 7.

In presenting his philosophical theism, John Fiske attempted to draw a sharp line between the function of science and the province of religion. It was his ambition to remove all possible conflict between the two. Science, he pointed out, deals with specifics, not final causes. Its business "is simply to ascertain in what manner phenomena coexist with each other, and the only kind of explanation with which it can properly deal is that which refers one set of phenomena to another set." Philosophical theism, on the other hand, regards "divine power as the immediate source of all phenomena alike." Consequently, it adds nothing for the scientist, as scientist, to explain actions and events by direct ascription to the Deity, any more, he might have added, than to explain a pain in a bodily organ as caused by the life of the organism!

CHAUNCEY WRIGHT AND EVOLUTIONARY NATURALISM

The attempt to free science from philosophy and religion (the tendency to explain phenomena within the universe by reference to elements beyond it) was carried farther by Chauncey Wright (1830-1875), a neglected figure in American philosophy. He was both mathematician and philosopher, earning his living as a computer for the *Nautical Almanac.* By working intensively, day and night, on his computations he would complete his annual task within a few months, thus freeing himself for uninterrupted attention to his primary interests in philosophy and science. He lectured occasionally at Harvard University and was a member of the famous Metaphysical Club which exercised a formative influence upon the early thought of Charles Peirce, William James, Oliver Wendell Holmes, and others who later contributed significantly to American thought. The reader will find helpful accounts of Wright in Joseph Blau's *Men and Movements in American Philosophy* (1952) and Herbert Schneider's *A History of American Philosophy* (1946).

In response to the question, "Why do we exist?" as posed by one of his correspondents, Wright replied, "All the ends of life are, I am persuaded, within the sphere of life, and are in the last analysis, or highest generalization, to be found in the preservation, continuance, and increase of life itself." He was skeptical as well of attempts to bring the data from all fields of science under one formula—as, for example, the evolutionary hypothesis. Evolution, which he considered fruitful as a biological hypothesis, he refused to accept as a cosmic hypothesis. In his *Philosophical Discussions* (1877), he wrote:

> We strongly suspect that the law of "evolution" will fail to appear in phenomena not connected, either directly or remotely, with the life of the individual organism, or the growth of which this law is an abstract description. And, heterodox though the opinion be, we are inclined to accept as the soundest and most catholic assumption, on grounds of scientific method, the too little regarded doctrine of Aristotle, which banishes cosmology from the realm of scientific inquiry, reducing natural phenomena in their cosmical relations to an infinite variety of manifestations (without a discoverable tendency on the whole) of causes and laws which are simple and constant in their ultimate elements.

Scientific advance, Wright believed, requires complete independence on the part of the scientist, with no entangling alliances with metaphysical, theological, or ethical systems. Only when scientifically neutral, and thus free to seek the truth as revealed by strict adherence to the methods of science, can the scientist do his best work. Similarly, he believed it was in the best interests of religion for the theologian to refrain from encroaching upon science. Again, in *Philosophical Discussions,* he wrote:

> The progress of science has indeed been a progress in religious truth, but in spite of false theology, and in a way which narrow theologians have constantly opposed. It has defined with greater and greater distinctness the boundary between what can be discovered and what cannot. It has purified religious truth by turning the moral consciousness to discover clearly in itself what it has obscurely divined from its own interpretations of nature. It has impressed on the mind of the cautious inquirer the futility, as well as the irreverence, of attempting a philosophy which can at best be but a finer sort of superstition, a real limitation to our conceptions of final causes, while apparently an extension of them.

For the proponents of special creation as well as for John Fiske, it will be recalled, the appearance of man in the evolutionary process was of special significance. Fiske went so far as to conclude that the emergence of self-consciousness in man marked the end of physical variations and assured for him continued progress psychologically and morally. In each instance, self-consciousness in man was viewed as different in kind from conscious behavior in animals.

Wright rejected these conclusions, insisting that here, as elsewhere in science, explanations of phenomena are to be found within rather than outside the processes of nature. Granted that mental behavior in man differs significantly from that of lower animals, its antecedents are nevertheless found in animal life and can be traced step by step in the evolutionary process. The distinction between instinct in animals and intelligence in man, for example, is less one of kind than of degree, and has been overstressed by students. Wright put it as follows, in *Philosophical Discussions:* "the distinction of instinct and intelligence, though not less real and important in the classification of actions in psycho-zoology, and as important even as that of animal and vegetable is in general zoology, or the distinctions of organic and inorganic, living and dead, in the general science of life, is yet like these, in its applications a vague, ill-defined distinction."

To Chauncey Wright, then, must be given credit for (1) a major contribution toward the emancipation of science from theology and ethics (an emancipation that many feel, in an atomic age, has gone too far, encouraging a spirit of neutrality, if not irresponsibility on the part of scientists to an extent that a highly sensitive and interdependent society can ill afford); and (2) an evolutionary and naturalistic psychology, one that was to undermine the validity of faculty psychology and, in the hands of William James, G. Stanley Hall, Edward L. Thorndike and others, affect profoundly both educational theory and practice.

WILLIAM GRAHAM SUMNER AND SOCIAL DARWINISM

Frequent mention has been made of the tendency in the eighteenth century to view the universe as a cleverly contrived machine, obviously designed by a beneficent Architect with the ends of man in mind. On this theory, what appear at first as evils and maladaptations, in their bearing upon man, are merely "not understood." When properly viewed, "all partial evil" becomes, in Pope's words, "universal good," and "whatever is, is right."

This manner of thought persisted well into the nineteenth century. Emerson, for example, saw in nature "the symbol of the spirit," a conviction that enabled him to assert in his *Essay on Nature* (1836) that "The moral law lies at the centre of nature and radiates to the circumference. It is the pith and marrow of every substance, every relation, and every process. All things with which we deal preach to us."

The story of evolution, as revealed by science, forced men to come to terms with quite a different theory of nature and its operations. According to Thomas H. Huxley, for example, writing in *Evolution and Ethics and Other Essays* (1896), man has become "the superb animal which he is" as a direct result of the struggle for existence. This has been a struggle in which he has succeeded better than his competitors "in the cosmic strife" by virtue of the qualities he shares with the ape and tiger: "his exceptional physical organization; his cunning sociability, his curiosity, and his imitativeness; his ruthless and ferocious destructiveness when his anger is roused by opposition." These are not exactly the moral qualities of a Christian ethics! But so firmly embedded in the minds of intellectuals was the assumption that the ways of nature are the ways of beneficent design and thus conform to a cosmic morality that, with the acceptance of evolution as a fact, it was inevitable some should attempt to justify ethically its central features.

Most influential of these interpreters of evolution was Herbert Spencer (1820-1903), of whom Henry Holt writes: "Probably no other philosopher ever had such a vogue as Spencer had from about 1870 to 1890. Most preceding philosophers had presumably been mainly restricted to readers habitually given to the study of philosophy, but not only was Spencer considerably read and generally talked about by the whole intelligent world in England and America, but that world was wider than any that preceded it." [4]

Widely influential also was Spencer's leading disciple in the United

---

[4] Henry Holt, *Garrulities of an Octogenarian Editor* (Boston: Houghton Mifflin Co., 1923), p. 298. For an excellent account of Spencer's influence in America upon the general public as well as philosophers, scientists, and the literary fold, see Richard Hofstadter, *Social Darwinism in American Thought* (Boston: Beacon Press, 1960), Chapter 2; also, Henry Steele Commager, *The American Mind* (New Haven, Conn.: Yale University Press, 1952), Chapters IV, V.

States, William Graham Sumner (1840-1910).[5] According to both Spencer and Sumner, evolution implies progress (the gradual selection of the fit and the elimination of the unfit as defined by a cosmic purpose), but the methods employed are ruthless, when viewed from the standpoint of the weak. Assuming with Malthus that population tends to exceed food supply, they also assumed that competition for survival is a universal law. In this competition, victory is awarded to the strong (identified with the "fit"), and the weak (the "unfit") tend to be eliminated. Since those who survive normally pass on their characteristics to their offspring there is an assurance of gradual improvement in the nature of individuals and society—provided the natural process of evolution is kept free from interference!

"Between them," remarks Henry Steele Commager, "Darwin and Spencer exercised such sovereignty over America as George III had never enjoyed." [6] And well might this be so, since economic society in the United States in the 1870's and 1880's "with its rapid expansion, its exploitable methods, its desperate competition, and its preemptory rejection of failure ... was like a vast human caricature of the Darwinian struggle for existence and survival of the fittest." [7]

What a comfort it was to those involved in the ruthless economic struggle of the period to receive scientific assurance that the work in which they were engaged was divinely ordained! John D. Rockefeller, for example, remarked in a Sunday-school address, "The survival of a large business is merely a survival of the fittest. . . . This is not an evil tendency in business. It is merely the working-out of a law of nature and a law of God."

Not only was the replacement of small business by large corporations cosmically justified by the theory of Social Darwinism, but the individuals who thus succeeded in dominating the economic scene—by virtue of what

[5] Sumner began his college work in 1859 at Yale as a student of theology and served for a few years both as the rector of the Episcopal Church in Morristown, New Jersey, and as editor of a religious newspaper. From 1872 to the end of his career, he occupied the position of Professor of Political and Social Science at Yale. Hofstadter, *op. cit.*, p. 54, remarks of him, "Although clerical phraseology soon disappeared from his style, his temper remained that of a proselytizer, a moralist, an espouser of causes with little interest in distinguishing between error and iniquity in his opponents."

[6] Commager, *op. cit.*, p. 87.

[7] Hofstadter, *op. cit.*, p. 44.

Chauncey Depew ascribed to their "superior ability, foresight and adapta-
bility"—constituted the elite of economic society. Thus Sumner insisted
that:

> The millionaires are the product of natural selection, acting on
> the whole body of men to pick out those who can meet the require-
> ment of certain work to be done. . . . It is because they are thus
> selected that wealth—both their own and that entrusted to them—
> aggregates under their hands. . . . They may fairly be regarded as
> the naturally selected agents of society for certain work. They get
> high wages and live in luxury, but the bargain is a good one for
> society. There is the intensest competition for their place and occu-
> pation. This assures us that all who are competent for this function
> will be employed in it, so that the cost of it will be reduced to the
> lowest terms.[8]

The logic of this argument precluded both interference on the part of
government with the operations of natural law in economic society and
private efforts at alleviating the conditions of the poor, the weak and the
handicapped. Of those who would remedy conditions that bear harshly
upon the weak, Sumner said:

> They do not perceive that . . . "the strong" and "the weak" are terms
> which admit of no definition unless they are made equivalent to
> the industrious and the idle, the frugal and the extravagant. They
> do not perceive, furthermore, that if we do not like the survival of
> the fittest, we have only one possible alternative, and that is the sur-
> vival of the unfittest. The former is the law of civilization; the latter
> is the law of anti-civilization. We have our choice between the two,
> or we can go on as in the past, vacillating between the two, but a
> third plan—the socialist desideratum—a plan for nourishing the un-
> fittest and yet advancing in civilization, no man will ever find.[9]

Not through attempts to modify the ways of nature, then, but through
faith in the ultimate outcomes of a gradual evolutionary process, can men
hope for improvements in society. "Every one of us," Sumner insisted, "is
a child of his age and cannot get out of it. He is in the stream and is

[8] William Graham Sumner, *The Challenge of Facts and Other Essays* (New Haven,
Conn.: Yale University Press, 1914), p. 90.
[9] Albert G. Davis and Maurice R. Davis (eds.), *Essays of William Sumner,* Vol. II
(New Haven, Conn.: Yale University Press, 1934), p. 56.

swept along with it. All his science and philosophy came to him out of it. Therefore the tide will not be changed by us. It will swallow up both us and our experiments. . . . That is why it is the greatest folly of which a man can be capable to sit down with a slate and pencil to plan out a new social world." [10]

THE CONCEPTS OF NATURAL RIGHTS AND EQUALITY REPUDIATED

Finally, in this summary of conclusions drawn from the "facts of evolution" should be mentioned the influence of Social Darwinism upon the eighteenth-century ideals of equality, natural rights, and democracy. First to be rejected was the concept of equality: equality either as fact or ideal. As fact, inequality, according to Spencer and Sumner, characterized individuals in the natural state. It is natural inequality, indeed, that constitutes a source of fruitful variations in individuals, variations that make for success or failure in the struggle for existence. Furthermore, equality is not acceptable as an ideal, since it runs counter to the ultimate welfare of society. Given liberty and freedom for all in the competitive struggle, those of "courage, enterprise, good training, intelligence, perseverance" will emerge on top.[11]

Natural rights, in the sense of rights possessed by men in a state of nature, likewise fail to pass the test of historical accuracy. Rather are they, according to Sumner, evolving folkways, rules of the game, peculiar to a given state of society and subject to change in the course of evolution: "The eighteenth-century notions about equality, natural rights, classes, and the like produced nineteenth-century states and legislation, all strongly humanitarian in faith and temper; at the present time the eighteenth-century notions are disappearing, and the *mores* of the twentieth century will not be tinged by humanitarianism as those of the last hundred years have been." [12]

So, too, with democracy. Given abundance of land and a sparce population, equality and democracy are temporarily possible. But let land become scarce and competition for survival keen, and the strong will emerge to assume direction of affairs. That is to say, democracy is only a passing phase in the evolution of society.

[10] *Ibid.*, Vol. I, from "The Absurd Effort to Make the World Over," p. 105.
[11] Sumner, *op. cit.*, p. 67.
[12] Davis and Davis (eds.), Vol. I, *op. cit.*, pp. 86-87.

THE WISDOM OF UNIVERSAL EDUCATION
ALSO QUESTIONED

What becomes of education in this view of society? What happens to Horace Mann's dictum that each child, to the extent of his ability, is entitled to free education by the state? Obviously, it becomes an impractical dream!

The Spencerian assumption that progress comes slowly—not through reform movements or the institutions of society, but through the gradual accretion of individual characteristics transmitted and perpetuated by inheritance—accords little influence to education as an institution. Sumner was not unalterably opposed to public education, as was Spencer, on the grounds that it undermines parental freedom and corrupts the body politic with the poison of public welfare. But he was far from friendly toward it, particularly on the higher levels, contending that the right to vote did not carry with it the right to free schooling.[13] Compulsory education he accepted, not so much for its contributions to social betterment as for its contribution to public order.

On the other hand, Sumner emphasized the importance of the family as an instrument in transmitting the qualities of character essential for success. Human progress, as he conceived it, is moral progress; and moral progress is largely dependent upon the individual acquisition of economic virtues. "Let every man be sober, industrious, prudent, and wise," he wrote, "and bring up his children to do likewise, and poverty will be abolished in a few generations." [14]

Is it not pertinent to consider what would have been the future of public education in the United States had the Spencerian conception of evolution been a formative influence in the early years of the nineteenth century? Fortunately this was not the case. As historians have indicated, there was much in Spencer and Sumner that appealed to the American mind in the 1870's and 1880's—to the acquisitive instincts, to the conviction that progress comes solely through the efforts of the able, and to the belief that the less government interferes with individual initiative the better. But, at the same time, as Commager has remarked, the American people "were logically and psychologically precluded from believing in a

[13] William Graham Sumner, *What Social Classes Owe to Each Other* (New York: Harper & Bros., 1883), pp. 40 ff.
[14] Davis and Davis (eds.), Vol. I, *op. cit.*, p. 109.

progress to which they made no contribution and which was divorced from their control." [15] It is not surprising, therefore, that further studies revealed a more responsible role in evolution for both the individual and the group.

LESTER WARD REASSERTS FAITH IN MAN

One of the first to challenge Social Darwinism was Lester Ward (1841-1913).[16] He agreed with Spencer that the laws of the cosmos bear upon the fate of man, but he repudiated the conclusion of both Sumner and Spencer that the way of wisdom is to accept passively the operations of nature and to adopt them as criteria of behavior in human relationships. On the contrary, Ward contended, civilization and progress in human affairs have come with man's determination to change the ways of nature, not with submission to his environment but with its transformation in harmony with need and desire. That is to say, with the advent of man, a new factor, a psychic factor, was introduced into the evolutionary process—a factor composed of consciousness, intelligence, purpose. Prior to man, the iron law of nature operated remorselessly in physical nature and animal life. With man, however, evolution and use of intelligence have made possible civilization; and civilization, in large measure, has resulted from the ability to reverse the course of nature and to free human beings from the fate to which other forms of life are subject.

The ability to use nature rather than merely to submit to its operations has been one of the primary contributions of physical science. Why, then, Ward inquired, should we not use the data of social science to better the state of man in society? The concepts of competition, of struggle for existence, and the selection of the "fit," as advocated by the Social Darwinians, thus became the objects of Ward's attack. In his *Psychic Factors of Civilization* (1893), he wrote:

[15] Commager, *op. cit.,* p. 90.
[16] Although largely self-educated, Lester Ward succeeded in acquiring a distinguished reputation as a botanist, paleobotanist, and sociologist. In 1883 he was appointed to the post of chief paleontologist in the United States Geological Survey. It was in this year also that he published his *Dynamic Sociology,* the first comprehensive sociological treatise written in the United States. General recognition of Ward's contributions came slowly for the reason, states Hofstadter, that he was so far in advance of his generation. Writing to Ward in 1903, the distinguished sociologist Albion Small stated, "You were not only ahead of us in point of time, but we all know that you are head, shoulders, and hips above us in many respects scientifically." Hofstadter, *op. cit.,* p. 84.

[Competition] has been the tyrant of nature. [And insofar as man] has progressed at all beyond the purely animal stage he has done so through triumphing little by little over this law and gaining somewhat the mastery of the struggle. Every implement or utensil, every mechanical device . . . is a triumph of mind over the physical forces of nature in ceaseless and aimless competition. All human institutions—religion, government, law, marriage, custom—together with innumerable other modes of regulating social, industrial, and commercial life are, broadly viewed, only so many ways of meeting and checkmating the principle of competition as it manifests itself in society.

Characteristic of man's intelligence, also, according to Ward, is the elimination of waste common to the natural process. Contrast, for example, nature's superabundance in producing organisms, its dependence upon wind, water, birds, and animals for the sowing of seed, as against the manner in which man selects seed, prepares the soil, eliminates weeds, plants at intervals, and harvests his products. With man in society, the situation is similar. To the extent that competition is controlled or eliminated, progress results. Left unrestrained, social waste and injustice result —in production of goods, in their distribution, in the rewards of industry.

Again, with government, there is a similar situation. Ward was willing to grant that the concept of laissez faire and noninterference on the part of government served a useful purpose when government was in the hands of an oligarchy and a monarchy. With the advent of representative government, however, and the direct participation of the people in determining their political and economic interests, laissez faire loses its validity and should be replaced by the applications of social intelligence. "Ignorance, poverty, drudgery and nameless misery," he believed, can be eliminated. But this requires the exercise of social intelligence on the part of legislators—of legislators, that is, who are properly equipped to legislate! According to Ward, "Before progressive legislation can become a success, every legislature must become, as it were, a polytechnic school, a laboratory of philosophical research, into the laws of society and of human nature. No legislator is qualified to vote on, or propose, measures designed to affect the destinies of millions of social units until he masters all that is known of the science of society. Every true legislator must be a sociologist."

To realize this objective involves a role for education quite different from that envisaged by Social Darwinism. For Ward, indeed, education was all-important in reversing the course of nature and in giving direction and purpose to the individual and his society. In organized society, he wrote in *Dynamic Sociology* (1883), "knowledge can no longer be left to chance and to nature." Its origin and its distribution "must be systematized and erected into true arts. Knowledge artificially acquired is still real knowledge, and the stock of all men must also consist chiefly of such knowledge. The artificial supply of knowledge is as much more copious than the natural as is the artificial supply of food more abundant than the natural supply."

Again, for Ward education was important for much the same reason that prompted Thomas Jefferson and Horace Mann to urge its support by the state. Unlike Sumner, Ward could not accept the assumption that class distinctions derive from differences in native ability. On the contrary, he believed with Jefferson that ability is found as commonly among the underprivileged and the poor as in the more favored classes. For example, in an article on "Social Darwinism" in 1907, Ward asserted that the only hope for society lies in the truth, "that so far as the native capacity, the potential quality, 'the promise and potency,' of a higher life are concerned, those swarming, spawning millions, the bottom layer of society ... are by nature the peers of the boasted 'aristocracy of brains' that now dominates society and looks down upon them, and the equals in all but privileges of the most enlightened teachers of eugenics." Furthermore, since he agreed with Spencer and many others of the period in the transmission of acquired characteristics, education loomed large in importance as an instrument with which to insure the steady progress of civilization.

COOPERATION BECOMES A FACTOR IN EVOLUTION

Although Ward's voice, for a time, was as one crying alone in the wilderness, he did not have to wait long for scientific evidence with which to support his view that Social Darwinism with its emphasis upon competition and the struggle for existence was one-sided not only in its applications to human society but to lower forms of life as well. Of particular importance in this connection were the contributions of Peter Kropotkin to the concepts of mutual aid and cooperation in the role of evolution. From his observations in Northern Asia, Kropotkin was impressed with the manner in which mutual aid, within the same species, rather than competition contributes to survival. Subsequent studies confirmed these observations. From ants and bees and beetles to birds and animals; from primitive man through societies ever more advanced—barbarian, medieval, and modern—Kropotkin compiled evidence to establish the fact that "competition is not the rule either in the animal world or in mankind."

Thus it was, by the late nineteenth century and the opening of the twentieth, that science, philosophy, and religion were once again in a position to view optimistically the resources in nature and human nature that man might use in order to raise the level of his civilization. The humane qualities—sympathy, generosity, benevolence, brotherly love, and the like—might be viewed as positive factors in human evolution, not as impediments to the realization of God's will!

For a time, in the 1870's and 1880's particularly, the opposite conclusion seemed inevitable. Scientific data, which seemingly established evolution as a fact, had suggested that men in society should discipline, if not root out, their altruistic impulses in order to conform to the laws of tooth and claw inherited from their animal ancestors. Data from the prehuman era were thus boldly used as criteria with which to oppose interference with economic, social, and political developments of the post-Civil War period: ruthless competition in business and industry, from which emerged, as though by a process of natural selection, huge aggregations of capital, industrial giants, eager to crush both labor and their competitors and to use government to safeguard and to promote their interests. There were leaders who sincerely believed, as George F. Baer boldly asserted during the strike of the United Mine Workers in 1902, that "The rights and interests of the laboring man will be cared for, not by the labor agitators, but by the Christian men to whom God in His infinite wisdom has given control of the property interests of the country." There were leaders, too, so concerned that the ways of God should operate without interference from misguided reformers that they fought vigorously all attempts through legislation to better the economic, social and political status of the masses. As ironmaster Abram S. Hewitt wrote at the time, "The problem presented to systems of religion and schemes of government is, to make men who are equal in liberty—that is, in political rights and therefore entitled to the ownership of property—content with that inequality in its distribution which must inevitably result from the application of the law of justice."

For a time, to repeat, Social Darwinism used the data of science—and the laws of nature supposedly established by these data—to discourage organized efforts on the part of reformers to improve conditions of labor or to better the lot of men, women, and children who were unable alone to breast the tides of rapid change. The latter included immigrants from abroad, rural families in process of flocking to the cities from their abandoned farms, and women and children forced to work long hours for meager wages under circumstances inimicable to health of body and mind and destructive of family life. In this atmosphere it was of no small moment that further study of the evolutionary process should provide data with which to redefine man's role in nature and society, and to confirm, through the use of intelligence and of education as a social institution, the possibility of transforming, even creating anew, when necessary, the institutions of his society in the image of the ideal.

Ward's contribution was to clear an intellectual trail that others might follow and improve—an old trail once familiar to Americans, but one which had suffered severely from neglect during the period of disillusionment and cynicism following the Civil War. But to profit from this renewed faith in man, and in education to give direction to change, it became necessary to re-examine traditional theories of learning and their implications for the school in the light of the concept of evolution. Consequently, we turn to the influence of evolution upon the psychology of learning and the curriculum of the school.

SUGGESTED READING

Beard, Charles, and Beard, Mary, *The Rise of American Civilization* (New York: The Macmillan Co., one-vol. ed., 1930), Chapter XXX.

Blau, Joseph, *Men and Movements in American Philosophy* (Englewood Cliffs, N.J.: Prentice-Hall, 1952), Chapter 5.

Cremin, Lawrence A., *The Transformation of the School* (New York: Alfred A. Knopf, 1961), Chapters 2-5.

Curti, Merle, *The Growth of American Thought* (New York: Harper & Bros., 1951), Chapter XXII.

Hofstadter, Richard, *Social Darwinism in American Thought* (Boston: Beacon Press, 1960), Chapters 2-4.

————, *Anti-intellectualism in American Life* (New York: Alfred A. Knopf, 1963), Chapters 9, 10.

CHAPTER 7
THE CONCEPTS OF MIND AND CONSCIOUS STATES ARE CRITICALLY EXAMINED

IN 1892 William James was invited to give a series of talks on psychology to the teachers of Cambridge, Massachusetts. This he was happy to do since it enabled him to apply to the problems of education revised conceptions of the nature of mind and mental processes which he had previously formulated and documented in his monumental work, *The Principles of Psychology*.[1]

Thus, for the conventional notion of an immaterial mind and its contents, James substituted his conception of the "stream of consciousness" and its functions. These functions, he pointed out, are intimately involved with the nervous system and have their origin in the practical necessities of living. "Our sensations are here to attract us or to deter us, our memories to warn or encourage us, our feelings to impel, or our thoughts to restrain our behavior, so that on the whole we may prosper and our days be long in the land." [2] That is to say, the original and primary function of consciousness is biological and related to survival—a point of view

---

[1] William James (1842-1910) was a pioneer in the United States in the attempt to establish psychology as a scientific discipline. In 1878 he entered into a publishing contract to write a text on psychology. The two-volume work, which he originally anticipated would take two years to complete, engaged him for twelve. It has since influenced profoundly not only psychology but other intellectual disciplines as well. See William James, *The Principles of Psychology* (New York: Henry Holt & Co., 1890).

[2] William James, *Talks to Teachers on Psychology: And to Students on Some of Life's Ideals* (New York: Henry Holt & Co., 1912), p. 24.

in direct contradiction to the classic tradition in philosophy, which held that "Man's supreme glory is to be a rational being, to know absolute and eternal and universal truth." Were the philosophers correct, said James, "withdrawal from the strife of human affairs would be not only pardonable but praiseworthy; and all that makes for quiet and contemplation should be regarded as conducive to the highest perfection." [3]

Credit for the practical emphasis in psychology, James attributed, in the main, to the theory of evolution and its contention that man has evolved from infrahuman ancestors, "in whom pure reason hardly existed at all." Mind "would appear to have been an organ" of adaptation to the environment, and "Consciousness would thus seem in the first instance to be nothing but a super-added biological perfection, useless unless it prompted to useful conduct, and inexplicable apart from that consideration." [4]

THE MIND-SUBSTANCE THEORY REFUTED

The stream of consciousness and its functions, to which James directed the attention of teachers, afforded a striking contrast to the mind-substance theory that had long dominated conceptions of learning and their implications for education. No matter how widely idealists and realists, rationalists and empiricists differed in their conceptions of the origins and nature of reality and knowledge, with few exceptions they had been in substantial agreement that man is unique in his possession of a "mind" or "soul" that somehow receives and employs psychic entities in the form of sensations, images, ideas, and the like.

For John Locke, the realist, it will be recalled, all knowledge comes from "experience," by which he meant that the original or primary elements of knowledge enter the mind by way of the senses. Once received, the mind has the power to combine simple ideas (or sensations) into representations of external objects; to recall past ideas; and to develop general ideas, concepts, and the like. Consequently, for Locke and his followers, the mind is also an active agent, capable of observing its own internal operations as well as outer objects and events and of drawing conclusions from them.

For Bishop George Berkeley, the mind is also active. In *Principles of Human Knowledge* (1710), he wrote:

[3] *Ibid.*, p. 23.
[4] *Ibid.*, pp. 24-25.

Besides all that endless variety of ideas and objects of knowledge [which we possess] there is likewise *something which knows or perceives them, and exercises diverse operations*—as willing, imagining, remembering—about them. This perceiving, active being is what I call *mind, spirit, soul,* or *myself.* By which words I do not denote any one of my ideas, but a thing entirely distinct from them, wherein they exist, or, which is the same thing, whereby they are perceived —for the existence of an idea consists in being perceived.

For Berkeley, however, there was no basis for concluding with Locke, or later, with the common-sense realists, who long exercised a dominant influence on American philosophy in the nineteenth century, that ideas "in the mind" testified to the existence of a material world (a material substance, in contrast with a spiritual substance). Since "to be is to be perceived," Berkeley concluded, the world of objects and events must be *ideas,* immediate sense qualities, in the mind—that is, perceived by God or men, or both.

From an inability to sense directly the external world (although it was precisely this that common-sense realists insisted we do), it was but a step to the realization that the existence of mind is also an inference, or, as Berkeley conceded, a "notion." One of the first to point out that we have no direct awareness of a self, or a mind, was David Hume in his *Treatise on Human Nature* (1740). "For my part," he wrote, "when I enter most intimately into what I call myself, I always stumble on some particular perception or other, of heat or cold, light or shade, love or hatred, pain or pleasure. I never can catch myself at any time without a perception, and can never observe anything but the perception."

It was not long before philosophers were ready to grant that our knowledge of a self, that is, of a mind or a soul, is indirect or a logical necessity, rather than an immediate experience. Thus, Francis Wayland opened his *Elements of Intellectual Philosophy* (1854) with words practically identical with those of Locke: "Of the essence of Mind we know nothing," and continued: "All that we are able to affirm of it is that it is *something* which perceives, reflects, remembers, imagines, and wills; but what that something *is* which exerts these energies we know not. It is only as we are conscious of the action of these energies that we are conscious of the existence of mind. It is only by the exertion of its own powers that the mind becomes cognizant of their existence."

Even as an inferred entity, however, the mind, or ego, was credited with the most essential of functions, that of serving as the source of personal identity and of providing continuity of experience as, for example, in giving the assurance that it was I who experienced the original of what now appears as a thing remembered. As John Stuart Mill put it, "This succession of feelings, which I call my memory of the past, is that by which I distinguish my Self. Myself is the person who had that series of feelings, and I know nothing of myself, by direct knowledge, except that I had them."

Others, less modest than Mill, attributed to the mind our feelings of self-determination and freedom of will. As an *active,* immaterial substance, minds were thus contrasted with material objects, which were envisaged as passive, capable of movement only when pushed or pulled from without. In looking back upon many an experience, wrote Joseph Haven, in his *Mental Philosophy* (1857), each of us becomes aware that it was in our power "to have thought, to have felt, to have acted differently." We are thus responsible for inclinations that lead to wrong choices and for opinions and views which influence feelings and dispositions insofar as they result from causes within our control.

Again, the mind enables us to form concepts and generalizations that outrun or go beyond the particular experiences from which they derive. For example, we utilize ideas of infinity, causation, energy, perfection, and force, the objects or alleged objects of which cannot be experienced directly and all of which go beyond or transcend the particulars from which they seem to be derived. Therefore, it was felt, we must assume the existence of a rational self that generates the concepts which serve as tools for the intellectual life.

And, finally, for many, a belief in immortality is only possible on the assumption that we possess a soul, or an immaterial self. Bishop Berkeley who, on this, agrees with Descartes, Newton, and Locke, wrote as follows, in *Principles of Human Knowledge:* "We have shown that the soul is indivisible, incorporeal, unextended, and is consequently incorruptible. Nothing can be plainer than that the motions, changes, decays, and dissolutions which we hourly see befall natural bodies (and which we mean by the *course of nature*) cannot possibly affect an active, simple, uncompounded substance; such a being therefore is indissoluble by the force of nature, that is to say—the soul of man is *naturally* immortal."

FACULTIES OF THE MIND AND THE
DOCTRINE OF FORMAL DISCIPLINE

Reference was made in Chapter 3 to the manner in which educators in the nineteenth century expanded upon Locke's conception of the mind and its powers. One group, closer, perhaps, to Locke, conceived of the mind as "one and indivisible" in its various operations—sensation, perception, memory, imagination, reason, and the like. For this group it was assumed that mental development is conditioned upon the exercise of the faculties. With use they improve; with disuse they decline in vigor. Since, however, the mind was conceived as a unit, it followed that improvement of one faculty through exercise would strengthen another (exercise of the memory, for example, would better not only memory but the reason, and vice versa), much as with the body the exercise of one member, such as the right arm, tends to strengthen other members, such as the left arm.

A second group, in contrast, conceived of the mind as a composite of separate faculties and thus concluded that improvement in one need not result in the improvement in another. As James Currie stated in his *Common School Education,* "The faculty of language is developed by speaking; of observation by observing; of imagination by imagining; and of reason by reasoning; if we exercise but one we shall educate but one; if we over-exercise one, the excess does not blow over to the benefit of another."

Both Rousseau and Pestalozzi accepted the theory of separate faculties, adding, however, the notion of their serial and chronological appearance in the life of the individual. For them, also, the order in which faculties appear served as a cue for parent and teacher in the education of the child. Since, for example, the child's first impulses and desires are of a sensuous character and relate primarily to his physical well-being, Rousseau insisted that his early training concentrate upon the physical. Thus it is with the mind. Since its first concern is with sensible objects and their relations, intellectual and moral education, involving as they do the faculty of reason, should be postponed until a later stage of development. Not until the age period of fifteen to twenty, according to Rousseau, is the nature of young people ripe for social and moral training.

A similar assumption gave character to the Pestalozzian system of object teaching—an effort to educate the child through the senses, on the assumption that they develop prior to other faculties. While this led both to the enrichment of the elementary school curriculum, with new materials in such fields as science, geography, arithmetic, and oral language, and to an emphasis upon child activity in learning, the results proved to be barren and formal.[5]

Two explanations may be given for this fact. First was the assumption that all minds are essentially alike, an assumption that encouraged teachers to impose identical methods and materials of instruction upon all of their charges. Insofar as differences of abilities were recognized at all, these were of degree only, one student being weaker, say, in mathematics than another. These differences, however, were not sufficiently evident (until individual differences received the attention of psychologists in the last decade of the nineteenth century) to affect curriculum content or method significantly. Second was the concept of formal discipline common to both the theory of the mind as a unit and that of the mind as composed of separate faculties. Formal discipline, or "transfer of training," as experimental psychologists later termed the theory, assumed that the exercise and training of a faculty, such as memory, with one type of material, let us say the memorizing of French verbs, will strengthen that faculty so that it will function the better, thereafter, in all situations calling for the use of memory.

Advocates of formal discipline were not altogether in agreement with respect to the sources of general training. For example, if one questioned that Mary should continue with her Latin because the content of the subject was foreign to her interests and future plans, he was assured that while this might be true there was, nevertheless, a discipline, a general intellectual power, that Mary must of necessity derive from Latin and Latin alone. On the other hand, if it were demonstrated that the intellectual power thus identified did not in fact transfer to Mary, then it was pointed out that there was an invaluable content within the disputed subject that all should possess. In each instance, the educational values involved were assumed to exist independently of the student, more or less as indigestion may be said to dwell within cold mince pies!

For many years, the doctrine of formal discipline was used to defend the traditional curriculum—the classics and mathematics—from the encroachments of new subjects—science, social studies, and practical subjects such as bookkeeping, accounting, industrial arts, and home eco-

[5] We return to the concept of inner development and its implications for the method and content of education in Chapter 9.

nomics. On the other hand, the doctrine also served as a temptation for the advocates of the new to defend their introduction by emphasizing their disciplinary value. For example, the advantages which students might derive from the teaching of drawing were described by one ardent advocate as follows:

> The visual and mental powers are cultivated in combination, the eye being trained to see clearly and judge accurately, the mind to think, and the hand to record the appearance of the object seen, or the conceptions formed in the mind. . . . The inventive and imaginative faculties are stimulated and strengthened in design, and the graphic memory is strengthened by practice in memory drawing. The aesthetic judgment is brought into use, the power of discerning beauty, congruity, proportion, symmetry, is made stronger; and the love of the beautiful, inherent more or less in mankind, is greatly increased.[6]

On the other hand, one might question the value of introducing vocational subjects into the curriculum when "The study of Latin language itself does eminently discipline the faculties and secure to a greater degree than that of other subjects we have discussed, the formation and growth of those mental qualities which are the best preparation for the business of life—whether that business is to consist in making fresh mental acquisitions or in directing the powers thus strengthened and matured, to professional or other pursuits." [7]

Probably the most authoritative statement in support of the doctrine of formal discipline was contained in the famous *Report of the Committee of Ten on Secondary School Studies* in 1894. This statement grew out of the attempt of the Committee to select from the multitude of subjects then included in the curricula of secondary schools those most appropriate for study by young people "who are going to college, for those going to a scientific school, and for those who, presumably, are going to neither," and to determine how these subjects might best be taught.

In answer to the first question, the Committee took the position that there is no essential difference in the content of subjects appropriate for those who intend to continue their education upon graduation and those

---

[6] From J. H. Morris, *Teaching and Organization*, as quoted in Edward L. Thorndike, *Educational Psychology, Briefer Course* (New York: Teachers College, Columbia University, 1917), p. 271.

[7] From Joseph Payne, *Lectures on Education*, as quoted in *Ibid.*, p. 270.

who do not so plan. The principle enunciated was that an education designed for the noncollege-bound is also best for the college-bound, although a careful reading of the recommendations of the various subcommittees suggests that with minor exceptions (such as the election of bookkeeping and commercial arithmetic and the substitution of "subjects thought to have practical importance in trade or the useful arts for some of the science in the third and fourth years of the English program") what influenced the committee was exactly the reverse. Consequently, it was not difficult for the Committee to draw a line of preference around the areas of English, Ancient and Modern Languages, Mathematics, Science, and History (including Civil Government and Political Economy).

In defense of its policy of limiting the curriculum to a few "well-selected subjects," the Committee stated: "Every youth who entered college would have spent four years in studying a few subjects thoroughly; and, on the theory that all the subjects are to be considered equivalent in educational rank for the purpose of admission to college, it would make no difference which subjects he had chosen from the programme—he would have had four years of strong, effective mental training."

The assumption of the Committee that the educational values of one subject can be equated with those of another and, by implication, that the approved subjects alone provide the "four years of strong and effective mental training" adequate for admission to college was challenged by one member, James H. Baker, President of the University of Colorado. In a minority report, Baker pointed out that the recommendations of the majority assumed as valid the doctrine that the mind is possessed of general powers—memory, imagination, reason, and the like—which, when trained by appropriate material, will function better thereafter in all situations calling for their exercise. To Baker and his minority report considerable credit is due for bringing the doctrine of formal discipline clearly to the fore. Out of the discussion thus stimulated in educational and psychological circles came investigation and experiment with respect to its validity. This brings us back to William James.

THE CONCEPT OF MIND AND ITS FACULTIES ENCOUNTERS EVIL DAYS

According to William James, one of the first to bridge the gap between an immaterial mind and a material body was Herbert Spencer. "On the whole," James wrote in 1897, "few recent formulas have done more service in psychology than the Spencerian one that the essence of mental life and bodily life are one, namely, the adjustment of inner to outer relations." [8]

In contrast with the traditional notion in psychology that mental states merely reflect the external world, James, following Spencer, stressed the *teleological* function of mental life. Our ability to form habits, to remember, to "abstract general properties from things" and to form concepts, he pointed out, "are exactly the faculties needed for steering us in the world of mixed variety and uniformity." So it is, too, with instincts, emotions and feelings. Phenomena of importance to us interest us. "Dangerous things fill us with involuntary fear; poisonous things with distaste; indispensable things with appetite. Mind and world in short have evolved together and in consequence are something of a mutual fit." [9]

Although James accepted Spencer's concept of adjustment as an original and primary function of mental activity, in contrast with Spencer, he conceived of adjustment as a *two-way process,* one in which the organism also transforms the environment in the process of "adjusting" to it. This was a difference of no small significance for education, as we shall see later!

Not only did James insist that mental states cannot properly be studied apart from the physical environment of which they take cognizance; he emphasized as well the intimate interrelationship of mental and physical activity. "All mental states, even mere thoughts and feelings," he asserted, "are motor in their consequences." He might have added, using the term "motor" figuratively, that they are motor in their nature, in order to dramatize his concept of mental life as "a stream of consciousness"—a concept he developed to replace both that of the mind and its faculties and the mind as a composite of psychic states.

For the mind as an entity (inferred, as we have seen, in order to account for the sense of personal activity, continuity of experience, an inward sense of freedom, and the like), James substituted the "passing thought." It is a patent fact of consciousness, he contended, that the "Thought" which I now have "knows its own predecessor" and requires no inference of a "Soul" or a "Transcendental Ego" in the background.

> Each pulse of cognitive consciousness, each Thought, dies away and is replaced by another. The other, among the things it knows,

[8] William James, *Psychology, Briefer Course* (New York: Henry Holt & Co., 1897), p. 4.
[9] *Ibid.,* pp. 4-5.

knows its own predecessor, and finding it "warm" ... greets it, saying: "Thou art *mine*, and part of the same self with me." Each later
Thought, knowing and including thus the Thoughts which went
before, is the final receptacle—and appropriating them is the final
owner—of all that they contain and own. Each Thought is thus born
an owner, and dies owned, transmitting whatever it realized as its
Self to its own later proprietor.[10]

Further analysis, supplemented by laboratory experiment, also enabled
James to refute the notion of separate faculties or general powers of the
mind, such as memory, imagination, and reason. Take memory, for
example. In order to determine whether a certain amount of daily training in the learning of poetry by heart would shorten the period required
to learn an entirely different kind of poetry, James undertook first to
memorize 158 lines of Victor Hugo's "Satyr." This required 131⅚ minutes.
He then devoted 20 minutes a day to the learning of the entire first book
of "Paradise Lost." This took 38 days. With this training, he went back to
Victor Hugo's poem and found it required 151½ minutes to memorize
158 additional lines.

To check the validity of his results, James persuaded a number of other
persons to repeat the test. From these results and other data, he concluded
that improvement in memory, when it occurs, results from improvement in
one's habitual methods of recording facts, not in a physiological reten-
tiveness, or a "faculty" of memory.

It remained for a former student of William James, Edward L. Thorndike, to strike the most decisive blow against the concept of formal discipline. In a series of investigations conducted by Thorndike and R. S.
Woodworth in 1901 and reported in detail in the *Psychological Review* of
that year, the experimenters concluded that improvement in any single
mental function as a result of training need not improve the ability in
functions commonly called by the same name.

Indeed, on occasion, the reverse is true. For example, Thorndike and
Woodworth had persons acting as subjects undergo training in operations
such as judging the areas of paper cards, judging of weights, striking out
certain letters from words on a printed page. Following a period of training, the subjects were given related tasks in order to determine the fruits
of their training. Once improved facility in striking out the letters *e* and *s*

[10] James, *The Principles of Psychology*, Vol. I, *op. cit.*, p. 339.

was acquired, the subject was asked to strike out other letters, such as *a* and *n*. Were faculty psychology valid, improvement acquired from practice in striking out the letters *e* and *s* should have carried over un-diminished to the striking out of *a* and *n*. Such, however, was not the case.

Multitudes of other experiments by other experimenters led to similar results—all of which seemed to confirm Thorndike's conclusion that "spread of practice occurs only where identical elements are concerned in the influencing and influenced function," identical elements, that is, of *method* and of *content*. (It remained for other students to question the meaning of the term "identical elements." What explains the fact, for example, that what is recognized as *identical* by one person is not so recognized by another?)

It also became clear, as Boyd H. Bode pointed out some years later, that faculty psychology had mistaken names for things.

> For example, a person may be quick to detect misspelled words; and if we are lazy or blinded by preconceptions we are tempted to explain this trait by saying that such a person has a faculty of "quick-ness." But such quickness, it was found, did not guarantee quickness in other respects, such as arithmetical processes. It does not follow that because we apply the word "quickness" to both operations, they are therefore the same thing and due to a faculty of quickness. We might as well say that the rattle of a fender in an automobile is identical with every other rattle in the car, and that an old car makes so much noise because by virtue of exercise it has acquired a highly developed faculty of rattling.[11]

By the end of the century, advocates of a mind possessed of faculties, each of which is subject to general improvement by training of a specific character, were clearly fighting a losing battle. The concept "mind" came to mean little more than a collective noun, a term used to designate a plurality of mental states, much as we use the term "woods" in speaking of a collection of trees. As against a faculty of memory, or imagination, or reason that men were once thought to employ, it was now concluded that they engage only in specific acts of memory, imagination, or reason. From this conclusion one group of educators developed a novel and ambitious program for education to replace the general training advocated earlier

[11] Boyd H. Bode, *Conflicting Psychologies of Learning* (Boston: D. C. Heath & Co., 1929), p. 47.

by the formalists. They proposed (1) to identify and classify the specific items of information relevant to the various subject matter areas, together with the most important specific habits, skills, and techniques employed in adult life; and (2) to impart these specific elements to young people by means of the most efficient methods psychology might devise! [12] Before we deal with these Herculean efforts at curriculum construction and the "psychology of adjustment" which prompted them, let us return to the development of a physiological psychology.

MENTAL STATES ARE SUBORDINATED TO THE BODY

One of the first in this country to draw attention to the influence of bodily conditions upon the "mind" was Dr. Benjamin Rush of Philadelphia. At a time when it was commonly assumed that mind and matter are two quite different substances, and the moral sense a source of insight into moral principles and specific moral decisions, Rush published a document on the *Influence of Physical Causes upon the Moral Faculty* (1786). In this he drew attention to the failure of children with brain defects to exercise memory, imagination, and judgment. He noted that a similar failure also occurred with moral behavior. A nervous fever, he pointed out, may not only cause loss of memory but influence the telling of truth. From numerous illustrations of the effect of physical injuries and illness upon moral decisions, Rush concluded that the cure of misbehavior is not found in punishment but in medicine and in informed treatment. Thus he pioneered in the diagnosis and treatment of mental illness, crime, and delinquency.

For example, Rush wrote as follows of the treatment of the criminally insane:

> It would be as absurd to inflict the punishment of death upon a fellow creature for taking away a life under a deranged state of the will, as for a surgeon to cut off an arm or a leg because in its convulsive motions it injured a toilet or overset a tea table. Now, while these morbid operations of the will may include in their consequences even theft and murder, yet they are to be considered, not as vices, but as symptoms of a disease. Therefore, for persons thus afflicted legislators should abolish the punishment of death, crop-

[12] See, for example, Franklin Bobbitt, *How to Make a Curriculum* (Boston: Houghton Mifflin Co., 1924), Chapter II.

ping, branding, and public whipping, and substitute for them confinement, labour, simple diet, cleanliness, and affectionate treatment. As is shown by the moral effects thus produced in the jail of Philadelphia, the reformation of criminals and the prevention of crimes can be better effected by living than by dead examples.[13]

As we observed in Chapter 5, the philosophy of materialism, which seemed for a time on the point of healthy development in the United States, was submerged by the rising tide of common-sense realism; and, with this, interest was lost in the scientific study of the interrelationships of mind and body. Not until the latter part of the nineteenth century did physiological psychology once more assume a dominant role in psychology, philosophy, and education. Major credit for this development should go to William James and the able students whom he either trained directly or influenced through his writings.

With the discrediting of a substantive mind and its faculties, many psychologists attempted to explain the behavior of mental states by means of the "laws of association." Thus the idea of thunder suggests the idea of rain by virtue of repeated connections in the past. To Franklin, lightning suggested electricity, because of the law of similarity and the like. Further analysis, however, revealed severe limitations in this type of explanation. Why, for example, do these "laws" operate on one occasion and not on another? Why is it that on one day Experience A suggests B, but on another, not B, but C? Why, James asked, do we strain for a solution of a problem all in vain for years and, one day, "walking in the street with our attention miles away from that quest, does the answer saunter into our minds as carelessly as if it had never been called for—suggested, possibly, by the flowers on the bonnet of the lady in front of us, or, possibly by nothing that we can discover?" [14] And why, continued James, do not the "laws of association of ideas explain the effects of fever, exhaustion, hypnotism, old age and the like?" Indeed, he concludes, "the pure associationist's account of our mental life is almost as bewildering as that of the pure spiritualist. This multitude of ideas, existing absolutely, yet clinging together, and weaving an endless carpet of themselves, like

[13] Quoted in Woodbridge Riley, *American Thought from Puritanism to Pragmatism and Beyond* (Gloucester, Mass.: Peter Smith, 1959), p. 112. See pp. 104-117 for an excellent summary of Rush's views on mental healing.
[14] James, *Psychology, Briefer Course, op. cit.,* p. 254.

dominoes in ceaseless change, or the bits of glass in a kaleidoscope—whence do they get their fantastic laws of clinging, and why do they cling in just the shape they do?" [15]

The associationists agreed with John Locke in ascribing the origins of ideas to the external environment. Sensations and perceptions were said to mirror external objects more or less accurately. But this was to admit dependence upon the body! Injure the optic nerve, and the mental representation of the object is either a distorted reproduction or it disappears, as far as that sense is concerned. This is to say that the nature and quality, even the existence, of sensations and their modifications through experience are dependent upon the nervous system and the brain.

The situation is similar with memory and past experience. The machinery of recall is "the same as the machinery of association, and the machinery of association . . . is nothing but the elementary law of habit in the nerve-centres." [16] Injure these, and no recall is possible.

Of particular significance in demonstrating the dependence of mental states upon physiological processes is James's discussion of emotions and instincts. Emotions, according to James, are tendencies to feel, and instincts are tendencies to act. In the first, the reaction called emotional terminates in the subject's own body; in the second, reaction tends to go farther and "to enter into practical relations with the exciting objects." Each may be set off by mere memory or an image, as well as by a concrete object or event. But, for our purposes, the important fact is that the consciousness which defines emotion or instinct derives from the bodily changes that follow upon the initiating perception.

As James put it, in speaking of an emotion, "Common-sense says, we lose our fortune, are sorry and weep; we meet a bear, are frightened and run; we are insulted by a rival, are angry and strike." The truth is, "the bodily manifestations must first be interposed between," and, therefore, "we feel sorry because we cry, angry because we strike, afraid because we tremble, and not that we cry, strike, or tremble because we are sorry, angry, or fearful, as the case may be. Without the bodily states following on the perception, the latter would be purely cognitive in form, pale, colorless, destitute of emotional warmth." [17]

For James, the reactions characterizing different emotions and instincts

[15] James, *The Principles of Psychology*, Vol. I, *op. cit.*, p. 3.
[16] James, *Psychology, Briefer Course*, *op. cit.*, p. 296.
[17] *Ibid.*, p. 376.

are explained in terms of evolution and their original survival value. This is another way of saying that inherited habits as well as acquired habits are facts of biology, and the consciousness accompanying them is married irrevocably to the body!

From the above it would seem to follow that mental phenomena are far from independent entities. Rather does their appearance and disappearance, even their existence, turn upon bodily activity. As James concluded, it is "safe to lay down the general law that no *mental* modification ever occurs which is not accompanied or followed by a bodily change." [18] Or, as psychologists quite generally came to insist, there is "no psychosis without neurosis."

One step more was required, in order to reduce mental states to a humble status. That was to challenge the assumption of their permanence. It was commonly assumed, for example, that sensations or perceptions, images, and ideas persist either in a "mind" or, in the associationists' theory, in association with others more or less permanently. The memory of a childhood event was thought of as the "same memory" on its various reappearances. It was assumed that there is a subconscious receptacle in which mental states dwell, ready to reappear in consciousness as occasion warrants. Similarly, repeated excitations of a sense organ by the same object were said to result in the "same" sensation.

The assumption does not hold, however, when we consider carefully the conditions under which sensations are received and past experiences and ideas recalled and used. Take the sensation of an object which we assume to be the "same" today as yesterday. It requires but little examination to reveal that "sameness" applies to the object experienced, remembered, or imagined, not to the mental phenomenon. "For an identical sensation to recur, it would have to occur the second time in an unmodified brain." [19]

What is true of sensations and perceptions would seem to apply equally to other mental phenomena such as emotions and ideas and concepts. The sameness and the permanence men have attributed to the "contents of the mind" are more accurately ascribed to the brain and the nervous system.

From this review of developments in psychology in the second half of the nineteenth century, we should not conclude that acceptance of

[18] James, *The Principles of Psychology*, Vol. I, *op. cit.*, p. 5.
[19] *Ibid.*, p. 232.

one theory followed upon the other in its application to education, that the concept of a mind and its faculties, for example, gave way to a psychology of mental states, and the latter to James's theory of a stream of consciousness. Rather are we to view these psychologies as essential elements in competing philosophies of education at a time when American education on all levels—elementary, secondary, and higher—was in process of phenomenal expansion and development. For example, far from giving up its ghost, the concept of the mind, or the Ego, under the influence of Hegelian philosophy and the dynamic personality of William T. Harris, not only gave character to the curriculum of elementary and secondary school in the period under review, but, as embodied in the reports of national curriculum committees, constituted a formative influence upon education well into the twentieth century.

Further, the concept of formal discipline and its influence upon school and college curricula was not completely eliminated. With surprising vitality it continued to influence teaching methods and curricular content in preparatory school and liberal arts colleges during the dominance of "education for adjustment" and experienced a vigorous revival in the 1930's.

So, too, the psychology of mental states persisted. Under the influence of Herbart and his distinguished American disciples, a mental states psychology, at the turn of the century, assumed prominence in the professional training of teachers and, thus, in teaching method and the organization of the curriculum in schools throughout the country.

Finally, the biological emphasis so prominent in James was continued in G. Stanley Hall and the culture epochs theory. In this theory the intimate interrelationship between physical and mental development was emphasized. On the assumption that "ontogenesis recapitulates phylogenesis," Hall and his associates evolved an elaborate plan for the education of the individual in which subject matters and method were to take their cue from stages of development in the individual—physical, intellectual, emotional, and social—which supposedly recapitulate corresponding stages of cultural development in the race.

A second development out of James continued to emphasize the dominance of the physical over the mental to the point at which, as in Thorndike, the latter was ignored for all practical purposes and, as in John Watson and other behaviorists in the twentieth century, mental phenomena were denied positive existence altogether.[20] Each of these developments, together with their implications for education, merits special consideration.

[20] It should be added that William James eventually rejected the concept of consciousness as something existentially distinct from bodily activity. In an article written for the *Journal of Philosophy, Psychology and Scientific Methods,* Vol. I, No. 18, September, 1904, and reprinted as Chapter I, "Does Consciousness Exist?" in his *Essays in Radical Empiricism,* James stated that for twenty years he had mistrusted "consciousness" as an entity. In denying consciousness as an entity, however, he insisted "most emphatically that it does stand for a function." That is to say, the subjectivity and the objectivity of an experience "are functional attributes solely, realized only when the experience is 'taken,' i.e., talked-of, twice, considered along with its two differing contexts respectively, by a new retrospective experience, of which the whole past complication now forms the fresh content." See William James, *Essays in Radical Empiricism* (New York: Longmans, Green & Co., 1912), Chapters I, II.

SUGGESTED READING

Bode, Boyd H., *How We Learn* (Boston: D. C. Heath & Co., 1940), Chapters I-VIII.

Butts, R. Freeman, and Cremin, Lawrence A., *A History of Education in American Culture* (New York: Holt, Rinehart & Winston, 1953), Chapter 10.

James, William, *The Principles of Psychology,* Vol. I (New York: Henry Holt & Co., 1890), Chapters VI, IX, X.

————, *Talks to Teachers on Psychology: And to Students on Some of Life's Ideals* (New York: Henry Holt & Co., 1912), Chapters II, III, XV.

Thorndike, Edward L., *Educational Psychology, Briefer Course* (New York: Teachers College, Columbia University, 1917), Chapter XVII.

CHAPTER 8
NINETEENTH-CENTURY
IDEALISM AND EDUCATION

IN March, 1857, Bronson Alcott spent several weeks at Yale College lecturing and conducting "Conversations" on Plato and Plotinus with small groups of undergraduates. This was not an altogether happy or successful experience for him, since Yale was still a stronghold of New England orthodoxy. Indeed, the most obvious result of his efforts was to hear himself preached against in the college chapel as a representative of "the new philosophical infidelity." Not until some years later was he to learn that his talks at Yale had served as a turning point in the intellectual career of a young man by the name of William T. Harris, who was to become one of his most able interpreters and defenders.

Harris (1835-1909) was at the time a Yale junior and in the throes of intellectual revolt against the orthodox Congregationalism in which he had been indoctrinated. Converted to Transcendentalism by Alcott, he quickly turned his back upon the "phrenological theories, mesmerisms, spiritualism, the water-cure, vegetarianism, socialism, and all manner of reforms" with which he had been toying, resigned from Yale in disgust, and decided to seek his fortune in the West. Shortly thereafter he became a teacher of shorthand in St. Louis, found employment in the public schools as a high school teacher, and, eventually, served as Superintendent of the St. Louis Public Schools from 1868 to 1880.[1] Under his direction,

---

[1] Nicholas Murray Butler once said of Harris, "The history of American education and of our American contribution to philosophical thought cannot be understood or estimated without knowledge of the life work of William Torrey Harris."

the schools of St. Louis attracted educational visitors from home and abroad by virtue of their excellence.

In 1889 Harris was appointed to the post of the first United States Commissioner of Education, occupying this position until 1906. In his work as Commissioner, together with his phenomenal activity as educational writer and speaker, he did much to give form and character to public school systems in the United States. At the same time, as a member of the St. Louis group of Hegelians, as founder and editor of the *Journal of Speculative Philosophy* (1867-1893), and as one of the organizers and participants of the Concord School of Philosophy (1879-1887), he contributed to the formulation of philosophical idealism in the United States and its applications to education. It was Harris who persuaded Bronson Alcott to meet with the St. Louis Philosophical Society, thus establishing a mutually stimulating relationship between New England Transcendentalism and St. Louis Hegelianisn.[2]

Several members of the St. Louis group had been impressed with Transcendentalism prior to their introduction to the philosophy of Hegel. Henry Brockmeyer, who might be called the originating genius of the group, had been attracted to Emersonian idealism some years before while on a brief sojourn at Brown University. Carrying "the transcendental notions of freedom, individualism, originality, and worship of nature to their extreme conclusions," [3] Brockmeyer retreated for a time to the backwoods of Missouri, where he lived the life of a hermit. Following his discovery of Hegel and the loss of his small fortune through the failure of an investment house, Brockmeyer returned to civilization and settled in St. Louis, where he served as an ardent interpreter of Hegelian thought and its applications to American culture. It was he who introduced Harris and other members of the philosophical society to Hegel's philosophy, and it was he who dominated the thinking of the group in his capacity as translator and interpreter of Hegel's logic.

Active also in the group that gathered around Brockmeyer and Harris, although never a convinced Hegelian, was Thomas Davidson, later characterized by William James in a memorial essay, "A Knight-Errant of the Intellectual Life." Others included George Holmes Howison, for many

---

[2] For an interesting and informative discussion of these two schools of idealism and the personalities that gave character to them, see Henry A. Pochmann, *New England Transcendentalism and St. Louis Hegelianism* (Philadelphia: Carl Schurz Memorial Foundation, 1948).

[3] *Ibid.*, p. 9.

years an eloquent exponent of "pluralistic personal idealism" at the University of California and Denton J. Snider, whose philosophical criticisms of literature were widely read in later years.

NEW ENGLAND TRANSCENDENTALISM AND ST. LOUIS HEGELIANISM COMPARED

Bronson Alcott proved to be a happy choice as a mediating influence between New England Transcendentalism and St. Louis Hegelianism. Although no match for Brockmeyer and his associates in abstract thought and argumentative ability, he was successful, to no small degree, in keeping in good repair a bridge of communication between the followers of Plato and Plotinus, with their proneness for poetic and intuitional methods of interpreting reality, and the disciples of Hegel who were wedded to more prosaic but rigorous dialectical reasoning. For example, on one occasion when argument waxed warm between representatives of the two groups at the Concord School of Philosophy, Alcott closed the meeting with this observation:

> The beauty of this school is that we have those who speak from . . .
> different aspects, so that we gather an idea of the different modes
> in which thought works. . . . Mr. Emerson puts his philosophy into
> warm tropes, and paints pictures with his words. But Hegel and that
> class of thinkers strip off the image and give you the pure, absolute
> truth as it lies in their minds. Mr. Emerson could not have had
> his influence in the world had he endeavored to do his work as
> Hegel did. . . . Imagination and reason are the opposite poles of one
> sphere. The poet and the philosopher work differently, but they do
> the same work.

It was easier for Alcott (especially when under the influence of his friend Harris) to accept the methods of both Plato and Hegel than it was for others more disposed to engage in rigorous thinking. If, on the other hand, we take Emerson as the representative of Transcendentalism, the differences between the two schools of idealism and their implications for education are substantial.

Contrast, for example, the conception of ultimate reality in Emerson's Over-Soul with that in Harris' Absolute Reason. For Emerson ". . . that Unity, that Over-Soul, within which every man's particular being is contained and made one with all other; that common heart, of which all sincere conversation is the worship, to which all right action is submission; that overpowering reality which confutes our tricks and talents and constrains every one to pass for what he is, and to speak for his character, and not from his tongue, and which evermore tends to pass into our thought and hand, and become wisdom, and virtue, and power, and beauty," is nevertheless an impersonal Being. "When it breathes" through the individual's "intellect, it is genius; when it breathes through his will, it is virtue; when it flows through his affection, it is love." That is, from the Over-Soul there flows into the receptive individual all that is good, and true, and beautiful and original; but the source itself is not to be confused with the finite or endowed with its characteristics. As Emerson wrote following an evening's conversation with Alcott in 1863: "Alcott defended his thesis of personality last night, but it is not quite a satisfactory use of words.... I see profound need of distinguishing the First Cause as superpersonal. It deluges us with power; we are filled with it; but there are skies of immensity between it and us."

For Harris and his fellow Hegelians, on the other hand, an essential characteristic of the Absolute, as Universal Reason, was that of a self-active personality which expresses itself at one and the same time as universal and particular. From Hegel, Harris derived the concept of the Universal as self-active Reason in which thought and will, subject and object are one. This resembles the pantheistic conception of Emerson in which the Over-Soul "breathes" through the particular but is not identical with it. Moreover, since self-activity characterizes the Absolute in both its universal and individual aspects, and thought and will are one, Harris felt warranted in believing not only in God as a person but in the freedom and immortality of the individual soul as well. For example, in a letter to Julia Ward Howe in 1901, Harris wrote,

> In the year 1858 I came to what seemed to me to be a real philosophical insight and all of my subsequent life has served to make me more certain of the validity of that insight. It amounted to seeing that self-activity or self-determining is presupposed by all dependent being, and even by time and space themselves as well as by all their contents. This insight recognized the activity of the first principle of the universe, and I could seem to see quite clearly that its activity must take the form of intellect and will, or else lose its independence and therefore come into the condition of presupposing another principle beyond it. One could not get rid of the first prin-

ciple in any event because the result of disproving a principle as original and primordial would be to place or presuppose another first principle above it.

The essential identity of the universal and particular as conceived by Harris suggests a second significant difference between the St. Louis Hegelians and the New England Transcendentalists with respect to the nature of the individual, his relation to society, and the conditions of his integrity and self-realization.

In an address on *Man the Reformer*, delivered in January, 1841, Emerson described some of "the practical impediments that stand in the way of virtuous young men ... on entering life." These "impediments" constitute a scathing indictment of the conditions of success in commerce and industry and the professions.

> The ways of trade are grown selfish to the borders of theft and supple to the borders (if not beyond the borders) of fraud. The employments of commerce are not intrinsically unfit for a man, or less genial to his faculties, but these are now in their general course so vitiated by derelictions and abuses at which all connive, that it requires more vigor and resources than can be expected of every young man, to right himself in them; he is lost in them; he cannot move hand or foot in them. Has he genius and virtue? the less does he find them fit for him to grow in, and if he would thrive in them, he must sacrifice all the brilliant dreams of his boyhood and youth as dreams; he must forget the prayers of his childhood; and must take on the harness of routine and obsequiousness.

Moreover, the professions do not afford a means of escape, for "the trail of the serpent reaches into all the lucrative professions and practices of man. Each has its own wings. Each finds a tender and very intelligent conscience a disqualification for success."

How, then, may one save his own soul? Emerson offered several suggestions, none of which implied conformity or adjustment to conditions as they are. Indeed, "Whoso would be a man must be a non-conformist." It is better to return "to primary relations" with nature; to farming, or to other forms of manual labor, if necessary; at least to simple conditions of living in order "to ransom" oneself "from the duties of the economy by a certain rigor and privation" in one's habits.

But above all, must we be receptive to new ideas; ideas that should enable us eventually "to revise the whole of our social structure, the state, the school, religion, marriage, trade, science, and explore their foundations in our nature. . . ;" ideas that come to one best in solitude, for there are "voices which we hear in solitude" that "grow faint and inaudible as we enter into the world." In solitude, moreover, and in nature rather than in society can we best serve as "receivers of truth" from the "immense intelligence" in whose lap we lie, and "allow a passage to its beams." (*Essay on Self-Reliance*)

According to Harris, in contrast with Emerson, one realizes his true nature through identification with society and its institutions. In the course of his development from childhood into adulthood, the individual evolves from a state roughly analogous to savagery into that of a civilized human being only insofar as he learns to merge his interests with the interests of others. "Man as a child, or a savage," Harris wrote, "is an incarnate contradiction; his real being is the opposite of his ideal being . . . His true human nature is Reason; his actual condition is irrational for it is constrained from without, chained by brute necessity, and lashed by the scourges of appetite and passion." [4]

Moreover, the child cannot "ascend above savagery" so long as he remains "isolated from the community." The one possibility "of amelioration for the natural man lies in the principle of combination. The individual must feel or perceive a common interest with other individuals. He must adopt for his own ideal the ideal of others . . . He learns to recognize his own essential aims and purposes in those of others, and more and more to make a common ideal the object of his strivings and endeavors." [5]

Identification with others, then, is a means for ascendancy "out of nature" into "human nature." In contrast with Emerson's emphasis upon originality to the point of nonconformity, Harris stressed a unique identification of self-activity of the one with the spiritual aspects of the whole as a condition of freedom. "It is through combination of man with man that the individual is able to achieve a rational existence. By combination each one is able to participate in the life of every other, forming a vast organism of institutions called human society; wherein each helps all and all help each." [6] To the significance of institutions in Harris' theory of education, we shall return in a moment.

[4] William T. Harris, *Psychologic Foundations of Education* (New York: D. Appleton & Co., 1898), p. 256.
[5] *Ibid.*, p. 257.
[6] *Ibid.*, p. 257.

As suggested earlier, the methods employed by these two schools in arriving at truth also differ. For the Transcendentalist, insight and knowledge, the acquisition of truth, result from a receptive attitude toward messages from without. Thus, for Emerson, analogy plays an important role in grasping truth. The "whole of nature," he wrote in his *Essay on Nature,* "is a metaphor of the human mind. The laws of moral nature answer to those of matter as face to face in a glass. 'The visible world and the relation of its parts, is the dial-plate of the invisible.' The axioms of physics translate the laws of physics. . . . Every property of matter is a school for the understanding,—its solidity, or resistance, its inertia, its extension, its figure, its divisibility. The understanding adds, divides, combines, measures, and finds nutriment and room for its activity in this worthy scene. Meantime, Reason transfers all these lessons into its own world of thought, by perceiving the analogy that marries Matter and Thought."

For Harris, too, mind and matter, when properly viewed, are but two aspects of one and the same thought, since he, in common with Hegel, assumed that thought and being, subject and object, are one. But the process of arriving at truth for the Hegelian involved more than intuition, or poetic vision, or mere reasoning by analogy. The self-activity of the Absolute manifests itself in nature as a dialectical process, a divine logic, the laws of which the finite mind must understand and observe if it would arrive at valid conclusions—a fact, as we shall see, that gives special import to the place of language, grammar and logic in education.

HARRIS AND THE PSYCHOLOGY OF EDUCATION

The importance of self-activity as the one essential characteristic of the universal and finite minds, Harris developed in his *Psychologic Foundations of Education.* In this work, he elaborated upon what he terms a "rational psychology" as against both faculty psychology and the newer physiological psychology with its tendency to subordinate the mind to the operations of the body.

Faculty psychology, with its emphasis upon cultivating such faculties as sense-perception, imagination, conception, and reasoning, Harris believed to be based upon a false analogy between the mind and body. "The defect of this mode of view," he wrote, "is that it leaves out of sight the genesis of the higher faculties from the lower ones. Muscles are not consecutive, the one growing out of another and taking its place, but they are co-ordinate and side by side in space, whereas in mind the higher faculties take the place of the lower faculties and in some sort absorb them." [7] Again, faculty psychology, with its inventory of the powers of the mind, fails to convey "insight into the genesis of the higher faculties of the mind."

Physiological psychology, according to Harris, is also limited in that it attempts to explain mind as a function of the body and "teaches that the soul has no subsistence apart from body: all individuality is corporeal." It thus rejects introspection, "our consciousness of the activity of the mind itself." This is serious, for the reason that it conveys a false understanding of the relationship between mind and body. That there is interaction between the two, all will admit, stated Harris. Modifications of the body are reflected in manifestations of feeling, knowing, and willing; and, on the other hand, the operations of feeling, knowing, and willing affect various bodily functions. The most that physiological psychology can do, however, is to investigate the relations of these two orders: to compare changes in the body with "the facts of mental action in the form of feelings, thoughts, and volitions," facts *known only by introspection*. "Introspection is therefore utterly indispensable to physiological psychology." [8]

But there is a second limitation to physiological psychology. It tends to put the cart before the horse, since it is mind and purpose—self-activity—in both a cosmic and an individual sense, that direct matter rather than matter, or the body, serving as the occasion for manifestations of mind.

This, continued Harris, is evident in evolution. "The evolutionary theory recognizes introspection as existing in the objective world—it sees in Nature a tendency to develop such beings as possess internality and energize to realize their ideals." [9] Indeed, "Nature is, in every particle of it, governed by ideals. Matter is heavy, and falls, for example, only because it obeys an ideal of which it is entirely unconscious, and yet which is manifested in it in the form of weight. Gravity is the manifestation of the unity of one body with another. The unity is potential, but its manifestation is real force, real attraction." [10]

Harris' concepts of self-activity and the function of "ideals" in evolution caused him to view evolution in a light different from the more mechanical conceptions of Herbert Spencer and Charles Darwin. Spencer, for example, conceived consciousness and will as products of nature or links in

[7] *Ibid.*, p. vi.
[8] *Ibid.*, Introduction, pp. 1-10.
[9] *Ibid.*, p. 21. Note the special meaning given to the term "ideals."
[10] *Ibid.*, p. 22.

a chain of causality rather than as forms of self-activity. Similarly, as against Darwin's theory of survival in the struggle for existence by means of natural selection, Harris conceived of evolution as a progressive development resulting from the "efforts" of plants and animals to adapt to their environments, efforts which lead those with greater will power or knowledge to survive.[11]

Plants exemplify self-activity on a somewhat higher level than inanimate matter, but are still "unconscious." Plants grow, put on new buds, leaves, branches, blossoms, fruit according to a pattern, or a directive energy of such a character that each individual realizes more or less perfectly the ideal of the species. That is, from the same elements such as soil and sunshine, plants of diverse species build up their "own individuality." They not only act, but they act for themselves. They are "self-related."

As we move up the scale of evolution from plants to animals, and from lower animals to man, expressions of self-activity increase in complexity. Plants, in reacting to their environment, as in nutrition, draw elements from the soil and transform these into elements of their own structure. Animals, on the other hand, add consciousness—feelings, emotions, desires, and the like. Thus their "individuality recoils from the attack made on the organism and reproduces its symbolic equivalent." This reaction is on the level of sense-perception.

In man, the self-activity leading to knowledge manifests itself on four levels of thinking, each of which conforms to Hegel's theory of dialectic. Sense-perception, the first stage of thinking, yields the world of independent objects as experienced by common sense through the application of past experience (a process, according to Harris, that involves syllogistic reasoning).[12] "Common sense assumes that experience has before it a world of complete individual things which either are or are not, and do not exist in a state of becoming or change, nor depend essentially upon one another." [13]

The second stage of thinking, however, reveals the error of common sense. By means of the critical process of attention, analysis, and synthesis, self-activity comes to view objects not as independent things but as related and independent upon each other, that is, as aspects or forms of energy.

[11] See William T. Harris, "Is Education Possible Without Freedom of Will?" *Education*, January, 1896; and "Herbert Spencer and His Influence on Education," in *Proceedings of the National Education Association*, 1904, pp. 47-48.
[12] Harris, *Psychologic Foundations of Education, op. cit.*, pp. 77 ff.
[13] *Ibid.*, p. 220.

"This stage of thinking," wrote Harris, "does not believe in *atoms* or *things;* it believes in *forces* and *processes*—called 'abstract ideas' because they are negative, and cannot be seen by the senses." [14] Abstract ideas, so conceived, give "more reality than the 'things' of sense-perception; the force is more real than the thing, because it outlasts a thing—it causes it to originate, to change, and disappear." [15] But this is not the last word.

On a third level of thinking, what were perceived as "forces," merge into one *"concrete idea,"* or "persistent force." "Persistent force, as taught by the scientific men of our day, is the sole ultimate principle, and as such it gives rise to all existence by its self-activity, for there is nothing for it to act upon. It causes all origins, all changes, and all evanescence. It gives rise to the particular forces—heat, light, electricity, magnetism, etc.—which in their turn cause the evanescent forms which sense-perception sees as 'things.' " [16]

But the concept of one persistent force as ultimate reality (the basis of pantheism) is not the final, satisfactory explanation. One step more leads us to the absolute idea, which is perceived by the reason as "self-determined." Analysis of the principle of "persistent force" establishes the *necessity* of the principle of personal being and thus the validity of the three essential outcomes of thinking—an absolute person, freedom, and immortality. "Since the 'persistent force' is the sole and ultimate reality, it originates all other reality only by self-activity, and thus is self-determined." But "self-determination implies self-consciousness and personality as the true form of its existence." [17]

"These four forms of thinking," concluded Harris, "correspond to four views of the world: (1) as a congeries of independent things; (2) as a play of forces; (3) as the evanescent appearance of a negative essential power; (4) as the creation of a Personal Creator, who makes it the theatre of the development of conscious beings in his image. Each step upward arrives at a more adequate idea of the true reality. Force is more real than thing; persistent force than particular forces; Absolute Person is more real than the force or forces which he creates." [18]

This final stage or "form" is, for Harris, "the only form which is consistent with a true theory of education," since it enables the individual

14 *Ibid.,* p. 211.
15 *Ibid.,* p. 211.
16 *Ibid.,* p. 212.
17 *Ibid.,* p. 227.
18 *Ibid.,* p. 227.

"to ascend by education into participation—*conscious* participation—in the life of the species. Institutions—family, society, state, church—all are instrumentalities by which the humble individual may avail himself of the help of the race, and live over in himself its life. The highest stage of thinking is the stage of insight. It sees the world as explained by the principle of Absolute Person. It finds the world of institutions a world in harmony with such a principle." [19] Here, Harris' conclusion affords an interesting contrast with the following passage in Emerson's *Essay on Politics* (1844): "Every state is corrupt. Good men must not obey the laws too well.... That which all things tend to educe, which freedom, cultivation, intercourse, revolutions, go to form and deliver, is character; that is the end of nature, to reach into this coronation of her king. To educate the wise man, the State exists; and with the appearance of the wise man, the State expires."

HARRIS VS. HERBERT SPENCER ON EDUCATION AND ITS PURPOSES

Idealism in the form of Transcendentalism exercised but a minor influence upon the structure of American school systems in the nineteenth century. Few schoolmen, for example, attempted to translate into subject matter and classroom method the implications of Emerson's concept of culture, as embodied in his image of the "semigod" in his poem "Culture":

... to his native centre fast,
Shall into Future fuse the Past,
And the world's flowing fates in his own mould recast.

Of Harris and his influence, by way of contrast, Merle Curti could write: "While it was Barnard and Mann who laid the foundations of the American public school system, it was William T. Harris who presided over the rearing of the structure. His most important achievement, however, was to furnish American education with a philosophy which helped the rank and file to adjust their thought and feeling to new activities without losing the sense of identity with older values and conditions." [20]

Central in Harris' thought was the concept of self-activity as an essential aspect of the Divine Reason and the mind of man. Accept this view

[19] *Ibid.*, p. 227.
[20] Merle Curti, *Social Ideas of American Educators* (New York: Charles Scribner's Sons, 1935), p. 310.

of man as basic, and it follows, as Americans had come to believe, that man is master of his fate and that *creativity*, rather than *adjustment* and *adaptation* to environment, becomes a distinctively human characteristic.

It was here that Harris found himself in fundamental opposition to Herbert Spencer and the latter's view of the origin and function of consciousness. Consciousness and will, according to Spencer, are products of nature, links in a series of natural causes, instruments of adaptation in the evolutionary process. The difference is, of course, basic but not novel in the history of thought. Shall we conceive the world as the cause of the contents of mind or as a reflection and the product of the latter?

In a *Journal of Education* article entitled, "The Danger of Using Biological Analogies in Reasoning on Educational Subjects" (1902), Harris gave his answer: "We must interpret the lower from the standpoint of the higher. The lowest is the incomplete and imperfect being. The higher is the more realized being, the more perfect, and it explains to us *the existence of the lower by showing its purpose*. The analogy of the lower order of being does not suffice to explain the higher order of being. The scale must be inverted before the human can be understood."

DIFFERENCES IN THEORY LEAD TO DIFFERENCES IN CURRICULUM

Harris' concept of self-activity and his resulting insistence upon the priority of spirit over matter, reason over nature, led him to oppose the early introduction of vocational education in the schools and to prefer the humanistic and social science subjects to the practical. Here, too, he differed radically from Herbert Spencer, whose influence, as we have seen, was widespread in both lay and professional circles during this period.

As early as 1859 Herbert Spencer had directed his guns at the conventional curriculum in school and college, charging that in the selection and the priority given subjects no adequate criteria were followed. Consequently he began his series of essays on education with the question "What Knowledge Is of Most Worth?" In answering this question, Spencer defined the purpose of education as preparation for "complete living.... Not how to live in the mere material sense only, but in the widest sense...."

Now, as applied to the curriculum, continued Spencer, this objective involves both knowledge and discipline; and the problem of education becomes, first, one of classifying "the leading kinds of activity which constitute human life" and, second, one of identifying those subjects which provide both the knowledge and discipline essential for the performance of these activities. The activities Spencer then classified as follows, in order of importance: (1) those that directly minister to self-preservation; (2) those "which, by securing the necessities of life, indirectly minister to self-preservation"; (3) those "which have for their end the rearing and discipline of offspring"; (4) those "which are involved in the maintenance of proper social and political relations"; and, (5) "those miscellaneous activities which fill up the leisure part of life, devoted to the gratification of the tastes and feelings."

From this listing Spencer concluded that consideration should be given, first, to the sciences of physiology, hygiene, physics, and chemistry; second, to the sciences and arts related to the securing of food, clothing, shelter, and the like; third, to the social sciences essential for one to become an intelligent citizen and neighbor; and, last, to the knowledge of literature, art, and aesthetics, including foreign language and literature. As he put it, since the latter "occupy the leisure part of life, so should they occupy the leisure part of education."

In an introduction to Spencer's *Essays on Education*, Charles W. Eliot noted the speedy reception of Spencer's ideas on education, as contrasted with the much slower acceptance of the teachings of earlier educational philosophers—Comenius, Montaigne, Rousseau. One reason for the differences, he stated, is that Spencer's ideas "have floated on a prodigious tide of industrial and social change, which necessarily involved wide-spread and profound educational reform," changes that have led large numbers of young people of both sexes to prolong their education beyond the elementary school and to prepare themselves for a great variety of new callings. These changes, together with the applications of science to agriculture, have stimulated the spread of vocational education and "free instruction" to "farmers, their farm-hands, and their children." Similarly, Spencer's emphasis upon education for parenthood and citizenship, his "advocacy of instruction in public and private hygiene," and the growing interest of the "free peoples" in the improvement of material conditions of living testify to a growing acceptance of Spencer's "principle that science is the knowledge of most worth." [21]

21 Charles W. Eliot, "Introduction," in Herbert Spencer, *Essays on Education*, Everyman's Library Edition (New York: E. P. Dutton & Co., 1910).

Radical as were Spencer's ideas, in the view of traditional educators, they appealed to the practical sense of large segments of the American people and were seemingly in tune with demands created by a rapidly expanding industrial society. To Harris, however, Spencer's contention that the social sciences, literature, and language should be subordinated to science was grossly erroneous. Far from relating merely or primarily to "the leisure part of life," he insisted, they serve as "windows of the soul." "In the language of a people," he wrote, "are revealed the internal logical laws or structural framework of its intellect and the conscious realization of the mind of the race, as they appear in the vocabulary, grammatical laws, or syntax. Grammar opens to the child his view of the inner workings of the mind of the race, and helps him in so far to a comprehension of his own spiritual self. Literature . . . is the most accessible, as well as the fullest and completest expression of the sentiments, opinions, and convictions of a people; of their ideals, longings, aspirations." [22]

Further, according to Harris, it is not correct to infer that physiology should be taught first to the child. If self-preservation be the criterion of selection, then we should bear in mind that the knowledge of how the individual can combine and cooperate with others is the first lesson to learn.

From this we should not conclude that Harris opposed science in the curriculum. Rather was it a matter of purpose served. In discussing the course of study, he mentioned "five windows of the soul which open out upon five great divisions of life. Two of these relate to man's comprehension and conquest of Nature, the realm of time and space." [23] In the elementary school, arithmetic and geography serve this purpose. The other three are history, language, and literature. Of the school in general, he stated:

> The studies of the school fall naturally into these five co-ordinate groups: first, mathematics and physics; second, biology, including chiefly the plant and animal; third, literature and art, including chiefly the study of literary works of art; fourth, grammar and technical and scientific study of language, leading to such branches as logic and psychology; fifth, history and the study of sociological, political, and social institutions. Each of these groups should be

[22] Harris, *Psychologic Foundations of Education, op. cit.,* p. 322.
[23] *Ibid.,* p. 322.

represented in the curriculum of the schools at all times by some topic suited to the age and previous training of the pupil.[24]

On the elementary and secondary levels the schools' basic concern is "education for culture." Not until later, preferably on the postgraduate and professional levels, should the aim be that of preparation for a vocation. As a practical administrator, however, Harris found it necessary to compromise and to accept the introduction of manual training and vocational education in the secondary level. He urged, however, as did John Dewey later, that vocational training not concentrate merely upon skills and techniques but emphasize, as well, the historical and cultural significance of trade and the vocations. Thus would it contribute not only to vocational efficiency but to spiritual self-realization as well.

A second contrast between Spencer and Harris derived from their interpretations of evolution and its bearing upon the individual. As we saw, in dealing with Social Darwinism, progress in human society was thought to result from the slow accumulation of individual differences in the struggle for existence. On this view, natural selection applies to mental characteristics as well as to physical, and to civilizations as well as to human individuals. Consequently, natural selection, rather than intervention on the part of the state, or by reform groups, will insure the survival of the fittest. Only by eliminating the unfit can we hope for progress. "If they are sufficiently complete to live, they *do* live; and it is well they should live. If they are not sufficiently complete to live, they die, and it is best they should die." [25]

Spencer thus emphasized the importance of individual variations for progress (minute and slow in accumulation as they might be) and the evils of state interference. Indeed, he "deplored not only poor laws, but also state-supported education, sanitary supervision other than the suppression of nuisances, regulation of housing conditions, and even state protection of the ignorant from medical quacks. He likewise opposed tariffs, state banking, and government postal systems." [26] Education, accordingly, should center upon developing the rugged individual, competent to make his own way in a society of tooth and claw and in a state

---

[24] *Ibid.*, p. 323. The reader will observe the similarity between this listing and the recommendations of the Committee of Fifteen on Elementary Studies in 1895.

[25] Herbert Spencer, *Social Statics* (New York: D. Appleton & Co., 1864), p. 415.

[26] Richard Hofstadter, *Social Darwinism in America* (Boston: Beacon Press, 1960), p. 41.

dedicated to the principles of laissez-faire—all in the hope that the process of adaptation might eventuate ultimately in a moral constitution fitted to a more humane society!

Harris, on the other hand, would use education not to confirm and develop the qualities of competition and of original nature but to transform the latter. "Out of the savage state," he wrote, "man ascends by making himself new natures, one above the other; he realizes his ideas in institutions, and finds in these ideal worlds his real home and his true nature." [27]

The institutions that humanize the individual are, of course, the home, civil society, the state, and the church ("taking the Church in a broad sense as the collective instrumentalities that teach the accepted view of the world as expressed in the prevailing civilization"),[28] institutions for which the school is to serve "as supplementary to the family, and propaedeutic to the State, the Church, and civil Society." [29]

Despite these differences between an individualistic and a social emphasis in education, Harris and Spencer were as one in their opposition to radical social reform. Spencer opposed it because it interfered with the operations of natural selection; Harris, because of his conviction that institutions and existing stages of society are, in their major characteristics, expressions of the Divine Mind to which accommodation (if not adjustment!) is a necessary preliminary to future progress.

As a Hegelian, Harris saw in the evolution of institutions the steady emancipation of the individual from the group, from forced conformity to voluntary cooperation in the civil community, the state, and the church. The advocates of socialism were in error, he thought, because they proposed to interfere with the self-activity of the individual, to destroy the gains that have come with private property, and thus to revert to the ancient subordination of the individual to the group. Not through socialism and general programs of reform but through the education of the individual and the discipline which schools can provide will young people acquire the qualities of character essential for social progress: habits of regularity and industry, perseverance, self-respect, and moral ideals, in-

[27] William T. Harris, "Nature vs. Human Nature, or the Spiritual," *American Journal of Education*, Vol. III, January, 1871, pp. 4-5.

[28] William T. Harris, "Social Culture in the Form of Education and Religion," *Educational Review*, Vol. XXIV, October, 1902, p. 229.

[29] William T. Harris, "The Church, the State, and the School," *North American Review*, Vol. CXXXIII, September, 1881, p. 216.

cluding respect for property, "the rights of organized industry," and the like.[30]

Unlike Spencer and William Graham Sumner, Harris emphasized the importance of universal education. As Curti points out, he would not grant that the industrial scrap heap was due to the profit motive of manufacturers. "He ascribed it merely to the lack of intelligence and education on the part of workers," and he believed that "with a 'knowledge of the rudiments' they should be able to re-adapt themselves in new luxury industries, the products of which they and their fellow workers were to consume." [31]

Harris also believed that the vocations which provide protection and comfort—such as medicine, insurance, teaching, art, drama, science, literature, and religion—could expand indefinitely and that members of all classes, by means of education, might therefore become active participants in this advance. As Harris stated in a letter to G. H. Howison in September, 1887: "The progress of man implies the increasing endowment of the individual with the consciousness of the experience of the whole race and with greater directive power, so that each sums up in himself the whole. This implies that the individual shall be educated to a higher and higher degree to the end that there shall be no such thing as caste, hereditary or compulsory, but only such caste as the individual is responsible for himself. How this can be anything but a democracy, I do not see." To insure a democracy so conceived, Harris would have elementary and secondary schools fit the young for participation in the cultural heritage and social cooperation of the race, leaving to higher and adult education the responsibility for a critical and comparative evaluation of human knowledge and the institutions of society.

RELATIONS OF CHURCH AND STATE

Finally, a word should be said of Harris' conception of religion, the relations of church and state, and the problem of religious instruction in public schools. "Religion," he declared in a paper before the American Philosophical Association in 1904, "is the foundation of social life insofar as that social life belongs to the history of civilization. Religion in the first

---

[30] See Merle Curti, *Social Ideas of American Educators* (New York: Charles Scribner's Sons, 1935), the chapter on "William T. Harris, the Conservator," for an excellent exposition of Harris' social philosophy.

[31] *Ibid.*, p. 329.

place is not merely the process of an individual mind, but it is a great social process of intellect and will and heart. Its ideas are not the unaided thoughts of individual scholars, but the aggregate results of the social activity of the intellect, so to speak, each thought of the individual being modified by the thought of his community, so that it comes to the individual with the substantial impress of authority."

Important as Harris conceived religion to be, and the invisible church as the archetype of all institutions, he nevertheless insisted that the functions of church and state are distinct and should be kept separate. Their methods differ even though their goals may be the same. The state is concerned with overt acts and seeks to secure free will through the administration of justice. The church, on the other hand, is concerned with the inner disposition of the soul and defines deviation from this ideal as sin. Were the church to assume the functions of the state, or the state those of the church, confusion would result.

> If it [the church] held firmly its standard of religion, and looked to the disposition of the heart, it would forgive overt acts in all cases where repentance is supposed to be sincere, and, on the other hand, it would punish malignant intention, even when there was no attempt on the part of the will to make it an overt act. This would destroy justice and undermine the state. No citizen would know what to expect, there would be no sure protection of person and property. If, on the other hand, the church adopted the standard of justice, borrowing it from the state, it would destroy religion. For if the church was to look to the overt act it would neglect the disposition of the heart, and give to its penances a meaning entirely unorthodox. . . . If the state undertook to regulate religious matters, the same confusion would occur, and the interests of justice, as well as those of religion, would suffer.[32]

As Superintendent of Schools in St. Louis and later as United States Commissioner of Education, Harris found ample occasion to express his views on the practical issue of religious instruction in public schools. Devoutly religious as he was, he nevertheless realized the difference between the church as an ideal expression of the Absolute and the interests of churches in the concrete. As the functions of church and state are

---

[32] William T. Harris, "The Separation of the Church from the Tax-Supported School," *Educational Review*, Vol. XXVI, October, 1903, p. 224.

different, so, he believed, their concerns should be kept separate—as evidenced by experience as well as theory.

Thus we find him contending that union between church and state, whenever tried, has led "to the corruption of the former and the weakening of the latter." Secondly, a mingling of the two tends to infringe upon freedom of conscience, the very cornerstone of free institutions.

More specifically, with respect to the school itself, Harris emphasized, first, that the school is a supplementary institution and that consequently it is a mistake to thrust upon it responsibility for "complete living." Secondly, he emphasized that the methods of religious instruction and secular teaching differ fundamentally. For example, he wrote: "The principle of religious instruction is authority; that of secular instruction is demonstration and verification. It is obvious that these two principles should not be brought into the same school, but separated as widely as possible. Religious truth is revealed in allegoric and symbolic form, and is to be apprehended not merely by the intellect, but also by the imagination and the heart. The analytic understanding is necessarily hostile and skeptical in its attitude toward religious truth." [33] Third, he noted that experience in St. Louis as well as in other sections of the country had confirmed the wisdom of excluding religious instruction from the public schools. As he stated of St. Louis in his *Seventeenth Annual Report* (1871): "I cannot find that our schools have ever since their foundation in 1838 permitted so much as the reading of the Bible in them. I believe their perfect secularity has done much to bring about the perfect intermingling of all in our schools which has existed so long."

The exclusion of religious instruction from the schools in no way lessened for Harris the responsibility of the schools for moral education. Indeed, he believed it clarified this responsibility by distinguishing between morality and religion. In a tract on *Morality in the Schools* (1871), he wrote:

> Morality involves behavior toward others and toward one's self and a ceremonial entirely different from that of religion; namely, the conventional ceremonial which we call the code of politeness, manners, and behavior toward others. The whole of this behavior can be taught, and is taught best, without bringing it into the same place and time with religious instruction. Moral behavior relates to

[33] *Ibid.*

details which appear unessential when placed side by side with the doctrine of man's relation to God. The strictly moral duties concern the relation of man to man, and for this reason are all finite when compared with the subject-matter of religion.

By developing moral habits, as it must do through its discipline and pervading atmosphere, the school lays a groundwork for religious education in other appropriate institutions. And, as we have seen, in discussing Harris' concepts of self-activity and the relation of the individual to the institutions of society, for him the primary function of subjects of study is to encourage the development of the free spirit through identification with the values implicit within these institutions.

HARRIS' UNIQUE CONTRIBUTIONS

Primary emphasis has been given to William T. Harris in this chapter because of his strategic position in education during a period in which the United States was undergoing a rapid transition from a rural and predominantly agricultural economy into one urban and industrial. These changes bore heavily upon the individual, transforming his ways of living and challenging long-accepted conceptions of his nature and the conditions of his self-realization. Free competition between individuals who could possess themselves of capital or stake off a claim in a public domain rich in soil, mineral, timber, or power had long given substance and validity to the ideal of a self-contained and rugged individualism. But the rapid disappearance of the frontier, the development of the corporate form of producing and distributing the necessities of life; the new relationships thus engendered between capital and labor, between industry and the public; the growing pains of government on local, state, and national levels; the growth of cities, with their wide extremes of wealth and poverty and novel problems of health and hygiene—all testified eloquently to the need for revising older conceptions of the individual, of the good society, and of a democracy.

It was Harris' mission to convince the layman as well as the educator that these stresses and strains were evidences not of disintegration but of a dialectical process that was certain to eventuate in a synthesis on a higher level of being; and that the means of realizing this better tomorrow was one not of revolution but of education, an education designed to identify the individual with the constructive aspects of evolving institutions. Harris and Denton J. Snider, for example, believed they saw in the United States, following the Civil War, a contest between rival forces of disintegration and concentration in the emergence of the principle of federalism or "the state-producing-state"—a Union which produces states and in which the states continuously recreate the Union.

Harris is also significant for a clear enunciation of the implications for education of the central tenets of idealism—a statement of position and the grounds for this position that have remained relatively unchanged to this day. He envisaged the ultimate nature of reality as mind, a creative intelligence, and individuals, in their valid and essential natures, as expressions of this mind. In its applications to the psychology of learning, at least two conclusions follow. First, the world of objects and events, including the physical nature of man, is subordinate to the mind and given character by it, rather than, as the materialist and the physiological psychologist would have it, being superior to, if not the cause of, "mind" and its conscious states. Secondly, Harris emphasized, as did later idealists, the spiritual and organic nature of society and its institutions and, consequently, the dependence of the individual for self-realization upon harmonious interrelationships between whole and part.

At the same time, he insisted that history records the progressive emancipation of the individual from domination by the group. Such progress is in the direction of mutually stimulating (organic) relationships between the institutions of the family, the civil community, and the state, on the one hand, and the individual, on the other; thus the relationships that have evolved are toward the democratic. He has been criticized for subordinating the individual to institutions in his scheme of education, and of overemphasizing adjustment. Perhaps this overemphasis is better ascribed to his attempt to correct what seemed to him an overly extreme individualism in the laissez-faire society of his day.

Finally, Harris is important for his contributions to the content of the curriculum—elementary, secondary, and higher. The vocabulary may have changed in the course of the years, but the conviction of idealists today that the "liberal arts" are of primary educational value and the sciences of secondary importance in the education of "free men" is grounded in assumptions analogous to those Harris employed in choosing subjects best designed to develop "self-active" and free individuals in essential harmony with the civilization in which they are born.

OTHER IDEALISTS OF THE PERIOD

Were we concerned with philosophic thought in the United States in the nineteenth century quite apart from its influence upon public education, we should dwell with some length upon the contributions of Josiah Royce (1855-1916), an absolute idealist, and Borden Parker Bowne (1847-1910), an advocate of personal idealism.[34] Both were eagerly read by many during a period in which both science and the "higher criticism" in religion were calling in question traditional doctrines. Influential as were both in philosophical and religious circles, lay and professional, they were not as immediately concerned with the curriculum of school and college as was Harris.

Reference should also be made to George Holmes Howison (1834-1916) of the University of California. Howison began his career as a member of the St. Louis group. He soon found it impossible, however, to accept the Hegelian concept of an Absolute Mind. This seemed to him to eliminate the significance and, ultimately, the *being* of the individual. In reaction to Hegelianism, he developed a pluralistic, personal idealism in which persons are conceived as irreducible, spiritual atoms in a society of spiritual beings or, as he termed it, an "Eternal Republic" or "City of God." A spiritual universe thus replaced the Absolute One, or God, of the Hegelians.

FELIX ADLER AND THE SPIRITUAL UNIVERSE

In Felix Adler (1851-1933), however, we have an attempt to relate a philosophy of personal idealism directly to educational theory and practice.[35] In formulating this ethical philosophy of life, Adler acknowledged

[34] The reader will find a brief but understanding discussion of both Royce and Bowne in Herbert Schneider, *A History of American Philosophy* (New York: Columbia University Press, 1946), Chapters 36, 37. See also Joseph Blau, *Men and Movements in American Philosophy* (Englewood Cliffs, N.J.: Prentice-Hall, 1952), Chapter 6.

[35] Felix Adler was a philosopher, educator, and social reformer. In 1876 he founded the Ethical Culture movement, and in 1878, the Ethical Culture School (until 1893 called the Workingman's School) in New York City. He was a member of New York's first tenement house commission in 1885 and for many years served as Chairman of the National Child Labor Committee. In 1902 he became professor of social and political ethics at Columbia University, where he taught his philosophy of ethical idealism for many years. His chief books were *Creed and Deed* (1877), *An Ethical Philosophy of Life* (1918), and *The Reconstruction of the Spiritual Ideal* (1924).

his indebtedness to Kant and Emerson and to the Hebrews' concept of holiness, or the worth of each individual. As against conventional systems of ethics, which, as he said, begin with nonethical data, an interest in science, or logic, or aesthetics and attempt to deduce from those fields principles applicable to ethics, Adler proposed to develop an ethical philosophy directly out of ethical data and distinctly ethical problems. These problems, he pointed out, have to do with relationships between people; with relationships of "the individual sacred as an end *per se* to other individuals no less sacred than himself." [36]

Central to Adler's ethics was his concept of the spiritual nature of the individual, "first as holy, in the sense of worth; second as irreducible, in the sense of uniqueness; thirdly, as organic," [37] in the sense that the *potentially unique* and indispensable nature of each person finds its expression through relationships that foster the unique and indispensable qualities in others. In contrast, then, with a one-God, a spiritual Absolute, Adler rooted his faith in a metaphysical concept of the one *in* the many. For example, in *The Reconstruction of the Spiritual Ideal*, he wrote:

> We speak no more of the God of Hosts, but, as it were, of the host as godhead. We speak of an infinite society, an infinite choir, a commonwealth of spiritual beings, each of which expresses the spiritual nature in a manner unlike all the rest. And this unlikeness . . . is irreducible. The integrity of each member is impermeable. How then can a host become a system? How can the unity of so vast a multitude of beings be conceived, each one of which, in the intimacy of his unlikeness, seems inaccessible to the rest? The unity is predictable only in the form that the unlikeness of each is such as to elicit the unlikeness in all the rest. And from the scheme of relations thus conceived, there is derived a new vital practical rule: Seek to elicit the best in others, and thereby you will bring to light the best that is in yourself; evoke the distinctive unlikeness of others, and thereby you will promote and produce the distinctive unlikeness which is your own essential self. [38]

[36] Felix Adler, *The Reconstruction of the Spiritual Ideal* (New York: D. Appleton & Co., 1924), p. 31.

[37] *Ibid.*, p. 57.

[38] *Ibid.*, p. 56. This ideal of ethical relationships Adler applied to relationships between husband and wife, and parents and children in the family; to vocational life (the ethical relations of employer and employee, the businessman to his customers, and the like); to relations between groups in social and civic life; and to relations between nations. See Chapters III-VI in this reference.

Just as Spinoza has been characterized as a God-intoxicated man, so may we speak of Adler as intoxicated with the idea of a spiritual manifold, a supersensible reality, in which each member gives expression to uniqueness through dynamic and creative interaction with other unique members. Adler thus substituted for a God in the singular, or the Deity as commonly conceived, the idea of a spiritual universe that serves as an ideal pattern for worthy relationships between individuals and groups in the empirical world.

If Adler were asked how he could justify attributing to the scoundrel as well as to the saint an essential nature as a timeless subsistence within a spiritual manifold, he would point to what he termed the "reality-producing functions" of the mind. "I do not *find* worth in others or myself," he asserted, "I attribute it to them and myself." If one attributes an ethical potency to others, he believed, they, as well as oneself, may succeed in rising to higher levels of sensitive, imaginative, and creative living.

Adler's affirmation of worth in each personality caught the imagination of many and inspired them to envisage in their immediate relationships within the family and in the daily functioning of social, civic, economic, and political institutions stimulating possibilities of reform. Many, for whom traditional religion no longer satisfied their spiritual needs, still longed for an active faith that would both stimulate and justify good works. This faith they found in Adler's vision of a democratic society patterned after a spiritual universe, a society organized on the principle that "within every human being" there is a spark of humanity which is to "be held more and more precious and be regarded with ever deepening reverence."

Moreover, the times were ripe for visions of positive reform. Unrestrained and rugged individualism, as we have seen, was producing ugly seams in American life with extremes of wealth and poverty and a conspicuous waste of both human and natural resources. The exploitation of children in mine and factory, the miserable products of slum existence, "the shame of the cities," as Lincoln Steffens characterized municipal government in 1904, the political and civic degeneration of community life, the impoverished and formal character of public education—all testified abundantly to the necessity of bettering human relations if the American dream were not to end in a nightmare.

Finally, reform, as Americans were prone to conceive of reform, demanded a corrective. Adler's insistence (in this respect, in common with

Harris) upon the mutual interdependence of human beings challenged the validity of the popular concept of the individual as an insulated atom and, as an atom, the architect of his own fortune. Contrast, for example, the implications of reform in Adler's principle that each person develops his own personality in the process of encouraging in others the expression of their distinctive natures with Emerson's essentially passive concept of reform. "The power, which is at once spring and regulator in all efforts at reform," wrote Emerson in *Man the Reformer* (1841), "is the conviction that there is an infinite worthiness in man which will appear at the call of worth, and that all particular reforms are the removing of impediments."

In other words, if we will but free the slave or remove the shackles from the limbs of the unfortunate and disadvantaged, the released will thereafter take care of themselves! Adler, on the other hand, recognized that release from bondage is but a first step and that time and patience, especially in education, may be necessary in order to assist the crippled to walk upright. Thus we *are* our brother's keeper!

In contrast with other educators whom we have considered—Horace Mann, Henry Barnard, William T. Harris—Adler was an active participant in social as well as educational reform. All-important as he considered the education of each individual to be, he was keenly aware of the fact that education in schools alone is insufficient to cure the ills of society.

In education, two aspects of Adler's philosophy were significant for mass education (for a program of education relevant to the needs of all types of mind and levels of ability): his concept of "culture" and his identification of "interest" with the unique potentialities of the individual. Both concepts were opposed to uniformity in curriculum content and to a lockstep method of instruction. Both were designed to bridge the gap commonly separating vocational from general education.

In a 1924 address, Adler stated:

> The reaching out toward culture is a spiritual necessity prompted by the desire to escape from the narrowing effects of specialism—of that excessive specialism which in every branch of human activity is becoming the fatal characteristic of modern civilization. For not only the factory operative, sentenced to the ever-reiterated performance of the same operation, is a victim of the division of labor, but the same principle crowds the scientist, the physician, the man of

affairs, into a restricted field. More and more men must content themselves to work in a single patch of the field, with the result that they tend to lose contact with the larger whole. Culture is the effort to escape from this diminution of both the work and the man.[39]

To become cultured, according to Adler, is to establish "contact with the larger whole" through the many potential radiations of a major interest. Thus, the businessman attains culture by becoming "internationally-minded" (that is, genuinely interested in the people of countries who may be affected by his business activity); "scientifically-minded" by following "the clues of science as it enters and fertilizes the field of industry"; and "ethically-minded" by sensing "the idea that business is a profession, a vocation, that the production and exchange of commodities, the proper function of commerce, is one of the great kinds of social service, and therefore that a man in business must think of himself as a social servant, as a vocational functionary."

The educator recognizes, of course, that Adler's ideal of culture in its application to an adult's vocation differs considerably from a student's *promising interest* or a potential vocational choice. But there is this in common: in each case the principle of procedure is functional. To the extent that one's peculiar forte, speciality, interest, or ability find fruitful expression in the related areas of art, literature, science, family life, vocational activity, community and civil undertaking, he is "reaching out toward culture" which "is a spiritual necessity prompted by the desire to escape from the narrowing effects of specialism."

As applied to the curriculum of the school this suggested an attempt to introduce a student in the secondary school to the most significant of life's functions, by means of his major interest. Take, for example, a student who possesses an interest and ability in art. In addition to the training which enables him to become efficient and competent in his field, he would be encouraged to move along the lines of his major interest into history (familiarizing himself with the role of the artist in various periods of history and the influence of these periods upon art), literature, science, language, music, and the other arts, and to participate by virtue of this

[39] Felix Adler, *The Ideal of Culture for Business Men* (New York: American Ethical Union, 1924). Observe that this is a positive phrasing of a criticism in John Dewey's *Individualism, Old and New* (New York: Minton, Balch & Co., 1930). See, for example, Dewey's chapter on "The Lost Individual."

same interest in the social, civic, and community undertakings in which the artist can serve society as citizen-artist.[40]

Adler's interest in education found its earliest expression in the establishment of a kindergarten in New York City in 1878, open and free to children of "the working-class." There was one significant difference, however, between Adler's concept of education and kindergarten education as conceived by Froebel and his followers. The spiritual potentialities of the child, which Froebel hoped to elicit through the use of the symbolism (the conventionalized materials and the stereotyped activities of the kindergarten) were envisaged as reflections of a spiritual unity. Consequently, while the kindergarten stimulated a reverence for child nature by virtue of the assumption that each child is a sacred personality, a replica of the Infinite Spirit, both the ends and the means of education were conceived as identical for all. For those inspired by Adler, in contrast, the essence of the child's nature is uniqueness. Consequently, the eye of the educator was encouraged to center upon distinctiveness of growth and upon the inner life of the individual, as well as upon outer behavior. Moreover, all acts of discipline, as all educational materials and methods, were evaluated in terms of their effects upon personality, thus subordinating the professional activity of the teacher, as the function of a parent, to an overarching ideal, an ideal at once individual and social.

Adler's concept of culture and its applications to education was far in advance of educational practice in the nineteenth century. Insofar as it was understood, however, it was in harmony, basically, with later developments in child study and the applications of psychology and psychiatry to education. But these had to wait upon the twentieth century.

[40] For a more complete discussion of the implications of Adler's concept of culture to the secondary school, see V. T. Thayer, "Secondary Education as Orientation," in Samuel Everett and others, A Challenge to Secondary Education (New York: D. Appleton-Century Co., 1935). For some years an attempt was made to apply Adler's general concept of culture to courses in the Fieldston School, the secondary division of The Ethical Culture Schools in New York City. However, the rigidity of college admission requirements as reflected in College Board examinations severely limited their development for students who wished both to enter college and to develop the cultural implications of their major interests.

SUGGESTED READING

Adler, Felix, *The Reconstruction of the Spiritual Ideal* (New York: D. Appleton & Co., 1924), Chapters I, II.

Cremin, Lawrence A., *The Transformation of the School* (New York: Alfred A. Knopf, 1961), Chapter 1.

Curti, Merle, *The Social Ideas of American Educators* (New York: Charles Scribner's Sons, 1935), Chapter IX. Also available in a paperback edition published in 1960 by Littlefield & Adams, Paterson, N. J.

Harris, William T., *Psychologic Foundations of Education* (New York: D. Appleton & Co., 1898).

Horne, Herman H., "An Idealistic Philosophy of Education," in *Philosophies of Education, Forty-first Yearbook of the National Society for the Study of Education* (Bloomington, Ill.: Public School Publishing Co., 1942), Part I, Chapter IV.

Leidecker, Kurt F., *Yankee Teacher: The Life of William Torrey Harris* (New York: Philosophical Library, 1946), Chapters VII, X, XIV, XV, XXII, XXIX.

Pochmann, Henry A., *New England Transcendentalism and St. Louis Hegelianism* (Philadelphia: Carl Schurz Memorial Foundation, 1948), Chapters I-VI.

Riley, Woodbridge, *American Thought: From Puritanism to Pragmatism and Beyond* (Gloucester, Mass.: Peter Smith, 1959), Chapter VIII.

Spencer, Herbert, *Essays on Education* (New York: E. P. Dutton & Co., 1910), Chapter I.

CHAPTER 9
PSYCHOLOGY PROVIDES
A DESIGN FOR EDUCATION:
G. STANLEY HALL AND
THE HERBARTIANS

CHAPTER 7 described the attempt of William James to substitute the concept of the "passing thought" for the traditional assumption of a mind, or a soul, as an entity separate and distinct from the psychic contents of experience. In denying the independent existence of mind, James also challenged long-accepted notions of its primary concerns. That man is a rational animal and that reason, as a faculty, occupies itself with problems superior to those of physical survival had been questioned by few since Socrates and Plato.

The development of physiological psychology cast doubt upon the aristocratic assumption that man's "theoretic life is his soul's genuine concern" and emphasized instead both the evolutionary origin of "mental phenomena" and their intimate connection with the physiological organism. It remained for G. Stanley Hall to take the concept of evolution as a fundamental principle and, with ideas derived from Herbert Spencer, Haeckel, Von Baer, Rousseau, and the Romanticists, to formulate a genetic theory of growth and development that influenced profoundly both the curriculum and the administrative organization of the school in the late nineteenth and early twentieth centuries.

GERMINAL IDEAS IN ROUSSEAU

As early as 1762 Jean Jacques Rousseau (1712-1778), in his *Emile,* had challenged the Puritan doctrine of the innate depravity of human nature and the corresponding assumption that children are "born in sin." Not in the child or in man's original nature is evil to be found, but in the institutions of society. In the opening words of *Émile*, Rousseau declared; "God makes all things good; man meddles with them and they become evil."

It follows that to educate the child properly we should take as our guide his native impulses and desires rather than attempt to adjust him to the institutions of society. The child, like the man, is an end in himself. He is too noble a being to serve as an instrument of others. Consequently, in planning his education, it should be borne in mind that "men are not made for their stations, but their stations for men."

A second germinal idea in Rousseau was the concept of stages of development through which the individual passes in his progress from infancy to adulthood. These stages, in the order of their appearance, are: sensation, physical activity, motor activity, memory, practical reason, theoretical reason, and social nature. As stated in *Émile*, "Since everything that comes into the mind enters through the gates of sense, man's first reason is a reason of sense experience. It is this that serves as a foundation for the reason of the intelligence; our first teachers in natural philosophy are our feet, hands, and eyes. To substitute books for them does not teach us to reason, it teaches us to use the reason of others rather than our own; it teaches us to believe much and know little."

Until the age of twelve, then, Rousseau would have the child's education concerned chiefly with physical activity and manifold relations with his sensible environment. Intellectual education (in the sense of the manipulation of abstract ideas and principles) would not begin until the age of twelve or fifteen, nor social and moral education, in any genuine sense, prior to the period of fifteen to twenty. By this time, but not before, the senses and the brain have developed to the point where it is appropriate and necessary to temper the heart. Again, as stated in *Émile*, "Man's proper study is that of his relation to his environment. So long as he knows that environment through his physical nature, he should study himself in relation to things; this is the business of his childhood. When he begins to be aware of his moral nature, he should study himself in relation to his fellow men; this is the business of his whole life, and we have now reached the time when that study should begin."

It is interesting to observe that although Rousseau would organize education in accordance with stages of development *common to all chil-*

dren he nevertheless repudiated the traditional concept of a typical mind, thus anticipating by more than a century the educator's concern for individual differences. Each mind, he insisted, has a form of its own which carries a moral for teacher and parent.

To Rousseau, then, credit should be given for formulating clearly and dramatically a theory of education more in harmony with a revolutionary future than with the educational practice of his day. Prior to *Émile* and, indeed, for nearly a century later, children were viewed as adults in miniature, different from older people in size and strength of the body and in maturity of mental faculties, but not in essential nature. Not until the nineteenth century, and the influence of the Pestalozzian and Herbartian movements in Europe, did Rousseau's concepts of child development and the basic principle that nature is right, and thus to be followed, seriously affect educational theory and practice.

Probably the most immediate effect of Rousseau's doctrines was felt in Germany, in the work of Basedow, Salzman, and Campe. In England Rousseau's influence was felt more in literature than in education. In France the rise of Napoleon and reaction to the French Revolution provided little encouragement for revolutionary developments in education.

G. STANLEY HALL (1846-1924)

Conditions in the United States during the second half of the nineteenth century were favorable to a thoroughgoing application of the germinal ideas expressed by Rousseau: that education is a natural process, that development from within provides the cue for subject matter and method, and that adequate preparation for life is one with the healthy expression of each of the several stages in an individual's progress from infancy to adulthood. And there was no one more competent to validate and apply these concepts to education than G. Stanley Hall and the students whom he inspired and influenced.

Hall was born in Ashfield, Massachusetts. Following his graduation from Williams College, he spent one year at the Union Theological Seminary in New York with the idea of entering the ministry, a plan more congenial to his parents than to him. Henry Ward Beecher was instrumental in his securing funds with which to study in Germany, and there he pursued a wide range of subjects, including theology, physics, philosophy of history, experimental psychology, and philosophy. Upon returning to the United States in 1871, he was refused a position as teacher of the history of philosophy in a midwestern university for the reason that his preparation indicated he would "unsettle men and teach them to hold no opinions."

A brief period of teaching in two private schools and tutoring in the family of a wealthy banker in New York City was followed by four years as an instructor in English, philosophy, and psychology at Antioch College, an instructorship at Harvard University, and further study abroad. In 1882 he was appointed to the professorship of "psychology and pedagogy" at Johns Hopkins University. There he developed laboratory work in psychology with a number of students who later were to become famous—John Dewey, Joseph Jastrow, J. McKeen Cattell, W. H. Burnham —and also established *The American Journal of Psychology,* the first in its field in English. In 1888 he was called to the presidency of Clark University, a position he held until his retirement in 1920.

It was at Clark that Hall established his reputation as an administrator and educator, attracting to the University outstanding men in their fields and stimulating students to undertake significant work in all aspects of psychology and education. Noted for his pioneer work in genetic psychology, he is appropriately called the father of the child study movement. To the study of growth and development in childhood and adolescence and to the theory and practice of education he brought the contributions of knowledge from many fields—biology, history, geology, comparative psychology—as well as conclusions drawn from firsthand observations and study of children. He and his students addressed thousands of questionnaires to all manner of individuals in all sections of the country, seeking data bearing upon childhood experiences which might serve as a basis of comparison with the results of direct observation of young people. Finally, he had the courage to draw conclusions from his investigations which seemed warranted by the data, even when these conflicted with traditional and conventional thought and practice.

To his work in child study Hall brought the results of wide and varied reading and training. For example, in his *Life and Confessions of a Psychologist,* he described the manner in which Trendelenburg's concept of "werden," or "becoming," Hegel's philosophy of history as God coming to consciousness in man, and Schelling's treatment of both inorganic and organic nature "as steps in the unfoldment of a mighty process" were confirmed in his mind by the writings of Darwin, Huxley, Spencer, Haeckel, and even Tyndall. "Inconsistencies troubled me little," he wrote, "but I was everywhere in avid quest of illustrations of developmental stages to span all chasms, and I conceived all creative processes as still active, all about me, and above all felt there was nothing really dead but that there was everywhere life abounding, filling all possibilities everywhere, which gave and still gives the deepest intellectual satisfaction I have ever known." [1]

Hall was convinced that psychology "had felt the influence of Darwinism vastly less than any other science that dealt with life." It consequently became his ambition to demonstrate that "there were just as many rudiments and vestiges in our psychic activity and make-up as in our bodies and that the former was just as much a product of slow evolutionary tendencies as the latter." [2]

THE DOCTRINE OF RECAPITULATION
APPLIED TO PSYCHIC LIFE

Not only did Hall and his students devise many of their own methods of investigation and experiment; they utilized as well generalizations from other fields. Thus from biology they derived the recapitulation theory, from psychology the theory of instincts, and from the social sciences the concept of stages of development through which all societies pass in their progress from primitive life to that of an advanced civilization. As we look back upon the early phases of the child study movement we can see that these doctrines became the lenses through which the movement read its data.

Take, for example, the recapitulation theory. In the hands of Ziller and G. Stanley Hall this theory gave new substance and form both to the culture epochs theory of the Herbartians and the developmental theory of Froebel. According to the biological theory of recapitulation of the time, each individual, prior to birth, passes through (recapitulates) well-defined physical stages reminiscent of that line of evolution to which he belongs. Thus, at one stage, the human embryo possesses a fishlike tail and gill slits which shortly disappear, to be replaced by still other non-human characteristics in its progress toward its eventual human structure. As expanded in Germany and by G. Stanley Hall in the United States, the concept of recapitulation came to mean that the individual

---

[1] G. Stanley Hall, *Life and Confessions of a Psychologist* (New York: D. Appleton & Co., 1923), p. 359.
[2] *Ibid.*, p. 360.

after birth and in the course of his development from infancy to adulthood passes through the cultural stages of racial experience, just as, *prior to birth*, in his embryological development he recapitulates the phylogenetic development of the species. In shorthand terms this theory affirmed that "ontogenesis recapitulates phylogenesis."

The recapitulation theory, thus conceived, gave definite and tangible meaning to the mystical Froebelian and idealistic conception of education as a process in which the individual expands, in the course of his growth, the germ of the infinite within him. It also allied itself with a serial and saltatory conception of child growth. According to these views, traits of mind and character (that is, inherited ways of thinking, feeling, and acting) arise more or less abruptly and follow each other in a definite order, thus giving unique and distinct characteristics to periods such as babyhood, childhood, and adolescence. For example, Hall said of adolescence:

> Adolescence is a new birth, for the higher and more completely human traits are now born. The qualities of body and soul that now emerge are far newer. The child comes from and harks back to a remoter past; the adolescent is neo-atavistic, and in him the later acquisitions of the race become preponent. Development is less gradual and more saltatory, suggestive of some ancient period of storm and stress when old moorings were broken and a higher level attained. The annual rate of growth in height, weight, and strength is increased and often doubled and more. Important functions previously nonexistent arise. Growth of parts and organs loses its former proportions, some permanently and some for a season. Some of these are still growing in old age and others are soon arrested and atrophy. The old moduli of dimensions become obsolete and old harmonies are broken. The range of individual differences and average errors in all physical measurements and all psychic tests increases. Some linger long in the childish stage and advance late or slowly, while others push on with a sudden outburst of impulsion to early maturity.[3]

According to R. W. Pringle, a follower of Hall, stages in the development of each individual—infancy, childhood, preadolescence, middle adolescence, and late adolescence—recapitulate the corresponding cul-

---

[3] G. Stanley Hall, *Adolescence*, Vol. I (New York: D. Appleton & Co., 1905), p. xiii.

tural stages which historians identify as prehistoric; patriarchal; tribal, feudal, with absolute monarchy; revolutionary, with constitutional monarchy; and republic, or self-governing.[4]

The recapitulation and culture epochs theories transform the educator into an investigator. He must observe children's interests and behavior and search the pages of history in order to secure the data with which to interpret their significance. Thus only can he identify the present stage of a child's development and organize the proper educational materials and experiences with which to foster its healthy expression.

RECAPITULATION AND THE CURRICULUM

In an address delivered before the National Council of Education in 1901 on the topic "The Ideal School as Based on Child Study," Hall described in short compass the applications of child development to the curriculum and the organization of the school. For example, he had discovered that from age eight or nine to puberty "there is a decreased rate of growth, so that the body relatively rests; but there is a striking increase of vitality, activity, and power to resist disease." This stage, he believed, corresponds to the period of human development well above the simian and before the historic period, "when our early forebears were well adjusted to their environment." It is a period therefore admirably adapted to "drill, habituation, and mechanism." Accordingly, the teacher should seek to establish the fundamentals of reading, writing, arithmetic, and the like. "Accuracy, which, when out of season, is fraught with so many dangers for mind and body, is now the order." Geography should be organized on the basis of the fact that a child's interest in primitive life and animals culminates in the ages of nine to ten, and interest in trade and government does not appear until from sixteen to twenty. Singing is important, "but far more time will be given to rote singing than to the singing from notes, especially at first," since the chief aim is "not to develop the power to read music but to educate the sentiments, and especially to attune them to love of home, nature, fatherland, and religion— the four chief themes of song in all ages, past and present."

Similar principles should determine the content of each and every subject in the school, according to Hall, since effective teaching requires the matching of subject matter with ways of thinking, feeling, and acting

---

[4] R. W Pringle, *Adolescence and High School Problems* (Boston: D. C. Heath & Co., 1922), pp. 16-17.

characteristic of stages of development in the life of the individual; stages of development that recapitulate the cultural history of the race.[5]

When we turn to methods of teaching and discipline advocated by Hall and his followers, we find the same adherence to the theory of using nature as a cue, a theory that suggests at one period the application of the most rigorous disciplinary measures and at another time a laissez-faire policy. For example, when speaking of the methods to be employed during the period between ages eight or nine to puberty, Hall insisted, "In most cases to try to explain brings self-consciousness and conceit. This method is the recourse of teachers and parents whose personality is deficient in authoritativeness. Obedience should still be a law, if not a passion." And, again, " 'Show,' 'demonstrate,' and 'envisage' should be our watchword, not 'explain.' . . . Even with respect to morals and conduct the chief duty of the child at this age is to obey."

Pringle gave similar advice, in speaking of the preadolescent:

> As to method, the statement sounds unpedagogical: much of the instruction may be dogmatic and authoritative, and often, to get the best results, the methods must be mechanical. It is not profitable always to try to appeal to the higher reasoning powers. Incitement and insistence on the part of somebody are needed. So far as many of the fundamentals are concerned, it is a case of drill and inculcation rather than true teaching. Duty on the part of the pupil consists largely in habitual and prompt obedience; for in giving lodgement to the fundamentals of knowledge, it is not practical to coquet with the child's likes and dislikes.[6]

On the other hand, with the dawn of adolescence, not only are rich and varied experiences imperative, but the manner of their presentation is of strategic importance. To drill at this stage is to retard development. Now is the time for encouraging the reasoning powers, thoughtfulness, and reflection.

In the realm of behavior Hall's theory of an intimate relationship between the child's instinctive nature and racial experience seemed to sanction a policy of noninterference with "nature." This policy found expression in the catharsis theory, according to which certain undesirable original

---

[5] See G. Stanley Hall, "The Ideal School," in National Education Association, *Proceedings and Addresses* (Washington, D.C.: the Association, 1901), pp. 474-488, for Hall's detailed description of subjects and methods.

[6] Pringle, *op. cit.*, p. 19.

tendencies must be given expression either because they are necessary preliminaries to, or correlates of, other quite different impulses or because their free expression in early life safeguards the individual from their appearance in later life.

To the layman the application of the catharsis theory to the discipline of the child could be shocking. Take, for example, the property instinct and its implications for parents and teachers as discussed by Kline and France and quoted by Hall:

> Selfishness is the corner-stone of the struggle for existence, deception is its very foundation, while the acquiring of property has been the dominant factor in the history of men and nations. These passions of the child are but the pent up forces of the greed of thousands of years. They must find expression and exercise, if not in childhood, later. . . . It does no good to make the child perform moral acts when it does not appreciate what right and wrong mean, and to punish a child for performing acts which his very nature compels him to do, is doing that child positive injury.
>
> During the period of adolescence, generosity and altruism spring up naturally. Then why try to force a budding plant into blossom? Instruct them by all means, teach them the right; but if this fails, do not punish, but let the child be selfish, let him lie and cheat, until these forces spend themselves. Do not these experiences of the child give to the man in later life a moral virility? [7]

SOME CONTRIBUTIONS AND LIMITATIONS OF THE CULTURE EPOCHS THEORY

One contribution of the culture epochs theory was to question the psychological appropriateness of the conventional administrative organization of public school systems at a time when education was undergoing severe growing pains at both elementary and secondary levels. Prior to the turn of the century, the elementary school had been the "common school" in the sense that for the large mass of young people graduation completed their education. Only a fraction of the school population anticipated further instruction. Consequently, the school was under no compulsion to organize its curriculum with an eye to subsequent work on the secondary

[7] Quoted in G. Stanley Hall, *Aspects of Child Life and Education* (Boston: Ginn & Co., 1907), pp. 166-167.

level. Nor would this have been an easy task, in view of the chaotic conditions of curricula in secondary schools of the period. From 1890 on, however, attendance records suggested that the high school would shortly become the common school, insofar as that term implies the enrollment of the bulk of the school population within a given age range and the point at which most young people terminate their formal education.

On the other hand, statistics of enrollment in the four years of high school were creating general concern. According to data provided by Alexander Inglis, the first year of public secondary schools in 1914-1915 included 40.86 percent of all pupils enrolled in these schools, but the fourth year only 13.99 percent. This fact suggested not only that something was wrong with the holding power of the secondary school but that the elementary school was failing to equip young people adequately for work on the secondary level.[8]

G. Stanley Hall and his disciples had a solution for both difficulties: create a new school unit attuned to the needs of the age group commonly served by the upper years of the elementary school and the first two years of high school, and organize both subject matter and instructional procedures for these years with an eye to the interests, needs, and future intentions of young people at this stage of growth and development. To be sure, other factors contributed to the emergence of the junior high school—including the need for "economy of time" in education, the concern of social reformers over the wastage in education resulting from the large percentage of dropouts in the early years of the secondary school, and the demands of business and industry for some form of vocational preparation of boys and girls at this point—but the psychological argument was most general in its appeal.

Thus it was that the junior high school came into being as a new school unit in which the subjects taught, extracurricular activities, methods of discipline, and instruction were all to be keyed to the needs of young people—intellectual, emotional, social, and vocational—in the early years of adolescence.

The demands for reform and the curricula they suggested were not altogether consistent. For example, the qualities of character possessed by young people in a stage of development analogous to that of feudal

[8] Alexander Inglis, *Principles of Secondary Education* (Boston: Houghton Mifflin Co., 1918), p. 121.

knights (cultural characteristics seemed to derive from the knights rather than from feudal serfs!) were hardly identical with those demanded by employers eager for "hands" to tend the industrial machine!

As indicated above, the recapitulation and culture epochs theories bore directly upon the curriculum of the school. Not only was new subject matter introduced on the elementary and junior high school levels—including art, music, and dramatic work as an inherent part of conventional subjects—but methods of teaching were vitalized by attempts to adapt subject matter and procedures to the interests and age levels of pupils.

In the junior high school, for example, it was observed that irregularities in physical growth are common, together with rapid changes in aptitudes and interests. This suggested a broad sweep of subject matter in contrast with narrow and specialized concentration upon one area or field. As a result, general science, general history, general mathematics, general literature, and "tryout" courses in the arts and crafts developed as a substitute for special subjects such as physiology and ancient history. Similarly, the budding social interests of this period, marked by new relationships between the sexes and keen sensitiveness to group approval or disapproval, suggested the introduction of socialized work (the "socialized recitation" and the project method) in the classroom and the organization of special-interest clubs, assemblies, dramatic work, and other valuable activities of an extracurricular nature. Again, since individual differences in interests and life goals tend to assume importance at this age, it was concluded that this called for differentiated curricula, including terminal courses of a vocational character for those not planning to continue with their education.

Unfortunately, in practice, this provision for individual differences eventuated all too often in varied curricula, such as a commercial curriculum, an industrial arts curriculum, or a general and a college preparatory curriculum. Each was designed to serve individual differences in interests and life goals as viewed from the administrative office, and from each it was often difficult for a pupil to transfer when necessary or advisable.

The theory of differentiated curricula represented progress. But it also involved assumptions of limited educational value. For example, the presentation of material "appropriate" to a given stage in the child's development was expected to exercise a magical influence by virtue of a preestablished connection between inner nature and outer stimulus. Thus

Indian life was studied in the early years of the elementary school, not so much because primitive life, in its simplicity, serves as a happy introduction to an understanding of the operations of a modern community—the providing of food, clothing, and shelter—but because it afforded channels of expression for the atavistic tendencies in the life of the young child.

Again, the assumption that stages of development in childhood and adolescence are instinctive rather than cultural in origin gave to child behavior an aspect of inevitability and imperativeness of serious import for discipline and child guidance. Take, for instance, a case of theft on the part of a child. How different the attitude and the responsibilities of a parent if, on the one hand, misbehavior is interpreted as an expression of racial experience compelled by nature and temporary in its effects, or, on the other hand, as an unhealthy response to factors operating in the immediate environment, perhaps aroused by feelings of deprivation or rejection or by unfortunate relationships that can be corrected once they are identified!

Extreme as the "instinctive" interpretation may seem to us today, it was of utmost significance that child behavior should no longer be equated with adult behavior. This laid the basis for a psychology of childhood and the development of a professional attitude toward children and child behavior.

Contradictory conclusions likewise apply to the effects of the recapitulation and cultural epochs theories upon teaching methods and the organization of subject matter early in the present century. To these should be given partial credit for the project method of teaching (later termed "units of work" or just plain "units") which in many schools came to replace the daily assignment and recitation of "lessons." [9] The project differed from the daily recitation in that it concerned itself with the solution of a problem, the understanding of a movement in history, a masterpiece in literature, or the operations of a social, industrial, or economic institution as a unified experience, in contrast with the daily nibbling process of assign, study, recite characteristic of the conventional lesson.

All of this was to the good, but when we examine the writings of one influential group of educators, who advocated the use of "real life projects," we discover their purpose was to introduce the child to present-

[9] For a discussion of the origin of the project method and influences leading to its development early in the century, see V. T. Thayer, *The Passing of the Recitation* (Boston: D. C. Heath & Co., 1928), Chapters XVI, XVII. For a quite different concept of the project as developed by William Heard Kilpatrick, see Chapter 12 to follow.

day life through a "progressive revelation of the world." This revelation was to be obtained by requiring the child to relive vicariously the experiences of his forebears who had built up the dominant institutions of society. Projects thus became reproductions of ideas which have found expression in social and industrial institutions. As one authority put it, "The world's experience and wisdom are gathered up and organized into these successful projects. They express the growing stages, the actual evolution of the main life processes in a practical world." [10]

Vital as this method of organizing instruction was, in contrast with the traditional piecemeal type of assignment and recitation, its Hegelian origin is clear. Of similar origin was the tendency (by thus "recapitulating" the growth and development of the institutions of society) to instill in the minds of children the conviction that the institutions of society are of divine origin and are, therefore, right!

SCIENCE UNDERMINES HALL'S THEORIES

For a goodly portion of his professional career, G. Stanley Hall experienced the satisfaction of seeing his ideas widely accepted and adopted by educational reformers in this country and abroad. Biology and psychology, anthropology and paleontology, and history as well seemed to confirm the recapitulation and culture epoch theories. Shortly before his death, however, these theories, together with their implications for child development and education, fell upon evil days. Further research in biology failed to sustain the recapitulation theory in the form accepted and applied by its child study advocates.

It was found, for example, that while the individual embryo may recapitulate the phylogenetic series to which it belongs, there are many gaps and omissions in this recapitulation. More serious was the fate that befell the theory of acquired characteristics (the theory that characteristics acquired during the lifetime of one generation or individual are transmitted in their original form to successive generations or individuals). Ironically, this was quickly replaced by its opposite, the germ-plasm theory of August Weismann, which emphasized the unbroken continuity of the germ plasm and its insulation from environmental influences in the life of a given individual. Finally, detailed comparisons of cultural periods in history with stages in the development of individuals have

[10] Charles McMurray, *Teaching by Projects* (New York: The Macmillan Co., 1920), pp. 50-51.

revealed only superficial resemblances between the two. Indeed, it soon became evident that the validity of the culture epochs theory varies inversely with a detailed knowledge of history and a careful, meticulous observation of child development!

A somewhat similar fate overtook Hall's generous list of instincts. As a result of Edward L. Thorndike's insistence that instincts be described in terms of the *specific* elements within a given situation to which *specific* responses in the individual are related, the number of instincts in human behavior began to shrink in number and, with their disappearance, the validity of the doctrine of catharsis. Moreover, as we shall see later, the influence of Thorndike's concept of habit formation and learning, together with the rise of behavioristic psychology, gave an entirely different turn to guidance in education from that implicit in the doctrine of catharsis and other theories of Hall. Although Hall had brought Sigmund Freud, Carl Gustav Jung, and other European psychoanalysts to the attention of American psychologists early in the twentieth century, not until after his death did their views of the unconscious give new direction to individual guidance and therapy.

As confidence in the theory of recapitulation weakened, psychologists began to search once more for explanations of children's behavior in the circumstances of their environment. Thus they began to draw conclusions quite different from those of the hereditarians with respect to the origins of interests and the use to be made of them in education.

CONDITIONS CALLING FOR REFORM IN EDUCATION AT THE TURN OF THE CENTURY

A number of factors, internal and external to the school, contributed to earnest demands for educational reform at the turn of the century. Several of these have received brief mention: the growing pains of adjustment between elementary and secondary schools as the latter gave promise, in terms of enrollment, of becoming the "common school"; lack of any general agreement with respect to curricular offerings in the secondary school either for college-bound students or for those who planned to terminate their education upon graduation; and heavy elimination of pupils between the eighth and ninth grades, plus a large proportion of dropouts between the ninth and twelfth. All were factors that seemed to confirm the contention of psychologists that neither the elementary nor the secondary schools of the country in their administrative structure or their instructional programs were geared to the developmental needs of children and adolescents.

Intimately related to the above were profound changes in the lives of people resulting from the rapid industrialization of American society. By 1890, for example, three-fifths of the population of the North Atlantic States had become city dwellers, and in sections of New England and the Middle Atlantic States many rural areas were falling into decay. Moreover, this shift from rural to urban living was proceeding at an ever accelerating pace.

For the educator these changes were of significance because of their impact upon young people and family life. Parents accustomed only to rural life were suddenly confronted not only with the problems of adjustment to new occupations but with those of rearing children under circumstances novel and disturbing. Children were not receiving from parents guidance in the many relationships of living that family life had long provided.

Severely handicapped in these respects were the rapidly increasing numbers of immigrants, handicapped not only by their rural backgrounds (a majority came from rural areas in Europe where they had earned their living, in the main, as farm laborers) but also by fundamental differences in the language, institutions, habits, and customs that distinguished the peoples of southern and eastern Europe from the original sources of immigration. Between 1880 and 1890, for example, 75.6 percent of all immigrants into the United States came from Great Britain, Germany, Ireland, Norway, Sweden, Denmark, and Canada. By 1901 this proportion had shrunk to 21.3 percent, while the percentage from Austria-Hungary, Italy, Russia, and Poland had increased from 17.6 percent of the total to 68.5 percent. Strangers in a strange land, subject frequently to exploitation at the hands of unscrupulous employers and employing agents, living under slum conditions, these people nevertheless strove in large proportions to provide their children with the open sesame to success in America, the advantages of a free education.

Not only were new developments in technology absorbing large proportions of the population, but change was invading the home and undermining the traditional family life through the employment of women and children. In 1900, 18.2 percent of all children between the ages of ten and fifteen were engaged in gainful occupations, and of the proportion of working children, one-sixth, or 17.2 percent, were under twelve years old.

Moreover, according to the census of 1910, 70 percent of all girls between the ages of ten and fifteen who were engaged in gainful occupations were so engaged outside the home.

These conditions weighed heavily upon the conscience of many Americans, and, eventually, laws were passed with an eye to improving both the working and living conditions of adults and, in the case of children, limiting the hours of labor and encouraging attendance at school. Compulsory school attendance laws, however, had the effect of rendering more complex the task of the educator. Into the schools there now flocked large numbers of young people of a type that had previously received little or no education, thus rendering obvious the need for fundamental revisions in curriculum content and new and more skillful methods of instruction.

These growing pains were manifest on all levels of public education, but the contrast between programs of education keyed, on the one hand, to the demands of the "inner nature" of the young and, on the other, to the immediate demands of personal, social, and economic adjustment were most obvious in the upper years of the traditional elementary school and in the newly organized junior high school. Here, genetic psychology was emphasizing the dynamic and instinctive potentialities of the young person, with the clear implication that nature was to be followed. But life outside the school, in home and community, in business and industry, emphasized the importance of "adjustment," the acquisition of those specific items of information, the habits, skills, emotions, and dispositions relevant to the "demands" of society. Confronted with this necessity of choice, educators turned to a psychology of control as formulated first by the Herbartians and, later, by Edward L. Thorndike and the behaviorists.

HERBART (1776-1841) AND THE HERBARTIANS

Important as was Pestalozzi's influence upon classroom teaching, it is probably to the Herbartians that chief credit should be given for professionalizing instruction. By 1890, as we have indicated, conditions were ripe for educational reform. And there was no lack of candidates for leadership in the reorganization of the curriculum, methods of teaching, and the administrative structure of the school. As we have seen, William T. Harris, G. Stanley Hall, Charles W. Eliot, and others were directing the attention of both laymen and the teaching profession to the task. Conspicuous amongst those who were to exercise a determining influence for some decades to come were Charles De Garmo, Frank McMurry, Charles McMurry, William C. Bagley, and John Dewey. A number of these men had studied in Germany and had become ardent disciples of Johann Herbart. All were profoundly impressed with the latter's psychology and its applications to education, even when, as with John Dewey, this served more as a foil than a guide for their own thinking. In 1892 they joined with others in the formation of the National Herbart Society, an organization that served both as a medium for the promotion of Herbartian theory and a general stimulus for the scientific study of education. (This society still functions as The National Society for the Study of Education.)

The opening words of Herbart's *Aesthetic Revelation of the World as the Chief Work of Education* run as follows: "The one and the whole work of education may be summed up in the concept—morality." "Virtue," or the development of character, was thus for Herbart the final aim of education.

But how can the attainment of virtue be assured? Herbart's answer was simple. Determine the content of interest. "The child enters the world," he wrote in *The General Principles of the Science of Education* (1806), "without a will of its own, and is therefore incapable of any moral relation. Consequently the parents (partly spontaneously, partly agreeably to the demand of society) can make themselves master of it as of a chattel."

Herbart agreed with Locke in denying the existence of innate faculties. He went farther in that he denied as well the existence of the mind as a substance. The soul, he insisted, is originally a *tabula rasa* without any form of life or "presentation." In it there are neither primitive ideas nor any predisposition to form them. "All ideas without exception are a product of time and experience." Indeed, the only form of mind he would grant was that of a logical entity with which to explain the beginnings of experience.

The soul (as this logical entity) seeks to preserve its existence. Hence, when acted upon through the nervous system, it responds either by attraction, repulsion, or indifference to "presentations." Sensations thus received and reacted to in one of these three ways respond in similar ways to subsequent "presentations," and thus, in accordance with the "laws" of association, a self is created. What men commonly term the "mind" is nothing other than the ordering, organizing, and reorganizing of experiences encountered since birth. As John Dewey remarked, "The 'furniture' of the mind," on this view, "is the mind. Mind is wholly a matter of content." [11]

Ideas that combine, that is, experiences that become organized in such a way as to reach out actively toward others of their kind, constitute interests. What men commonly call the "mind" is, in fact, merely a collective noun, used more or less as the term "woods" is used to designate a group of trees. The same is true of the terms for the faculties of memory, reason, will, and the like. These are names used to describe ways in which ideas function and are related. We have not a faculty of memory, but specific memories; not a reason, but instances of reasoning; not a faculty of will, but individual volitions. Accordingly, we find the Herbartians, in common with William James, Edward L. Thorndike, and others, subjecting the notions of "mind," its "faculties," and instincts to critical study and investigation, but, more radical than the latter, concluding, to their own satisfaction, that the child begins experience with nothing other than what his environment provides.

Since, according to this view, the success of parent and teacher in forming the character of children turns upon both the content and the form of experience (the *way* in which the new is related to the old as well as the nature of the new), the scientific study of children's minds became all-important in education; as important, indeed, as it was for G. Stanley Hall and his fellow investigators, although from quite different assumptions as to the origin and the meaning of what might be found.

Under the influence of the Herbartians, the attention of educators thus centered upon the significance of children's interests in the selection of subject matter and methods of instruction. Interests, as the Herbartians envisaged them, are ideas that reach out for other ideas or experiences. Since for them, also, there are no faculties, no feelings, or volitions separate and apart from an idea, an interest is an idea with at least two aspects: a core of content and an emotional or volitional aspect. Hence, it also follows that mere information is not enough. Knowledge must encourage the pursuit of further knowledge and, ideally, eventuate in virtuous action.

What this involves for the teacher was well stated by Charles De Garmo in his *Essentials of Method* (1889):

[11] John Dewey, *Democracy and Education* (New York: The Macmillan Co., 1916), pp. 81-82.

His primary function is to impart knowledge in such a way that it can be most rapidly, securely, and profitably assimilated, and this is the problem of concrete apperception. . . . He must know something of the child's previous knowledge and interests in order to utilize them; he must select his materials of instruction with respect to ultimate purposes and the pupil's comprehending powers; he must arrange the subject-matter, not only with respect to the pupil's acquired experience, but also with respect to that which he is going to acquire, i.e., the studies must be brought into the best coordinate relation to one another, and he must adapt his teaching processes so as to secure the quickest apprehension and the longest retention of the matter taught. All this has to do with the acquisition of new experience upon the basis of that already acquired.

This conscientious attempt to determine the substance and form of children's minds directed attention not only to the subjects of most worth (the content of the curriculum) but to the manner in which subjects might be related and correlated to advantage. Further, attention was directed not merely to determining the most effective methods of presenting material to young minds but, eventually, to improving all phases of the learning process—assignment, study, and recitation.

Thus far we have used the terms "ideas," "interests," and "experiences" more or less interchangeably. This in no way does violence to Herbart who conceived the mental life of the individual as evolving through the various processes of association from simple "presentations" of sense-perception to the more complex generalizations, concepts, and judgments. It should be observed, however, that this conception is possible only by ascribing a threefold nature to ideas: (1) In the beginning they are the *reactions* of a logical entity, the soul, to physiological occasions. (2) They become reactions which attract, repel, and associate in various ways (according to the "laws" of association) with other "reactions" and are thus *psychological entities* in their own right (nouns, not verbs). (3) As interests, feelings, volitions, and the like, in relation to objects and events in the external world, they are *relationships*. That is to say, "ideas" are at once reactions, entities, and relationships out of which one forms his mental life and creates his character!

HERBARTIAN INFLUENCE UPON CURRICULUM AND METHOD

Despite their differences with respect to the origins of experience (the strict Herbartians repudiating the theory of inherited characteristics and instincts) there was much in common between G. Stanley Hall and his followers and the Herbartians. Both groups conceived of education as primarily concerned with character formation, that is, with the child's emotional and volitional nature as well as his intellect. Both emphasized the supreme importance of history, literature, and the arts in giving form to emotion and disposition and thus contributed to the enrichment of the curriculum in elementary and secondary education. Some, however, as Francis W. Parker, emphasized science as of equal importance in the "revelation" of reality.

Impressed as they were with *method,* with the form as well as the substance of ideas, the Herbartians were not content to keep subjects in watertight compartments. Soon, therefore, "correlation" as an objective in teaching loomed large in educational discussions of the day.

"Virtue," we have said, was for Herbart the final aim of education. As a means for realizing this end he stressed the significance of interest and appreciation. Had pedagogues taken these doctrines seriously in their applications to individual children, they would have been impressed with the significance of individual differences in pupils' backgrounds and interests and the consequent necessity of modifying traditional group instruction. This was done eventually, with the introduction of "supervised study," schemes for "individual instruction," and other novel devices designed to encourage young people to progress at their own rates and thus to offset some of the disadvantages of lockstep instruction in groups.

The first effect of the Herbartian movement, however, was to accentuate the importance of the teacher's direction of children's learning in order to mould performances in accordance with the assumed patterns of "thought processes." Thus Herbart's description of the way the mind works in acquiring new material and in organizing a subject as a whole was converted into a method of instruction that required pupils to move in unison through five stages: (1) Preparation, (2) Presentation (lecture, textbook, and the like), (3) Comparison and Abstraction (including questions and answers, discussions leading to generalizations), (4) Generalization, and

(5) Application (which, like Presentation, might be direct or indirect and consequently somewhat elastic in method and consumption of time). At first, ideally, these five steps were to be completed in one day. With the later development of the project method of teaching and the introduction of larger units of study, however, these five steps often occupied weeks of classroom work.

The Morrison Plan, for example, developed at the Laboratory School of the University of Chicago in the late 1920's and early 1930's abandoned the daily recitation in favor of units of work that might consume weeks in effecting the proper "adaptations" in skills and attitudes and eventual "mastery" of subject matter. The Plan involved five different types of instruction, the most influential being the "science type" of unit (in no way confined, however, to science materials). This science type consisted of (1) *exploration* on the part of the instructor in order to determine through question and answer, discussion or pretest, the students' readiness for the subject; (2) the *presentation* of what lay ahead, frequently in the form of lecture; (3) the *assimilation period,* in which students worked individually in mastering common materials, with special provision for individual differences in rate of work, interests, and the like; (4) *organization,* in which each individual summed up in writing what he had learned and demonstrated by passing a comprehensive test that he had acquired the proper understanding and adaptation; and, finally, (5) the *recitation,* consisting of an oral presentation by members of the class, group discussions, "floor talks," "written recitation," and the like, all with a view to demonstrating that the learning anticipated by the instructor had actually taken place. With minor variations this plan is still widely followed in unit methods of instruction in secondary schools.[12]

TWO TRENDS IN HERBARTIANISM

From this brief summary of Herbartian psychology and its influence upon curriculum and method, it is clear that it contributed to two contradictory lines of development. Interests, in the hands of the schoolmaster, became the end points of his efforts. As he saw it, upon him rested the responsibility of moulding children's minds, of determining for them the ideas that were to move them. And this was a natural assumption, if

12 For an excellent discussion of the evolution of teaching procedures, see Harold B. Alberty and Elsie J. Alberty, *Reorganizing the High School Curriculum* (New York: The Macmillan Co., 1962), Chapter 9, on "The Modern Concept of Unit Teaching in Its Historical Setting."

one believed with Herbart that "virtue," or character formation, is the "one task, and the whole task of education" and "all ideas without exception are the product of time and experience." On the other hand, once interests became central in education, it was inevitable that their original and dynamic character should receive attention, as, indeed, was already the case with G. Stanley Hall and the geneticists in psychology. Skillful teaching, on this second view, involved identifying the interests of children and providing ways and means for their worthy expression and development. This endeavor eventually transformed many a teacher-centered institution into a child-centered school.[13]

The Herbartian emphasis upon teaching method likewise stimulated two quite opposite trends in teaching procedure: (1) the development of the lockstep method of group instruction, such as the Herbartian "steps" referred to above; and (2) experiments with individual instruction—the Winnetka, Dalton, Miller, and Morrison and other plans. Some of these, such as the Winnetka Plan, organized instruction almost exclusively with an eye to individual differences in rate of learning. Others attempted to combine individual and group instruction in order to provide for both social and individual development.

Finally, to the Herbartians should go major credit for directing attention to the way in which children learn, to the influences that operate upon them in mastering assignments prior to the "recitation." Thus did they enlarge the function of the teacher to include the direction of the learning process as well as that of a hearer of "lessons," a function sociological in its application as well as psychological in its concerns. For example, the Supervised Study Movement in the first quarter of the twentieth century had in mind factors such as the necessity of offsetting unfortunate home conditions under which young children are often required to study, their confused memories of assignments made, and the greater efficiency that would result were studying done in school under the eye of the teacher and immediately following the "assignment" period. Indeed, supervised study received the enthusiastic support of the lay public as well as professional educators, as evidenced by the following incident published in the *Ladies' Home Journal* (January, 1913) under the title "The Widow Who Was Dead Right."

[13] Out of the debates respecting the nature and place of interest in education came John Dewey's monograph on *Interest as Related to Will* in 1895, later expanded into the educational classic, *Interest and Effort in Education* (Boston: Houghton Mifflin Co., 1913).

A widow wrote the superintendent of schools as follows: "I have four little girls attending your schools. I am up at five o'clock in the morning to get them off to school and to get myself off to work. It is six o'clock in the evening when I reach home again, pretty well worn out, and after we have had dinner and have tidied up the house a bit it is eight o'clock. Then, tired as I am, I sit down and teach the little girls the lessons your teacher will have them say over on the following day. Now, if it is all the same to you, it would be a great help and favor to me if you will have your teachers teach the lessons during the day, and then all I would have to do at night would be to hear them say them over."

In sum, it may be said of the Herbartians that they attempted with considerable success to professionalize education and to make of teaching a science. At the same time, beginning, as they did, with a concern for children's interests as a guide for educators, they ended with catalogs of ideas, skills and adjustments, selected emotional and social aspects of life that children were expected to incorporate in their natures. They began with a study of the details of the learning process, an inquiry into the origins and operations of experience. They ended with stereotyped methods, a Procrustean bed of educational procedure. They began with an emphasis upon the dynamic life of the learner and ended with an elaborate plan of educational control. The voice was the voice of Jacob, but the hands were the hands of Esau!

SUGGESTED READING

Alberty, Harold B., and Alberty, Elsie J., *Reorganizing the High School Curriculum* (New York: The Macmillan Co., 3rd ed., 1962), Chapter 9.

Bode, Boyd H., *Conflicting Psychologies of Learning* (Boston: D. C. Heath & Co., 1929), Chapter VII.

Curti, Merle, *The Social Ideas of American Educators* (New York: Charles Scribner's Sons, 1935), Chapter XII. Available also in paperback: Littlefield, Adams & Co., Paterson, N.J., 1960.

Hall, G. Stanley, "The Ideal School," in National Education Association, *Proceedings and Addresses* (Washington, D.C.: the Association, 1901), pp. 474-488.

————, *Life and Confessions of a Psychologist* (New York: D. Appleton & Co., 1923).

Thayer, V. T., *The Passing of the Recitation* (Boston: D. C. Heath & Co., 1928), Chapter V.

PART III

CONFLICTING CONCEPTIONS OF EDUCATION IN THE TWENTIETH CENTURY

CHAPTER 10
EDUCATION AS ADJUSTMENT:
EDWARD L. THORNDIKE
AND THE PSYCHOLOGY
OF BEHAVIORISM

THE contributions of Edward L. Thorndike (1874-1949) to psychology and education were monumental. While properly known as the father of educational measurements, he began his career by subjecting to critical examination and laboratory experiment the most common assumptions in the educational psychology of the late nineteenth and early twentieth centuries, e.g., the concept of general faculties, the concept of formal discipline, the theory of instincts and its corollaries, the recapitulation theory, and the doctrine of catharsis.

So successful was he in his attack upon the concept of faculties of the mind and the allied doctrine of formal discipline that he severely weakened their influence upon the curriculum and teaching method for well over a generation. And he was similarly successful in attacking the psychology of instincts. By insisting that instincts be defined in terms of innate responses of a specific character to specific elements in the stimulating situation, Thorndike reduced drastically the number accepted by psychologists.[1] This insistence upon definiteness was also a decisive factor in undermining the recapitulation theory and its corollary, the catharsis doctrine, in education and child guidance.

[1] These accomplishments did not prevent Thorndike from retaining a large number of original tendencies "concerned with food-getting, habitation, fear, fighting, and anger," which later psychologists tended to question in whole or in part. These included, for example, "acquisition and possession," "collecting and hoarding," "fighting," "motherly behavior," "gregariousness," "rivalry," "jealousy," and others.

THE S→R BOND CONCEPT AND ITS IMPLICATIONS

But Thorndike's procedure also involved an assumption! His assumption was that behavior in animals and men can be explained in terms of what he termed S → R bonds. That is to say, for what had previously been vague and general descriptions of essentially occult forces Thorndike now attempted to substitute an inventory of specific "responses" *natively connected* with specific "situations" in the environment. In a widely studied work, he wrote:

> Any man possesses at the very start of his life, that is, at the very moment when the ovum and spermatozoon which are to produce him have united—*numerous well-defined tendencies to future behavior*. Between the situations which he will meet, and the responses which he will make to them, *pre-formed bonds* exist. It is already determined by the constitution of these two germs, that under certain circumstances *he will see and hear and feel and act in certain ways*. His intellect and morals, as well as his bodily organs and movements, are in part the consequences of the nature of the embryo in the first moment of his life. What a man is and does throughout life is a result of whatever constitution he has at the start and of all the forces that act upon it before and after birth.[2]

The central facts in educational psychology for Thorndike were thus S → R bonds. Inherited tendencies, such as reflexes and instincts, and learned acts, such as those of skill or complicated acts of thought, were explained and reduced to situations (S) and responses (R) and the *connections* that unite these situations and responses. The presence or absence of inherited connections between potential responses to potential situations was said to determine the character of an individual and to set the limits of his education!

[2] Edward L. Thorndike, *Educational Psychology, Briefer Course* (New York: Teachers College, Columbia University, 1917), p. 3. Italicized terms are mine. I refer to this early volume of Thorndike's for the reason that it was written during the period of his most potent influence upon American education. By virtue of the large number of students who studied under him, Thorndike's psychology became for many years virtually the official psychology in schools of education. Not until after 1920 were his views seriously challenged in educational circles. It is interesting to observe, for example, the manner in which Kilpatrick (who eventually repudiated the concept of S → R bonds) struggled manfully to use Thorndike's "laws of learning" as a vehicle for his more creative and organismic conception of the learning process. See William Heard Kilpatrick, *Foundations of Method* (New York: The Macmillan Co., 1925).

The real concerns of the educator were thus with S → R bonds. The original responses of the human being, commonly called instincts, were to be carefully noted and the situations provoking them patiently catalogued. Hence, as we shall observe later, the significance of intelligence tests loomed large as a means of determining in advance of a child's education (1) the potentialities and the limitations in his original makeup, and (2) the program of education best suited for him.

The importance of these original S → R bonds as starting points in learning Thorndike made clear in the following statement:

> The original connections may develop at various dates and may exist for only limited times; their waxing and waning may be sudden or gradual. They are the starting point for all education or other human control. The aim of education is to perpetuate some of them, to eliminate some, and to modify or redirect others. They are perpetuated by providing the stimuli adequate to arouse them and give them exercise, and by associating satisfaction with their action. They are eliminated by withholding these stimuli so that they abort through disuse, or by associating discomfort with their action. They are redirected by substituting, in the situation-connection-response series, another response instead of the undesirable original one; or by attaching the response to another situation in connection with which it works less or no harm, even positive good.[3]

The original situations to which the individual is natively responsive Thorndike designated original "satisfiers" and "annoyers." As such, however, they are composed both of situations within and outside the body. A catalog of these would contain the ultimate sources of values. "The original basis of the wants which so truly do and should rule the world is the original satisfyingness of some states of affairs and annoyingness of others. Out of such original satisfiers and annoyers grow all desires and aversions; and in such are found the first guides of learning."[4]

S→R BONDS AND THE LAWS OF LEARNING

When the character of an individual's original makeup is known in terms of situation-response units, the further problem in his education becomes that of manipulating these in accordance with the laws of learn-

3 Thorndike, op. cit., p. 3.
4 Ibid., p. 50.

ing. And the laws of learning are, in turn, no more than specific statements of the conditions under which "connections" are perpetuated, eliminated, modified, or redirected in accordance with the Principle of Readiness and the Laws of Exercise and Effect (Thorndike further subdivided these Laws into the "Law of Multiple Response to the Same External Situation," the "Law of Set or Attitudes," the "Law of Analogy," and the "Law of Associative Shifting").[5]

An illustration or two should render clear Thorndike's use of the S → R bond concept. For example, in discussing the instinct of fear, he made the point that we should not speak of this instinct in general terms, as psychologists were prone to do, but should define its character precisely. "Practically," he wrote, "it makes a great difference whether a man responds only with discomfort, palpitations, and the inner subjective fear, still shooting at the enemy, or also runs and hides. Theoretically, it makes a great difference whether the situations involved are regarded as producing indiscriminately a vague X, fear, which then may at random produce any assortment of its various 'expressions,' or are regarded as each producing, under the same conditions, an effect proper to it and to nothing but it." [6] Accordingly, we should describe the instinct of fear in terms of the specific situations which provoke the specific response "fear"; and there are as many "fears" as there are discrete responses and allied situations. "Fearful sounds rarely provoke turning the head away and covering the eyes, but fearful sights often do."

A similar insistence upon specific situation-response relationships characterized Thorndike's description of the learning process. We shall illustrate first with a simple case of learning and, second, with the acquisition of a concept.

The simplest case of animal learning that Thorndike used was that of a chick finding its way out of a maze. The maze is confusing because it furnishes the chick several different paths to follow, of which but one leads out of the maze. When it succeeds in getting out of the maze, however, the chick is rewarded by being with other chicks, by "eating, and being in its usual habitat." On the other hand, if it follows a blind alley, it "has the discomforts of thwarted effort." Learning is evidenced by following the path out, immediately after being placed in the maze. The situation for the chick is, "in essence, *Confining walls and absence of other*

[5] *Ibid.*, Chapters X, XI.
[6] *Ibid.*, p. 21.

chicks, food, and familiar surroundings." The responses consist of "running around, making loud sounds, and jumping at the walls." When the chick runs to the correct place it gets out. In the process of learning it reduces the number of useless movements and shortens the circuit between the situation and the successful response.

Thorndike therefore concluded that learning is a matter of "strengthening and weakening of bonds between a situation present to sense and responses in the nervous system, which issue then and there in movement." That is to say, the correct responses become fixed by exercise and the resulting satisfaction, while the unsuccessful responses are dulled or eliminated by virtue of the dissatisfaction which they engender. Since, however, the learning actually consists in no more than selecting for emphasis, certain responses which the chick makes out of its repertory of inherited situation-response connections, it may be viewed as habit formation. Nothing has really been added either to the situation or the response. Nothing has been created. Learning has merely resulted in a realignment of units of response with which the animal was originally endowed. Responses, such as jumping up or running around, have been subordinated or completely submerged, and the response of following the correct path directly upon being placed in the maze has assumed the role of major importance.

We now turn to a higher form of learning, to the development of concepts. Does learning of this character involve anything new, or is it essentially the same as learning for the chick?

In describing the subtler forms of analysis or learning, Thorndike explained how we secure an abstract idea, such as "fiveness." This, he pointed out, is accomplished in at least three ways. The first consists "in having the learner respond to the total situations containing the element in question with the attitude of piecemeal examination, and with attentiveness to one element after another." [7] By naming five boys, five girls, five pencils, and the like, and having the learner respond in such a way as to favor "the partial and predominant activity of 'how-many-ness' as far as may be," a bond is ultimately established between the element "fiveness" and the response to "fiveness" on the part of the learner. A second way in which a connection between the desired element in the situation and the response is effected, according to Thorndike, is by means of dissociation of varying concomitants. By associating a response of "five" to a variety of situations such as five pencils, five boys, and five girls, which differ in

[7] *Ibid.,* p. 159.

all respects except in the element "five," the element of "fiveness" in the situation finally becomes distinctly associated with the response. And, thirdly, "fiveness" may be learned by having a child respond to "situations which, pair by pair, present the element in a certain context and present that same context with the *opposite of the element in question,* or with something at least very unlike the element." [8] Thus a child being taught to respond to one-fifth of a pie, a cake, or the like will have the bond between situation and response brought out and strengthened by contrasting five pies, or five cakes, for example.

Observe that in this description of the ways in which the concept of "fiveness" is learned, nothing new has really been learned. Thorndike found the response of "fiveness" waiting in the nervous system for the proper element in the situation. As he wrote: "These means utilize the laws of connection-forming to disengage a response-element from gross total responses and attach it to some situation element." [9] Consequently, in the case of the acquisition of a concept as in the case of the chick's learning the correct exit from a maze, it is presupposed that every element learned is, strictly speaking, not learned. It is embodied in our first total reaction to a situation, and learning is merely a name for the fact that what hitherto have been implicit S → R connections are finally made explicit. All learning, for Thorndike, is habit formation. The simplest physical act and the most complicated and original thought process are classified under the same category.

This holds true even when it appears that "In human thought and action a situation often provokes responses which have not been bound to it by original tendencies, use, or satisfaction." [10] When acts of thought which seemingly involve novel data, association by similarity, and purposive behavior are carefully analyzed, we discover previously existing but subtle bonds between elements in the situation and the response. In the process of learning, connections between situations and responses may shift so that a response to one element may be transferred to another element and vice versa, but the laws of learning are confined to operations upon responses with which man is originally endowed and upon elements within situations to which he is originally sensitive. Within the

[8] *Ibid.,* p. 160.
[9] *Ibid.,* p. 161.
[10] *Ibid.,* p. 108.

range of original endowment the utmost variation is possible, but novelty is confined to confirming, establishing, or eliminating connections between what are originally inherited responses and elements in situations to which one is originally sensitive. From the inventory of inherited satisfiers and annoyers, then, according to Thorndike, come all ideas and preferences. "We trust to the laws of cerebral nature to present us spontaneously with the appropriate idea, and also *to prefer that idea to others.*" [11]

In reducing learning to habit formation, Thorndike seemed to ally himself in spirit, if not in theory, with Herbart and to reaffirm the dominating position of the teacher. It is true, of course, that Herbart denied the existence of instinctive tendencies. For Herbart the mind is originally a *tabula rasa;* for Thorndike inherited tendencies constitute the raw materials of education, and educational procedure must take into consideration their peculiar character. In each instance successful teaching turns upon a careful manipulation of the learner. Herbart would have the teacher determine the content of the child's mind, his apperceptive systems of ideas, as a basis for the presentation of new ideas; Thorndike, the child's working capital in the form of inherited and acquired S → R bonds. For each, education involves an external operation upon the child. Method, far more than the spontaneous activity of the learner, becomes the chief hope of the educator.

FROM WHENCE CAME S→R BONDS?

In discussing "Democracy and Human Nature," John Dewey pointed out "that the popular view of the constitution of human nature at any given time is a reflex of social movements which have either become institutionalized or else are showing themselves against opposing social odds and hence need intellectual and moral formulation to increase their power." [12] Thus Plato turned to the society of his day (a society composed of three classes—a laboring class, a citizen soldiery class, and a legislative class) in order to describe the constitution of human nature. This he found to be of a threefold nature—the base appetites, the generous-spirited impulses, and reason. Similarly, in the seventeenth and eighteenth centuries, when philosophers undertook to validate the principles

[11] *Ibid.,* p. 172.
[12] John Dewey, *Freedom and Culture* (New York: G. P. Putnam's Sons, 1939), Chapter V, p. 107.

of political democracy and economic individualism in opposition to an earlier organic conception of man and society, they did so by means of a psychology that insisted "all social phenomena are to be understood in terms of the mental operations of individuals, since society consists in the last analysis only of individual persons." Or, as John Stuart Mill put it, "The laws of the phenomena of society are and can be nothing but the laws of the actions and passions of human beings united in the social state."

Dewey's theory suggests that the nature of human nature is not easily determined—that even philosophers and scientists see through colored lenses. Consequently, when the scientist undertakes, as did Thorndike, to describe its character, he cannot isolate it entirely from the society in which it is embedded. Nor can he free himself from assumptions!

Take, for example, Thorndike's conception of $S \rightarrow R$ bonds. From whence did he derive them? Surely not from observed fact! No scientist has been privileged to observe under his microscope the specific original responses and situation-elements to which man is originally sensitive and that later become organized into a complicated language response. And none has detected the original units in the way of responses and situations that become associated in such a complicated and original thought pattern as Newton's conception of the Law of Gravitation. From whence, then, did Thorndike derive his theory?

Cole and Bruce offer one suggestion. They point to the similarity between Thorndike's concept of trial-and-error learning in the individual and the Darwinian concept of evolution through "the survival of the fittest." They write:

> Just as in nature there is a prodigality that produces myriad forms of life, some fit and others not adapted to survive, and then a ruthless weeding out of the unfit, so the learner produces a galaxy of random responses, most of which are beside the mark, only one being the chance "success."
>
> And, like nature, the learner seems blind, the selection process slow. But the steady pressure of biological needs, the satisfactions and tension reductions, cause the successful acts to "reproduce their kind." Let nature alone and the needed response will be discovered, and survive. Thus, while Darwin's contemporaries were preaching a laissez-faire economics, that in free competition the best systems

work themselves out, and while Darwin was glimpsing a similar order in nature, Thorndike came to a laissez-faire theory of learning.[13]

This similarity is suggestive as to the milieu from which Thorndike derived his concept of learning. Born in 1874, his formative years were spent in a period when Darwinism had at last become a decisive influence in the social as well as the natural sciences. Furthermore, as a student of William James, Thorndike might be expected to develop further the relations of psychology to physiology and biology.

Certain it is that in pulverizing human experience and limiting educational procedure to the manipulation of S → R bonds, Thorndike, as his predecessors in the child study movement, drew his inspiration from biology. Biologists had become absorbed with the processes of heredity and in seeking to explain the fact of inherited characteristics had hit upon the concept of unit characters. Specific physical characteristics in animals as well as plants were supposed to reside within the germ cell. The discovery of Mendelian laws, according to which *certain* characteristics of one generation, such as the color of the eyes, reappear in succeeding generations in ways that can be predicted by mathematical formulae, easily led to the assumption that this holds true of *all* characteristics. And from the assumption that all *physical* characteristics derive from determiners in the germ plasm, it was but one more step to assume this holds true as well of *psychological* traits. How heavily Thorndike leaned upon this biological position is apparent from our first quotation bearing upon preformed bonds (see p. 214).

Consider also the following statement by one of his disciples:

Life begins with the fertilization of the ovum, a microscopic but very complex cell. Contained in the germ cell are certain elements or "determiners" out of which the various bodily organs and functions develop. Certain determiners grow into certain sense organs, others become particular bones, others become teeth and so on. Even for the most minute traits, the color of the eyes, the shape of the lobe of the ear, a particular notch in a tooth, there exist determiners in the germ cell. Except for the occasional congenital dis-

[13] Lawrence E. Cole and William F. Bruce, *Educational Psychology* (Yonkers, N.Y.: World Book Co., 1950), p. 458.

turbance of the severe types mentioned, the differences among infants which appear at birth are *native* in the sense that they are the result of the unfolding, innate growth of determiners which exist in the germ cell from the beginning of life.[14]

It thus appears that what Thorndike assumed to be man's original equipment of responses to situations were the psychological correlates of what biologists termed "unit characters." And such a conception of human nature had implications for learning eagerly welcomed by many educators who were striving manfully to meet the novel problems of mass education in towns and cities of rapidly mounting enrollments.

SOME APPLICATIONS OF THORNDIKE'S PSYCHOLOGY

Mention was made in Chapter 9 of changes in American society that were giving rise to severe problems: heavy immigration of peoples from abroad whose language, customs, and ways of living were foreign to those encountered here; the steady drift of Americans of rural background to urban centers; and a rapid increase in child labor. As more and more children went to work, there was the attending threat that large numbers of the younger generation would attain adulthood and assume the responsibilities of citizens in a democracy untrained, even stunted in their development.

To meet this threat reformers had striven with considerable success to secure the passage of child labor laws and compulsory school attendance legislation. This success was speedily reflected in school enrollments. For example, a high school enrollment that in 1890 consisted of only 1.6 percent of the total elementary and secondary school population increased by 1926 to 15.2 percent of this population. The employed proportion of all youth between the ages of ten and fifteen fell from 18.4 percent in 1910 to 8.5 percent in 1920. Conspicuous also was the rapidity with which enrollments were increasing above as well as within the age of compulsory school attendance. In 1918, for instance, the secondary school enrolled 28.29 percent of the population between the ages of fifteen and eighteen. By 1926 this proportion had grown to 53.12 percent.

These developments confronted school systems with the baffling prob-

---

[14] Arthur I. Gates, *Psychology for Students of Education* (New York: The Macmillan Co., 1923), p. 111.

lem of finding teachers trained and competent to educate a type of young people for whom little or no education had previously been available. The conventional curriculum was inadequate in that, at best, it met the needs of the academically minded for an academic education only and failed to equip young people of all types of mind to meet the demands of life other than academic. New subjects as well as new criteria for the selection of material within the traditional subjects seemed essential. Thus "civics," which had previously concerned itself with forms of government and matters exclusively political, was transformed into "community civics" as one means of acquainting young people with the agencies, institutions, and problems of the local community as well as state and nation. In the elementary school, particularly, the need for health education seemed obvious as one means of correcting the neglects and the mistakes of parents. Still again, as a result of the exodus of women from the home and the early employment of girls outside the home, home economics (chiefly cooking and sewing) gained entrance into the curriculum. For both boys and girls, urgent calls from business and industry for "hands" suggested modifications of academic subjects and the introduction of vocational and prevocational courses that would fit them for economic activity.

But what were the needs of young people in a population of diverse abilities and plural backgrounds? To many seeking an answer to this question, Thorndike's psychology came as manna from heaven. For one thing, it encouraged the use and development of intelligence tests with which to identify different levels of native ability in children in advance of their education and thus determine the probable limits of their schooling. For a time, it looked as though these tests would serve as much to raise roadblocks to the progress of the "dull" as to open roads of opportunity for the "able." There were, for example, school systems in which alert supervisors undertook to administer intelligence tests to children in the primary grades with a view to their assignment in groups according to "native intelligence," a procedure which, it was assumed, would render teaching more efficient. Fortunately, however, confidence in the tests as adequate indicators of "raw brain power" eventually weakened, and they came to be used instead as instruments with which to gauge a young person's present working capital, without dogmatic inference as to its original source.

SPECIFIC OBJECTIVES AND THE CURRICULUM

The early years of the twentieth century were conspicuous in the applications of science to all phases of business and industry. It was applied not merely to the invention of new products and processes but to the details of organization and management designed to promote economy and efficiency. Experts trained in "scientific management" studied carefully the performances of workers on the job with results so fruitful in economy and efficiency that many came to see in "job analysis" possibilities of application not only to vocational education but to the reform of other aspects of education as well. All that was needed, it seemed, was to identify the specific outcomes to which a school subject should lead and to provide for these outcomes by insuring that pupils engage in the activities certain to eventuate in the proper habits and skills, information, attitudes, ideals, and the like.

The new emphasis in the selection and organization of subject matter received definite formulation in 1918 with the report of the National Commission on the Reorganization of Secondary Education. This Commission stated the areas of concern, or the functions of the secondary school, in the form of Cardinal Principles. Its preliminary statement read: "In order to determine the main objectives that should guide education in a democracy, it is necessary to analyze the activities of the individual. Normally he is a member of a family, of a vocational group, and of various civic groups, and by virtue of these relationships he is called upon to engage in activities that enrich family life, to render important vocational services to his fellows, and to promote the common welfare."

Then followed the well-known principles that were to guide schoolmen in the reorganization of subjects and curricula: health, command of fundamental processes, worthy home membership, vocation, citizenship, worthy use of leisure, and ethical character. The insistence of the Commission upon organizing secondary education with reference to the needs of actual living, together with the assumption that learning is a matter of cementing specific responses to the appropriate specific stimuli, or situations, encouraged efforts to organize the curriculum in terms of "scientifically determined specific objectives."

Consider the task that confronted educators! All life was to be analyzed into its simple components; traits of mind and character that each child should acquire were to be identified and classified; and the ways and means were to be devised for inducing him to make these traits his own! Nevertheless, as one industrious worker put it,

> The central theory is simple. Human life, however varied, consists in the performance of specific activities. Education that prepares for life is one that prepares definitely and adequately for these specific activities.... This requires only that one go out into the world of affairs and discover the particulars of which these affairs consist. These will show the abilities, attitudes, habits, appreciations, and forms of knowledge that men need. These will be the objectives of the curriculum. They will be numerous, definite, and particularized. The curriculum will then be that series of experiences which children and youth must have by way of attaining those objectives.[15]

Insistence upon definiteness and specificity was not without beneficial results. The prescientific era in education had encouraged the accumulation of much useless subject matter and questionable methods. The new emphasis was practical. Each item of subject matter was required to present its credentials before securing employment. Directly or indirectly each was required to further a specific item of knowledge or trait of character which clearly pointed the way toward effective adult life.

This practical approach was of benefit alike to the young and inexperienced teacher in a crowded schoolroom and to the children who were taught under these unfavorable conditions. Many of the latter were either foreign-born or the offspring of foreign-born. An analysis of their requirements in the way of facts, skills, personal habits, and social outlooks gave relevance to school activities that might otherwise have been lacking. The traditional gap between school and community was partially bridged.

On the other hand, the applications of "science" were often superficial and of limited value. One school system, for example, undertook to organize its own course of study in history. Its method was to release a number of its teachers from their classroom duties and assign them to the task of searching through contemporary magazines for references to historical figures and events in order to determine quantitatively the relative value of the items of information pupils were to digest. In another community the appropriate material for a course in physics was identified by asking the parents of pupils what applications of the facts and prin-

15 Franklin Bobbitt, *The Curriculum* (Boston: Houghton Mifflin Co., 1918), p. 42.

ciples of physics they had made in their daily lives. Whatever the method followed, the general tendency was to emphasize subject matter that pertained to adult life rather than to young people growing up and to accept the status quo, the existing state of adult culture, as the criterion for deciding what the future adult should know and do.

These applications of science in education were not limited to the elementary or secondary schools on the one hand or to trade and vocational education on the other. They were applied as well to the junior college years when it became evident in the 1920's and 1930's that the junior college, as a terminal institution, was designed to serve large numbers of students who were beginning to engulf the senior high school and to encroach upon the lower levels of college and professional school. To meet these new demands upon education, terminal courses were devised for the junior college period much as they had originated earlier in the century in the junior high school. These courses operated in large measure on the assumption that vocational preparation should be of a specific character and lead to the acquisition of specific skills and operations.

A similar point of view influenced the organization of courses in "general education" in the first two years of college and the lower divisions of universities. One example was the survey course in the first year of college. This evolved out of a desire to read unity and consistency of pattern into the student's education, to give him an overview of representative fields of knowledge or an equally complete introduction to the facts and principles and activities within a functional area of living. As an introduction to fields of knowledge, this movement probably reached its culminating point at Colgate University, where students in their freshman year were required to devote two-thirds of their time to five survey courses: surveys of the physical sciences, the biological sciences, the social sciences, the fine arts, and philosophy and religion. President Cullen wrote of these courses: "Colgate is aware that it did not invent the survey course, but it believes it is the first to carry the idea to its logical conclusion, and that its five courses spreading over the whole domain of human knowledge, and required of all freshmen, constitute a departure in college education." [16]

[16] Quoted from a Survey by the American Association of University Women, in *Thirty-first Yearbook of the National Society for the Study of Education* (Bloomington, Ill.: Public School Publishing Co., 1932), Part II, pp. 46-47.

A second type of survey course undertook to introduce students to "functional areas of living." Thus Stephens College, a woman's college in Missouri, under the direction of W. W. Charters, attempted to determine the activities in which women actually engage and the problems and the needs they encounter in the course of their daily lives. These returns were classified into seven areas of activities and problems, and courses were designed to enable the students of Stephens to acquire the principles and facts and skills essential for functioning adequately as women.

Goucher College engaged in a similar attempt to make education functional. Taking its cue from the procedure of the United States Department of State in establishing standards of eligibility for departmental posts by analyzing "records of usage" which reveal the duties actually performed by the office in question, the college attempted to determine "what qualifications, preparation, and training would be useful to a Goucher graduate in living her life." Eight objectives of general education were formulated which the college believed to relate directly to the life activities of women.[17]

Mention has been made of the rapid increase in secondary school enrollments during the first quarter of the century. The inundation of the secondary school was met first by the introduction of vocational courses, on the assumption that the primary purpose of the school was twofold— to train young people for their future occupations and to provide general education of a college preparatory character. By the 1940's many educators had become convinced that these two functions of the school neglected the needs of some 60 percent of the secondary school population. The reason lay in the decreasing need for any special type of preparation for many jobs in the world of work. Indeed, in many instances, business and industry preferred to train young people on the job, asking only that the schools provide them first with a good general education. Following a study by the Vocational Education Division of the United States Office of Education, a national conference was held in Washington in May, 1945, and the following resolution was adopted:

It is the belief of this conference that, with the aid of this report in final form, the vocational school of a community will be able better

[17] For a discussion of experiments in curriculum organization on the college level as well as in elementary and secondary education during the period under review, see the *Twenty-sixth Yearbook* and the *Thirty-first Yearbook of the National Society for the Study of Education.*

to prepare 20 per cent of the youth of secondary school age for entrance upon desirable skilled occupations; and that the high school will continue to prepare another 20 per cent for entrance to college. We do not believe that the remaining 60 per cent of our youth of secondary school age will receive the life adjustment training they need and to which they are entitled as American citizens—unless and until the administration of public education with the assistance of the vocational education leaders formulate a similar program for this group.[18]

In 1946 five regional conferences, made up of school superintendents, secondary school principals, state directors and supervisors of vocational education, and representatives of state departments of education and teachers colleges, were held under the auspices of the United States Office of Education to consider the educational needs of this 60 percent. It was agreed at these conferences that secondary education was failing to provide adequately and properly for a major proportion of young people of secondary school age and that "functional experiences in the areas of practical arts, home and family life, health and physical fitness, and civic competence" were essential for this group. Moreover, it was assumed, as one of the leaders of this movement for life adjustment education later wrote, that "it is a hopeless task to subject those of below-average and even average intelligence to the same pattern of studies the brighter ones can profitably pursue." [19]

This diagnosis of the nature of that large segment of the secondary school population which was neither college-bound nor qualified for admission to the run-of-mine vocational class led to earnest efforts throughout the country to organize new courses of a "life adjustment" character and to the revision of traditional subjects from a similar point of view. Thus came into being the life adjustment education movement out of which critics of American schools in the 1950's were to make a national issue. To these criticisms of public education and education for life adjustment we shall return later.

[18] United States Office of Education, *Life Adjustment Education for Every Youth,* Bulletin 1951, No. 22 (Washington, D.C.: U.S. Office of Education, Federal Security Agency, n.d.), p. 15.
[19] Carl G. Franzen, "What Has Happened to Life Adjustment Education?" *Phi Delta Kappan,* March, 1960, p. 248.

METHODS OF TEACHING ALSO REFLECT
THE S→R BONDS THEORY

The Herbartian emphasis upon methods of learning, as we have seen, led school systems to experiment with ways and means of improving instruction. To it we gave credit for the supervised study movement, attention to individual differences in interests and in pupils' rates of learning, and widely publicized plans or methods of teaching such as the Winnetka, Dalton, and Morrison plans. Strict accuracy requires a division of credit between the Herbartians and the followers of Thorndike in the development of methods of teaching that emphasized the careful identification of the end results (ideas for the Herbartians, habits for the followers of Thorndike) and meticulous direction of the learning process. Since, for Thorndike, all learning was a matter of habit formation, the problem of instruction for the teacher involved analyzing carefully the subject matter to be taught into the steps pupils were to take in translating the information, skills, habits, dispositions, and the like into fixed S → R bonds.

As Morton's *Teaching Arithmetic in the Primary Grades* (1927) informed teachers who might use it, "Teaching the fundamental facts of arithmetic is a habit-forming process. What we desire to do is to form bonds in the child's nervous system between stimuli and responses."

In Winnetka, Illinois, for example, elementary school subjects were organized in such a way that each child might proceed at his own rate. Subjects confronted children in the form of "goals" and were planned in such a way that when one goal, or a portion of a goal, was completed the pupil took a self-administered test in order to determine whether he was ready to submit to the teacher's examination, the final criterion for determining fitness for the next task.

The Winnetka Plan of individual instruction was more than a method of teaching, since it involved as well criteria for the selection and organization of subject matter. It was significant also in calling attention to the wide range of abilities among school children with respect to rates of learning and the need to adapt instruction to individual differences. Its limitations were twofold: (1) the individual differences provided for were differences in rate of learning only; and (2) in its emphasis upon mastery of facts and skills (the "essentials" in each subject "scientifically" determined), it tended to separate knowledge and techniques from attitudes, ideals, and appreciation. It assumed, for example, that it is more essential to know the number combinations than to possess the right attitude toward mathematics and that historical facts quantitatively determined are more necessary for the child to master than the development of the disposition to solve social problems reflectively. Finally, in its attempt to prepare children for the adult world, it separated the "hard-work subjects" of the morning (studied individually and corresponding to the working day of the adult) from the social and group activities of the afternoon (analogous to the leisure time and social life of the adult).

More widely adopted in this country and abroad than the Winnetka Plan, in part because it involved less radical deviation from traditional subject matter and method, was the Dalton Plan. It differed from the Winnetka Plan in that its curriculum was less severely compartmentalized and, consequently, made less distinction between mastery of common essentials in the form of knowledge and skills, apart from other desirable learning products. Further, while it allowed each child to progress at his own rate, it required him to budget his time (as adults must learn to do!) in order to complete the jobs required each month in all of his subjects. For example, he was not privileged to begin the second month's assignment in one subject until he had finished the first month's assignment in all subjects.[20] In both plans, however, emphasis was placed upon the mastery of one step before undertaking the next, thus avoiding the evils of partial learning. Grades were thus unnecessary.

This same conscientious attention to detail and to habit formation in child rearing was extended to parent education. For example, Gary Cleveland Myers advised parents: "Be always present when the child is exposed to the particular dangerous thing you have selected to work upon. Let him always have the opportunity to touch it. Then always give him pain immediately. You are not interested in keeping the child from that dangerous thing just this time. . . . But you are interested in creating in his nervous system a permanent association with the forbidden act or thing."[21]

[20] For contemporary descriptions of these two plans, as well as other experiments in curriculum organization and teaching methods, see *Twenty-fourth Yearbook of the National Society for the Study of Education* (Bloomington, Ill.: Public School Publishing Co., 1925), Part II. Also, for a contemporary appraisal of their contributions and limitations, see V. T. Thayer, *The Passing of the Recitation* (Boston: D. C. Heath & Co., 1928), Chapters XIII, XIV.

[21] Gary Cleveland Myers, "Babyhood," *Child Study Magazine*, September, 1930, p. 18.

IDEALS, TOO, ARE REDUCIBLE TO SPECIFICS!

For a time, the stimulus-response theory of learning gave assurance of simplifying the task of moral education and the teaching of life's ideals. As one authority put it, in writing on the teaching of ideals, "Conduct and behavior are specific.... One does not act honestly in general; he performs a thousand specific acts of honesty. He tells the truth about the sharpened tool he ruined, about the dime lost, or about the window he broke in play. By an accumulation and integration of these thousand acts, he becomes an honest person." [22] That is to say, ideals, like faculties of the mind, are under suspicion, and he who would develop character in young people must deal in specifics. He must analyze the virtues he would have children acquire into the specific traits of which these virtues are composed, and then select the situations best calculated to fuse the two! To quote our authority again:

> "Honor thy father and thy mother ..." is an easy Commandment to memorize, but often the glibbest parrot in a church school has not the faintest idea of how to put the principle into practice. Children have to be taught these trait actions one by one. Only in a series can pupils learn to apply a principle. The individual actions must be patiently taught them. At one time they must learn to honor their father and mother by saying: "Yes, father"; at another time by placing the mother's chair; or at still a third time by offering the father the favorite seat. No mere knowledge of the general rule or deep desire to follow the ideal is a substitute for this detailed training in specific forms of action.[23]

The author of this injunction recognized that specific acts prompted by emotion and thought tend to come to a head eventually in a principle or an ideal of behavior, which, in turn, may initiate and direct action. Less discerning students of conduct and moral education were less tolerant of the function of ideals and principles in teaching. Indeed, they viewed the latter as useless verbal luggage, as mere abstract and collective nouns, serving a convenient purpose in discourse, perhaps, but lacking potency and reality apart from the particulars they designate. The real business of education centered upon developing in children the myriad of specific

[22] W. W. Charters, *The Teaching of Ideals* (New York: The Macmillan Co., 1927), p. 106.
[23] *Ibid.*, pp. 107-108.

responses essential to finding their way around in a world of discrete and specific events.

Finally, this psychology of learning carried an inherent appeal to superintendents of schools and supervisors charged with the grave responsibility of directing inadequately trained teachers in the art of teaching large class groups and measuring the results of their teaching. The steps required were clear and definite, at least in theory. Bring together in manageable form the relevant and pertinent facts, skills, and statements of abilities which children are to acquire and teachers to demonstrate in their work; provide teachers with suggestions for inculcating the requisite facts and skills; and then test from time to time the effectiveness with which both teacher and children have followed the plans thus formulated. Do this faithfully, and efficient results will follow.

THE TRANSITION TO BEHAVIORISM

We have spoken of Thorndike as the father of educational measurements. He should also be credited with laying the foundations of behavioristic psychology, a psychology that rejects introspection and introspective data—mind, conscious states, goals, purposes, and the like—and insists instead upon explaining learning and thinking in terms of what is "external and observable."

Thorndike, himself, did not directly deny mind and conscious states as such. He merely ignored earlier formulations by describing his concept of S → R bonds as "tendencies to behavior." "Connections," commonly thought of as "ideas," became for him "situation-response units," more complicated to be sure than simple reflex actions, but neural *responses* nevertheless. "Ideas" that lead to knowledge, "in the popular sense of the term," he pointed out in discussing analytic learning, are "situation-response bonds where one term, at least, is the inner condition in a man which we call an idea or judgment or the like." [24]

From this point it was but a step to a description of (1) *thinking* as a form of "verbal activity" operating in accordance with the rules of language or grammar and inductive and deductive logic, and (2) *all learning* as "the building, more or less permanently, of new associations between a response (already tied to one stimulus) and a new stimulus or between a response (untied) and a stimulus that has not been associated

[24] Thorndike, *op. cit.*, p. 141.

together before." Thus was achieved a description that involves no reference to "internal, unobservable, mental processes." [25]

In educational circles, at least, this transition from Thorndike to outright behaviorism involved a further reduction of instincts and rigid adherence to Thorndike's concept of inherited S → R bonds, with a corresponding faith in the plasticity and educability of man. For example, following his experimental work with infants in the Maternity Ward of Johns Hopkins Hospital in Baltimore and other locations, John B. Watson (1878-1958) announced to the world, "The behaviorists believe that there is nothing from within to develop. If you start with a healthy body, the right number of fingers and toes, and the few elementary movements that are present at birth, you do not need anything else in the way of raw material to make a man, be that man a genius, a cultured gentleman, a rowdy, or a thug." [26]

The above quotation was written for laymen, particularly parents, upon whom Watson wished to impress that (1) all learning is habit formation, and (2) environment rather than heredity determines what a man becomes. When writing more precisely for the profession, he admitted the existence of original, simple reflexes such as the reaction of the eye to light, sucking, hunger contractions, arm and leg movements, and the like, out of which later and more complex behavior develops. But, he insisted, "it is difficult to say how much of the act as a whole is due to training or conditioning." [27] Moreover, Watson attributed no scientific validity to what earlier psychologists had termed instincts—fear, anger, emulation, constructiveness, play, jealousy, and others—or to so-called inherited "aptitudes," mental characteristics, special abilities and the like. He insisted that they are, in fact, learned responses. Moreover, acknowledged unlearned responses such as fear, rage, and smiling, he pointed out, are responses of a general character rather than specific and are capable of being aroused by a variety of situations rather than by tied-in stimuli. That is, for Thorndike's assumption of original S → R bonds, Watson substituted the concept of multiple responses to multiple stimuli.

[25] C. D. Hardie, "Some Concepts in Education in the Light of Recent Philosophy," *Studies in Philosophy and Education,* Summer, 1962, p. 216.

[26] John B. Watson, *Psychological Care of Infant and Child* (New York: W. W. Norton and Co., 1928), p. 41.

[27] See John B. Watson, *Behaviorism* (New York: The People's Institute Publishing Co., 1925), Chapters V, VI, for his discussion of the question "Do instincts exist?"

Not original nature, then, but the ways of man to man determine the potentialities and the limitations of human nature. To the quality of our relations with our associates are we indebted for the kinds of people we become; and character and personality are developed in a manner not unlike that in which the South Sea islanders are said to make their living —namely, by taking in each other's washing!

Although Thorndike and Watson differed in their emphasis upon the relative importance of heredity and environment, they were in essential agreement in ascribing all learning to habit formation. Watson was more explicit, however, in his repudiation of mental phenomena as factors in behavior. Thus thinking was for him an exclusively physiological activity. Insofar as it involves words, it hinges upon word *conditioning:* the association of a word with an object or an event and the later substitution of the word for the object or event in effecting a response. Thinking begins when the child "reacts not only to words spoken by others and to words read in books, but also to words he himself silently speaks." [28] This silent talking to oneself (thinking) Watson termed *implicit behavior,* a type of behavior that includes words and talking to oneself, but also other representative bodily activity, such as the nod of the head in response to a question, the raising of the eyebrows, a shrug of the shoulder, or the catching of the breath. As he put it, "We think with the whole body. . . . But since the human solves most of his problems with words, so most of our implicit behavior is verbal." [29]

Watson drew heavily upon physiologists. Other behaviorists, as Albert P. Weiss and Clark Hull, preferred to describe human behavior in terms of physics and physical energy rather than as physiological activity. Stimulus and response were thus described as an interaction "between different forms of stress." As Weiss explained,

The stimulus is to be regarded as one form of stress in the environment. The sense organs are also systems of stresses. The interaction between these two kinds of stresses (light waves and the chemical changes in the sense organs for instance) are the antecedents of a third type of change known as a nervous process. Finally, a fourth type of change occurs, the contraction of a series of muscle fibers,

[28] John B. Watson, *The Ways of Behaviorism* (New York: Harper & Bros., 1928), p. 82.
[29] For a brief statement of Watson's explanation of thinking as physiological behavior, see *Ibid.*, Chapter V, on "How We Think: A Behaviorist's View."

which produce movements of the body or parts of the body. These movements in turn may bring about changes in the environment such as sound waves and speech sounds, which in turn may act as stimuli for the sense organs of other persons and release a similar cycle, *ad infinitum.*[30]

The categories of explanation thus differed, some behaviorists substituting physics and others physiology and biology for psychic phenomena. But there was and is still an essential agreement among behaviorists that human nature is best understood and described in terms of observable behavior rather than by means of states of consciousness.

DETERMINISM IN EDUCATION

In severely reducing the number of inherited response units with which human beings are assumed to begin life, Watson carried farther a trend for which Thorndike should be credited in his criticisms of G. Stanley Hall. Moreover, in emphasizing the significance of learned responses in contrast with native endowment and the manner in which the simplest reflexes are modified by experiences early in life, Watson and other critics of the S → R bond concept performed a valuable service to education. Their contribution came at a propitious time, for the period following World War I was one of disillusionment with respect to democracy and severe questioning of the wisdom of universal and free education.

This skepticism regarding education was reinforced by the success that seemed to attend the use of intelligence tests during the war in the selection of leaders and the elimination of the unfit from the army. With the publicizing of these results, not only seasoned psychologists and learned journals but popular magazines and the daily press undertook to convince the public that intelligence tests were well-nigh infallible instruments with which to predict the future of young people. Thus, psychologist L. M. Terman wrote in a paper on "The Intelligence of School Children" (1919):

> The relative permanency of the I.Q. enables us to predict with some degree of approximation the mental level a child will attain by a given age. . . . Facts have been presented which show that the limits of a child's educability can be fairly predicted by means of

[30] See Albert Paul Weiss, *A Theoretical Basis of Human Behavior* (Columbus, Ohio: R. G. Adams & Co., 1925).

mental tests in the first school year. By repeated tests these limits can be determined accurately enough for all practical purposes by the end of the child's fifth or sixth school year. This early, at least, vocational training and vocational guidance should begin.[31]

Terman's conclusions had serious implications for public education, since they came at one and the same time that the friends of democracy were urging the enactment of child labor legislation and more stringent enforcement of compulsory school attendance laws. Moreover, in response to these urgings, communities throughout the nation were in process of enlarging their facilities in order to accommodate a rapidly increasing secondary school population.

But education was not the only area affected by intelligence tests. They were also used to establish the thesis of the Social Darwinists of the 1870's and 1880's to the effect that economic status, wealth and poverty, and social class merely reflect native talent. Consequently, efforts at social reform and attempts to better the lot of the underprivileged through social legislation were said on "good authority" to run counter to science.

No one was more alert to the implications for democracy and public education in this trend than Professor William C. Bagley, who stated in part:

> It is since the World War closed that a radical skepticism of the influence of education has been most clearly revealed. When the Allies and their associates girded up their loins to crush the imperialistic ambitions of the Central Powers, it was the safety of democracy and of democratic institutions that became the rallying cry. . . . As long as the guns roared on the Western Front, nothing was too good for the common man, whether he was in the trenches, or on the transports and supply-ships, or in the essential industries at home; but when no sooner had the echoes of the last gun died away than the rallying cry of democracy lost much of its intensity and far more of its sincerity. The loss has been progressive ever since. . . .
>
> There is little wonder, then, that determinism of the hereditarian variety has spread far beyond academic circles. At first the "highbrow" magazines took it up; then the widely-read weekly journals.

[31] Quoted in William C. Bagley, *Determinism in Education* (Baltimore, Md.: Warwick & York, 1929), p. 20.

Books like those of Lothrop Stoddard have had a wide vogue, and the theory of Nordic supremacy is now a commonplace.[32]

Bagley performed a valuable service in examining critically the tenets of the hereditarians. For example, from his analysis of the results of the army intelligence tests he demonstrated that these established a far more convincing relationship between education and ability than between ability and native endowment. Thus, "the states which had good schools in 1900 and thereabouts made good records in the Army tests in 1918, while the states that had poor schools in the former years made poor records." This was true of both whites and Negroes but particularly true of the latter where "the median Negro scores when distributed by states show a closer resemblance to school conditions in those states in 1900 than do the white scores." Indeed, to the discomfort of many, Bagley was able to demonstrate that Negroes in northern states with good school systems scored higher on the tests than did whites from southern states with poor school systems.[33]

A typical expression of the pessimistic attitude toward the potentialities of the common man was found in Ross Finney's A Sociological Philosophy of Education, written, as he stated in his Preface, to establish the "sociological point of view in education" in contrast with individualistic psychology. "The basic idea" he sought to promote was "the tendency of human minds to learn from one another, through a sort of semipassive mentation that results naturally from the social process. This is education in the broadest sense of the word; and from it result human nature and social organization, which are but two aspects of the same thing."

For Finney, however, education is important. "Whatever is put into the school process of today comes out in the social process of tomorrow. Within limits, education is the guiding factor in social change. Therefore, the educators are running not merely the schools, but, in the long run, the world itself."

The educators run the world, provided, of course, they recognize frankly the "telic" function of education and the character of the material with which they must work! Finney frankly described the nature of this material in his chapter on "Followership and the Duller Intellects." One

---

[32] Ibid., pp. 47, 48.
[33] Ibid., p. 125.

extract will illustrate his basic thesis: "Both history and psychology seem to be with the pessimists, for democracy never has worked, except temporarily. The leadership of the wise and the good has never been anything more than a beautiful wish. In practice it has almost always given place to the drivership of the strong. To date, in western society, the mobilization of the masses has never been secured except by force—or superstition."

This situation is far from ideal, however. "Successful democracy demands the ascendancy of the wise and the good; that old ascendancy of the strong and the selfish is the very thing democracy aspires to get away from." To insure "leadership by the intelligent," followership "by the dull and ignorant must somehow be assured." But how can it be assured? Ross Finney's solution was simple. Make use of education!

> It is not enough that we teach children to think, we must actually force-feed them with the concentrated results of expert thinking. To this end there is immense occasion for memoriter training and sheer drill. Ours are the schools of a democracy, which all the children attend. At least half of them never had an original idea of any general nature, and never will. But they must behave as if they had sound ideas. Whether those ideas are original or not matters not in the least. It is better to be right than original. What the duller half of the population needs, therefore, is to have their reflexes conditioned into behavior that is socially suitable. And the wholesale memorizing of catchwords—provided they are sound ones—is the only practical means of establishing bonds in the duller intellects between the finding of social scientists and the corresponding social behavior of the masses. Instead of trying to teach dullards to think for themselves, the intellectual leaders must think for them, and drill the results, memorites, into their synapses. For the dullards it is that or nothing.[34]

Watson opposed what he considered an overemphasis upon inherited traits and the limitations this imposed upon education; but he was one with Ross Finney in stressing the all-importance of external control and of conditioning in learning, as our first quotation from *Psychological Care of Infant and Child* clearly indicates. Consider also the manner in which the impersonal relationships of an adult society unconsciously function

[34] Ross Finney, *A Sociological Philosophy of Education* (New York: The Macmillan Co., 1929), Chapter XX, pp. 386-395.

in his advice to mothers on how to avoid the dangers of excessive mother love!

> There is a sensible way of treating children. Treat them as though they were young adults. Dress them, bathe them with care and circumspection. Let your behavior always be objective and kindly firm. Never hug and kiss them, never let them sit in your lap. If you must, kiss them once on the forehead when they say good night. Shake hands with them in the morning. Give them a pat of the head if they have made an extraordinarily good job of a difficult task. Try it out. In a week's time you will find how easy it is to be perfectly objective with your child and at the same time kindly. You will be utterly ashamed of the mawkish sentimental way you have been handling it. . . .
>
> In conclusion won't you then remember when you are tempted to pet your child that mother love is a dangerous instrument? An instrument which may inflict a never healing wound, a wound which may make infancy unhappy, adolescence a nightmare, an instrument which may wreck your adult son or daughter's vocational future and their chances of marital happiness.[35]

GESTALT PSYCHOLOGY MODIFIES THEORIES OF LEARNING

In 1924, Robert Morris Ogden of Cornell University translated Kurt Koffka's *Grundlagen der Psychischen Entwicklung* (1921) into English under the title of *The Growth of the Mind*. This undertaking, he modestly stated in the Preface to his own volume, "afforded me an opportunity to become intimately acquainted with the point of view of Gestalt psychology and its application to child study." [36] It may also be said to mark the date when the psychological contributions of German scientists provided sound reasons for Americans to renew their faith in democracy and the unique potentialities within human beings! Shortly after Ogden's translation of *The Growth of the Mind* and the publication of his own book, a distinguished group of Gestalt psychologists who had been forced to flee from Hitler's Germany began to infuse new blood into American psychology and education.[37]

[35] Watson, *Psychological Care of Infant and Child, op. cit.*, pp. 81-82, 87.

[36] Robert Morris Ogden, *Psychology and Education* (New York: Harcourt, Brace & Co., 1926), p. v.

[37] Kurt Koffka, Wolfgang Köhler, Kurt Lewin, and Max Wertheimer.

Ogden and his fellow Gestaltists contended that Thorndike's formulation of the laws of learning was of limited application because of the very nature of the experiments from which they were first derived—experiments with animals under conditions artificial and novel and of a type that rendered difficult, if not impossible, "sizing up" the whole situation. To test the nature of learning accurately and the use or failure to use "intelligence," argued Ogden, subjects should be put in natural situations, situations in which they are at home, and then confronted with obstacles, hindrances, novel circumstances, and problems requiring solution.

When tests were carried out accordingly, it was found that learning is by no means exclusively a matter of conditioning or of trial and error of a mechanical character. Nor is it solely a matter of establishing "connections" between specific elements of a situation and specific responses. For example, when chicks were "conditioned" to prefer the darker of two grains (a stimulus we may term S_2 in preference to S_1) and later confronted with a choice between S_2 and a still darker grain (S_3) the chicks promptly pecked the latter. As a result, the experimenters concluded that the response was to a *relationship* ("darker-than") rather than between a specific S and a specific R.

Again, from a series of experiments involving problems of increasing difficulty, problems, some of which all chimpanzees could solve but all of which no one of them could solve, Köhler concluded that learning is of neither the piecemeal nor the blind trial-and-error character assumed by Thorndike. Rather is it a response to a total situation that undergoes reconstruction in the course of trial and error; errors as well as successes are often used to bring about an eventual solution. That is to say, learning involves the sensing of relationships, a reorganization and reconstruction of situations in the course of responses, and, on occasion, "insight" that leads immediately to a solution.

Cole and Bruce illustrate this point by describing the manner in which Köhler's chimpanzees solved one of their food problems. "The chimpanzee," they write, "has a special taste for acid fruit, which he prefers to all others; and so he also relishes formic acid. If he passes close by a board or beam covered with ants, he simply rolls his tongue along and gathers them in! On this beam around the wire netting he could not pursue this primitive method, as the ant stream was *outside* the wire netting. So, first one of our animals, then another, and then the whole company, began to stick twigs and straws out through the meshes, and drew them in immediately, covered with ants, which were promptly devoured." [38]

From a comprehensive review of contemporary theories of learning (which they classify broadly as (1) the mechanistic "connectionist-conditioned-response theory," and (2) "the Gestalt-and-problem-solving view"), Cole and Bruce concluded that neither explains adequately *all learning*. They write:

> What seems to be needed, therefore, is the ability to recognize the kinds of learning in which the special contributions of one theory or the other will be of particular help. . . . Our task is to build an educational psychology that will draw from each of the two views a single broad set of suggestions directly applicable to the various needs of the learner in school and home. . . . In some respects the Gestaltists have shown us what learning *ought* to be like. Instead of slow, plodding, repetitious learning of the conditioning experiment, we *ought* to find a way of handling our learners and materials that would lead to flashes of insight.[39]

These are measured statements of psychologists following a survey of some fifty years of careful experimentation with learning in animals and men. They cannot convey adequately the significance of the Gestalt movement at a time when a mechanistic psychology and a deterministic theory of learning were undermining confidence in universal education and faith in the potentialities of the common man. The Gestaltists confronted scientific evidence of man's unfitness for democracy with scientific evidence to the contrary.

But they were not alone in this. They merely reinforced a conception of human nature and of learning that clearly contrasted with the views of the conditioned reflex and trial-and-error schools of learning. As against the notion that all learning is habit formation of an essentially mechanical character—the result of external forces operating upon the organism—it was boldly asserted that the individual is born with "a primary equipment of impulse, of tendency forward, of innate urgency to do." Moreover, in contrast with the conception of thinking as "mere" verbal activity of an essentially habitual character, or a complex organization of habitual

[38] Cole and Bruce, *op. cit.*, p. 467.
[39] *Ibid.*, pp. 482-483.

responses, this new view defined thinking as the use of "intelligence" and intelligence as a process in which past experience is employed in novel ways to meet novel situations. The chief spokesman of this movement in education was John Dewey, to whose views we now turn.

SUGGESTED READING

Alberty, Harold B., and Alberty, Elsie J., *Reorganizing the High School Curriculum* (New York: The Macmillan Co., 3rd ed., 1962), Chapters 3, 9.

Bagley, William C., *Determinism in Education* (Baltimore, Md.: Warwick & York, 1929), Chapters I-IV.

Bode, Boyd H., *How We Learn* (Boston: D. C. Heath & Co., 1940), Chapters XI-XIII.

Cole, Lawrence E., and Bruce, William F., *Educational Psychology* (Yonkers, N.Y.: World Book Co., 1950), Chapters 10-13.

Cremin, Lawrence A., *The Transformation of the School* (New York: Alfred A. Knopf, 1961), Chapter 6.

Hofstadter, Richard, *Anti-intellectualism in American Life* (New York: Alfred A. Knopf, 1963), Chapter XIII.

Parkhurst, Helen, *Education on the Dalton Plan* (New York: E. P. Dutton and Company, 1922).

Thayer, V. T., *The Passing of the Recitation* (Boston: D. C. Heath & Co., 1928), Chapters VI, VII.

Thorndike, Edward L., *Educational Psychology, Briefer Course* (New York: Teachers College, Columbia University, 1917), Chapters I, II, X-XII.

Watson, John, *The Ways of Behaviorism* (New York: Harper & Bros., 1928), Chapters II, V, VI.

CHAPTER 11
JOHN DEWEY
AND EXPERIMENTALISM
IN EDUCATION

IN considering John Dewey (1859-1952) and experimentalism in American education, we are dealing with influences more exclusively American than heretofore. Not that experimentalism is without roots in European philosophy—indeed, one may find elements of similarity in Aristotle and John Dewey with respect to their conceptions of knowing and the relation of the human organism to its environment.[1] Nor is it difficult to identify a community of spirit, despite fundamental differences in theoretical formulation as to the nature of reality, experience, and truth, in Dewey, on the one hand, and English philosophers, particularly of the empirical and utilitarian schools, on the other. After granting a generous measure of credit to the effects of European thought upon John Dewey (including that of Hegel, as we shall see in a moment), it still remains true that in him we have an original synthesis of influence distinctively American.[2]

[1] See, for example, John Herman Randall, Jr., *Aristotle* (New York: Columbia University Press, 1960), p. 105.

[2] Were we dealing more fully with Dewey's philosophy rather than with his contributions to educational theory and practice, we should preface our discussion with the pragmatism of William James and Charles Peirce, the social philosophy of George Mead, and the influence of Darwinism and the critics of Social Darwinism, particularly Lester Ward and Albion Small. Our primary interest in education also explains our use of the term "experimentalism" rather than "pragmatism" and "instrumentalism," terms more specifically applicable to Dewey's conception of the nature of truth.

THE CONQUEST OF THE CONTINENT
AND MAN'S CONCEPT OF HIMSELF

There is, for example, the optimistic concept of human nature and its native resources that emerged out of the repeated experience of generations of Americans in transforming their physical environment and changing the material and social status in which they were born. In one of his essays Stuart Chase states that before America was settled a squirrel might have climbed a tree at the point now known as the Battery in New York City and traveled without touching ground to the shores of Lake Michigan where Chicago is now located. Consider the changes the hands of men have wrought since then!—the land cleared slowly and painfully, the canals dug, the railroads built, the cities and towns grown up with their diversified populations and industries—all these changes within a comparatively short period. Consider, too, the contrast between the view that meets the eye today from the cliffs overlooking Salt Lake City, Utah, and the barren waste of desert sand that greeted the eyes of Brigham Young and his Mormon followers in 1847, after their trek across desert and over mountains from their burned-out homes in Missouri. Within a few years of his famous declaration, "This is the place," the desert was made to blossom as the rose, rich in soil irrigated from mountain stream, heavy with fruit and grain.

From these and other experiences of like nature in man's transformation of his physical environment and, of equal importance, creation of his own institutions—economic, social, political—together with their modification from time to time, as new need became evident, evolved the conviction that institutions are born of man and are to be evaluated in terms of their effects upon people. These experiences emboldened Dewey to reinterpret the Protagorean principle that man is the measure of all things.[3] He spoke of man in the concrete, that is, not of abstract man or of abstract society, but of people as persons and of persons in association. Here was a conviction quite the opposite of one that would seem equally

---

[3] For Dewey, as we shall see later in this chapter, the phrase, "man is the measure of all things," did not imply, as it did in Plato's criticism of Protagoras, that moral judgments are wholly subjective, that each individual is a law unto himself and determines "truth" according to his own private experience. Rather did it mean that morals originate in human experience and are validated in terms of their effects upon people.

natural in a society with institutions and mores dating from a period beyond the memory of man.

Intimately associated with the above development was accent upon change and the effects of change upon concepts of law and morals. Acceptance of change as an inherent aspect of life led to superficial assumptions—to the assumption, for example, that the new is of necessity better than the old—and it led to the total rejection of the time-honored, if misleading, dictum that the old are wise and the wise are old. But from the common experience of Americans in the creation of new communities and the devising of regulations and laws that were to govern these communities, there emerged ample evidence in support of the far more radical conclusion that law and morals are of this world's origin— made for men by men.

Two statements on the nature of law will illustrate the transformation that took place in the legal mind within a half-century. The first is from an address delivered in 1836 by the distinguished jurist Chancellor James Kent: "The law, as a science, is only a collection of general principles, founded on the moral law, and in the common sense of mankind, and applied to particular cases as they arise, by the diligence of the bar and the erudition of the courts." The second is from lectures on *The Common Law* delivered at Harvard in 1880 by Oliver Wendell Holmes:

> The growth of the law is legislative. And this in a deeper sense than what the courts declare to have always been the law is in fact new. It is legislative in its grounds. The very considerations which judges most rarely mention, and always with an apology, are the secret root from which the law draws all the juices of life. I mean, of course, considerations of what is expedient for the community.... And as the law is administered by able and experienced men, who know too much to sacrifice good sense to a syllogism, it will be found that, when ancient rules maintain themselves in the way that has been and will be shown in this book, new reasons more fitted to the time have been found for them, and that they gradually receive a new content and at last a new form, from the grounds to which they have been transplanted.

It has been easier and far more common for Americans to derive from their experience the concept of law as subject to change in response to human needs than to conclude the same of the principles of morality. In practice, they seem to have lived fairly comfortably with two inconsistent convictions: (1) that moral codes are defined for man and are connected with supernatural commands, rewards, and punishments; and (2) that moral principles should be applied with an eye sensitive to specific situations, since their primary purpose is to refine and better the quality of human relationships. Consequently, Dewey drew directly upon practice as well as theory when he stated that "morals is the most humane of all subjects" and "that human nature exists and operates in an environment. And it is not 'in' that environment as coins are in the box, but as a plant is in the sunlight and soil. . . . Moral science is not something with a separate province. It is physical, biological and historic knowledge placed in a human context where it will illuminate and guide the activities of men." [4]

DEMOCRACY AS A WAY OF LIFE

In "Creative Democracy—The Task Before Us" (an address prepared for delivery at a dinner in celebration of his eightieth birthday in 1939), John Dewey drew attention to the fact that the country, while not entirely in a pioneer state at the time of his birth, was still, save perhaps in a few large cities, "so close to the pioneer stage of American life that the traditions of the pioneer, indeed of the frontier, were active agencies in forming the thoughts and shaping the beliefs of those who were born into its life." Prominent among these beliefs was that of democracy as a *way of life*, not merely as a political structure. Today, continued Dewey, conditions of living have so profoundly changed that we have "to re-create by deliberate and determined endeavor the kind of democracy which in its origin one hundred and fifty years ago was largely the product of a fortunate combination of men and circumstances."

What were some of the characteristics Dewey felt we should "re-create"? One, already mentioned, was the belief in democracy as "a personal way of life" as well as a form of government. Second was the belief that the institutions of democracy, as an organized society, are created by the people to serve the needs of people and that the means employed toward this end are those of mutual consultation, persuasion, equality of participation in decisions, and freedom of thought and expression. Or, as Lincoln so effectively summarized out of his experience on the frontier,

[4] John Dewey, *Human Nature and Conduct* (New York: Henry Holt & Co., 1922), pp. 295-296. We shall return to Dewey's concept of moral values later in this chapter.

a democracy is "a government of the people, by the people, and for the people."

Dewey recognized, of course, with Boyd H. Bode, that life in the local community often fell short of the ideal, that pressures for conformity in thought and action frequently denied equality and freedom to some members of the community to the extent even of "downright tyranny" and "unjustifiable prying into private affairs." As one man complained, "It is getting so in this community that a widower cannot even get his shoes shined without having all the neighbors say that he might have waited a while longer." [5] But, as Bode also pointed out, the social controls thus exercised were commonly accepted because they originated "within the community itself and did not represent an authority reaching in from the outside," the difference being analogous "to the difference between being ordered about by a policeman and being ordered about by one's wife." Furthermore, there was always a safety valve, the opportunity to move on to another location.

The freedom to change both place of residence and means of earning one's living without penalty no longer exists to the same extent as yesterday. But so convinced was Dewey that "mutual consultation and conviction reached through persuasion" constitute the heart of democracy and "make possible a better quality of experience than can otherwise be provided on any wide scale" that he repeatedly emphasized its central importance in education.

THE EFFECTS ON PERSONALITY OF AN INDUSTRIAL AND URBAN CIVILIZATION

In discussing the nature of aims in education, in his *Democracy and Education*, Dewey stressed the "futility of trying to establish *the* aim of education—some one final aim which subordinates all others to itself." Such efforts are useless for the reason that *statements* of aims are matters of emphasis at a given time in response to situations peculiar to that time. Consequently, they tend to omit factors that require little or no emphasis and to highlight defects and needs.[6]

This observation is of interest in connection with Dewey's description

---

[5] Boyd H. Bode, *Democracy as a Way of Life* (New York: The Macmillan Co., 1943), p. 21.

[6] See John Dewey, *Democracy and Education* (New York: The Macmillan Co., 1916), Chapter VIII, also p. 130.

of the status of the individual in a society predominantly industrial and urban in contrast with that in which he was born and reared. In the latter, economic processes were relatively simple and relationships between the participants—employer, employee, customer—predominantly personal. By the close of the nineteenth century and the early years of the twentieth, however, the picture was strikingly different. The United States had become one of the leading industrial nations of the world. Large-scale industry and the corporate form of business organization were transforming traditional forms of production and distribution, ownership and management. Economic society composed of a working class with one set of interests and a business group (including the professions) with another was much as a house divided against itself. Within these groups, moreover, specialization of function was robbing activity of the fullness of meaning, social as well as economic, it once possessed.

These negative influences in what had become a "money culture," Dewey described in detail in his *Individualism, Old and New*.[7] The change from a simpler society into one in which "quantification, mechanization, and standardization" are characteristic has its good side, he granted. "External conditions and standards of living are undoubtedly improved." But their effects "have invaded mind and character and subdued the soul to their own dye." Loyalties that once held individuals, and gave them support, direction, and unity of outlook on life, have become for many "hollow or are openly repudiated, and they drift without sure anchorage." In consequence "individuals are confused and bewildered." They "vibrate between a past that is intellectually too empty to give stability and a present that is too diversely crowded and chaotic to afford balance or direction to ideas and emotion."[8]

Moreover, these ill effects are not limited to one class. They influence all members of economic society—the captains of finance and industry who "exercise leadership surreptitiously and, as it were, absentmindedly" as well as the laboring people few of whom "know what they are making or the meaning of what they do."

Lawrence A. Cremin has pointed out that these negative influences loomed large in Dewey's mind when he came to consider the responsibilities of the modern school.[9] Dewey was also impressed with the efforts of

---

[7] John Dewey, *Individualism, Old and New* (New York: Minton, Balch & Co., 1930).

[8] *Ibid.*; see chapter on "The Lost Individual," pp. 51-73.

[9] See Lawrence A. Cremin, *The Transformation of the School* (New York: Alfred A. Knopf, 1961), Chapter III.

Jane Addams in Chicago, Lillian Wald and John Elliott in New York, and others in social settlement work. Common to all was the attempt to create a sense of community and to humanize relationships between people in an otherwise impersonal environment. Also common to all, but expressed most eloquently by Jane Addams, was the hope that working people might be educated and conditions of their labor modified so as to give greater meaning and a sense of social significance to their activities. "It takes thirty-nine people to make a coat in a modern tailoring establishment," she wrote in *The Spirit of Youth and the City Streets* (1909), "yet those same thirty-nine people might produce a coat in a spirit of 'teamwork' which would make the entire process as much more exhilarating than the work of the old solitary tailor, as playing in a baseball nine gives more pleasure to a boy than is afforded by a solitary game of handball on the side of a barn."

Objectives of this character led Dewey to urge the introduction of "occupations" into the elementary school. By so doing, he believed the school would provide an education analogous to that provided by home and community when young people were made to feel they were both sustained and sustaining members of a "social whole."

The education provided would be analogous and more, since to the values indicated above might be added an educational content often absent from real life. "You can concentrate the history of all mankind into the evolution of the flax, cotton, and wool fabrics into clothing," Dewey wrote in *The School and Society*. "It is not only that the occupations, the so-called manual or industrial work in the school, give the opportunity for the introduction of science which illuminates them, which makes them material freighted with meaning, instead of being mere devices of hand and eye; but that the scientific insight thus gained becomes an indispensable instrument of free and active participation in modern social life." [10]

Dewey developed these views in three lectures delivered before the parents of his experimental school at the University of Chicago in April, 1899. In the first of these he described the household of several generations earlier, when it "was practically the center in which were clustered all the typical forms of industrial occupation." In this household, he emphasized, each member had his own task. "It was a matter of immediate and personal concern, even to the point of actual participation,"

[10] John Dewey, *The School and Society* (Chicago: University of Chicago Press, 1900), pp. 36-37.

involving "training in habits of order and of industry, and in the idea of responsibility, of obligation to do something, to produce something in the world."

In the second lecture, entitled "The School and the Life of the Child," we have his frequently quoted description of the "ideal school":

> If we take an example from an ideal home, where the parent is intelligent enough to recognize what is best for the child, and is able to supply what is needed, we find the child learning through the social converse and constitution of the family. There are certain points of interest and value to him in the conversation carried on; statements are made, inquiries arise, topics are discussed, and the child continually learns. He states his experiences, his misconceptions are corrected. Again the child participates in the household occupations, and thereby gets habits of industry, order, and regard for the rights and ideas of others, and the fundamental habit of subordinating his activities to the general interest of the household. Participation in these household tasks becomes an opportunity for gaining knowledge. The ideal home would naturally have a workshop where the child could work out his constructive instincts. It would have a miniature laboratory in which his inquiries could be directed. The life of the child would extend out of doors to the garden, surrounding fields and forests. He would have his excursions, his walks and talks, in which the larger world out of doors would open to him.
>
> Now, if we organize and generalize all of this, we have the ideal school.[11]

It was the same conviction as to need and opportunity in education that prompted Dewey to urge provision for vocational education on the secondary school level, but organized in such a way as to insure both technical efficiency and a liberal education.

DEWEY AND THE "GOLDEN MEAN" IN EDUCATIONAL DISCUSSION

Among the papers received by editor William T. Harris for possible publication in his *Journal of Speculative Philosophy* was one from an unknown young man by the name of John Dewey. So cordial and helpful was Harris' response that Dewey ventured to solicit the older man's judgment as to whether he possessed sufficient ability to make a profession of philosophy. We assume the answer was encouraging!

[11] *Ibid.*, pp. 51-52.

Dewey's early acceptance of the Hegelian philosophy continued to influence his method of thinking long after his rejection of the substance of Hegelian and neo-Kantian idealism. Take, for example, the characteristic manner in which he analyzed the recurring issues in education. This began by opposing thesis to antithesis, laying bare the partial truth contained in each of two competing theories, together with their limitations, exaggeration, and neglected aspects, and concluded with a synthesis so much richer and relevant to the problem that it constituted a new and original contribution. Eduard Lindeman once called this the method of the "golden mean."

In the 1890's and the early years of the twentieth century, the debate waxed loud and furious in educational circles between the Herbartians, who gave central place to interest as a means to learning, and the traditionalists, who valued effort with or without personal satisfaction or visible reward as a means to discipline. Dewey's attempt to resolve this conflict constructively appeared first as a supplement to the *First Yearbook of the National Herbart Society* (1895), under the title of *Interest as Related to Will*, and, some years later, in more popular form in a small volume entitled *Interest and Effort in Education* (1913).

Beginning with a summary of the "briefs" of the two parties in the "lawsuit," Dewey followed with a critical appraisal in which he made clear that each was "strong in its negations rather than in its position" and that both erred in their use of the common assumption that what is to be learned or mastered is external to the self.

> Because the object or end is assumed to be outside self it has to be *made* interesting; to be surrounded with artificial stimuli and with fictitious inducements to attention. Or, because the object lies outside the sphere of self, the sheer power of "will," the putting forth of effort without interest, has to be appealed to. The genuine principle of interest is the principle of the recognized identity of the fact to be learned or the action proposed with the growing self; that it lies in the direction of the agent's own growth, and is, therefore, imperiously demanded, if the agent is to be himself. Let this condition of identification once be secured, and we have neither to appeal to sheer strength of will, nor to occupy ourselves with making things interesting.[12]

[12] John Dewey, *Interest and Effort in Education* (Boston: Houghton Mifflin Co., 1913), p. 7.

Following this analysis, Dewey introduced a concept of educational practice that enlists both interest and effort but excludes alike superficial and sensational appeals to interest (the sugarcoating of tasks) and insistence upon effort unrelated to meaning and purpose.

THE CHILD VS. SUBJECT MATTER

In *The Child and the Curriculum* Dewey again attempted to find solid ground between two groups of educators; between the ardent advocates of child nature and those who place first the acquisition of the cultural inheritance. Advocates of the first position, he stated, insist:

> The child is the starting-point, the center, and the end. His development, his growth, is the ideal. . . . Not knowledge or information, but self-realization is the goal. To possess all the world of knowledge and lose one's own self is as awful a fate in education as in religion. Moreover, subject-matter never can be got into the child from without. Learning is active. It involves reaching out of the mind. It involves organic assimilation starting from within. Literally, we must take our stand with the child and our departure from him. It is he and not the subject-matter which determines both quality and quantity of learning.[13]

The second group centers upon the importance of subject matter "as compared with the contents of the child's own experience."

> It is as if they said: Is life petty, narrow, and crude? Then studies reveal the great, wide universe with all its fullness and complexity of meaning. Is the life of the child egoistic, self-centered, impulsive? Then in these studies is found an objective universe of truth, law, and order. Is his experience confused, vague, uncertain, at the mercy of the moment's caprice and circumstance? Then studies introduce a world arranged on the basis of eternal and general truth; a world where all is measured and defined. Hence the moral: ignore and minimize the child's individual peculiarities, whims and experiences. They are what we need to get away from. . . .
>
> Subdivide each topic into studies; each study into lessons; each lesson into specific facts and formulae. Let the child proceed step by step to master each one of these separate parts, and at last he will have covered the entire ground. . . .[14]

[13] John Dewey, *The Child and the Curriculum* (Chicago: University of Chicago Press, 1902), p. 13.
[14] *Ibid.*, p. 12.

Having stated the case for each position, Dewey defined the problem as one of getting rid of the assumption, common to each, that there is a gap in kind, "as distinct from degree," between child experience and appropriate subject matter.

> Abandon the notion of subject-matter as something fixed and ready-made in itself, outside the child's experience; cease thinking of the child's experience as also something hard and fast; see it as something fluent, embryonic, vital; and we realize that the child and the curriculum are simply two limits which define a single process. Just as two points define a straight line, so the present standpoint of the child and the facts and truth of studies define instruction. It is continuous reconstruction, moving from the child's present experience out into that represented by the organized bodies of truth that we call studies.[15]

Again there followed a discussion that stressed the importance in teaching of bringing into fruitful connection the powers, capacities, and attitudes of the young person and race-experience as embodied in the curriculum.

In view of the fact that Dewey reverted frequently to what he insisted was a false dichotomy between a concern for the inner life of the child and a concern for the mastery of organized subject matter, it is difficult to explain the repeated criticism of critics that he discounted the importance of the latter. For example, in an article written in 1926 for *The Journal of the Barnes Foundation* and reprinted in 1947, he criticized the lack of guidance in child-centered schools in words unusually sharp for him. Said he, "Such a method is really stupid. For it attempts the impossible, which is always stupid; and it misconceives the conditions of independent thinking." Again, in 1928, we find him insisting that the systematic organization of subject matter is a first essential for achieving individuality and that teachers, by virtue of their greater maturity, experience, and background, are obligated to assist in its mastery.[16]

The Way Out of Educational Confusion (The Inglis Lecture for 1931) dealt in a similar manner with the multiplication of subjects and courses in school and college and the conflict this has engendered between the advocates of a liberal and cultural education and those favoring the intro-

---

[15] *Ibid.*, p. 16.

[16] John Dewey, "Progressive Education and the Science of Education," *Progressive Education*, Vol. V (July, August, September, 1928), pp. 197-204.

duction of practical and vocational subjects and courses in the curriculum. This dispute, Dewey indicated, results in part from the phenomenal increase in knowledge, together with recent trends toward interrelationships between fields once separate and distinct, and in part from developments within modern society that have so saturated the arts and technologies "with applied science that the routine apprenticeship methods of the past no longer serve." Thus he concluded that new organizations and new syntheses of subject matter are called for that will both liberalize practical and vocational education and relate more meaningfully the cultural and humanistic subjects with "the interests and activities in which the mass of men and women must perforce engage." [17]

Dewey's Phi Delta Kappa Lecture on *Experience and Education* will serve as a final illustration of his proneness to seek the "golden mean" in the solution of educational issues. In this lecture he addressed himself to the issue of traditional vs. progressive education. Traditional education, he said, is based on the following assumption:

> The subject-matter of education consists of bodies of information and of skills that have been worked out of the past; therefore, the chief business of the school is to transmit them to the new generation. In the past, there have also been developed standards and rules of conduct; moral training consists in forming habits of action in conformity with these rules and standards. Finally, the general pattern of school organization (by which I mean relations of pupils to one another and to the teachers) constitutes the school a kind of institution sharply marked off from other social institutions.[18]

Proponents of the progressive school criticize this type of education as one "of imposition from above and from outside. It imposes adult standards, subject-matter, and methods, upon those who are only growing slowly toward maturity" and thus does violence to their experience.[19] Consequently,

> To imposition from above is opposed expression and cultivation of individuality; to external discipline is opposed free activity; to learning from texts and teachers, learning through experience; to acqui-

[17] John Dewey, *The Way Out of Educational Confusion* (Cambridge, Mass.: Harvard University Press, 1931); see pp. 9-17, 23-41.

[18] John Dewey, *Experience and Education* (New York: The Macmillan Co., 1938), p. 2.

[19] *Ibid.*, p. 4.

sition of isolated skills and techniques by drill is opposed acquisition of them as means of attaining ends which make direct vital appeal; to preparation for a more or less remote future is opposed making the most of the opportunities of present life; to static aims and materials is opposed acquaintance with a changing world.[20]

Dewey resolved the conflict between traditional and progressive education by reference to the nature of experience and its *full* implications for education. The traditionalists err, he believed, because of indifference to the relationship between the knowledge, skills, and techniques they would have the child acquire and his inner attitudes and dispositions. The progressives, despite their concern for the inner life of the individual, his interests, felt needs, and desires, tend to ignore the twofold nature of experience: the fact that the *quality* of experience derives from the *interaction* between environment and internal conditions. "Learning through experience" as an educational objective thus requires attention to environmental factors (subject matter and activities carefully planned) in relation to the personal needs, desires, purposes, and capacities of the student. In further amplification of the principles of continuity and interaction as essential aspects of experience and education Dewey devoted some five chapters to "Criteria of Experience," "Social Control," "The Meaning of Purpose," and "Progressive Organization of Subject-Matter."

JOHN DEWEY'S RADICALISM

If it be correct to state that Dewey habitually sought the golden mean in resolving educational issues, how do we explain the partisan spirit in which his own position is so frequently discussed? A superficial answer might be that few participants in a controversy welcome a peacemaker whose method is to call attention to the weak points of each! But more accurate is the fact that Dewey's educational philosophy derived from

[20] *Ibid.,* pp. 5-6.
Dewey's method of formulating educational issues has exposed him to careless misrepresentation. A glaring illustration is Mortimer Smith's widely read volume, *And Madly Teach* (Chicago: Henry Regnery Co., 1949), pp. 19-23. Smith, one of the founders and leaders of the "basic education" movement, devotes a chapter to "The Philosophical Basis of Modern Education," which is none other than the thought of John Dewey, the "godfather" of this "false" philosophy. As evidence of Dewey's "concrete proposals of educational reform," Smith quotes the above passage from *Experience and Education* and also our quotation from *The Child and the Curriculum,* beginning with the words "The child is the starting-point." In each instance, of course, the passage quoted states an extreme position in contrast with which Dewey develops what he considers to be a sounder position.

premises that challenged traditional concepts in philosophy and education.

Take, for example, the concept of experience, to which brief reference was made above. This differs radically from the dualistic assumption of a mind that receives impressions from an outside world and from behaviorism with its concept of "connections" established between well-defined or self-contained situations in the environment and equally specific responses within the nervous system. It also differs from the critical realism of the period which insisted that the mind is nothing other than the brain, a bodily organ, that brings about adjustments between "cerebral events" and "atomic and electronic forces" outside the body.

The difference between Dewey and these extremes resulted from his concept of man as an organism and the relation of an organism to its environment. This involved a wholehearted acceptance of the theory of evolution and man's place in nature. Thus Dewey's position set him apart from idealists who insisted that evolution applies only to man's physical nature, not to his mind or soul, and from realists of the materialistic school who conceived of man as a complex organization of physical and chemical constituents or, in physiological terms, merely a high-grade animal whose behavior can be explained in mechanical terms.

Neither view, as Dewey saw it, does full justice to man's nature, since there is more "mind" in body than the realist grants, and more body in mind than the idealist can see. What is needed in each instance is a revised understanding of the relation of an organism to its environment.

THE RELATION OF AN ORGANISM
TO ITS ENVIRONMENT

The relationship of an organism to its environment, according to Dewey, is not one of two separate and distinct kinds of objects. Rather is the experience of an organism the resultant of two interacting and interpenetrating influences—an interaction or, as he termed it, a *transaction* in which biological inheritance and environmental factors merge to determine the outcome—experience.

The human being, as all organisms, lives *within* an environment and by means of it. Breathing, as Dewey once put it, "is an affair of the air as truly as of the lungs." It takes its specific character from the condition of each. So is digestion an affair of food as truly as of the tissues and secretions of the stomach. Walking involves not only legs and muscles but the surface walked upon. The one cannot be described accurately without reference to its relation to the other. "Speech demands physical air and human companionship and audience as well as vocal organs."

Experience as a transaction between organism and environment holds true on all levels of organic life; and the nature and the quality of experience vary with the structure of the organism on the one hand and the environment to which structure is sensitive on the other. Or, we might say, in the course of evolution structure and environment have grown up together in a mutually creative relationship.

On the purely physical level, objects are in external relationship (as a piece of iron placed in a wet spot develops rust). Unlike organisms, however, they do not interact with their surroundings so as to preserve their identity. Organisms, in contrast, have interests and act to realize these interests. Their relations with objects and events involve sensitivity and organized response. A response, however, varies with structure. In the most primitive organisms, environment consists of the immediately present. On a higher level, distance receptors (eyes, ears, nose, for example) introduce a more complicated environment. Still higher are organisms capable of anticipating events and responding to the future, a future modified by the past. And, finally, in an ascending series of increasingly complex interrelationships between environment and response, are animals that employ symbols, gestures, signs, and—as in man—language and meanings that introduce an intellectual and social environment no longer bound to the physical,[21] or restricted to the particulars of time or space.

On all levels of evolution, then, the important thing to observe in understanding Dewey is the twofold origin and content of experience. Human nature in general, as mind and character of individuals in particular, results from interplay between organic equipment and stimulating conditions. As Dewey once stated, qualities of character such as honesty, chastity, malice, peevishness, courage, triviality, industry, and irresponsibility are not exclusively personal. "They are working adaptations of personal capacities and environing forces."

Dewey's insistence upon experience as both subjective and objective

21 This is a hurried and limited description of developments to which an entire book would hardly do justice. A more adequate description is given in John Childs, *American Pragmatism and Education* (New York: Henry Holt & Co., 1956), Chapter 4.

explains his impatience with an exclusively child-centered education, or an education that deprives young people of the funded experience of others. But it caused him to object equally to the introduction of subject matter unrelated to the background and experience of the learner.

A REVISED CONCEPT OF INSTINCTS AND HABITS

Early in his career, Dewey studied under G. Stanley Hall and was doubtless influenced by the latter in his conceptions of evolution and the nature of instincts. Indeed, faint traces of the recapitulation theory appear in *The School and Society*, as evidenced by the argument that one advantage attending the introduction of "occupations" into the school curriculum is that in them "the historic development of man is recapitulated." [22] But by 1923, when G. Stanley Hall came to write his autobiography, we find him expressing puzzlement over Dewey's rejection of the concept of recapitulation.

Dewey similarly revised his concept of instincts. In *The School and Society* Dewey spoke of the social instinct, the constructive instinct, the instinct of investigation, and the expressive or art instinct as "the natural resources, the uninvested capital, upon the exercise of which depends the active growth of the child." [23] Instincts so conceived, however, differed in plasticity and generality from Thorndike's inherited connections between specific elements within a situation and specific responses of the individual. Moreover, for Dewey, they continued to lose in specificity. By 1922, with the appearance of *Human Nature and Conduct*, he identified instincts with impulses that take their character more from situations in which they find expression than from heredity. For example, in a footnote to his chapter on "Plasticity of Impulse," he wrote that he was using the words "instinct" and "impulse" as practical equivalents intentionally. "The word instinct taken alone," he wrote, "is still too laden with the older notion that an instinct is always definitely organized and adapted—which for the most part is just what it is not in human beings. The word impulse suggests something primitive, yet loose, undirected, initial." [24]

It is not difficult to identify the reasons for Dewey's decision to subject the theory of instincts (conceived as inherited ways of thinking, feeling,

[22] Dewey, *The School and Society, op. cit.*, p. 34.
[23] *Ibid.*, pp. 59-61.
[24] John Dewey, *Human Nature and Conduct* (New York: Henry Holt & Co., 1922), p. 105.

and acting in response to typical life situations). The early years of the twentieth century were years of economic, social, and political ferment. Instinct psychology seemingly confirmed the conservative contention that institutions reflect a human nature that remains unchanged in its essential aspects from age to age, and it followed that attempts to alter human institutions fundamentally are utopian. On the other hand, if the opposite conception be valid, and human nature is originally "wholly empty and passive," the reformer might envisage the reshaping of man and society.

The intellectual as well as the social climate was thus ripe for Dewey once again to exercise his genius for finding the golden mean between two extreme positions. "Curiously enough," he wrote, "both parties rest their case upon just the factor which when it is analyzed weakens their respective conclusions." The "radical reformer" underestimates the influence of habits and of institutions in shaping raw human nature, and the conservative errs in his conception of the nature of instincts.[25]

His examination of these two positions involved an analysis of both instinct and habit. In a chapter entitled "No Separate Instincts," Dewey equated the psychologist's belief in instincts, such as fear, anger, rivalry, love of mastery, sexual drive, and maternal love, with the early tendency of scientists to explain phenomena by reference to special forces, such as nature's abhorrence of a vacuum and the "force" of combustion. So "we tend to regard sex, hunger, fear, and even much more complex active interests as if they were lump forces, like the combustion or gravity of old-fashioned physical science." Eventually, we came to understand that what were termed "forces" are "only the phenomena over again." A similar conclusion seems warranted in psychology.[26]

Moreover, when we examine concrete instances of instinctive behavior, we find first "that no activity (even one that is limited by routine habit) is confined to the channel which is most flagrantly involved in its execution. The whole organism is concerned in every act to some extent and in some fashion, internal organs as well as muscular, those of circulation, secretion, etc." And the state of the organism is not twice the same in an instinctive act such as hunger, sex, or fear. "Even physiologically the context of organic changes accompanying an act of hunger or sex makes the difference between normal and a morbid phenomenon." Secondly, continued Dewey, the environment in which a so-called instinctive act takes

25 *Ibid.*, p. 107.
26 *Ibid.*, p. 150.

place is never twice the same, and, therefore, the *meaning* of the act is never the same. That is, its meaning is never the same in terms of its effects upon the organism as well as the situation. "A child gives way to what, grossly speaking, we call anger. Its felt or appreciated quality depends in the first place upon the condition of his organism at the time, and this is never twice alike. In the second place, the act is at once modified by the environment upon which it impinges so that different consequences are immediately reflected back to the doer." [27]

It is a matter of great importance educationally to recognize three possibilities in the career of an "impulse activity." It may find "a surging, explosive discharge—blind, unintelligent"; it may be sublimated—"that is, become a factor coordinated intelligently with others in a continuous course of action," as when anger is converted into a determination to right social injustice or when "sexual attraction" reappears in art or in tranquil domestic attachments and services; or, finally, it may be suppressed, "turned inwards, to lead a surreptitious, subterranean life." In each instance it is the situation rather than "inborn tendencies to respond" that gives quality and meaning to the response. Analysis of the nature of instincts thus undermines the rigid position of conservatives "who argue that social and moral reform is impossible on the ground that the Old Adam of human nature remains forever the same."

But what of the opposite contention? What becomes of John Watson's assertion, quoted in our last chapter, that given a healthy body, the right number of fingers and toes, and the few elementary movements that are present at birth, it is possible to make of man what we will? This, too, is a gross oversimplification, in part, because it ignores aspects of instinct and impulse to which we shall turn in a moment and, in part, because it underrates the influence of habits and customs in the environment over which our high-grade animal trainer has little control!

Although they are first in time, wrote Dewey of impulses, "they are never primary in fact; they are secondary and dependent." [28] The child begins life with vague, random, and undefined impulses. But these are quickly shaped by the habits and customs of his family and the culture in which he lives, moves, and has his being. This conception of habit differs radically from the dualistic psychology according to which a mental state sets off a physiological response of a channeled, routine character. No

[27] *Ibid.*, p. 152.
[28] *Ibid.*, p. 89.

more than instincts are habits the resultants of psychic forces. To conceive them so is to put the cart before the horse. What are commonly termed sensations and ideas do not come to an empty mind fully formed. Far from being original elements in experience, sensations and perceptions are the products of prior activity. "To be able to single out a definite sensory element in any field is evidence of a high degree of previous training, that is, well-formed habits. A moderate amount of observation of a child will suffice to reveal that even such gross discriminations as black, white, red, green, are the results of some years of active dealings with things in the course of which habits have been set up." [29]

What is true of simple perceptions is much more relevant to ideas and purposes. "There is no immaculate conception of meanings and purposes." Contrary to the assumptions of ordinary psychology, "The act must come before the thought, and a habit before an ability to evoke the thought at will." This conclusion is of profound import, in Dewey's thought, for moral education, since it undercuts the popular notion that verbal instruction prior to and unrelated to active experience can be effective.

Moreover, habits are not to be considered mere bodily or physiological responses, since they are not confined to the body. They are "affairs" of organism and environment. They are *arts* in that they involve "skill of sensory and motor organs, cunning or craft, and objective materials." And they are arts also because they include behavior that is flexible and adjustable to changing conditions. They are not mere tendencies to act; they are predispositions.

Dewey recognized that he was introducing into educational discussion a novel conception of "habit." Nevertheless, he retained the term for two reasons: (1) He wished to correct the notion that habits are triggered reactions of a mechanical character. Such actions exist, but their role in conduct is far more limited than commonly thought. (2) He considered that "we need a word to express that kind of human activity which is influenced by prior activity and in that sense acquired; which contains within itself a certain ordering or systematization of minor elements of action; which is projective, dynamic in quality, ready for overt manifestation; which is operative in some subdued subordinate form even when not obviously dominating activity." [30]

[29] *Ibid.*, p. 31. Dewey illustrated this point further by reference to illusions, experiences in which habits are primary in determining perception.
[30] *Ibid.*, p. 41.

THE ROLE OF INSTINCT AND HABIT IN LEARNING

On the surface it would seem that Dewey was in substantial agreement with the dictum that all learning is habit formation. But agreement with behaviorists is verbal only. For them habit is analogous to a coiled spring waiting to be released. For Dewey, as we have seen, habits are active and flexible ways of cooperating with the environment—cooperative activity in which each contributor helps to define and give character to the other. Take, for example, the interaction between stimulus and response in the process of solving a picture puzzle. In cases of this character, what began as an unrecognized and meaningless relationship between lines gradually takes on form and character, ending as a clearly defined picture. Much the same relationship exists between two people in the process of establishing a friendship. The kind of person each becomes in the eyes of the other is the result of a mutually creative process. Consider also the manner in which a thought develops in the course of revising a paragraph that ultimately gives adequate expression to what the author has in mind.

Habits, so conceived, are all-important in learning. They provide the discipline, the "know-how" with which to cope with the various situations of life—the novel as well as the familiar. It is habit, a focusing of the results of past experience upon what is critical in the present that enables the sailor to cope with a storm at sea just as it is habit, funded experience, that enables the scientist in his laboratory or the scholar in the library to engage in fruitful research. And, of course, one indispensable function of the school is to provide young people with appropriate experiences within the various fields of knowledge out of which they may develop the essential intellectual disciplines.

But habits, even as Dewey conceived them, can inhibit progress. They tend to perpetuate themselves. "Existing institutions impose their stamp, their superscription upon impulse and instinct" and thus easily become impediments to progress. Often, indeed, it is the most scholarly individual, the one best-equipped with the heritage of the past, who resists suggestion for reform. It is this tendency to resist change, on the part of the intelligent members of society as well as the uninformed, that leads, on occasion, to blind revolt and revolution.

The tendency for institutions and ideas to become fixed and rigid gives significance to impulse and instinct in education. Impulse, as we have seen, is quickly channeled by habit and custom, but not altogether! Take language, for example. Original impulses of expression elicit response and direction from a child's elders and eventually become the instruments of communication, but not to the point of total exclusion of individual differences in the pronunciation of words or in their meanings. Words, as means of communication (as habits), change significantly with time and in response to circumstance, as the criticism leveled at lexicographers amply demonstrates upon the appearance of each new edition of a dictionary! The young "are not as yet subject to the full impact of established customs. Their life of impulsive activity is vivid, flexible, experimenting, curious." [31] These are facts of which education should take full advantage in a changing society and in a democracy where progress depends upon maintaining an appropriate balance between the influences of stability and change. One function of the school, insisted Dewey, is to provide an environment in which the young can acquire the discipline (the habits) with which to meet the challenges of change. He wrote significantly in this connection:

> In order that education of the young be efficacious in inducing an improved society, it is not necessary for adults to have a formulated definite ideal of some better state. An educational enterprise conducted in this spirit would probably end merely in substituting one rigidity for another. What is necessary is that habits be formed which are more intelligent, more sensitively percipient, more informed with foresight, more aware of what they are about, more direct and sincere, more flexibly responsive than those now current. Then they will meet their own problems and propose their own improvements.[32]

To serve as needed, however, the school must concern itself with the nature and the role of reflective thinking or "intelligence" in education.

THE NATURE OF THINKING AND ITS IMPLICATIONS FOR EDUCATION

Dewey used the term "reflective thinking" in order to distinguish it from the process of "mere thinking," the uncontrolled, unregulated and undirected coursing of ideas through one's head—as in daydreaming or reverie. Reflective thinking arises out of a "forked-road situation"—an ambiguous and confusing situation, a dilemma that requires resolving, or a difficulty or problem that presses for solution. It involves the mind

[31] *Ibid.*, p. 127.
[32] *Ibid.*, p. 128.

and consciousness, not as immaterial substances or psychic energies but as *minding* operations in which the present, past, and future are intimately involved.

To the nature of reflective thinking and the implications of a complete act of thought for education, Dewey devoted an entire book, *How We Think*.[33] Briefly summarized, a complete act of thought, according to Dewey, involves five stages. As indicated above, it begins with or grows out of a "perplexed, troubled, confused situation." Action or thought or both are blocked or interrupted. This leads to an attempt to locate the difficulty, obstruction, frustration, or source of doubt, as the case may be. Secondly, suggestions occur to mind or are searched for as possible solutions. These involve past experience and prior knowledge as resources upon which to draw. The third stage involves relating suggestions back to the problem in an effort to determine their relevance and appropriateness as possible solutions. "Given a genuine difficulty and a reasonable amount of analogous experience to draw upon," wrote Dewey, "the difference, *par excellence*, between good and bad thinking is found at this point." Reflective thinking thus requires patience and endurance, an unwillingness to accept a suggested solution lightly, and the determination to suspend judgment when necessary and to search for additional suggestions. The fourth stage involves further testing of a worthy hypothesis; the fifth, some form of verification or corroboration of the accepted solution. Obviously not all problematic situations require all five stages. Some problems are resolved by merely identifying the source of confusion or trouble. Similarly resolution can occur at each succeeding stage. On the other hand, each stage or phase may consume long periods of time.

Dewey's analysis of thinking had profound implications for both philosophy and education. For the latter these implications bordered upon the revolutionary, since they inaugurated reform in methods of instruction and principles of selection of subject matter (the project and problem methods of teaching, for example) as well as in organization of the curriculum and the life of the school. They likewise challenged the validity of traditional psychology with its dualistic explanation of learning.

"It would be impossible," wrote Dewey in *Democracy and Education*,

[33] John Dewey, *How We Think* (Boston: D. C. Heath & Co., 1910; rev. ed., 1933). Both the 1910 and the 1933 editions were intended as textbooks in education, as was *Democracy and Education, op. cit.* The latter volume devoted Chapters XI-XIV specifically to the nature of thinking and its applications to methods of instruction and subject matter organization. Dewey's *Logic: The Theory of Inquiry* (New York: Henry Holt & Co., 1938) was, of course, a much more technical examination of the nature of thought and its implications for philosophy.

"to state adequately the evil results which have flowed from this dualism of mind and body, much less to exaggerate them." [34] In school practice, he continued, it has led to the assumption that bodily activity is an intruder in the classroom. Consequently, the greater the extent to which such activity can be suppressed, the better. "A premium is put upon a physical quietude," and the teacher's responsibility is to insist "on silence, on rigid uniformity of posture and movement; upon a machine-like simulation of the attitudes of intelligent interest." [35] For the very young child this assumption is most serious, since manipulation and physical expressions of native curiosity are conditions of his learning, of his acquiring ideas. For the older person, as well as the young, it neglects the part played by the senses, the muscles, the vocal cords, and other bodily organs not only in the elementary activities of reading, writing, figuring, and the like but, on a much higher level, in the conduct of experimentation and research.

The senses, he pointed out, "are avenues of knowledge not because external facts are somehow 'conveyed' to the brain, but because they are *used* in doing something with a purpose." [36] Again, the separation of "mind" and body "leads to emphasis upon *things* at the expense of *relations* or connections," whereas the measure of the value of an experience lies in the perception of relationships or continuities to which it leads. Grasping the meaning of a thing does not come from combining impressions or perceptions viewed as mental states. A wagon, for example, "is not perceived when all its parts are summed up; it is the characteristic connection of the parts which make a wagon." It is the use to which it is put and the purpose it serves that identify and give it meaning. Thinking is thus an activity—the "intentional endeavor to discover *specific* connections between something we do and the consequences which result, so that the two become continuous." [37] The failure to realize this fact leads easily to the fallacy of identifying words with ideas.

Thus Dewey attacked the evils that follow upon the application of the mind-body concept to education. More positively, he emphasized the identity of the processes of thinking and steps in learning. That is to say, since "thinking is the method of an educative experience," it follows that the essentials of method are "identical with the essentials of reflection." These steps, or phases, as we have seen, are:

[34] Dewey, *Democracy and Education, op. cit.*, p. 165.
[35] *Ibid.*, p. 165.
[36] *Ibid.*, p. 167. Note also that for Dewey ideas are not mere psychic entities, images, and the like, but plans for action, anticipated solutions of problems.
[37] *Ibid.*, p. 170.

... first, that the pupil have a genuine situation of experience—that there be a continuous activity in which he is interested for its own sake; secondly, that a genuine problem develop within this situation as a stimulus to thought; third, that he possess the information and make the observations needed to deal with it; fourth, that suggested solutions occur to him which he shall be responsible for developing in an orderly way; fifth, that he have an opportunity and occasion to test his ideas by application, to make their meaning clear and to discover for himself their validity.[38]

Here is a description of the nature and purpose of the learning process (of education) that contrasts with traditional education. The young person is no longer viewed as a passive and compliant recipient of information, habits, skills, and standards as defined and imposed by adults. Rather is he conceived as active by nature and quite properly a voluntary participant in his own learning. Moreover, subject matter is no longer adequately conceived as "pre-digested," to adopt a term later used by Kilpatrick. Organized knowledge and funded experience constitute indispensable grist for the educational mill, but not necessarily, indeed seldom for the young child, as classified subjects and insulated compartments of knowledge. Again, a vital learning experience involves an intellectual acquisition, but its effects bear as well upon attitude, disposition, and will. Finally, its end results and the test of its success embrace far more than a correct answer in the back of a book or a favorable grade on an examination paper. The successful educational experience involves nothing less than the "reconstruction or reorganization" of experience, a reconstruction that adds to the meaning of experience and enhances one's ability to add to the course of subsequent experience. In short, it is growth that leads to further growth.

Inspired by Dewey's philosophy and his own pioneer efforts at the University of Chicago, educators throughout the country were soon engaged in novel experiments in democratic school administration and curriculum organization. And, under the guiding spirit of William Heard Kilpatrick, the project method of teaching came into widespread use.

DEMOCRACY AND THE NATURE OF MORAL IDEALS

In the aforementioned birthday address, "Creative Democracy—The Task Before Us," Dewey remarked,

---

[38] *Ibid.*, p. 192.

I have been accused more than once of an undue, a utopian, faith in the possibilities of intelligence and in education as a correlate of intelligence. At all events, I did not invent this faith. I acquired it from my surroundings as far as those surroundings were animated by the democratic spirit. For what is the faith of democracy in the role of consultation, of conference, of persuasion, of discussion, in formation of public opinion, which in the long run is self-corrective, except faith in the capacity of the intelligence of the common man to respond with common sense to the free play of facts and ideas which are secured by effective guarantees of free inquiry, free assembly, free communication?

This passage, together with other portions of Dewey's address, on this occasion in which he described democracy as a *"personal* way of individual life," signifying "the possession and continual use of certain attitudes, forming personal character and determining desire and purpose in all the relations of life," suggests the similarity in his view between the methods of intelligence and those of education for democracy. Democracy, as he conceived it, is a moral ideal.

But what are moral ideals? First, let us consider what they are not. They are not otherworldly in origin and authority; that is, they are not injunctions originating outside human experience and depending for their effectiveness upon rewards and punishment in this world or the next. Nor are they principles derived from an ideal world, as distinct from the actual and made known to us by a special faculty of the mind. Both of these views fail to do justice to human nature—the first by conceiving of man's nature as infected by original sin; the second by conceiving of it as "sensuous, impulsive, subject to necessity, while natural intelligence is such that it cannot rise above a reckoning of private expediency." [39]

Unsatisfactory also is the assumption of Herbert Spencer and the Social Darwinians that "natural laws are themselves moral," that transgression brings its own penalty while conformity brings "the reward of increased

---

[39] Dewey, *Human Nature and Conduct, op. cit.,* p. 295. In this respect Dewey, who differed from Alexander Meiklejohn on many subjects, would nevertheless agree with these words from the latter's *Education Between Two Worlds* (New York: Harper & Bros., 1942), p. 202: "The truth is . . . human prophets have perceived in human nature itself the beauty of holiness, the strength of humility, the magnificence of wisdom. And these qualities seemed to them so great, so significant in their authority over the beliefs and conduct of men that, without knowing what they were doing, they created the myth of divine origins and divine sanctions. That myth is now fading away. But the human truth to which it gave untenable expression still remains. Courage, beauty, freedom, justice, honesty, are still the original facts. The myth was the secondary thing."

vitality and happiness." Inherent in this view is the assumption that the processes of evolution in the far-off future will harmonize egoistic desires and the necessities of the environment, that the function of reason is "to acknowledge the evolutionary forces and thereby refrain from retarding the happy day of perfect harmony. Meantime, justice demands that the weak and ignorant suffer the effects of violation of natural law, while the wise and able reap the rewards of their superiority." [40]

There are faults in the assumption that what is, is right and must, therefore, be accepted. It fails to recognize that perception of things as they are, is, for human beings, but the first step toward changing them and making them better; that morality "resides not in the perception of fact, but in the *use* made of its perception"; and that the one unique function of intelligence is "to tell when to use the fact to confirm and perpetuate, and when to vary conditions and consequences." [41]

Opposed to each other as the preceding concepts are in important respects, they are similar in conceiving of morality as consisting of principles to which man must conform but which he must not create. They are thus *objective* in their independence of human experience. A third type errs, in Dewey's view, in the opposite direction, in its subjective emphasis. This holds that moral judgments are expressions only of personal feelings as contrasted with statements of fact. Or, as a recent writer puts it, value statements "are not statements in the ordinary sense but are part of the utterer's verbal behavior which is attempting to control behavior in other people. They are means used by parents, teachers, preachers, politicians, judges to secure behavior that is acceptable to society." [42] This statement downgrades, if it does not ignore, both the social origin and the social reference of "the utterer's verbal behavior."

Basic to an understanding of Dewey's conception of morality is the social origin of its principles. Man, we have said, is an organism. But the human organism, for Dewey, is far more than a biological organization.

[40] Dewey, *Human Nature and Conduct, op. cit.,* p. 298.
[41] *Ibid.,* pp. 298-299.
[42] C. D. Hardie, "Some Concepts in Education in the Light of Recent Philosophy," *Studies in Philosophy and Education,* Vol. II, Summer, 1962, p. 231. For a more adequate discussion of the "emotive theory of values," see A. J. Ayer, *Language, Truth, and Logic* (London: Victor Gollancz, Ltd., 1949), Chapter VI; and Charles L. Stevenson, *Ethics and Language* (New Haven, Conn.: Yale University Press, 1945). For Dewey's most incisive analysis and critique of the "emotive theory," see his "Theory of Valuation," *International Encyclopedia of Unified Science,* Vol. I, No. 4 (Chicago: University of Chicago Press, 1939).

It absorbs into itself aspects of the culture in which one is born and develops—science, morals, religion, art, industry, and law, which is to say, "The stuff of belief and proposition is not originated by us. It comes to us from others, by education, tradition, and the suggestion of the environment. . . . Our thoughts of our own action are saturated with the ideas that others entertain about them, ideas which have been expressed not only in implicit instruction but still more effectively in reaction to other acts." [43]

As Dewey conceived them, moral injunctions are not without sanction and authority over and above the whims of the individual who seeks to impose them upon others. Dewey and Tufts wrote as follows in their joint work on *Ethics:*

> The essence of the claim which Right puts forth is that even if the thing exacted does not appeal as his good to the one to whom it is addressed, he *should* voluntarily take it to be a good; that, in short, it should *become* his good, even if he does not so judge it at the time. . . . The solution of the apparent contradiction between that which is not now judged good and yet *should* be judged good points the way to the criterion of which we are in search. Does the conduct alleged to be obligatory, alleged to have an authority of moral law behind it, actually contribute to a good in which the one from whom an act is demanded will *share?* . . . If the claim is, then, of the kind which he himself puts forth, if it serves a good which he prizes for himself, he must, in the degree in which he is fair-minded, acknowledge it to be a common good, and hence binding upon his judgment and action.[44]

The fact that our ideas of right and wrong are social in origin, the products of human experience (in contrast with principles of divine and ideal origin), in no way guarantees their validity in specific situations. Selfishness as well as generosity, prejudice and passion as well as moral thoughtfulness are equally products of social experience. Even principles that have been tested in many varying situations in the past must needs square themselves with novel circumstance. In other words, moral problems are similar to other situations in which funded experience conflicts with impulse, principle with principle, long-established behavior with change. Consequently, frustration, confusion, and contradiction challenge

[43] Dewey, *Human Nature and Conduct, op. cit.,* pp. 314-315.
[44] John Dewey and James H. Tufts, *Ethics* (New York: Henry Holt & Co., rev. ed., 1932), pp. 250-251.

thought, which is another way of saying that, for Dewey, moral problems are not different in kind from other problems demanding reflective thought.

It follows that character education should not be relegated to a separate category. "All education that is fit to be called education is a form of character education," from which it follows also that mere verbal instruction in ethics and morality is inadequate, although it is highly important that young people be encouraged to evaluate their experiences and arrive at fruitful conclusions regarding the relative merits of one type of experience, principle, or course of action in contrast with another. Indeed, as against reliance upon praise and blame (which to be sure have their educative influence), Dewey stressed the educational value of experiences "which enable an individual to see for himself what he is doing, and which put him in command of a method of analyzing the obscure and unavowed forces which move him to act." [45]

The foregoing emphasizes the importance of adult guidance fully informed "by the method and materials of a science of human nature." As Dewey remarked in *Experience and Education,* there is little point in the educator's being more mature than the young if he fails to use his greater insight and mature experience to help organize the conditions of the experience of the immature. [46]

Although Dewey objected to the terminology of Freudian psychology and its dualistic emphasis, he welcomed its contributions to the understanding of human behavior. His own recognition of the role played by emotional and social factors in personality development and in education was influential in broadening the concept of guidance to include more than academic and vocational concerns alone. Without judgments on conduct permeated by the materials and methods "of a science of human nature," he wrote in 1922, "the best-intentioned attempts at moral guidance and improvement of others often eventuate in tragedies of misunderstanding and division, as is so often seen in the relations of parents and children." [47]

[45] Dewey, *Human Nature and Conduct, op. cit.,* p. 321.
[46] See Dewey, *Experience and Education, op. cit.,* p. 32.
[47] *Ibid.,* p. 321.

REFLECTIVE THINKING, DEMOCRACY, AND SOCIAL CHANGE

Moral education is thus no simple matter. Far from being an incidental responsibility of the school, of one department, of one subject, or of one aspect of a subject, it is all-embracing. It is more than a matter of instruction in conscious principles of conduct (though these are important as generalizations from experience and the content of the curriculum—art, science, literature, history, and the like) which young people may employ as major premises in a syllogism. To such instruction must be added rigorous training in all other aspects of reflective thinking.

Moreover, since democracy is a "personal way of individual life," there is a striking similarity between the methods of reflective thinking and the processes of democracy, for democracy, as an organized society, puts a premium upon values roughhewn from the past, upon respect for the worth and integrity of the individual, and upon commitments to the ideal of equality and to ordered change. But it conceives of these values, precious as they are, more in the nature of formulas than as absolutes to be employed without respect to circumstance. Of and by themselves values are dehydrated. Only when caught up in the actual stream of events do they take on specific meanings, meanings which derive from the specific situation as well as from their abstract formulation. This is another way of saying that the happy solution of problems in a democratic society is uniquely dependent upon the methods of reflective thinking. And education of the young for effective participation in a government "of the people, by the people, and for the people" requires repeated experience in classroom and school in the exercise of reflective thinking as individuals and as groups.

Again, a democratic society, for Dewey, is an open society, one in which problems are solved and decisions arrived at through the exercise of freedom of thought and expression and majority decision. It is also a society keyed to change, to change that is ordered, controlled, and directed insofar as possible by the cooperative thought and action of its members.

What does this concept imply as regards the responsibility of the school? Three positions put forth by educators were rejected in whole or in part by Dewey. The first, indoctrination and education for conformity (be it conservative or radical), he opposed completely, on the ground that it violates integrity of thought and denies to young people their right to acquire the intellectual and moral discipline without which a free and open society cannot long survive.

A second position assumes that secondary as well as elementary school pupils are too young and inexperienced to understand adequately, let alone solve, the problems related to the growing pains of society; that disciplined methods of thinking are best developed by dealing with problems of the past or with problems in areas where facts are salted down and the validity of conclusions can be accurately checked. While, in the eyes of its advocates, this method has the advantage of avoiding the criticism that frequently accompanies the consideration of controversial issues in the school, it fails to provide an essential discipline—that of dealing with problems in which reason must cope with emotion and passion.

Third is the position that the school, as an institution representative of all the people, must confine itself to training students in "how to think but not in what to think." If by this is meant the exclusion of officially sanctioned solutions of problems the answer to which the future alone can validate, Dewey was agreed. But he urged, nevertheless, that such exclusion not take away from individuals the privilege and the responsibility involved in arriving at conclusions that have run the gauntlet of thorough classroom study, investigation, and discussion. To deny students the right to adopt what seem to them warranted conclusions and to close discussion without answers (if this were possible!) is to abort a complete act of thought. Consequently, Dewey could not accept fully an educational program that attempted to cope with problems of change without arriving at conclusions.

But whose conclusions are warranted—those of the instructor, those of a class consensus, or those of members of the group as individuals? On this point there is some vagueness, if not contradiction, in Dewey's writings. Ideally, he would have the teacher, when dealing with problems—economic, social, political—on which the community is divided, follow a procedure analogous to that of the natural sciences. There we find no sharp distinction between what to think and how to think. For example, before a student attempts to conduct research on a problem in physics, chemistry, or biology, for example, he must acquire as rich a background as possible, including prior research and competing theories, all on the assumption that present knowledge is inadequate. The period of the 1930's was one in which, for many students, the foundations of American society gave evidence of crumbling, and Dewey, along with others, was convinced that a new social order was impending. Consequently, he believed the school was obligated to acquaint the student with the data bearing upon trends that spelled a future different from the present, even though these data might weight decisions contrary to the status quo.

For example, addressing himself to the problem of methods of instruction that avoid "undemocratic inculcation of ready-made conclusions on the one hand and aimless vagueness on the other," Dewey wrote:

> If the relation between the economic organization of society and the realization of the democratic principle is simply a matter of adoption of "a specific reform," then insistence, if it should exist, that educators should use the schools to promote this reform conflicts with the professed democratic aim. But the "if" covers a good deal of ground. The belief that there is an *inherent* connection between the *realities* of a democratic society, under present conditions, and a change in economic affairs in the direction of greater control and planning exercised in the social interest does not seem to be correctly described as a specific social and economic reform. . . .
>
> If teachers who hold that there is an intrinsic relation between actualization of democracy and social planning of economic institutions and relations hope to bring others to the same conclusions by use of the method of investigation and free cooperative discussion, I see nothing undemocratic in the procedure.[48]

The suggestion that instruction in the social sciences follow a procedure analogous to that in the natural sciences has its difficulties. For one very good reason, the facts and the relevant data in the two fields are not analogous. It is not surprising, therefore, to find Dewey's followers divided on the proper course for the school to follow when dealing with problems on the cutting edge of the future. One group adheres strictly to the principle of neutrality—open discussion and a fair hearing for all points of view, with conclusions left entirely to the students as individuals. A second attempts to distinguish between fundamental principles which the school is obligated to instill in students and specific applications of these principles to issues in controversy. With respect to the latter, they are in agreement with the first group. Still a third group is convinced that "neutrality" is no longer in tune with the critical nature of the times. They say what is needed on the part of the school today is the exercise of a

[48] John Dewey, "Education, Democracy, and Socialized Economy," *The Social Frontier*, December, 1938, pp. 71-72.

"justifiable partiality" that will lead young people "to build the widest possible consensus about the supreme aims which must govern mankind in the reconstruction of the social order." [49] In Chapter 13 we shall return to these divergent conceptions of the role of the school in contemporary society.

[49] Theodore Brameld, "Philosophies of Education in an Age of Crisis," *School and Society,* June 21, 1947, p. 451.

SUGGESTED READING

Childs, John L., *American Pragmatism and Education* (New York: Henry Holt & Co., 1956), Chapters 4-6.

Cremin, Lawrence A., *The Transformation of the School* (New York: Alfred A. Knopf, 1961), Chapters III, V; pp. 135-142.

Dewey, John, *The Child and the Curriculum* (Chicago: University of Chicago Press, 1902).

———, *Democracy and Education* (New York: The Macmillan Co., 1916), Chapters XI, XII.

———, *Experience and Education* (New York: The Macmillan Co., 1938), Chapters I-III, VII.

———, *How We Think* (Boston: D. C. Heath & Co., 1910; rev. ed., 1933), Chapter I.

———, *Human Nature and Conduct* (New York: Henry Holt & Co., 1922), Part I, Sections I-V; Part II, Sections I, II, V-VII; Part IV, Sections II, IV.

Edman, Irwin, *John Dewey, His Contributions to the American Tradition* (New York: The Bobbs-Merrill Co., 1955), Chapter VIII.

Geiger, George R., *John Dewey: In Perspective* (New York: Oxford University Press, 1958), Chapter 9.

CHAPTER 12
EDUCATION
BETWEEN TWO WARS

FEW contrasts are more striking than those of attitude and conviction in the American people immediately preceding and following World War I. In 1901, the Supreme Court of the United States, in a five-to-four decision, approved the annexation of the Philippine Islands and the acquisition of Puerto Rico. These additions of territory, together with that of Hawaii in 1900, marked what has been called a "watershed in American history." The United States had become a world power with some 11,000,000 subjects of colonial status. William Jennings Bryan and other "anti-imperialists" feared that the nation could "not endure half republic and half colony." But the vast majority of the people who voted to reelect McKinley in 1900 seemed to agree with Senator Beveridge, who stated in a speech before Congress (January 9, 1900) that the "God in Heaven marked the American people as His chosen nation to finally lead in the regeneration of the world." To be sure, there were cynics who identified imperialistic ambitions of American business lurking beneath this rhetoric; but others sincerely believed the time had come for the United States to change the course of its history, assume the white man's burden, and share the fruits of a superior civilization with the "inferior and torpid" peoples of the earth.

By 1918, under the leadership of Woodrow Wilson, these messianic impulses were directed toward the promotion of international order and the rescue of European civilization from the "Huns." On January 5, 1918, came Wilson's declaration of his famous "Fourteen Points" (including his proposal for a League of Nations that would afford "mutual guarantees of political independence and territorial integrity to great and small states alike"). And there is little doubt that his words seemed to his fellow countrymen to follow logically and appropriately from those in his war message of 1917. At that time he had said: "The world must be made safe for democracy.... We are saying to all mankind, 'We did not set this Government up in order that we might have a selfish and separate liberty for we are now ready to come to your assistance and fight out upon the field of the world the cause of human liberty.'"

Then followed the disillusionments of peace, accentuated by revelations of secret treaties entered into between Russia, France, England, and Italy prior to and during the war, together with the restrictive clauses of the Treaty of Versailles. By March of 1920, little protest could be marshaled in opposition to the Senate's rejection of both the Treaty and the proposed League of Nations. "Countless Americans," wrote Charles and Mary Beard, "who in 1914-18 had yearned for a 'brave new world' at the conclusion of the war were disheartened by the proofs of sinister purposes running against their dreams."[1] In November, 1920, Warren G. Harding's plea for a return to "normalcy" received the endorsement of the electorate, and, by common agreement, European nations in particular and foreigners in general were left "to stew in their own juice."[2]

DEMOCRACY AN "ILLUSION"

Confidence in democracy suffered a similar deflation in the 1920's, an inevitable aftermath, perhaps, when we consider the pathetic outcomes of a war so costly in terms of lives lost and treasure expended. In addition, there was the increasing pressure of special interest groups upon state and national legislatures, to which the "muckrakers" earlier in the century had drawn public attention. These developments now led many political scientists openly to question whether democracy could withstand the pressures. And, finally, there were the widely publicized results of intelligence tests administered during the war, to which attention was called in Chapter 10. In the eyes of educators and the intelligentsia particularly,

[1] Charles Beard and Mary Beard, *Basic History of the United States* (Philadelphia: The Blakiston Co., 1944), p. 442.

[2] A slogan popular in the 1920's and expressive of the sentiment of the period. Mention should also be made of the Immigration Act of 1924, with its quota system, cleverly designed to restrict immigration.

the tests established clearly the futility of expecting the masses to cope successfully with the complicated problems of self-government, a conviction documented to the satisfaction of the "civilized minority" by the writings of Henry L. Mencken in the *American Mercury*, the scientific determinists in philosophy and psychology, and the "new humanists" of the Paul Elmer More and Irving Babbitt school.

The significance of these changes in attitudes toward democracy will be appreciated if we recall the enthusiasm with which the Progressives in the first two decades of the century undertook to bring government close to the people by means of measures such as the direct primary, the "initiative," the "referendum," and the "recall." (By 1916, for example, forty-five states had enacted laws providing for the direct primary in the selection of party candidates.) Contrast these accomplishments in democracy with the state of mind of a people that permitted the *Training Manual* of its Army, in 1928, to define democracy as follows for the enlightenment of its recruits! "A government of the masses. Authority derived through mass meeting or any other forms of 'direct' expression. Results in mobocracy. Attitude toward property is communistic—negating property rights. Attitude toward law is that the will of the majority shall regulate, whether it be based upon deliberation or governed by passion, prejudice, and impulse, without restraint or regard to consequences. Results in demagogism, license, agitation, discontent, anarchy."

AMERICAN BUSINESS AND A NEW SOCIAL ORDER

Equally startling was the reversal in popular attitude toward American business and the fruits of the capitalistic system. The first decade of the century was one of exposure of the "nefarious activities" of American business, as represented by the Standard Oil Company, the insurance companies, the meat trust, drug and food combinations, the railroads, the "money trust," and their corruption of governments, local, state, and national, conditions that prompted Theodore Roosevelt to inveigh loudly against the "malefactors of great wealth" and to initiate governmental action designed to correct abuses and to restore the natural resources of the country to the people.

This was also the heyday of the "muckraking" magazines (*McClure's, Everybody's, Cosmopolitan, Arena,* and *Hampton's,* to mention the most prominent). They increased their circulation phenomenally in the first decade—*McClure's,* for example, from 307,000 to more than 750,000 between 1900 and 1906. Prominent writers were Ida Tarbell, who exposed the monopolistic activities of the Standard Oil Company; Lincoln Steffens, famous for *The Shame of the Cities* and other works; Ray Stannard Baker, who wrote *The Right to Work;* Thomas W. Lawson, author of *Frenzied Finance;* and David Graham Phillips, who wrote *The Treason of the Senate.*

The campaign for various reforms—to end the malpractices of corporations, to ease the competitive position of small business in relation to the large corporation through government regulation, and to abolish abuses attendant upon the labor of women and children—was continued well into the first administration of Woodrow Wilson. Between his election in 1912, however, and the outbreak of World War I, muckraking entered upon a rapid decline. Merle Curti attributes this decline in part to weariness of the public, in part to the influence of bankers and advertisers upon the muckraking magazines, and in part to the feeling that the extension of government control over business through legislation had remedied the most flagrant of abuses.[3]

To these factors, following the War, should be added the conviction of economists that the United States had entered upon a new economic era, one of surplus capital in contrast with that of scarcity. This theory—widely publicized by high-pressure salesmen, newspaper columnists, and fiction writers—emphasized spending as the key to prosperity. "In spending, so the argument ran, one not only enjoyed the comforts and luxuries now available through the magic of mass production; one also fed the springs of prosperity by insuring the indefinite expansion of producer's goods industries."[4] As early as 1918, E. W. Howe had written, in *The Blessing of Business,* "The man who does me most good is the one who sells me necessary supplies and conveniences at a low price, because of economics of production."

By 1928, American business had not only regained respectability; it had become the recognized agent of a new and better social order, an order characterized by "prosperity, mass production, high wages, high-pressure selling, installments, service, bigger and betterism."[5] Even Lincoln Steffens, the muckraker of twenty years before, was now moved to

[3] Merle Curti, *The Growth of American Thought* (New York: Harper & Bros., 1951), pp. 621 ff. For an excellent survey of American thought preceding and following the war, see Chapters XXIV-XXVII.
[4] *Ibid.,* p. 697.
[5] *Ibid.,* p. 693.

suggest that the goals of socialism might be achieved under the auspices of a beneficent capitalism! But nothing, perhaps, reveals more accurately the new conception of business than the fact that Bruce Barton's book *The Man That Nobody Knows* (1925), picturing Jesus as the prototype of a modern man of business, enjoyed the status of a bestseller for a period of some two years.

EDUCATION TAKES BUSINESS AS A MODEL

Nowhere was business in its corporate organization and methods of operation admired more than in public education. The reform movement of the first decade of the century had resulted in the adoption of child labor legislation by some forty-three states. These laws not only governed hours and conditions of labor but defined the minimum age for leaving school. Supplemented and strengthened as they were in many states by compulsory school attendance laws, school enrollments began to increase phenomenally. With these developments came growing pains in the administration and organization of school systems.

Not the least of these pains was that resulting from lay administration by large school boards. This problem followed from the manner in which city boards of education tended to evolve—for just as the city itself grew in size and population by absorbing communities on its fringes, so its board of education was commonly enlarged by the steady absorption of local school committees. Add to this the general practice of administering school affairs through subcommittees, and it is not difficult to understand the waste, inefficiency, and, frequently, the corruption that beset school administration in the first two decades of the twentieth century. In 1902, for example, the board of education in the city of Philadelphia contained some 500 members. And in Rochester, New York, lay members of the board of education once served on the following committees: finance, qualification and employment of teachers, organization of schools and grievances, textbooks, library and apparatus repairs, buildings, supplies, fuel and fire fixtures, printing, salaries, janitors, and law apportionment.[6]

It is not strange that reformers turned to business organization for suggestions. The business corporation seemed to possess merit at precisely those points where municipal government had failed. In contrast with the large city councils and boards of education with their waste of time,

[6] Samuel Dutton and David Snedden, *Administration of Public Education in the United States* (New York: The Macmillan Co., 1915), p. 141.

logrolling, and subordination of public interest to factional selfishness, the governing boards of large corporations evidenced an enviable singleness of purpose and a capacity to distinguish between essential policies and details of administration. A similar comparison between the "democratic" administration of the schools (if we equate democratic with lay administration!) and the internal structure of the corporation seemed to favor the latter. The general manager appointed the heads of his department on the basis of merit and held them responsible for results. No consideration of politics or special favoritism stood in the way of increasing output or the lowest cost of production. Centralized responsibility and control, clearly defined functions, and single-hearted concentration of each member of the organization upon his work seemed indeed an ideal and a method worthy of incorporation in the conduct of school affairs.

Out of these comparisons came the small board of education concerned, in ideal at least, with the formulation of policy rather than with details of its administration. Within the school system came clean-cut divisions of labor and authority running from the board of education to the superintendent and from him to associate or assistant superintendents, to principals and supervisors, to heads of departments, to teachers.

The appeal to business as a model for the reform of public education likewise received support from constructive elements in public opinion. It carried conviction to the public-spirited businessman predisposed to favor suggestions derived from his own successful experience. For quite different reasons, social reformers supported programs of efficient school management. Their concern for child life led them to support policies that would lead ultimately to the insulation of the school from outside influences, whether these influences were the plunderings of politicians, the self-seeking purposes of pressure groups, or the baneful effects of an industrial civilization.

On the administrative side, as the social reformers saw it, the first essential was to secure an honest and efficient conduct of public education. To safeguard children for a necessary period of healthy growth and development, they fought for and secured legislation which raised steadily the age of compulsory school attendance and protected the young in other respects from the blighting effects of their environment. Not until some years later did it become evident that in freeing the school administration from lay interference and patterning the administrative structure upon that common to business organizations reformers had insured that children would attend autocratically managed schools—schools which attempted the impossible task of educating young people for active participation in democratic life under conditions that denied to them ways of living consistent with this preparation!

As we saw in Chapter 10, scientific management in industry, together with the assumptions of behavioristic psychology, also exercised a decisive influence upon the minds of educators concerned with methods of instruction and the curriculum. Job analysis, activity analysis, and functional analysis were used by curriculum experts to identify the specific activities in which children should engage in order to acquire the specific items of information, ideas, habits, and skills essential for effective performance in adult life. Subjects of study, such as spelling, arithmetic, handwriting, geography, history, and literature were subjected to detailed analysis in order to determine what each might yield in the way of specific knowledge and skills. In each instance, the criterion of approval was social utility or actual use in the "real business of living."

For example, an investigation of words used by adults and children in the writing of letters led to a reduction of words in spelling lists from some 10,000 to 4,000. Similarly, the tabulation of problems actually encountered by farmers, bankers, housewives, shoppers, and the like was used to determine the appropriate content of textbooks in arithmetic. One who participated actively in studies of this character, prior to a radical change of heart, later remarked:

> Rarely the educational technicians questioned the existing order.... They started with the *status quo*. They accepted school subjects. They were willing to permit algebra, arithmetic, spelling, geography, and science their definitely allotted places in the school program. They did not see American life and its problems on the one hand and the growing child and his needs on the other as important units to be integrated. Even to these new educational scientists reorganization was to be piecemeal.[7]

From the analysis of conventional subjects to an analysis of life situations in which young people require competence, but for which traditional subjects gave no preparation, was, of course, but a step. Consequently, it is not surprising that educators, at a time when the "melting pot" concept was also popular, should extend their techniques to areas other than the academic—first, to vocational education and, later, to the social, civic, and

[7] Harold Rugg and Ann Shumaker, *The Child-centered School* (Yonkers, N.Y.: World Book Co., 1928), p. 30.

personal areas of "adjustment." Particularly did this extension seem relevant on the secondary school level for that steadily increasing proportion of boys and girls who did not plan to attend college.

These considerations led to what was first termed the "enrichment" of the curriculum, but was later termed, in the 1940's and 1950's, the "corruption" of the curriculum by the introduction of "life adjustment" subjects of a nonacademic character. These included nonvocational as well as vocational subjects, when, as in the 1930's and 1940's, it became evident that vocational training alone would not solve the problems of the non college-bound student in a world in which there was decreasing need of special training in order to enter upon many types of jobs. By 1949, for example, vocational and nonvocational subjects enrolled nearly as many students as did mathematics, science, and foreign language combined.[8]

Finally, brief mention should be made of attempts to apply the principles of scientific management to problems of supervision. As we have said, the period was one of phenomenal increases in school enrollments. By 1920, for example, 90 percent of all children in the population from ages seven to thirteen were enrolled in school. Between 1918 and 1926, the proportion of young people between the ages of fifteen and eighteen enrolled in high school increased from 28.29 percent to 53.12 percent.

These developments confronted school systems with novel and baffling problems of educating children of widely different abilities and backgrounds with teaching staffs increasingly difficult to recruit in numbers and qualifications adequate for the task. One solution suggested was "divide in order to conquer." Accordingly, children were grouped in instructional groups on the basis of "ability," as determined, in some instances, by intelligence tests alone and, in others, by a combination of factors—"intelligence," teachers' appraisal of ability, previous grades, and the like. Various devices were likewise adopted in order to standardize teaching performance so as to enable a supervisor to control and direct better the activities of his staff. One or two illustrations will have to suffice.[9]

---

[8] John F. Latimer, *What's Happened to Our High Schools?* (Washington, D.C.: Public Affairs Press, 1958), pp. 120-121.

[9] The literature of the 1920's abounds in descriptions of plans and experiments in "scientific supervision." One excellent source of illustrations is *Scientific Method in Supervision, Second Year Book of the National Conference of Supervisors and Directors of Instruction* (New York: Teachers College, Bureau of Publications, Columbia University, 1929).

In Minneapolis, time studies were made of the various types of reading activities in the primary grades, with a view to standardizing the time teachers might properly devote to each phase. In another instance, the teaching of arithmetic was analyzed into steps and a "kit of tools" devised for the supervisor to use in testing the results of instruction, diagnosing outcomes, and applying remedial procedures. The "kit" in this instance consisted of some eight different "tools." Common to virtually all of these plans for effective supervision was the assumption that uniformity and efficiency are identical twins. Children were caught up in a lockstep performance which required them to proceed at a uniform rate, to acquire identical items of information, or to perfect identical skills in identical ways. Teachers were required to operate within an autocratically organized school system in which they as well as their pupils subordinated individual talent to the dictation of their superiors.

THE CULT OF THE CHILD

Not all Americans in the 1920's were satisfied with the prevailing emphasis upon the superiority of the American way of life, its mass production and consumption, material values, conformity and standardization of thought, and surface recreation. Thus a warm reception was accorded such prominent writers of protest as H. L. Mencken, Ellen Glasgow, Eugene O'Neill, Sherwood Anderson, Edmund Wilson, John Dos Passos, Sinclair Lewis, and Theodore Dreiser. Disillusionment assumed different forms: withdrawal from politics in the face of the trend toward "normalcy" and the failure of parties of protest to win public support; flagging interest in social work and social reform, when these efforts also gave little evidence of long-term results; and rejection of the standards of conventional morality. "The cult of self-expression and pleasure, especially in the realm of sex," writes Merle Curti, "and the corresponding reaction against so-called Puritanism and Victorianism constituted one of the most obvious patterns among both intellectuals and the 'flaming youth' of the middle classes." [10]

It was primarily laymen of this frame of mind—middle-class and upper-middle-class businessmen, professionals, writers, artists—who first joined with disillusioned educators and teachers to establish schools in which

[10] Curti, *op. cit.*, p. 710. For a vivid description of "The Revolt of the Highbrows," see Frederick Lewis Allen, *Only Yesterday* (New York: Bantam Books, 1946), Chapter 9.

children might be recognized and treated as individuals, each with a unique personality and possessed of unique needs. For the regimented school of large classes and lockstep procedures were substituted groups small in size, in which children worked and played in an atmosphere free from restraint. As against standardization and uniformity, the new schools emphasized creativity and self-expression—self-expression in the arts, conspicuously, but in other areas of learning as well—on the assumption that each individual is endowed with an "innate capacity" for creative activity and expression which it is a primary function of the school and the home to cultivate. Instead of teacher-dominated situations, fixed schedules, and arbitrary subjects (reading, arithmetic, geography, history, etc.), attention centered upon "real life situations"; children's interests and needs; group initiative in suggesting, planning, and executing "projects" and "units of work"—sometimes as outgrowths of conventional subjects, sometimes as organizing centers of activity occupying an entire year—in which "skills" were developed "on the side" as essential tools with which to achieve major objectives. Finally, in contrast with the old school with its mass-education machinery, its formal methods, and authoritarian atmosphere, the new schools undertook to deal with children as individuals and to foster their personal and social development through the cooperative and social relationships of each child with his peers.

This novel approach to education yielded interesting results. It revealed hitherto unsuspected possibilities within children. In a friendly and sympathetic atmosphere they astonished observers with original and creative productions. Children who had previously been passive and overly docile began to manifest initiative and self-direction. Subject matter, also, underwent revolutionary change. As children's interests in the world about them became grist for the teachers' mill, young folk began to explore, inquire, and investigate into their environment with a freshness of spirit and—within limits—with a thoroughness superior to that of the conventional school. And although the habits and skills, and even the information thus acquired, were often partial and lopsided when laid against the standards of adequate discipline, this disturbed not at all the nonconformist hearts of teachers who were themselves in rebellion against the old.

Although friendly to the emphasis upon creative work in the "child-centered" schools, Harold Rugg emphasized that "the chief weakness of these schools is conspicuous intellectual waste. *Child activity is regarded altogether too frequently as an end in itself, rather than as a means to growth."* [11] One who spoke in defense of less emphasis upon formal education in the early years and more upon ample provision for constructive play, art, music, shop, and the like was Elizabeth Irwin of The Little Red School House. She once explained that children from intelligent homes in the modern urban environment have ample opportunity to acquire at home such skills as reading, writing, and arithmetic, but that since their homes lack the facilities and the ability to provide other essentials for development these become the responsibility of the school.

Although a number of leaders in the "child-centered" school movement were acquainted with John Dewey's thought and, in some instances, had studied under him, progressive education in the early 1920's was more in the tradition of Rousseau and G. Stanley Hall than of Dewey. Social reform and the revitalization of democracy through education was less a loving concern than to insure for each child healthy channels of expression for the unique and creative potentialities with which it was assumed he is natively endowed. As Lawrence A. Cremin points out, the sources of their inspiration were primarily expressionism in art and Freudian psychology with its insights into the unconscious and its mechanisms.[12]

This distinction between the new education as conceived by Dewey, on the one hand, and the proponents of the child-centered schools, on the other, is important to observe in order to appraise the influence of William Heard Kilpatrick, in whom, in many respects, the two are blended.

THE CONTRIBUTIONS OF WILLIAM HEARD KILPATRICK

It is interesting to speculate how fundamentally Dewey's thought would have influenced education in this country and abroad had he not found in William Heard Kilpatrick a brilliant and persuasive expounder of his philosophy in its applications to educational theory and practice. It is said that it was Professor Kilpatrick who persuaded Dewey to write *Democracy and Education* (1916), probably the most comprehensive statement of the latter's philosophy in relation to education.

In 1909 Kilpatrick accepted the position of professor of educational

---

[11] Harold Rugg, "A Critical Appraisal of Current Methods of Curriculum-Making" in *Twenty-sixth Yearbook of the National Society for the Study of Education* (Bloomington, Ill.: Public School Publishing Co., 1927), Part I, p. 436.

[12] For a brief but enlightening description of these two influences, see Lawrence A. Cremin, *The Transformation of the School* (New York: Alfred A. Knopf, 1961), pp. 201-215.

philosophy at Teachers College, Columbia University, a post he occupied until his retirement in 1938. During this period, students flocked to him from all parts of the Union and, increasingly, from other countries, as his reputation as a teacher and expounder of the philosophy of experimentalism grew to enviable proportions. Of this influence Dewey once wrote:

> In the best sense of the words, progressive education and the work of Dr. Kilpatrick are virtually synonymous. I say in the best sense because the phrase "progressive education" has been and is frequently used to signify any kind of school theory and practice that departs from previously established scholastic methods.... The aims and processes of learning, which have been so fully and concretely stated by Dr. Kilpatrick form a notable and virtually unique contribution to the development of a school society that is an organic component of a living, growing democracy.[13]

SOCIAL CHANGE AND EDUCATION

What have been the "aims and processes" of education to which Kilpatrick has drawn attention over the years?[14] In a very real sense, Kilpatrick's primary concern throughout his educational career has been character development. He has believed, however, that for education to develop character most effectively it is necessary to transform schools and schooling in ways relevant to the needs of young people who are called upon to play a responsible role in a changing and a democratic society.

In 1926 Dr. Kilpatrick delivered three lectures at Rutgers University under the title of *Education for a Changing Civilization*.[15] In these lectures he drew attention to the major characteristics of modern society and their implications for education. These characteristics are variations upon the theme of rapid change. The implications drawn involve new conceptions of subject matter and its purposes, new methods of working with young people, and the transformation of the spirit and atmosphere of the school in harmony with the ideals and purposes of democracy.

Traditional education, he stated, assumed that the future, in all essential aspects, will resemble the past. Consequently the task of the school

13 John Dewey, "Introduction," in Samuel Tennenbaum, *William Kilpatrick, Trail Blazer in Education* (New York: Harper & Bros., 1951).
14 For a list of articles, pamphlets, and books written by William Heard Kilpatrick, see *Studies in Philosophy and Education*, November, 1961, pp. 220-230.
15 William Heard Kilpatrick, *Education for a Changing Civilization* (New York: The Macmillan Co., 1926).

was to transmit the cultural heritage. It professed to prepare for adult life, but did not do so, thus failing in two respects. "It has not prepared for the present adult life, and it has ignored the unknown future adult life." [16] Again, the older school recognized a split in education. Life outside the school provided the "real life situations," the vital experiences, "the language of daily life, domestic duties, means of livelihood, and such moral and social attitudes and customs as would be learned by the simple process of living the group life." The school supplemented this education with instruction in subject matter "fixed-in-advance," and concerned primarily with the transmission of information, skills, and habits of thought keyed to a static society.

It was thus life outside the school that provided the most vital education, education through firsthand experience. Today, however, this situation no longer obtains. The home and community no longer enlist the young in the economic and social activities or in the intimate cooperative relationships that once made of them institutions and agencies "for inducting the child into industrial activity or for giving him insight into the basic economic-social processes or for building in him those cooperative moral-social attitudes and habits that underlie social life." [17] Since family and community fail to provide the "inherent" education they once did, continued Kilpatrick, it must be furnished by the school. "This demands that the school become more truly a place of actual experiencing, for only in and from such experiencing can the child get the inherent close-to-life kind of education formerly given by his home and community. Since it is life with inherent educating that has been lost, it is life with inherent education that must now be provided." [18]

Changes in fundamental ways of living and attitudes associated with these ways likewise affect moral education. "Less and less do the young yield themselves to the mere word of their elder's command. Less and less do they accept existing custom and convention as binding. More and more do they insist on why's that shall be to them convincing." [19]

These are stubborn facts. It is a condition and not a theory that confronts us. With external authority gone and mere verbal instruction a feeble instrument, the school must help young people "to find the only

[16] *Ibid.*, p. 61.
[17] *Ibid.*, pp. 63-64.
[18] *Ibid.*, p. 96.
[19] *Ibid.*, p. 80.

real authority that can command respect, the internal authority of 'how it works when tried.' " [20]

What is true of morals and moral education applies also to education for democracy. The commitment of the American people to democracy requires them to reject the authoritarian school and the attitudes of mind and character fostered by it. "Possibly one reason for the disappointments of democracy," wrote Kilpatrick, with his mind's eye upon the times, "is that we have never really tried it." We "do not learn what we do not practice."

Finally, Kilpatrick called attention to science and the role of science in modern life. By science, he meant the methods of "tested thought." To tested thought and its methods we owe the transformation in man's attitude toward himself, the transformation from want of confidence in his natural faculties and the results of his own thinking to one of confidence and reliance upon both. From this confidence and the applications of science as a method in all areas of living have come the revolutionary changes of the modern world, including the ability to control and direct change itself. Consequently it is important to acquaint young people with this indispensable tool of scientific method, to help them acquire the habits of mind and character its use involves, which is another way of saying, "Our duty is so to prepare the rising generation to think that they can and will think for themselves, even ultimately, if they so decide, to the point of revising or rejecting what we now think. Our chosen beliefs will have to stand this ordeal." [21]

The above summary, brief as it is, should answer, in part at least, those critics of Kilpatrick who contend he centered so exclusively upon the presumed "needs" of children that he neglected the equally important demands of society upon education. On the contrary, the transformations in modern society to which he drew attention render imperative for him a new conception of the task of the school. "The old notion," he wrote, "contemplated a static civilization with problems already solved. . . . That curriculum was, at its best, the ordered arrangement of past-achieved solutions. Learning was acquiring these age-old solutions. A passive acceptance constituted 'docility,' the highest of youthful virtues. But we now face an unknown future. We must prepare in a different fashion." [22]

[20] *Ibid.*, p. 82.
[21] *Ibid.*, p. 60.
[22] *Ibid.*, p. 123.

Fundamental changes in the nature of society and the effects of these changes upon young people render imperative a new education. The "laws of learning," as interpreted by Kilpatrick, also require that the school become a place of "actual experiencing."

KILPATRICK'S TWO THEORIES OF LEARNING

One year prior to the publication of *Education for a Changing Civilization* (1926), Kilpatrick published his widely used text *Foundations of Method* (1925).[23] This book is of interest today as evidence of his earnest and ingenious attempt to translate Thorndike's psychology of S → R bonds into a dynamic theory of learning. It was an attempt which he eventually abandoned in favor of an "organismic psychology," a psychology more in harmony with Dewey's concept of experience as a process of interactions between organism and environment.

In his early acceptance of Thorndike's psychology, Kilpatrick stressed the identification of learning as an active process, a way of behaving in contrast with the traditionally passive emphasis. "To learn," he insisted, "is to acquire a way of behaving." Translated into S → R bonds, this means the strengthening of existing bonds or the joining of a new R to an old S.[24] The correct conception of subject matter, or "desirable learnings," he also interpreted as potential ways of behaving which one acquires best as needed.

Kilpatrick gave a similar interpretation to the "laws of learning," to fundamental laws of exercise and effect, and their specific applications as the laws of readiness, set and attitude, satisfaction and annoyance, multiple response, associative shifting, and the like. These "laws" he employed effectively to emphasize the importance of practice in living situations. "What we learn we must practice." The law of set and attitude is identified with the significance of will, purpose, self-direction. The facts of multiple response to multiple situations emphasize the significance of "incidental" and "associated learnings"—of attitudes and appreciations that color and permeate not only the acquisition of knowledge and skills but the situations and conditions under which learning takes place.

By 1935, however, Kilpatrick was ready to abandon what he then

---

[23] William Heard Kilpatrick, *Foundations of Method* (New York: The Macmillan Co., 1925).
[24] See *Ibid.*, Chapters II, III, for Kilpatrick's detailed analysis of learning in terms of Thorndike's psychology.

characterized as an atomistic psychology attempting to be "scientific." Though concerned primarily with living persons, he stated, advocates of this psychology tried, "in order to be 'objective,' to banish from the educative process both personality and life. They analyzed life into small separate pieces as impersonal as possible—facts, habits, skills—and studied these in separation, as if they could be put back together and get persons and life. They called these small pieces 'educational objectives' and would make a curriculum out of them. They memorized nonsense syllables, as if they would tell them how persons learn in life." [25]

"In direct contrast" with this psychology, based upon physiology and seemingly "but body, non-thinking and mechanistic," Kilpatrick now turned to a psychology that takes its cue from biology. In the following passage, he described this "better psychology":

> [It] gives full sway to all the organism can do; away from atoms like $S \to R$ or the conditioned reflex to the organism acting as a whole, with thinking, feeling (emotion), impulse, physical movement, glandular action, etc., as aspects (not separable parts) of one organic action. In particular, this better psychology rejects such an analytic procedure as grants the same behavior to small pieces in separation as when in living contexts. Learning is increasingly seen as creative of its own subject matter, not simply an acquisition of what was already there.[26]

The new "organismic psychology" conceived of education as valid only when it is "primarily the conscious pursuit of personally felt purposes with ever more adequate self-direction as the goal." The proper unit of the curriculum is thus "an instance of self-directed purposive living, not as formerly a selected portion of subject-matter-set-out-to-be-learned." [27]

The transition from a mechanistic to an organismic psychology reinforced Kilpatrick's original commitment to education through real life situations. "The newer education," he wrote, "finds its unit in terms of the newer psychology which starts with life as the pursuit of ends or purposes. A desirable educative experience is present whenever a person faces a challenging situation and undertakes responsibly to deal with it." [28]

[25] William Heard Kilpatrick, *Remaking the Curriculum* (New York: Newson & Co., 1936), p. 16. This book was based on a series of articles written for the *NEA Journal*, beginning in November, 1935, and ending in May, 1936.
[26] *Ibid.*, p. 18.
[27] *Ibid.*, p. 18.
[28] *Ibid.*, p. 33.

THE PROJECT METHOD

Few teachers have enjoyed for as long a period the influence that Kilpatrick exercised upon theory and practice during the years of his active teaching. To his classroom at Teachers College, Columbia University, came students from all over the world, and from it went forth earnest disciples—supervisors and teachers, principals and superintendents, instructors in schools of education—eager to apply what they had learned in the form of the "project method" of teaching.

The term "project" was first used in vocational education to describe an assignment that supplemented regular classwork. In agriculture, for example, the instructor might assign a real life problem as a home task (feeding and caring for stock, planting and raising a crop, and the like), involving the concrete application of principles previously learned in school. The term quickly spread to other areas in order to describe any *supplementary* activity of a *practical* character involving the *application* of a principle learned. What Kilpatrick and his followers undertook to do was to reverse earlier procedures by giving central importance to the problem or the project, on the assumption that its real life character would insure the essential mastery of knowledges and skills once the pupil identified himself wholeheartedly with the task in hand.

In the hands of skillful teachers and competent supervisors the project (later more commonly termed a "unit of work," or "center of interest") stimulated badly needed reorganization of elementary education. As we have seen, elementary school enrollments increased phenomenally during the first third of the century. An urban and industrial civilization was no longer dependent upon child labor in the city or in the country (for science and technology were also revolutionizing life on the farm). Childhood had become a unique stage of development with new needs and new potentialities to which the school thus far had given too little attention. As these needs gained recognition, attempts were made to serve them by the introduction of additional subjects taught in the traditional manner.[29]

The project method gave not only unity and meaning to these otherwise

[29] By the turn of the century, for example, the curriculum of a "good" elementary school included some ten or more separate subjects: reading, writing, spelling, arithmetic, geography, history, nature study, physiology or hygiene, music, and drawing. See Ralph W. Tyler, "The Curriculum—Then and Now," *The Elementary School Journal*, April, 1957, pp. 364-374.

unrelated subjects but significance and purpose as well to the mastery of the "minimum essentials" of habits and skills and information. In the better schools the work of each grade came to center upon general organizing themes [30] for a year or a portion of a year. From the "wholehearted" pursuit of these themes, teachers succeeded in developing not only academic knowledge, skills, and attitudes in a manner equal to, or superior to, the accomplishments of the traditional school but, in addition, fruitful relations between school, home, and community. Attention was thus directed to the all-round development of children—emotional and social, as well as academic—a concern that gave rise to the phrase "the whole child." What was meant, at best, was not, as frequently charged, that the school assumed direct responsibility for the total development of the child, thus replacing the home and other institutions, but that work in school should take its character from its relation to all essential aspects of growth and development. Implied, of course, was a curriculum sensitive as well to the characteristics (assets and debits) of each community.

Unfortunately, in this country, demand has always outstripped supply of competent teachers who combine a rich and varied background with a professional knowledge of child growth and development. As a consequence, in all too many instances, Kilpatrick's philosophy was superficially interpreted and misapplied. His condemnation of subject matter planned in advance and without reference to the needs of young people or the peculiarities of a situation ("pre-digested subject-matter") was used to justify anti-intellectualism and undirected classroom experiences for children.

Lawrence A. Cremin quite properly contends that Kilpatrick's discussion of the project method in his *Foundations of Method* encouraged a dichotomy between teaching children and teaching subjects, to the disadvantage of the acquisition of organized knowledge. "The resultant child-centered emphasis," writes Cremin, "calls to mind the very position Dewey himself rejected, first in *The Child and the Curriculum* (1902) and later in *Experience and Education* (1938)." [31] The present writer attended many an educational conference in the 1930's at which the phrase "mere subject matter" was used in a manner to suggest that the school's responsibility for organized knowledge was something to be avoided

[30] For illustrations of "centers of interest" and a criticism of their advantages and disadvantages, see Rugg and Shumaker, *op. cit.*, Chapters VI–X.
[31] Cremin, *op. cit.*, pp. 218–220.

at all costs. Many an objector to the doctrine of formal discipline during this period seemed to assume, nevertheless, that the method of thinking acquired in a real life situation, however trivial, would enhance thought in all other situations!

Furthermore, there was no shortage of "experts" to promote the doctrine that a curriculum designed to meet the needs of a specific group of children can only be planned appropriately "on the spot," by teachers and pupils jointly. On occasion, the words of Kilpatrick might be interpreted as favoring a curriculum of this character. But he was usually careful to qualify his approval with the suggestion that the program should reflect "the cooperative efforts among all who deal with the child both during any one year and throughout successive years." This differs from a plan whereby each class and its teacher is free "to gallop off in all directions." [32] All too often the outcomes, in terms of educational values and learning products, particularly in the hands of teachers of meager background and experience, were such as to encourage the savage criticism of the 1950's.

THE DEPRESSION OF THE 1930'S
AND THE NEEDS OF YOUTH

Child labor legislation reinforced by compulsory school attendance laws in the first and second decades of the century were major factors in changing the character of the elementary school population and, with this change, in drawing attention to the need for educational reform. The depression of the 1930's served a similar purpose with respect to secondary education.

So severe were the depression years in their effects upon the employment of young people above the age of compulsory school attendance that the generation in school and college at that time was frequently referred to as "the lost generation." Between 1930 and 1935, for example, the proportion of all employed youth between the ages of sixteen and twenty-four decreased by approximately 30 percent.[33]

Opportunities that in the 1920's seemed to beckon youth diminished rapidly in the 1930's. From studies of conditions in widely separated

[32] See Kilpatrick, *Remaking the Curriculum, op. cit.,* pp. 95-96. The more extreme position found expression in L. Thomas Hopkins' *Integration: Its Meaning and Application* (New York: D. Appleton-Century Co., 1937).

[33] The data on unemployment and school attendance used in this section are taken from Homer P. Rainey, *How Fare American Youth?* a preliminary report prepared for the American Youth Commission (New York: D. Appleton-Century Co., 1937).

cities and states—from New York to Houston to Denver, from Connecticut to Pennsylvania to Minnesota—it was possible to conclude, as did Rainey, that the depression had produced a large crop of "square pegs in round holes." There was a steady increase in the proportion of high school graduates for whom only jobs of a manual and unskilled character were open. Opportunities in the professions were not consistent with the aspirations of youth. Professor Harold F. Clark estimated that of 400,000 youth who left school in 1936 with hopes of entering the professions only 87,500 succeeded in so doing.

A new stage of development was plainly being created by the exclusion of young people above the age of compulsory school attendance from other than blind-alley occupations. And this new stage was one with both cultural and psychological characteristics, for which only the emergence of childhood in an earlier period provided an analogy. Just as early in the century children below age fourteen were being excluded from the activities of home and community which once provided an "inherent education," so now in an urban and industrial society, adolescents were being confronted with a similar fate. Thus it was becoming clear to educators and others concerned with the problems of youth that here was a new stage of development with novel implications.

For adolescents, however, and the society of which they were members, the implications of this new stage were quite different from those attendant upon the earlier "emancipation" of children. As one group of observers pointed out at the time:

> Decreasing economic opportunity has not only brought defeat to large portions of the population and deeply felt insecurity to all; indirectly, through this defeat and insecurity, it has brought in its wake the profoundest threats to which democracy in this country has been subject. The situation is peculiarly crucial with respect to adolescents. They remain without status, on the one hand pressed by the culture to establish themselves on the basis of economic participation, and on the other hand denied the opportunity to work. Without status, it is difficult for them to accept themselves or others as persons. Unless the school discovers some way to help these young people find and accept new roles and new status, new relationships with others, new missions in life, democracy may disappear. All this calls for a reinterpretation of educational goals and procedures.[34]

[34] V. T. Thayer, Caroline B. Zachry, and Ruth Kotinsky, "A New Education for Youth," *Progressive Education*, October, 1939, p. 398.

These remarks were based upon the findings of the Adolescent Study of the Commission on the Secondary School Curriculum of the Progressive Education Association. On the basis of data secured from a study of over 600 adolescents in schools, colleges, and out-of-school situations, this study attempted to provide a more meaningful description of adolescent development for the purposes of education than had previously been available. The study likewise pooled its resources with committees of school and college teachers who worked with the Commission in various subject matter areas.

THE TIMES DEMAND A NEW SECONDARY EDUCATION

Rapidly mounting enrollments in secondary school and college reflected these changes in the status of youth. By 1935, approximately 65 percent of the population aged fourteen to eighteen were enrolled in school; and a secondary school population that had numbered some 700,000 in 1900 had increased to more than 6,000,000 by the mid-1930's. Moreover, this increase was not restricted to the secondary school. During the same period, enrollments in institutions of higher education increased from some 237,500 to about 1,260,000.

But what was the reaction to the education and training available to American youth in the light of this new situation? Few authorities, at the time, disagreed in theory with the following statement by Homer P. Rainey:

> It is perfectly clear that the old secondary education which stressed the selective and college preparatory functions is no longer suited to modern conditions. Secondary education is not now to be regarded as a privilege for a selected minority. It is rather to be thought of as a common experience for practically all youth between 14 and 18 years of age. In the past we have referred to the elementary grades as the "common school." This concept must now be revised to include the entire field of secondary education, which embraces the junior and senior high school and the junior college. The primary function of a secondary education for the period ahead is to provide a common education for all at these higher levels.[35]

Although educators were inclined to agree with Rainey in theory, the schools that succeeded in translating theory into practice were few indeed.

[35] Rainey, *op. cit.*, p. 46.

The curriculum in the vast majority of secondary schools was still keyed to the requirements for admission to the conventional college and thus to a level and a type of academic ability denied to some 50 to 60 percent of the school population. Professor Terman, for example, estimated that an intelligence quotient of at least 110 was required for success in the traditional high school, while some 60 percent of American youth ranked below that score. It was concern for this lower group that gave impetus to "education for adjustment" in harmony with the specific "demands" of society as interpreted by behavioristic psychology.[36] Conditions within as well as outside the educational system thus seemed to call for the reorganization of education, vocational as well as general.

Studies conducted by the American Youth Commission clearly demonstrated the inadequacy of vocational preparation of a narrow and specific character. As one of these studies emphasized, "The great majority of the entrants into occupational life today must possess qualities of adjustability and adjustment, must know how to do not one thing but many things, must be able to transfer from one job to another, must be capable of sustained attention and quick reaction, must be more intelligent, and must be able to get along with people, to work with them, to direct them and to serve their needs." [37]

In contrast with the prevailing tendency in vocational education to train for specific operations and positions, the American Youth Commission urged an interrelationship between vocational and general education. For example, it was pointed out that "all vocations which deal with machinery have a common background in physical science. All the vocations which are of a type commonly classified as commercial have a background in economics. The learned professions have a background in history and literature." [38] This statement reminds one of the following words of John Dewey:

> Conflict between the cultural, or liberal, and the practical will continue with result of confusion as long as both of them are narrowly conceived. I can hardly go into the philosophy of American life, but I do not see how anyone can doubt that as long as the humanistic is set off as something by itself, apart from the interests and activi-

[36] See Chapter 10 of this volume.
[37] American Council on Education, *Equal Educational Opportunity for Youth* (Washington, D.C.: the Council, 1939), p. 139.
[38] Rainey, *op. cit.*, p. 56.

ties in which the mass of men and women must perforce engage, it will grow thinner, more and more reminiscent, a struggling survival of what Santayana calls the "genteel tradition." It is equally true that as long as the actual occupations of men, with the exception of a few professions labelled "learned," are not affected by a larger outlook and the fuller background presented by the ideal for which the liberal in education stands, they will be narrow and hard, tending not merely to the "utilitarian" in its restricted sense, but even toward the brutal and the inhuman.[39]

Since it was becoming evident, as World War II and later trends confirmed, that in industry and agriculture, particularly, training programs below the semiprofessional level might be reduced to "short, intensive units immediately prior to employment,"[40] the Commission urged that education prior to the beginning of the senior high school period be "general and uniform for all, with emphasis upon a general or liberal education."[41] It was recognized, of course, that no one rigid rule should govern vocational education and training to the exclusion of conditions peculiar to communities. What the Commission had in mind was that vocational education should become, so far as possible, the hub of a wheel with many spokes (the spokes representing specific vocations) related intimately to general education. Obviously these recommendations carried implications for general as well as vocational education above the level of the junior high school.

THE GENERAL EDUCATION MOVEMENT

As we have seen, enrollments in both secondary school and college had increased rapidly since the turn of the century, rendering acute growing pains on both levels. One response was the emergence of the junior college, public and private, much as earlier a similar influx from elementary school into high school had created the junior high school with provisions for both vocational and general education. Indeed, by 1930, junior colleges, both public and private, numbering some 400 or more, had been organized in every state in the Union and the District of Columbia, with

[39] John Dewey, *The Way Out of Educational Confusion* (Cambridge, Mass.: Harvard University Press, 1931), p. 26.

[40] See Hollis L. Caswell and others, *The American High School: Its Responsibility and Opportunity* (New York: Harper & Bros., 1946), Chapter IX.

[41] Rainey, *op. cit.*, p. 54.

the exception of Nevada, Vermont, and Wyoming.[42] On the whole, however, by the early 1930's, the results of the junior college movement were far from revolutionary, and for a reason similar to that blocking reorganization on the senior high school level: the insistence of standardizing agencies that junior colleges wishing their graduates admitted to senior colleges duplicate work offered in the lower divisions of colleges and universities. Consequently, progress toward reform in large measure was forced to wait upon changes in the curriculum of the latter.

Vocational education in junior colleges also tended to be specific, following the pattern of education for adjustment and the methods commonly followed in trade schools of a lower order. Only here and there, by the 1930's, were beginnings made in the organization of semiprofessional courses basic to both professional and semiprofessional training.[43]

Reorganization on the college level began with the introduction in the freshman year of courses under the varied titles of orientation, survey, and general education. Orientation courses originated, as the name suggests, in an attempt to adjust freshmen to the complexities of college life but, like college life itself, became increasingly complex and plural in their objectives. One early purpose was to offset the specialization and fragmentation in knowledge resulting from the multiplication of courses in college and university and the evils of uneven and skewed development associated with the elective system. The methods adopted varied, with the result that the spirit of experimentation spread widely, centering attention eventually upon the wider problem of what education best serves the needs of young people of school and college age.

One answer was the survey course to which reference was made in Chapter 10. This was akin in spirit to the method of job analysis in vocational education, in that it attempted to identify the facts and principles in representative fields of knowledge that might serve as a basis for a student's subsequent work in college. Gradually more functional criteria were employed, as evidenced, for example, in the statement of Dean John J. Coss of Columbia University in describing the course on "Contemporary Civilization" at that institution. This course, wrote Dean Coss, is an attempt "to ask: What are our social and intellectual worries; how

---

[42] For a picture of their offerings, see Doak S. Campbell, *A Critical Study of the Stated Purposes of the Junior College* (Nashville, Tenn.: George Peabody College, 1930).

[43] For a description of these trends, see Robert J. Leonard, "Professional Education in Junior Colleges," *Teachers College Record*, Vol. XXV, May, 1925, pp. 717-733.

do we come to have them; what attitudes can we take toward them; what promising solution can we find for them?" [44]

This functional emphasis was also apparent in the orientation courses of the University of Chicago. Thus the objectives of the course in biology were (1) to cultivate "a familiarity with, a respect for, and some facility in the scientific method"; (2) to give the student the biological information he needs as a citizen and a parent; and (3) to arouse an interest "in the grand machinery of the organic world" and the large concepts that have proved useful in biology.

In a similar but more thoroughgoing manner, as described in Chapter 10, Stephens College, Missouri, undertook on the basis of a survey to plan the content of courses so as to enable the students to acquire the principles and facts and skills essential to function adequately as women.

Still a third method was to use the concept of orientation to provide educational guidance of the individual student, rather than to insure his mastery of materials and processes formulated in advance. This involved programs of study for students in small groups or for individuals, if necessary, in the light of individual analysis, as, for example, at Bennington, Sarah Lawrence, and Black Mountain colleges. In more conventional colleges, as, for example, Vassar and Converse, individual courses ("Euthenic" at Vassar, "The Family" at Converse) were occasionally organized with direct reference to the students' needs rather than upon the basis of prescribed ground to be covered.

This is by no means a complete description of attempts at reorganization of the curriculum on the college level prior to the full onslaught of the depression in the 1930's. It is hoped, however, that enough has been said to indicate the emergence of new criteria for the organization of the curriculum and the selection of subject matter for courses in the first two years of college. These criteria were less the scholarly interests of advanced workers in the field, as formerly, and more the assumed needs of students as indicated by the demands of society and revealed by objective analysis. Except for the minority of experimental colleges, emphasis was not so much upon the individual, his interests, background, or particular situation, as such, but, rather, upon what an objective analysis of society seemed to indicate should be inculcated in him.

[44] From John J. Coss, "A Report of the Columbia Experiment with the Course on Contemporary Civilization" in William S. Gray (ed.), *The Junior College Curriculum* (Chicago: University of Chicago Press, 1929).

There was a similar placement of emphasis in the psychological assumptions giving character to these courses. The student was viewed either as a mind to absorb subject matter prepared in advance or as an organism to be conditioned to think, feel, and act in ways revealed as essential by "social analysis."

It is also hoped that this brief reference to general education in the two years beyond high school will indicate the relationship between these efforts at educational reform and earlier attempts to transform elementary education. Indeed, the schools of philosophy and psychology that found expression in reforms as different as the great books curriculum at St. John's College in Annapolis, Maryland, the social functions procedure at Stephens College, the survey courses at Chicago, Colgate, and elsewhere, and the emphasis upon the individual in the more radical experimental colleges were identical with those used earlier to give form and shape to elementary education. As we shall see in a later chapter, the "common human nature" which the great books curriculum at St. John's College was designed to inform and to discipline was but another name for the "mind" of traditional education with which William T. Harris and other educators of the nineteenth century were concerned. The social functions procedure accepted Kilpatrick's thesis that real life situations should give character to work in the school, but differed radically from Kilpatrick in its applications. Analysis of contemporary society rather than the interests and concerns of young people was to reveal the "areas of living" or "social functions" that should determine the content and organization of the curriculum.

THE EDUCATIONAL POLICIES COMMISSION REDEFINES THE FUNCTIONS OF EDUCATION IN AMERICAN DEMOCRACY

Probably the most widely quoted definition of "areas of living" in this period was that of the Educational Policies Commission of the National Education Association, entitled *The Purposes of Education in American Democracy* (1938).[45] On the expressed assumption that the purposes of

[45] Educational Policies Commission, National Education Association, *Policies for Education in American Democracy* (Washington, D.C.: the Association, 1946). This volume includes the 1938 statement together with two other general statements by the Commission: *The Unique Function of Education in American Democracy* (1937), and *The Education of Free Men in American Democracy* (1941). Page references are to the 1946 volume.

education in any society "reflect and interact with the purposes which permeate the life of the people," that is, their "system of values," the Commission boldly asserted, "The general end of education in America at the present time is the fullest possible development of the individual within the framework of our present industrialized society." [46] It then promised "to set down in some detail a description of the necessary and desirable elements of information, skill, habit, interest, and attitude which most surely promote individual development and encourage democratic ways of living among the people of this country." [47] The areas of "behavior" selected as most relevant for this modest undertaking were four: *Self-Realization, Human Relationships* (Home, Family, and Community Life), *Economic Efficiency,* and *Civic Responsibility.* Each of these areas was then analyzed further into the activities of the educated person who succeeds in giving evidence of its realization.

As one rereads this document, the influence of functional and activity analysis and behavioristic psychology are evident. The promised goal of specificity with respect to the information, skills, habits, and the like upon which a teacher of a given subject might center is never quite realized, despite suggestive general discussions of each trait listed under the four major objectives. From this point of view, the report is no more realistic than its definition of the "system of values" of American society, a limited definition when measured against the full range of values that were actually operating in the lives of American citizens.

Primarily, the significance of the report at the time derived from the fact that an authoritative body, such as the Educational Policies Commission, at a most critical period in American life, undertook to define on a national scale the major purposes of public education in terms far broader than (1) the traditional emphasis upon the three R's in elementary education, or (2) a choice between specific vocational training and general education of a college preparatory character in the secondary school, or (3) a distinction between professional and semiprofessional training and a liberal education in college and university. Educational institutions were now conceived as supplementary institutions in a most vital sense—as society's instruments for envisaging the all-round development of the individual in a democratic society—not with the intention of replacing other institutions, but rather of reinforcing and assisting them

[46] *Ibid.,* p. 186.
[47] *Ibid.,* p. 187.

in such a way as to insure, as far as possible, equality of opportunity for each young person in the development of his talents and abilities.

Secondly, the report was of the utmost importance in reasserting the democratic ideal in American education. As we have seen, the 1920's had been years of disillusionment and cynicism for large numbers of people with respect to democracy. The rise of totalitarian states in Europe under Mussolini and Hitler, together with the destructive effects of the depression at home, with its challenge to the American people to meet the crucial needs of the period with instruments of their own creation, once more aroused general interest in and concern for democracy. In a companion report on *The Unique Function of Education in American Democracy* (1937), the Educational Policies Commission urged schools and colleges to reexamine their administrative structure and their instructional programs in the light of their responsibilities and potential contributions to the democratic way of life. The importance of this challenge at the time will be appreciated when we recall the imminence of World War II and the impending confrontation of the democratic and totalitarian powers.

THE CONCEPT OF NEEDS ASSUMES IMPORTANCE

Much closer to the individual school and the individual student, in their recommendations, were two commissions of the Progressive Education Association in the 1930's. The first, *The Commission on the Relation of School and College,* entered into a special arrangement between some thirty secondary schools and over three hundred colleges according to which the former were freed for a period of eight years to experiment with their curricula without jeopardizing the admission of their students into college. The second, *The Commission on the Secondary School Curriculum,* undertook through committees composed of school and college teachers and members of the staff of the Adolescent Study (a subcommittee of the Commission) to suggest materials and methods of instruction in subject matter areas in the light of a personal-social conception of the needs of young people of secondary school age.[48]

[48] Each Commission issued a number of publications dealing with various aspects of its work. A general overview of the activities of the Commission on the Relation of School and College was presented in Wilfred M. Aiken, *The Story of the Eight-Year Study* (New York: Harper & Bros., 1941); and in *Thirty Schools Tell Their Story* (New York: Harper & Bros., 1943). The findings and conclusions of the Commission on the Secondary School Curriculum and the Adolescent Study are reviewed in V. T. Thayer, Caroline Zachry, and Ruth Kotinsky, *Reorganizing Secondary Educa-*

This is no place to discuss the work of these two commissions in detail. What should be emphasized is, first, that their concerns were in no way confined to the college-bound student alone. Experiments in the reorganization of the curriculum of the secondary school, for example, as conducted under the auspices of the first Commission, had in mind all types of students of secondary school age. Similarly, the data on the needs of adolescents, as formulated by the Adolescent Study and interpreted by the subject matter committees of the second Commission, were based upon the study of some 650 young people in school, college, CCC work camps, and other out-of-school groups by a staff of sociologists, anthropologists, and trained psychiatric social workers.

The conception of "needs" as interpreted by these two commissions was an application of John Dewey's theory of the nature of experience, experience as a mutually defining interrelationship, a "transaction" as Dewey termed it, between the individual and his surroundings. It thus differs from "needs" viewed as the demands, requirements, and standards of society which continue to serve as a basis for the organization of courses of study and curricula in a large number of schools today. It also differs from the social functions approach to curriculum organization as commonly applied in the elementary school.[49] As the Committee on the Function of Science in General Education put it, "To speak of a need without including both its *personal and social* aspects is to leave out an indispensable element. Merely to say that Johnny wants something or that teacher X believes Johnny needs a particular piece of knowledge, is to leave out the element of interaction between the two necessary components."[50]

In line with this dual conception of experience and of needs, the Com-

tion (New York: D. Appleton-Century Co., 1939); and Caroline Zachry and Margaret Lighty, *Emotion and Conduct in Adolescence* (New York: D. Appleton-Century Co., 1940). The reports of the various subject matter committees (all published in New York by D. Appleton-Century Co.) were: *Science in General Education* (1938), *Language in General Education* (1940), *The Visual Arts in General Education* (1940), *Mathematics in General Education* (1940), and *Social Science in General Education* (1940). Two other documents related to the curriculum were Lawrence Conrad, *Teaching Creative Writing* (New York: D. Appleton-Century Co., 1937); and Elbert Lenrow, *Prose Fiction in General Education* (New York: D. Appleton-Century Co., 1940).

[49] For an excellent review of the social functions concept in the secondary school in the 1930's and since, see Harold B. Alberty and Elsie J. Alberty, *Reorganizing the High School Curriculum* (New York: The Macmillan Co., 3rd ed., 1962), Chapter 8.

[50] *Science in General Education, op. cit.,* p. 26.

mission on the Secondary School Curriculum concluded that curricular experiences should meet the following criteria:

First, they must relate meaningfully to the prevailing desires, inclinations, and quests of the particular students for whom they are designed, since needs are personal in reference. Curricular experiences, in other words, must have identifiable connection with the individual student's desires for a sense of security, of belonging, of achievement, and the like, and must contribute to their fulfillment in socially desirable ways.

Second, they must be relevant to significant current social, economic, political, and cultural trends as they bear upon the adolescent, since needs are also always social in reference. In other words, they must further the individual's adjustment within the basic relationships of living.

Third, they must further the realization of democratic values since education cannot meet needs without giving direction to their expression. Curricular experiences must be conducive to the growth of that kind of personality which is capable of democratic living under modern conditions.[51]

With these criteria before them, various subject matter committees associated with the Commission undertook to examine the resources of their fields—science, social studies, mathematics, language, literature, art—with a view to suggesting materials and methods appropriate for meeting the needs of young people in the four areas of Immediate Personal-Social Relationships, Social-Civic Relationships, Economic Relationships, and Personal Living. Each of these "basic relationships" was further analyzed in terms of needs which it was hoped administrators, guidance workers, and teachers would find helpful in the conduct of school and classroom and the organization of subject matter.

For example, the needs emphasized in *Economic Relationships* were: (1) the need for emotional assurance of progress toward adult status, (2) the need for guidance in choosing an occupation and for vocational preparation, (3) the need for wise selection and use of goods and services, and (4) the need for effective action in solving basic economic problems. The *Immediate Personal-Social Relationships* (referring to the adolescent's relationships in home and family life and with his schoolmates and friends) stressed the importance of healthy emancipation from ties with

[51] Thayer, Zachry, and Kotinsky, *op. cit.*, p. 415.

the family and fruitful relationships with his peers. The needs stressed were (1) the need for increasingly mature relationships in home and family, and (2) the need for successful and increasingly mature relationships with the age-mates of both sexes. How a subject matter group might employ these analyses is well illustrated in the volume *Science in General Education* and in Elbert Lenrow's *Prose Fiction in General Education*—to mention but two publications of the Commission.

A more recent formulation of this same basic concept of needs and its implications for education will be found in Robert J. Havighurst's *Human Development and Education*. Havighurst, who worked intimately with both commissions, now prefers the term "developmental task" to "needs." "A developmental task," he writes, "is midway between an individual need and a societal demand." [52] It is a task that "arises at or about a certain period in the life of the individual, successful achievement of which leads to his happiness and to success with later tasks, while failure leads to unhappiness in the individual, disapproval by the society, and difficulty with later tasks." [53] In this volume, Havighurst analyzes the developmental tasks from infancy throughout life and discusses the biological, sociological, and cultural nature and basis of each; the manner in which they are related to lower-, middle-, and upper-class cultures; and their implications for the curriculum.

No one type of curriculum organization emerged from the work of these commissions. Some schools continued with the conventional subject matter organization but modified both content and method in the light of new criteria. Others adopted what was termed a broad fields curriculum (for example, English, social studies, science, mathematics, as a substitute for insulated and diverse subjects such as composition and literature, biology, chemistry, physics, geography, history, algebra, and geometry). Still others adopted the core curriculum and unified subject approach. The core curriculum was usually a basic course required of all students, and two or more periods a day were commonly devoted to it. Organization was around broad themes or problems which took their character from needs common to all students of a given grade level or age group. By their very nature these problems cut across traditional subject matter lines. Integrated courses of this kind tended to enlist the

[52] Robert J. Havighurst, *Human Development and Education* (New York: Longmans, Green & Co., 1953), p. 332.
[53] *Ibid.*, p. 2.

cooperative efforts of a group of teachers from different fields in determining the needs of participating students and in the marshaling of the resources of their particular areas for the purpose of meeting the educational needs of the group. Supplementing the core course were the so-called special fields courses of the conventional curriculum. In some schools, the core curriculum was carefully planned in advance with respect to the problems or "units of work" undertaken. In others, it became an "experience curriculum," planned jointly by teachers and students. As such it resembled the project method as envisaged by William Heard Kilpatrick.[54]

The results of the Eight-Year Study were significant as determined by the experience in college of graduates from the Thirty Schools. In a comparison of 1,475 of these graduates with matched pairs of graduates from conventional schools, it was found that the former excelled in all subject matter fields with the exception of foreign language; received slightly more academic honors; were judged to be more precise, systematic, and objective in their thinking, more resourceful in meeting new situations; and equalled or excelled their peers in other essential areas of college experience.[55] Despite these verified outcomes, the Eight-Year Study has had comparatively little influence in changing either the character of the curriculum in secondary schools or the requirements of admission to college. The "lost generation" of the 1930's became the indispensable means for the survival of democratic nations in the 1940's. And the preoccupations of a people at war constituted an atmosphere unfavorable to suggestions for fundamental reorganization of their educational systems. Furthermore, the conclusion of the "hot war" merely marked the beginning of a "cold war" with its fear of communism and the subversion of American institutions. Such fear was better adapted to conformity of mind and attempts to perpetuate the status quo than to efforts at change, as evidenced in the 1950's by attacks upon education in which progressive education in any of its forms was identified by many as an alliance with "collectivism" or, even, the clever designs of communism.

Before we turn to the postwar period, however, and its influence upon

[54] For a recent discussion of the structure of the curriculum, see Alberty and Alberty, *op. cit.*, Chapters 5, 6, and 7. For Kilpatrick's concept of the curriculum of the 1930's, see his *Remaking the Curriculum, op. cit.*

[55] For a more detailed comparison of the two groups, see Aiken, *The Story of the Eight-Year Study, op. cit.*, pp. 110-112, and Dean Chamberlain and others, *Did They Succeed in College?* (New York: Harper & Bros., 1943).

education, we should consider more fully the revived interest in democracy in the 1930's and its implications for education as viewed by contrasting schools of educational thought. We now turn, therefore, to a discussion of rival conceptions as to the school's function in a rapidly changing democratic society.

SUGGESTED READING

Alberty, Harold B., and Alberty, Elsie J., *Reorganizing the High School Curriculum* (New York: The Macmillan Co., 3rd ed., 1962), Chapters 4, 8.

Childs, John, *American Pragmatism and Education* (New York: Henry Holt & Co., 1950), Chapter 7.

Cremin, Lawrence A., *The Transformation of the School* (New York: Alfred A. Knopf, 1961), Chapter 7.

Curti, Merle, *The Growth of American Thought* (New York: Harper & Bros., 1951), Chapters XXIV-XXVII.

Kilpatrick, William Heard, *Education for a Changing Civilization* (New York: The Macmillan Co., 1926).

———, *Remaking the Curriculum* (New York: Newson & Co., 1936).

Rugg, Harold, and Shumaker, Ann, *The Child-centered School* (Yonkers, N.Y.: World Book Co., 1928), Chapters V-X.

Thayer, V. T., Zachry, Caroline B., and Kotinsky, Ruth, *Reorganizing Secondary Education* (New York: D. Appleton-Century Co., 1939), Chapters II-III.

CHAPTER 13

THE RELATION
OF THE SCHOOL TO
THE SOCIAL ORDER

ON the whole the 1920's were years of prosperity and optimism. The business boom that began in 1924 and lasted until 1929 was one of the longest in American history. The period was also one of phenomenal opportunity for large numbers of Americans to invest their profits and their savings in the securities of attractive new industries—the automobile industry, aviation, new applications of electricity, and the chemical industry (stimulated by the war, later by the assignment to American firms of German patents, and by high tariffs on European chemical products) —in addition to conventional avenues of investment such as farms, real estate, and railroads.[1]

Only here and there were voices to be heard questioning continuous progress. A majority, as evidenced by their ballots in November of 1928, were in agreement with Herbert Hoover's declaration on August 11 of that year that "We in America today are nearer to the final triumph over poverty than ever before in the history of any land."

---

[1] In 1926 Congress voted mail subsidies and other forms of assistance to the airlines, with the result that commercial aviation quickly developed into a big business. By 1929 the chemical firms of DuPont, Allied Chemicals, and Union Carbide exceeded in size any similar firm in Europe. In 1920 there were about 9,000,000 automobiles registered in the United States. By 1930 registrations had increased to nearly 30,000,000. For a summary of this period of "boom and bust," see William Miller, *A New History of the United States* (New York: George Braziller, 1958), pp. 362-368.

Then came the stock market crash of October, 1929, and the long depression of the 1930's. Between March, 1930, and March, 1931, unemployment grew from 4,000,000 to 8,000,000, and these totals were not limited to the unskilled. They involved all classes and all vocations—professional workers, such as artists, writers, physicians, teachers, architects, research workers, as well as farmers, small businessmen, factory workers, and the like. Soon large numbers of the dispossessed began to inhabit flophouses and to construct shacks out of tin and tar paper, discarded packing boxes, and old car bodies, thus forming throughout the nation communities ironically called "Hoovervilles." Bread lines and soup kitchens were common. "Citizens of Chicago," wrote Arthur Schlesinger, Jr., "in this second winter, could be seen digging into heaps of refuse with sticks and hands as soon as the garbage trucks pulled out. On June 30, 1931, the Pennsylvania Department of Labor and Industry reported that nearly one-quarter of the labor force was out of work." [2] Clarence Pickett, of the Friends Service Committee, found Pennsylvania schools in which 85, 90, and 99 percent of the children were underweight, drowsy, and lethargic. " 'Have you ever heard a hungry child cry?' asked Lillian Wald of the Henry Street Settlement in New York City. 'Have you seen the uncontrollable trembling of parents who have gone half-starved for weeks so that the children may have food?' " [3]

Tragic also was the inability of many leaders to envisage adequate means of relieving distress. At one and the same time that the head of President Hoover's Organization on Unemployment Relief (Walter S. Gifford, president of the American Telephone and Telegraph Company) was declaring as his "sober and considered judgment" that federal aid would be a disservice to the unemployed, and "the net result might well be that the unemployed who are in need would be worse instead of better off," [4] public and private resources available for relief were rapidly shrinking. In New York City, for example, family allowances were averaging $2.39 per week for relief. Similar conditions existed in other cities, while in many rural areas no relief was available at all. Small wonder that Wallace B. Donham, Dean of the Harvard Graduate School of Business Administration, was moved to write in 1932 that "capitalism is on trial

[2] Arthur M. Schlesinger, Jr., *The Crisis of the Old Order* (Boston: Houghton Mifflin Co., 1957), p. 89.
[3] *Ibid.*, p. 171.
[4] *Ibid.*, p. 174.

and on the issue of this trial may depend the whole future of western civilization." [5]

Some of the effects of the depression upon youth were mentioned in the last chapter. Speaking of these young people in its issue of February, 1940, *Fortune Magazine* stated, "At least six million of the nine million 'unemployed,'" during the ten-year industrial depression, "were neither tractored off the farm nor rationalized out of the roundhouse nor spray-gunned off the scaffold nor mechanized out of the mines nor even eroded onto the highways. Six million, as a statistical matter, have never had jobs at all. They are the net increase in the working population.... Such in simplified form is the problem that like the ghost of his guilt freezes the tongue of any honest American who is otherwise proud of his economic system.... For nearly one-fourth of the population there is no economic system—and from the rest there is no answer."

Moreover, graduation from school and college was no longer the open sesame to success it once had been. In many communities manual and unskilled labor alone afforded what few jobs were available to high school, even college graduates, and these on a diminishing scale. Financial stringency, moreover, soon began to undermine education both in quantity and in quality. Public schools in numerous instances were forced to shorten their terms. Sixteen small colleges closed their doors, and hundreds of others reduced salaries.[6] Not until Congress under the New Deal began to provide aid through work relief (the Works Progress Administration), jobs for young people in school (the National Youth Administration), and other devices for stimulating the economy, did light begin to break through darkness. Despite the unfavorable conditions of the depression decade, secondary school enrollments for the country as a whole increased from 4,800,000 in 1929–1930 to 7,100,000 in 1939–1940.

The full implications of these facts for the future were not lost upon educators. A few of the implications for curriculum of school and college were discussed in our last chapter. In the minds of many, however, these changes fell short of what was essential in order to meet the realities of a society obviously in process of disintegration. To center upon the indi-

[5] Wallace B. Donham, *Business Looks at the Unforeseen* (Boston: Whittlesey House, 1932), p. 207.
[6] Merle Curti, *The Growth of American Thought* (New York: Harper & Bros., 1951), p. 719.

vidual, as progressive schools and colleges were doing, is excellent, wrote the most vigorous of these critics, George Counts, but "it brings into the picture but one-half of the landscape."

Nor was there time to waste. Both Italy and Germany provided object lessons of the manner in which frustrated youth might repudiate democracy and adopt the "leadership principle" in their search for security. Moreover, a fear that fascism and national socialism might "happen here" gained probability with the appearance of Huey Long in Louisiana, advocating his program of "share the wealth," and with the growing popularity and influence of Father Coughlin in Detroit, of fascist organizations, such as the Silver Shirts, the Crusaders, the Khaki Shirts, the National Watchmen, and of other "patriotic" societies of an antiliberal and antilabor bias.

Opposed to revolution under the leadership of the elite were those who saw in Marxism and the dictatorship of the proletariat in Russia an example the United States might well follow. "The success of the Five-Year Plan in Russia," writes Merle Curti, "in contrast to the economic breakdown at home, seemed to prove the inability of the middle-of-the-road liberals to accomplish reconstruction. Students of economics, sociology, history, and philosophy, including Lewis Corey, Max Lerner, Louis Hacker, Dr. Henry Sigrist, and Sidney Hook, related Marxism both to historical developments and to the current American scene." [7] In all fairness, it should be added that many writers and educators of this period who found in Russia suggestions for a solution to the economic and political problems of this country were eventually disillusioned with the communist "experiment" and labored diligently to inform Americans of the dangers it held for democratic institutions. Others, however, merely exchanged one form of dogmatism and intolerance for another, devoting their talents not only to opposing communism but liberal movements as well!

Still a third group was convinced that the depression marked the disintegration of capitalism and the emergence of a new economic and social order, one that promised to develop into a new feudalism if uncontrolled, but which, if properly directed, might be made to evolve into a collectivistic and cooperative democracy. To tip the balance in favor of democracy, this group turned to the schools.

[7] *Ibid.*, p. 731.

THE RELATION OF THE SCHOOL
TO A "NEW" SOCIAL ORDER

For the school to play a role in achieving a new social order was, of course, to reverse the traditional function of public education in American society. As we observed in Chapter 5, the fathers of the American public school saw in it an instrument for the conservation of values and the creation of unity out of diversity, by which was meant, of course, the values of the dominant group or class in society. Indeed, in their attempt to justify taxing one man for the education of another man's child (that is, general taxation in support of education) Henry Barnard, Horace Mann, Thaddeus Stevens, and others repeatedly emphasized that a major purpose of public education was to give stability to the status quo. In so doing they were no more than reaffirming the agelong and accepted mission of the school in relation to the society it has attempted to serve. Schools, traditionally, have been established for the purpose of conserving the knowledge, skills, and values of groups homogeneous in character and in which change was not anticipated or, if anticipated, was to be resisted. As Horace Kallen puts it, "West or East, education is overwhelmingly a work of culture, the old repeating themselves in the young, projecting their past as youth's future. Change, new directions, new goals, are forced, not chosen." [8]

Horace Mann, to be sure, recognized the increasing heterogeneity of American society, and he saw in the school one means of overcoming divisiveness. It was the danger of divisiveness, indeed, that led him to oppose sectarian religious instruction in public schools, while, in a country predominantly Protestant, he would have the schools continue to promote those tenets of religion acceptable to all. His formula for political education was similar: teach the principles common to all political parties. Should, by chance, a textbook include matters in controversy, he would have the teacher read it without comment or "at most ... say that the passage is the subject of disputation, and that the schoolroom is neither the tribunal to adjudicate, nor the forum to discuss it." [9]

With John Dewey and William Heard Kilpatrick, ideas in conflict be-

[8] Horace Kallen, *Philosophical Issues in Adult Education* (Springfield, Ill.: Charles C Thomas, 1962), p. 84.
[9] Horace Mann, *Twelfth Annual Report* (1848), in Lawrence A. Cremin (ed.), *Horace Mann on the Education of Free Men* (New York: Teachers College, Columbia University, 1957), p. 97.

came valuable grist for the educational mill. Change was no longer feared. Indeed, for both, change is a fundamental characteristic of reality. Consequently, a primary task of the school is to help young people forge instruments of mind and character with which to cope with change. For both, also, the methods of thinking employed in scientific investigations constitute the most valuable of these instruments. Finally, since in both Dewey and Kilpatrick the traditionally optimistic attitude of Americans toward change was strong, they could see only good resulting from exercising the minds of the young upon problems related to the future. Indeed, as Kilpatrick emphasized in *Education for a Changing Civilization*, "we must look as far into the future as we can to catch its problems." It is our duty as teachers "to prepare the rising generation to think that they can and will think for themselves, even ultimately, if they so decide, to the point of revising or rejecting what we now think." If the ideas thus challenged are worthy ones, he continued, they will survive this test. If they cannot thus survive, the probabilities are they ought not to, and the school will have contributed fruitfully to change. "As soon as we take the lid off the universe our claim to fasten our conclusions on our children vanishes. We must free our children to think for themselves." [10]

High on the list of priorities of procedure for both Dewey and Kilpatrick, however, was integrity of process for both student and teacher. The teacher's obligation—"with proper care for age and interest"—was to acquaint young people with the growing pains of their society, since problems of this kind constitute "the best intellectual subject-matter they can have." Furthermore, "that teachers do not know the answers to the problems will help, not hurt, the work." That is to say, both student and teacher should realize that judgments as to the future are of necessity tentative—thus are precluded dogmatic conclusions on the part of students and indoctrination on the part of teachers.

Looking back upon the controversies of the 1930's, Kilpatrick wrote in 1951, "A decade or two ago there was positive demand that the schools help build a new social-economic order. If this means that teachers should plan such an order and then by specific indoctrination raise up a new generation committed to the new order so planned, we cannot accept this program." [11] At the same time Kilpatrick consistently rejected the formula

[10] William Heard Kilpatrick, *Education for a Changing Civilization* (New York: The Macmillan Co., 1926), p. 60.

[11] William Heard Kilpatrick, *Philosophy of Education* (New York: The Macmillan Co., 1951), p. 124.

that the school should teach "how to think rather than what to think." This dictum was used all too often to justify an evasion of ideas in conflict on the apparent assumption that training derived from dealing with noncontroversial or "safe" subject matter would transfer, when needed, to problems in socially sensitive areas.

GEORGE S. COUNTS AND A CALL TO THE TEACHERS OF THE NATION

To many educators, profoundly disturbed by the disintegrating effects of the depression upon American society, this "neutral" attitude seemed out of tune with the pressing needs of the time. Indeed, as George Counts emphasized in his widely read and widely publicized pamphlet, *Dare the Schools Build a New Social Order?* [12] this group believed that the school, unless it now seized the initiative and proceeded to educate boldly for a new social order more in harmony with the principles of a truly democratic society, would continue to serve the interests of but one class, as it had in the past, as against the interests of the "masses" of the people.

Counts thus brought squarely into the foreground the question of the nature of the responsibility of the teaching profession to the young and to the society it serves. Should the profession attempt to mould the minds of the young in ways it considers relevant and appropriate to the future, or, should it continue, as in the past, "in the grip of conservative forces . . . serving the cause of perpetuating ideas and institutions suited to an age that is gone"? [13]

Opposition to Counts's thesis of indoctrination came first from progressive educators. Consequently, it was to the limitations and "fallacies" of progressive education that he first addressed himself.

Valuable as he recognized the contributions of progressive schools to have been—in focusing attention upon the child and the importance of his interests, in defending the thesis "that activity lies at the root of all true education," in conceiving of "learning in terms of life situations and growth of character," and "in championing the rights of the child as a free personality"—they nevertheless failed for want of a theory of social

[12] George S. Counts, *Dare the Schools Build a New Social Order?* (New York: The John Day Co., 1932). This pamphlet was based upon three papers read at national meetings of three educational associations in February of 1932: the Progressive Education Association, the Department of Superintendence of the National Education Association, and the National Council of Education.

[13] *Ibid.*, p. 5.

welfare, "unless it be that of anarchy or extreme individualism." Progressive schools were also limited, he insisted, by virtue of the clientele they served—a liberal-minded, upper-middle class, "persons who are fairly well-off, who have abandoned the faith of their fathers, who assume an agnostic attitude towards all important questions, who are full of humane sentiments in general" but are insensitive "to the accepted forms of social injustice," who "are content to play the role of interested spectators in the drama of human history," and who "in the day of severe trial will follow the lead of the most powerful and respectable forces in society and at the same time find good reasons for so doing." [14] To be genuinely progressive, Counts concluded, education must emancipate itself from the influence of this class, face social issues courageously, establish organic relationships with the community, "develop a realistic and comprehensive theory of welfare, fashion a compelling and challenging vision of human destiny, and become less frightened than it is today at the bogus of imposition and indoctrination." [15]

Then followed an analysis of some ten fallacies which Counts believed "to underlie the theoretical opposition to all forms of imposition." Briefly stated, these fallacies were: that man is born free; that the child is good by nature; that he lives in a world of his own; that education is "a pure and mystical essence that remains unchanged from everlasting to everlasting"; that the school should be impartial in its emphases; that "the great object of education" is to produce "the individual who adopts an agnostic attitude toward every important social issue" and "can balance the pros against the cons with the skill of a juggler"; that education is primarily intellectualistic in its processes and goals; that the school is an all-powerful educational agency; that ignorance rather than knowledge is the way of wisdom (with the result that progressive education wishes to build a new world through the education of the child "but refuses to be held accountable for the kind of world it builds"); and, that the major responsibility of the school is to prepare the individual to adjust to social change without responsibility for giving direction to change.[16]

Each of these fallacies, when examined, proves to be an overstatement and, when reduced to proper size, justifies the conclusion that growing up involves of necessity a high degree of imposition and indoctrination

14 *Ibid.*, p. 7-8.
15 *Ibid.*, pp. 9-10.
16 *Ibid.*, pp. 13-27.

of the young. Counts then posed the question: "Assuming that the child will be imposed upon in some fashion by the various elements in his environment, the real question is not whether imposition will take place, but rather from what source will it come." [17]

His answer was a clarion call to the teachers of the nation to organize as a profession, "reach for power and then make the most of their conquest," and boldly transform the schools into "centers for the building, and not merely for the contemplation of our civilization." To insure this outcome, however, it was necessary that the profession itself (which includes "scientists and scholars of the highest rank, as well as teachers working at all levels of the educational system") come "to grips with the problem of creating a tradition that has its roots in American soil, is in harmony with the spirit of the age, recognizes the facts of industrialism, appeals to the most profound impulses of our people, and takes into account the emergence of a world society." [18]

In his pamphlet on *Dare the Schools Build a New Social Order?* Counts distinguished, none too clearly to be sure, between his own private analysis of the causes and cures of the contemporary predicament of society and the tasks of the school. As he saw it, the times required that a society well on its way toward economic feudalism be refashioned in harmony with the American democratic tradition. This, in turn, implied the adoption of a formidable list of specific reforms, including "as a last resort," if need be, a willingness "to follow the method of revolution." [19] On the other hand, immediately following the assertion that the schools must become centers for the building of our civilization, he stated, "This does not mean that we should endeavor to promote particular reforms through the educational system. We should, however, give to our children a vision of the possibilities which lie ahead and endeavor to enlist their loyalties and enthusiasm in the realization of the vision. Also our social institutions and practices, all of them, should be critically examined in the light of such a vision." [20]

Less modest in its demands upon the profession was A *Call to the Teachers of the Nation*, issued in 1933 by the Committee on Social and Economic Problems of the Progressive Education Association.[21] The style

[17] *Ibid.*, p. 17.
[18] *Ibid.*, p. 39.
[19] *Ibid.*, pp. 41-42.
[20] *Ibid.*, p. 37.
[21] Progressive Education Association, Committee on Social and Economic Problems, *A Call to the Teachers of the Nation* (New York: The John Day Co., 1933).

of this pamphlet suggests generous contributions from Counts, who served as Committee chairman. The *Call* begins with a description of the plight of the American people in the fourth year of the depression. Even though they are in possession of the earth's richest resources and are "masters of the most advanced technology, they stand confused and irresolute before the future. With everything needful to banish poverty, to inaugurate an economy of plenty, and to clear the way for unbounded cultural advance, they tolerate an economic system . . . [that] makes a hollow mockery of their most cherished ideals." [22]

At bottom, according to the Committee, the causes for the present "phenomena of prosperity and depression, poverty and riches, production and extravagance, starvation in the midst of plenty" are to be traced "to a conflict between the social forms of production and the private system of distribution." [23] And this conflict, in turn, has been "re-inforced" by a confusion in values and purposes resulting from an "irreconcilable conflict" between two traditions, the one democratic and concerned for the well-being of the common man (the Jeffersonian tradition), the other aristocratic and with little faith or concern for the mass of the people (the Hamiltonian tradition). It is with the Jeffersonian tradition, reinterpreted in harmony with the characteristics of an industrial and technological society, that the teaching profession should ally itself. "In the great battle of ideas and values precipitated by the advance of industrial civilization the teachers of the country are inevitably and intimately involved." From this analysis, the Committee concluded that as "guardians of childhood, bearers of culture," and as "loyal servants and spiritual leaders of the masses of the people" the teachers of the nation "cannot evade the responsibility of participating actively in the task of reconstituting the democratic tradition and thus working positively toward a new social order." [24]

That the vast majority of the teachers of the nation did not accept this *Call* was not surprising. Indeed, Counts himself confessed to some misgivings as to the probable outcome of his appeal in his pamphlet on *Dare the Schools Build a New Social Order?* More surprising for many was the fact that the American economic and social order did not collapse as anticipated. On the contrary, it quickly regained sufficient vitality, first, to aid our European allies and, later, to engage directly in a life-and-death struggle with both Hitler and Mussolini in Europe and the Japanese

[22] *Ibid.*, p. 6.
[23] *Ibid.*, p. 11.
[24] *Ibid.*, pp. 18-19.

in the Far East. The conclusion of World War II found the American people in quite a different mood from that of the early 1930's. By 1950, the producing classes, whose interests Counts had urged the schools to serve, were far more preoccupied with the material comforts and the lure of "middle-class values" than with plans for the democratization of industry, economic planning, and political and social reform. Moreover, far from organizing for the purpose of taking over control of the schools and promoting revolutionary doctrines, members of the teaching profession, by and large, were offering little resistance to attacks upon academic freedom and charges of "subversion" within the profession directed against public education by Senator McCarthy and other opponents of liberal democracy. Indeed, the 1940's and 1950's seemed to confirm the thesis advanced by Nathaniel Peffer in replying to Counts and others: "When indoctrination for a new social order is practicable, it will no longer be necessary, for then the new order will have surrendered or been converted. Whatever education may be culturally or as a concept, as an institution it is not independent or self-sufficient. It cannot create; it can only reflect. It cannot generate new social ideas; it can transmit only those which are already accepted. It must always bend to the collective will around it." [25]

THEODORE BRAMELD AND RECONSTRUCTIONISM IN PHILOSOPHY

Not all voices in favor of a fundamental reconstruction of society through education were silent following World War II. For the past twenty years, Theodore Brameld, in season and out, in periods of prosperity as boldly as during cycles of depression, has courageously called upon the schools to examine and reexamine their curricula, their methods of instruction, and their administrative organization in the light of their potential role as creators rather than mere reflectors of the culture. To define his position in contrast with conventional education and conservative influences in the philosophy of education, on the one hand, and progressive education or experimentalism on the other, Brameld early adopted the term "reconstructionism." While less inclined today to insist upon this as a label,[26] he has in no way altered his conviction that the mission of a

[25] Nathaniel Peffer, "Educators Reaching for the Stars," *Harper's Magazine*, January, 1934, pp. 230-238.

[26] See Theodore Brameld, *Education for the Emerging Age* (New York: Harper & Bros., 1961), p. 1.

philosophy of education is to point the way toward the reconstruction of a culture, "which, left unreconstructed, will almost certainly collapse of its own frustrations and conflicts."

Brameld agrees with Counts in two respects: (1) that we live in a highly critical period in human history, and (2) that education in the United States should play a creative role in giving shape to the future. He objects, however, to what he calls the "naive" notion that his is a mere restatement of Counts's program. In the first place, "the domestic and world situation" is vastly different today from what it was in the 1930's. America was then absorbed chiefly "in its internal problems of poverty, unemployment, and insecurity." Today, humanity "is caught in the throes of a planetary transformation." Consequently, he believes the indignation and vision of the "social frontier" educators need to be redirected not so much toward ourselves as "toward the desperate plight, growing power, and emerging goals of the underdeveloped areas of the world, inhabited by the bulk of the world's population." [27]

Again, for the schools to be transformed "into powerful institutions of cultural change toward the goal of a planet-wide democratic order," a much more sophisticated and comprehensive theory of learning is called for than either Counts's conception of "imposition" or the experimentalist's preoccupation with methodology—methodology of "how to think" to the exclusion of hoped-for conclusions. Valuable as are the techniques of reflective thought and scientific method it employs, experimentalism, contends Brameld, "is defective in the respect that it focuses too much upon means at the expense of ends; it expresses the typical experimental spirit of open-minded, tolerant consideration of all sides of all questions, but fails to answer clearly the question of where we are going. In this concern of *how* we *do* think it has insufficiently helped us to discover for *what* we *should* think. Thus it is the counterpart of a culture developing by trial and error, with subordinate concern for clear-cut purposes or goals." [28]

In other words, the weakness of experimentalism, according to Brameld, is that it "expresses the mood, the values, and the practices of a culture *in transition* between two greatly different eras of modern history." The first was one of "industrialism, nationalism, capitalistic democracy, and individualistic liberalism." Appropriate to this period was the progressive's emphasis upon problem solving as an individualistic method. The emerg-

[27] *Ibid.*, p. 15.
[28] *Ibid.*, p. 26.

ing age is characterized by these fundamental features: "a largely automatic, integrated technology powered increasingly by atomic energy; a world population sufficiently educated to regulate its own growth according to available resources; a publicly planned and directed system of distribution of these resources so that physical and spiritual deprivation due to inequitable distribution of goods is eliminated; and an *enforceable* international government under democratic and, as far as possible, decentralized control." [29]

Brameld is also convinced that recent contributions of psychology, together with other social sciences, particularly anthropology, provide a more culture-centered concept of learning than either Dewey or Kilpatrick envisaged. Anthropology, for example, pictures man as unique among animals in his capacity for culture building. It also reveals that people everywhere possess similar endowments and similar wants, some of the latter "physiological, some psychological, some social." It thus supports "the prime political assumption of democracy that people of every race, nationality, religion, or social status are sufficiently alike in their basic structures, energies, potential abilities, to reach a vastly higher level of competence, self-reliance, and achievement than social opportunity has thus far typically offered." [30] Not the least in importance of the basic drives is "the desire for self-government," which, presumably, justifies the assumption that an adequate realization of these wants and needs on a worldwide scale requires a democratic association of the peoples of the earth.[31]

As Brameld sees it, then, both the critical nature of the times and a culture-centered theory of learning call for a philosophy of education that strives to give positive direction to an emerging society. This philosophy, "built out of the needs, wants, and interests" common to all people "should attempt to establish by discussion and consensus the institutional patterns needed now and in the future, in order that human beings may achieve utmost fulfillment of those values they possess most universally." [32]

Perhaps it should be pointed out, parenthetically, that Brameld's critics question the proposition that the existence of basic wants and needs common to all people is better calculated to bring about, eventually, an era

[29] *Ibid.*, pp. 31-32.
[30] *Ibid.*, p. 83. See p. 128 for a detailed list of these "common denominators" of human behavior and the implications Brameld draws from them for a world order.
[31] *Ibid.*, p. 83. See also Chapter 12 on "The Human Roots of World Order."
[32] *Ibid.*, p. 139.

of peace on earth and good will toward men than is the existence of un-shared wants, needs, and interests. In each instance, peace or the reverse turns upon the manner of their interaction. Indeed, continue the critics, when we consider the varied, at time contradictory, expressions these assume in different cultures, their similarities tend to fade away both with respect to the objects of their satisfaction and the conditions of their realization. Be this as it may, it is Brameld's conviction that the needs, wants, and interests "common to all people" can be used to give direction to an "emerging society." It is this conviction that defines the task of edu-cation both with respect to the design of the curriculum and to methods of instruction.

On the assumption that the junior college properly includes the period extending from the junior year of the high school through the second year of college, Brameld would have the curriculum center upon "the problems and prospects of reorganizing democracy" and its institutions with an eye to an evolving social order. This means, "not that other important areas are to be neglected, but that these be related to the hub as spokes are to the wheel." "Let us consider a new type of junior college," he writes, "open to all average young citizens from about seventeen to twenty years old. The four-year curriculum would be organized around one central theme: 'What kind of world can we have and do we want?' Each semester would consider different dimensions of this question: political, economic, scien-tific, moral, aesthetic, religious, and many others." [33]

THE METHOD OF "DEFENSIBLE PARTIALITY"

In an earlier volume, Brameld contrasts the method of reconstruction-ism with that of experimentalism. "Reconstructionist education," he states, "takes sides. It encourages students, teachers, and all members of the community not merely to *study* knowledge and problems crucial to our period of culture but also *to make up their minds* about the most promis-ing solutions and then to act concertedly. Its emphasis on *commitment* to agreed-upon future-looking goals thus raises the old problem, once more, of bias and indoctrination." [34]

What emerges, however, from a careful reading of Brameld, is his in-

[33] *Ibid.*, pp. 34-35. For a more detailed discussion of the design of the curriculum, see his Chapter 18 in full.

[34] Theodore Brameld, *Patterns of Educational Philosophy* (Yonkers, N. Y.: World Book Co., 1950), p. 558.

sistence, when dealing with the problematic and controversial, upon the method of group dynamics, carried, if possible, to the point of class consensus and conviction. Only thus, he believes, can schools avoid "one of democracy's greatest weaknesses," its pride in "open-mindedness and tolerance." The experience of commitment and conviction, it would seem, constitutes a value in itself. On the other hand, indoctrination, in the form of a deliberate marshaling of data, the omission of vital considerations, the use of propaganda, or the conscious playing upon prejudice with a view to a skewed conclusion is equally condemned by a philosophy which holds "that men should build positive convictions only by public inspection of and testimony about all pertinent and available evidence and by exhaustive consideration of alternative convictions." [35] Conclusions are *defensible*, then, only when they are "able to stand up against exposure to open unrestricted criticism and comparison" and are *partial* "insofar as these ends and means still remain definite and positive to their democratic advocates after the defense occurs." [36] One may question whether this fully elucidates the phrase "defensible partiality." Is it identical with Dewey's "warranted assertion"? Or is it a tentative conclusion which one may hold, even act upon, until evidence to the contrary appears? Or does it mean commitment (intellectual and emotional) so *defensible* that a class group, clearly identified with the school, may engage as partisans in a controversy in which the community is as a house divided against itself?

The reader, as others, may have difficulty in understanding in what way group consensus, as a practical objective, of necessity contributes toward cultural renewal, or to a consistent program of planned change. Obviously, on crucial issues involving long-established habits, emotions, customs, and the like, the "facts" leading to a consensus in one class group may very well lead to a consensus of a different character in another group. The experimentalist, with his faith in intelligence, does not object to this outcome. It is less clear how it should gladden the heart of the reconstructionist. Indeed, the experimentalist is satisfied with Dewey's oft-quoted observation: "Let us admit the case of the conservative: if we once start thinking no one can guarantee where we shall come out, except that many objects, ends, and institutions are doomed. Every thinker puts some portion of an apparently stable world in peril, and no one can wholly predict

[35] Brameld, *Education for the Emerging Age, op. cit.*, pp. 156-157.
[36] *Ibid.*, p. 157.

what will emerge in its place." Evidently the reconstructionist insists on knowing in advance the shape of things to come!

Finally, some see operating in Brameld's insistence upon commitment and consensus the influence of factors in contemporary life to which he is otherwise opposed—influences that shape the mind of the "organization man" and encourage conformity. To be sure, these critics admit, the *ends* are in no way identical. The reconstructionist hopes to bring about a radical transformation of society through consensus. Others utilize consensus in order to insure conformity with institutions and conditions as they are. But do the *means* differ? Granted the voice is the voice of Jacob, may not the hands prove to be the hands of Esau?

I. B. BERKSON AND CONSERVATIVE RECONSTRUCTION

I. B. Berkson's *The Ideal and the Community* represents reconstructionism in a more conservative vein. Berkson agrees with Brameld that "neutralism" is no longer applicable to the critical position in which the United States finds itself today. "Underlying the contemporary conflict of educational theory," he writes, "is a recognition of the need of a definite philosophical basis for education, of clearly formulated aims resting on accepted or acceptable principles." [37]

Berkson also believes that neither Dewey's conception of education as growth nor Kilpatrick's insistence upon identifying learning with the "biological life-process" provides sufficient direction for education today. They afford a one-sided view, only, of the educative process, thus underestimating "the part played by institutions in maintaining the existing democratic order." This will no longer do. "The aggressive ideologies of our day cannot be fought with vague statements on the merit of 'the democratic process'; they must be met with forceful counter-ideas. Democracy must become a cogent, compelling belief, capable of inspiring commitment and loyalty." [38]

As a reconstructionist, Berkson turns from "a biological-social interpretation" of learning "to an historical-cultural approach" with emphasis upon "institutional achievements and the enduring ideals of civilization at the center of consideration." [39] Here, of course, he repudiates the doctrine

---

[37] I. B. Berkson, *The Ideal and the Community* (New York: Harper & Bros., 1958), p. 3.
[38] *Ibid.*, p. 18.
[39] *Ibid.*, p. xi.

that the aims of education are derived from experience and the needs and wants of individuals. Rather do they flow from the ideas and the value judgments that give form and character to the culture in which the individual lives, moves, and has his being.

This is not to say that "needs" and the understanding of child growth and development are unimportant. On the contrary, Berkson insists they are indispensable guides for method and the grading of subject matter. As he puts it, "Method is always important, but what its significance is can only be gauged in relation to aims. It is only *after* we have decided *what* to teach that we may discuss the question of method." [40]

It follows that the scope and content of education provided by the school will vary with time and place, with the political and economic conditions of a people, and with their ethical and religious ideals. It does not follow, however, that the school should encourage blind conformity to the past or the acceptance of conditions as they are! "Every institution," Berkson emphasizes, "fulfills a need, embodies a norm of practice, and expresses an ideal," but since the institutions of American society are plural, the needs thus served are many, and the ideals of one institution are frequently in conflict with those of another. Occasions for stimulating moral growth through the equating of practice with ideal, as well as ideal with ideal, are thus not wanting. And the task of the school is not rendered easier by the fact that it is called upon, as the servant of more than one master, at times to help young people resolve the conflicting claims of the local community, the larger society, and the accepted principles and ideals of a still higher authority.

In the field of knowledge, the school's obligation "is to present the most accurate, the most comprehensive, the most advanced achievement as agreed upon by competent students in each field." In personal behavior, "it should represent the approved manner and the good taste of the community as against actual practices when these fall short. In the field of ethics, which involves belief as well as action, its mission is to cultivate the ideal—the ideal of the society of which it is a part but at the same time transcends—the ideal as expressed in the writings and pronouncements of its leaders and its statesmen." [41]

[40] *Ibid.*, p. 235.
[41] *Ibid.*, p. 222.

THE SCHOOL'S ROLE IN THE RECONSTRUCTION OF SOCIETY

Education, continues Berkson, "has a double responsibility: one of conservation and one of reconstruction." Thus, in certain areas, the school is charged with responsibility for the indoctrination of the young, although he prefers the term "nurture" as "more in accord with democratic assumptions and psychological conceptions." [42]

The two functions in education—conservation and reconstruction—are organically related, since it is from the past that "frames of reference" used in moulding the future are derived. And Berkson goes on to warn:

> There is danger in this era of transition as democracy tends to move forward—that the imponderable insights which endow it with spirit will be dissipated and the structure of values on which it rests will be weakened. Education today must emphasize anew the heritage of the humanities, the classic literatures, and the political, philosophic, and religious ideas which exemplify Western civilization. To this traditional and essential work of education another purpose of paramount importance must be added: to aid in bringing the new democratic world order into being. This will involve the study of contemporary social problems in the light of our national ideals.[43]

Now, just because there are wide differences "on basic presuppositions as well as in normative conclusions" in the social studies, it is important that the "corpus of ideas and practices" constituting the democratic frame of reference be made clear for students. "An indispensable function of educational leadership is to formulate its directives—its established principles and ideal aspirations—as a basis for school policy." [44] Among the established principles, Berkson includes the following as a minimum: "adherence to the principles and procedures of the Constitution; a renewed emphasis on the Bill of Rights; a consistent implementation of racial equality; the furtherance of economic welfare for the nation as a whole; the promotion of a democratic international order based on the Universal Declaration of the Rights of Man."

Armed with these principles and ideals as basic assumptions, or major premises in thought and discussion, Berkson would have the school deal

[42] *Ibid.*, p. 209. See also pp. 253-254.
[43] *Ibid.*, pp. 209-210.
[44] *Ibid.*, p. 256.

fully and fairly with all aspects of problems relating to the future. But, in contrast with Brameld's striving for a group consensus to be followed by "concerted action," he would conclude discussion with full allowance "for differences of views with reference to means and measures designed to achieve the goals set forth." That is to say, Berkson distinguishes carefully between the promotion (indoctrination) of common principles and ideals and the specific conclusions to be drawn from their application. As the representative of the community as a whole, the school cannot become the partisan advocate of one section of opinion in that whole.

Indoctrination, then, as Berkson sees it, is not wrong when it involves "positive teaching." It is wrong only when employed "in situations which call for initial analysis of important differences of opinion." [45]

Berkson also questions the validity of methods commonly used in dealing with controversial issues in the classroom. Thus, he writes:

> Indoctrination of an undesirable kind may be carried on in many ways and need not be conscious or deliberate. A usual form is to present only one view of a controversial issue or to present alternative views in a deprecatory fashion. Another method is to carry on group discussions on issues far beyond the knowledge or the capacity of the learners who miraculously arrive at a consensus in complete harmony with the views of the teacher. Indoctrination becomes inevitable when insufficient time is allowed for critical analysis, when the process of reasoning is short-circuited in situations where it is important to encourage it. Indoctrination is not avoided by substituting "pupil-centered" for "teacher-dominated" methods. At the high school or college level, student participation may be a means of guarding against biased teaching. But where the teacher provides accurate knowledge, supports conclusions by evidence, gives consideration to contrary views, formal presentation may involve less indoctrination of the undesirable sort than the method of discussion when it circles around the raw opinions of unprepared students.[46]

The school's position on indoctrination defines as well its attitude toward academic freedom. Berkson considers the latter a professional obligation rather than a right guaranteed by the Constitution. "It makes demands on self-restraint, on intellectual integrity, on respect for colleagues and students." [47] It is a "corollary of the belief in the value of

45 *Ibid.*, p. 254.
46 *Ibid.*, pp. 254-255.
47 *Ibid.*, see particularly pp. 257-260.

scholarship and scientific inquiry for the extension of knowledge and the service of human welfare. In substance, it makes the ethics of the profession of scholars and scientists supreme over the arbitrary control of outside forces—of the state, the church, the political party, and, not least, of public opinion."

This conception of academic freedom as primarily a moral obligation resting upon the profession requires teachers to run counter, on occasion, to local prejudice and special interests. For example, legal opposition to the doctrine of evolution (as in Tennessee) "does not affect the moral right and the duty of the teacher to expound the theory of evolution as a warranted scientific conclusion." Similarly, the principle that all men are created equal "gave the American teacher warrant to draw inferences" and to oppose racial discrimination and segregation, even before the decision of the United States Supreme Court in May, 1954.[48] But how, in plain fact, teachers can thus defy state and local authority in this manner, and at the same time maintain an educational atmosphere in the classroom, leave alone retain their positions, we are not told. Elementary and secondary school teachers are far more vulnerable in this respect than are college and university instructors. The latter are afforded some protection by both the American Association of University Professors and the regional associations of colleges and universities, which have power of accreditation.

One explanation for Berkson's hasty treatment of academic freedom below the college level follows from his conviction that "abstract ideological issues," such as capitalism vs. communism, "should be avoided." Discussions in secondary schools he would have center upon "concrete proposals made in legislative bodies, by welfare organizations, by scientific associations." Instruction in the social studies in the elementary school, he believes, "should be predominantly descriptive and exploratory, designed to supply information and develop general attitudes rather than to analyze or discuss proposals." And he optimistically concludes that academic freedom on these lower levels applies more "to organization of the curriculum and the use of textbooks than to problems of the teacher in the classroom." [49]

The solution proposed is obviously too easy. When organized groups bring pressure upon a board of education to ban from the classroom

[48] *Ibid.*, p. 260.
[49] *Ibid.*, p. 260.

specific materials or the discussion of certain topics (as was done in Los Angeles several years ago with respect to the United Nations, material carefully prepared by responsible educators, and as is common in southern schools today with respect to problems of segregation) it is difficult to see in what respects this is less serious for the teacher in a secondary school than it is for an instructor in a college classroom.

To insist, as does Berkson, that academic freedom is a moral responsibility is helpful. But in education the moral can hardly be divorced from the educational. How valid a procedure is it educationally, for example, for a teacher "to expound the theory of evolution as a warranted scientific position," or to assert dogmatically that racial differences have no valid status in anthropology, when community sentiment views the one as religious heresy and the other as a communist tenet designed to undermine the southern way of life? Moreover, as we shall see later, the problem of academic freedom is not solved either educationally or morally by evasion or by yielding passively to pressure groups, be they religious, political, economic, or social.

In some respects, the problem confronting schools today is not unlike that of the 1930's, although the sources of pressure are different. Many believed then that the integrity of instruction in the classroom was in danger of being undermined by the radical left, by groups that sincerely believed the salvation of American society depended upon indoctrinating young people in the principles of a new social order. Today, it is the "radical right" that threatens academic freedom most conspicuously, fully convinced, as was George Counts in 1932, that "since the child will be imposed upon in some fashion by the various elements in his environment, the real question is not whether imposition will take place, but rather from what source it will come." [50]

Conservative pressures assumed prominence in the 1950's as one aspect of a larger movement commonly referred to as the "McCarthy period." With the decline of Senator McCarthy's influence, attempts of lay groups to control the selection of textbooks, to ban the consideration of certain topics from the classroom, and to exclude "objectionable" books, magazines, and other materials from the school library, continued unabated, but with less attention from the public press and magazine. Thus, as Paul Goodman writes, "Rival world views, whether folk, traditional, sectarian, or artistically and philosophically heretical, are less and less

[50] Counts, op. cit., p. 27.

available" to the high school student. "He is not likely to know of other possibilities of philosophy, political dissent, religious faith, artistic tradition, free science." [51]

IN SUMMARY

In this chapter we have attempted to review representative conceptions of the responsibility of the school in a democratic society with respect to problems of change. Traditionally, the accepted function of the school has been conservative—to transmit in orthodox form (that is, "to impose") the ideas, habits, customs, and ideals of the society it serves. This seemed an obvious policy in a homogeneous society and in periods of little change. It was not challenged seriously in the United States until the accepted facts of heterogeneity in religion confronted educators with the problem of the place of religion in public education. Horace Mann and others attempted to solve this problem by means of nonsectarian religious instruction—instruction that emphasized items of common agreement and carefully excluded the controversial. With the advent of serious disagreements in other areas—economic, political, social—in American society, the principle underlying nonsectarian instruction seemed to most educators the appropriate one to follow until well into the twentieth century. At this time there emerged a more dynamic and creative conception of the nature of "mind," and a keener appreciation of the type of intellectual discipline required for intelligent participation of the individual in a society at once democratic and changing began to influence educational practice. Experimentalism now emphasized the importance of objective consideration of controversial issues but with careful avoid-

---

[51] Paul Goodman, "Don't Disturb the Children," *The New Republic*, March 16, 1963, pp. 19-20. For a discussion of censorship of textbooks in its bearing upon schools and the problems this engenders in the 1960's for teachers, superintendents of schools, library committees, and textbook publishers, see *NEA Journal*, May, 1963, pp. 19-28. In an introductory statement on "What Is the Problem?" Jack Nelson (a Pulitzer Prize winner) points out that textbooks came under fire in nearly a third of the state legislatures between 1958 and 1962. These attacks come chiefly from such groups as the John Birch Society, an organization called "America's Future" (which publishes *Operation Textbook*), the Daughters of the American Revolution (which busily distributes its *Textbook Study*), the Sons of the American Revolution, and other ultraconservative organizations. These groups distribute each other's propaganda and carry on concerted campaigns against what one publication (*What's Happened to Our Schools?* published by America's Future) envisages as "a planned, slyly executed, and almost successful attempt to deliberately under-educate our children in order to make them into an unquestioning mass who would follow meekly those who wish to turn the American Republic into a socialistic society."

ance of indoctrination. Implicit was the assumption that the task of the school is to render the young sensitive to the growing pains of society and to develop skill in coping with these pains, while scrupulously refraining from imposing upon them an officially approved cure.

In the 1930's, under the impact of the depression, this "neutral" policy was challenged by George Counts and others of like mind in the interests of "realism." Since, as they saw it, indoctrination from some source is inevitable, the teaching profession, as the most competent and, potentially, the most adequate representatives of the masses of the people, should boldly educate for a new social order. Despite insistence that his program of "defensible partiality" differs from that of Counts (which we may grant it does insofar as its goals are international rather than domestic), Brameld's education for commitment through consensus would seem to differ only in sophistication and refinement. Berkson, in contrast, would have the schools give shape to the future, first, by identifying the young with the "enduring" principles and ideals of their cultural inheritance and, second, by training them in the application of these constants to the problems of the future without official commitment to specific solutions. Finally, in recent years there has been a resurgence of conservative influences determined to enforce conformity of instruction in harmony with their parochial conceptions.

Is the public school back where it started? Are we to conclude that it "cannot create; it can only reflect ... the collective will around it," as Nathaniel Peffer insisted in the 1930's? This conclusion, however, accords neither with professional judgment of today nor with the responsibilities of the school as defined by the courts. May we consider the latter first.

There is constitutional authority for the principle that in matters upon which the public is divided the function of the school is not to take sides but to maintain an attitude of "wholesome neutrality." This principle was clearly enunciated in 1943 by the United States Supreme Court in *West Virginia Board of Education* v. *Barnette* (319 U.S. 624). Said the Court: "If there is any fixed star in our constitutional constellation it is that no official, high or petty, can prescribe what shall be orthodox in politics, nationalism, religion, or other matters of opinion or force its citizens to confess by word or act of faith herein."

In recent years, the Court has applied this principle of neutrality more specifically to the area of religious instruction. In two cases involving the reading of the Bible and reciting the Lord's Prayer at opening exercises in public schools, the Supreme Court affirmed the appropriateness of the "study of the Bible or of religion, when presented objectively as a part of a secular program of religion." But it stated clearly that the "machinery of the state," in this instance the school, cannot be used, "nor can a majority of the people use the machinery of the state, in order to promote or practice religious instruction." [52]

Obviously, what holds true of religion, in principle at least, applies to other areas in which the public is as a house divided against itself. It would seem, then, that there is sound basis for Berkson's remark to the effect that "As a member of a profession the teacher is never merely the employee of the educational institution which engages him or of the board of education. He is the servant of society in the broadest sense, a representative of the cultural heritage, of the community as its highest achievements and aspirations. The loyalty of the educational profession is due to the nation as a whole, to the fundamental principles of the democratic society." [53]

But what, more specifically, does this "loyalty to the nation as a whole" imply for the pupil, the teaching staff, and the relations of the latter to the community? For the young person it clearly implies the right to receive guidance in acquiring the intellectual and moral discipline essential for effective participation in a changing and a democratic society. This discipline will not come from a school policy of evasion and of by-passing matters in controversy. On the contrary, it is best developed when problems for which there is no answer in the back of the book, or which the future only can resolve, are consciously used as grist for the intellectual mill. When students are involved repeatedly in situations in which they are called upon to state objectively rival points of view, to gather data in support of competing positions, to serve as moderators and critics of class discussions, there is reason to believe they will acquire eventually the habits and the skills, the logic and the discipline, essential for decision making in a free and open society.

Discussion within professional circles of the problem of "indoctrination" in the classroom have rendered clearer than thirty years ago the plural responsibilities of the teaching profession. First, there are areas in which the school, as the home, quite properly centers upon the acquisition of specific facts, habits, and attitudes. The manner in which this is done

[52] *School District of Abington Township* v. *Schempp*, 374 U.S. 203 (1963).
[53] Berkson, *op. cit.*, p. 258.

marks the difference between good and poor teaching; but *what* is learned is, ultimately, of more importance than the methods employed. Acquiring habits of personal hygiene, learning how to read, mastering the fundamental operations of arithmetic, and other elements of a basic and general education fall within this category.

Secondly, there are traits of character, such as the common virtues, that constitute the social cement of all human associations. Here the psychologists have helped both parent and teacher to appreciate the importance of harmony between the inner feelings and the emotions of the young person and the qualities of mind and character they would have young people make their own. Consequently, method assumes greater importance than in the first category. (Included in this category also are the basic values and principles of the culture—those which are quite properly "taught" at one stage but which, at a later and mature stage of development, the student should be called upon to examine freely and responsibly.)

Third, there is the area in which good teaching is concerned that the student familiarize himself with the present state of knowledge within a specific field as a basis for further study and research, but that he carefully avoid unquestioned allegiance to theories, concepts, and facts. Here the major goal is the process of reaching valid conclusions, the logic peculiar to the field of inquiry (as in science, history, and the like), devotion to truth for its own sake. As John Locke wrote long ago in his *Conduct of the Understanding* (1697): "To be indifferent which of two opinions is true, is the right temper of mind that preserves it from being imposed on, and disposes it to examine with that indifferency till it has done its best to find the truth; and this is the only direct and safe way to it."

Finally, we come to that difficult area in which, as Bertrand Russell has said, one must learn to live without certainty and yet not be paralyzed by hesitation. Conclusions are important but should be held tentatively and with due consideration for the convictions of others. Emotions cannot be excluded, nor should they be, as in our third category, since they give vitality and sustaining power to actions that may flow from decision. But they require control and direction from reason. As suggested above, the teacher's primary concern with problems that fall within this area is not to promote his own views or an officially sanctioned conclusion but to assist young people to acquire the discipline of democratic decision making. To further this aim, it is obvious that textbook, library, and other sources of information should provide the student with material bearing upon all relevant points of view, not excluding those of the instructor when the latter is convinced his students are sufficiently mature to consider them on a par and on a par only with other reference material.

Passions and emotions, as we have said, cannot be eliminated entirely from issues that deeply involve both students and the out-of-school community. The problem is rather to control and direct them. On occasion, when emotions run high and the partisans of different points of view are unwilling to listen to their opponents, the instructor will serve the cause of education best by suspending further class discussion until such time as the class gives evidence of a more mature attitude.

The problem is similar in the relations of school to community. Not all communities are sufficiently mature or favorably committed to the principles of democratic discussion to permit untrammeled study in school of critical issues. The remedy is hardly for the school to insist with Berkson that academic freedom and the higher loyalty of the teacher make "the ethics of the profession of scholars and scientists supreme over the control of outside forces. . . ." Rather is it to seek ways and means of educating the community. This the school can attempt in various ways. One is to alleviate parental fear of biased instruction in meetings with parents at which the school explains its educational policy and the relation of this policy to the principles of American society.[54]

Obviously, cooperation of school and community turns upon confidence in the integrity of the teaching staff. The teacher must therefore distinguish carefully between his rights as a citizen and his responsibilities as an educator. What the latter may dictate will vary with situations. If a primary teacher, at one extreme, or a college professor, at the other, engages in outside activities of a controversial nature, or affiliates with movements and causes which seriously divide the community, such activities will have less influence upon work in the classroom than if he taught students in the upper years of the elementary school or the high school. Thus, though the teacher's responsibilities as an educator do not of necessity preclude the discharge of his obligations as a citizen, or prevent

[54] The problems of freedom to learn and freedom to teach are discussed more fully in V. T. Thayer, *The Role of the School in American Society* (New York: Dodd, Mead & Co., 1960), Chapters 21, 22.

his following the dictates of his conscience, they do become a legitimate item for his "prayerful" consideration.

Quite different is the situation when an instructor on any level becomes a partisan in the classroom and substitutes propaganda and subtle means of skewing instruction for unbiased guidance. Different also is the situation when a teacher affiliates himself with organizations outside the school —be they religious, political, economic, or whatnot—that presume to control his activities as a teacher.[55]

One of the distinctive characteristics of a democracy is the fact that it subjects its participating members to a continuous educational experience. In the process of electing its officials and holding these officials responsible for their actions, in conscientiously studying issues and passing judgment upon them, there are opportunities for growth unequaled in other forms of political and social organization. To realize these opportunities most fully, the schools of a democracy are charged with the task of developing in each successive generation the discipline of the open mind, on the assumption, as Justice Frankfurter once put it, that "Without open minds there can be no open society, and if there be no open society the spirit of man is mutilated and enslaved." This, we take it, defines the major responsibility of the American school in its relation to the social order.

[55] This question was widely discussed several years ago in connection with the problem of whether or no communists and "fellow travelers" should be permitted to teach in schools and colleges. The point here is that the principle involved has implications other than merely political.

SUGGESTED READING

Berkson, I. B., *The Ideal and the Community* (New York: Harper & Bros., 1958), Chapters 1, 2, 5, 12, 13, 15.

Brameld, Theodore, *Education for the Emerging Age* (New York: Harper & Bros., 1961), Chapters 1-3; 10-12.

Counts, George S., *Dare the Schools Build a New Social Order?* (New York: The John Day Co., 1932).

Hook, Sidney, *Education for Modern Man* (New York: Alfred A. Knopf, 1963), Chapter 5.

Taylor, Harold, *On Education and Freedom* (New York: Abelard-Schuman, 1954), Chapter VII.

Thayer, V. T., *American Education Under Fire* (New York: Harper & Bros., 1944), Chapters IV, VII.

Thayer, V. T., *The Role of the School in American Society* (New York: Dodd, Mead & Co., 1960), Chapters 21, 22.

CHAPTER 14
PUBLIC EDUCATION
COMES UNDER FIRE

IN discussing "the revolutionary transformation of the American high school" between 1900 and 1950, James B. Conant remarks that only recently have the American people become aware of the changes that have taken place in their schools in the past fifty years. So occupied were they in the 1930's "that few laymen fully realized that a revolutionary transformation of the schools had just occurred." Not until "the post-war adjustment" had been made, continues Conant, "did any large number of articulate Americans wake up to what had happened. And as often is the case with those suddenly awakened from a deep sleep, the first exclamations were not too closely related to the actual situation." [1]

EDUCATION FOR FREEDOM

This statement ignored one significant group of "articulate Americans" who were very much awake to changes in American education as early as 1936. With the publication of Robert Maynard Hutchins' *The Higher Learning in America* [2] in that year, a vigorous attack was launched upon "anti-intellectualism" in American life and the assumptions and practices of American schools and colleges, which, it was felt, were largely responsible for perpetuating a general "lack of respect for the mind." This

[1] James B. Conant, *The Child, the Parent, and the State* (Cambridge, Mass.: Harvard University Press, 1959), p. 84.

[2] Robert M. Hutchins, *The Higher Learning in America* (New Haven, Conn.: Yale University Press, 1936).

volume, and others that followed in the 1940's and 1950's, urged the American people to reform education and, through education, their civilization by a return to an emphasis upon "the intellectual virtues" and the "training of the mind." [3]

Virtually the root of all evil in American society Hutchins attributed to materialism. "Materialism has captured our culture. It has captured the state. It has captured education." [4] This materialism accounts for the major ills of school and college education. The love of money, as exemplified in the scramble for endowments and gifts, and the dependence upon student fees and legislative grants have led to a service station conception of education. Materialism prompts course offerings designed to appease pressure groups and to encourage large numbers of students to continue their education beyond the point of their intellectual competence. It leads inevitably to the introduction of practical "life adjustment" courses and a narrow vocationalism, and it equates the values of an education with superficial criteria for success in life. Other errors related to materialism include overemphasis upon facts and trivial data to the exclusion of basic principles and ideas; upon empirical science, narrow vocationalism, professionalism, and specialization to the neglect of the permanent studies; and upon spontaneous interests and education through direct experience rather than upon the training of the mind and the pursuit of knowledge that alone insures wisdom.

Materialism thus reigns supreme. Only by a "moral, intellectual, and spiritual reformation for which the world waits" can we be saved, and such a reformation depends "upon true and deeply held convictions about the nature of man, the ends of life, the purposes of the state, and the order of goods." [5]

Little has happened since 1936 to change Hutchins' indictment of American education. For example, in a discussion following an address before the Modern Forum of Los Angeles in 1963, he charges:

> The educational system has steadily deteriorated; the mass media have steadily deteriorated. Since we cannot assume that they have

---

[3] See, for example, Robert M. Hutchins, *No Friendly Voice* (Chicago: University of Chicago Press, 1936), consisting of some twenty-four addresses; *Education for Freedom* (Baton Rouge, La.: Louisiana State University Press, 1943); *Morals, Religion, and Higher Education* (Chicago: University of Chicago Press for Kenyon College, 1950); and *The Conflict in Education* (New York: Harper & Bros., 1953).

[4] Hutchins, *Education for Freedom, op. cit.,* p. 42.

[5] *Ibid.,* p. 47.

no influence, we must assume that they have a bad influence. This is the assumption that I make. The educational system has turned into a program of accommodating the young until we are ready to have them go to work. The object of American education is to get everybody into school and to keep them there as long as possible. Since they are there and must stay there, they have to do something. What they do is to learn what Dr. James B. Conant calls "marketable skills," to the acquisition of which he thinks 85 per cent of our school children are destined. This is in spite of the fact that Dr. Conant knows perfectly well that by the time they graduate the skills will be unmarketable. Either the skill will not be in demand at all, or it will be in demand at an entirely different level. This means that the pupil who spends his time acquiring a marketable skill will have nothing to market.[6]

Hutchins was quickly joined by others eloquent in their condemnation of existing systems of education in schools and colleges.[7] For example, in 1942, Stringfellow Barr, President of St. John's College, charged American schools and colleges with the responsibility for grave errors of judgment, such as the delay of the United States in entering the war against the Axis powers and failure to appreciate the merits of Streit's plan for "Union Now!" These specific mistakes, he argued, sprouted from an education based upon false intellectual premises much as weeds spring up in a neglected garden. To save America, it was imperative to restore to the colleges "the kind of education which many American colleges had furnished well into the nineteenth century."[8]

As we shall observe in a moment, Barr as well as Hutchins advocates a curriculum that centers upon the "great books" of western civilization. Just how this is identical with the kind of education furnished by American colleges "well into the nineteenth century" or with "liberal education" as understood by a third advocate of "Education for Freedom," Mortimer Adler (who states he means by liberal education "precisely what was understood by it in our colonial schools and colleges"), is not clear. Nor have these writers clarified in what way bringing back the

[6] Robert M. Hutchins, *A Conversation on Education* (Santa Barbara, Calif: Center for the Study of Democratic Institutions, 1963), p. 11.

[7] Under the caption of "Education for Freedom," the title of a series of addresses on the radio in the 1940's.

[8] Stringfellow Barr, "The Education of Free Men," *The New Republic*, August 31, 1942, pp. 248-250.

kind of education once "furnished by American colleges" would eliminate the materialism from American life it was once powerless to prevent from becoming dominant.

So much for the evils of contemporary society and the mistakes of education. How can education be reformed, and, through education, American society regenerated?

Here again Hutchins' answer today is as it was twenty years ago: Recognize that the "cultivation of the intellect" is the "first duty" of the educational system. Thus, in replying to the query, "What in your opinion is the ideal education?" he states, "Ideal education is the one that develops intellectual power. I arrive at this conclusion by a process of elimination. Educational institutions are the only institutions that can develop intellectual power. The ideal education is not an *ad hoc* education, not an education directed to immediate needs; it is not a specialized education, or a pre-professional education; it is not a utilitarian education. It is an education calculated to develop the mind." [9]

Unlike James B. Conant, who boldly repudiates the assumption that a program for American education can best be deduced from an abstract concept of education,[10] Hutchins started with the philosophical premise that "One purpose of education is to draw out the elements of our common human nature. These elements are the same in any time and place. The notion of educating a man to live in any particular time or place, to adjust him to any particular environment is therefore foreign to a true conception of education." [11]

Perhaps we should add that Hutchins was aware of a seeming contradiction in his argument. Up to this point he had demonstrated the manner in which education reflects the character of the society it serves. Now he proposed to transform society through education. His answer in *Education for Freedom* was that we must not assume a defeatist attitude. "The only way to a spiritual revolution is through education. . . . If one college and one university—and only one—are willing to take a position contrary to the prevailing ideology and suffer the consequences, then conceivably, over a long period of time, the character of our civilization may change." [12]

9 Hutchins, A Conversation on Education, op. cit., p. 1.
10 Conant, op. cit., p. 1.
11 Hutchins, The Higher Learning in America, op. cit., p. 66.
12 Hutchins, Education for Freedom, op. cit., p. 59.

What Hutchins meant by the elements of "our common human nature" should not be confused with the "common denominators" in human behavior that Brameld would have men use in order to construct a new world order of shared experiences and common agreements. For Hutchins and the Education for Freedom group our common human nature is a metaphysical substance, an essence in man, not a potential relationship or association. It is a faculty of mind or reason containing within itself slumbering ideas or principles that only one kind of subject matter and discipline can bring into being. As Mark Van Doren wrote in his *Liberal Education:* "Aldous Huxley calls liberal education abstract. If he means that it is general, or occupied with a nature always assumed to be the same, he is right. . . . In these pages it still is to be defined, but when the moment comes for that it should already be clear that liberal education is nothing less than the complete education of men as men; it is education of persons; or, ideally, it is education." [13]

The concern to educate what is common in man prompted Hutchins and his associates to revive two assumptions in education that most educators had come to believe Edward L. Thorndike and other opponents of formal discipline had finally buried early in the century. These were the assumptions (1) that there is a subject matter for teaching best adapted for all students without respect to differences; and (2) that this subject matter, when properly taught, will develop in students an intellectual power "capable of being applied in any field whatever."

EDUCATION AND THE GREAT BOOKS

Hutchins had little to say specifically of education below the age of sixteen other than to reject completely the experience curriculum and a child-centered education. Education of this character, he believed, had succeeded only in ruining the schools. Attempts to relate the school to life, to enrich the curriculum with firsthand experience, or to promote character development through "learning by doing" evidenced a shallow and superficial pedagogy. "Today as yesterday," he asserted, "we may leave experience to other institutions and influences and emphasize in education the contribution that it is supremely fitted to make, the intellectual training of the young." [14]

From ages sixteen to twenty, or, roughly speaking, from the junior year

[13] Mark Van Doren, *Liberal Education* (New York: Henry Holt & Co., 1944), p. 29.
[14] Hutchins, *The Higher Learning in America, op. cit.,* p. 69.

in high school through what is now the second year of college, he considered to be the period of "general education." And by general education he meant the kind that "everybody should have."

Hutchins was as convinced in 1936 as he is today that economic conditions require provision of some kind of education for all young people up to the twentieth year. And he has not been blind to the problem this raises with respect to the "one-third" who "cannot read from books." He believes, however, if we but put our minds to it, we shall discover ways of providing a general education for "the hand-minded and the functionally illiterate" as well as for the two-thirds who can read. Vocational education and technology have no place in general education and can be justified only "because we discover certain principles can best be communicated through technical work." [15]

The subjects of study basic to this general education program are (1) those from which men may glean the eternal and immutable ideas—valid major premises—for use in solving the problems of living in any society, at any time, and in any place; and (2) those that communicate "our intellectual tradition" and insure the cultivation and use of the "intellectual virtues." "This means understanding the great thinkers of the past and present, scientific, historical, and philosophical. It means a grasp of the disciplines of grammar, rhetoric, logic and mathematics; reading, writing, and figuring. It does not, of course, mean the exclusion of contemporary materials. They should be brought in daily to illustrate, confirm, or deny the ideas held by the writers under discussion." [16]

Most spectacular of the attempts to apply Hutchins' thesis was the program of St. John's College in Annapolis, Maryland. Under the leadership of Stringfellow Barr, as President, and Scott Buchanan, as Dean, the undergraduate period of St. John's was organized around one hundred of the "great books" of western civilization. These books were grouped in both historical and disciplinary sequence. When organized chronologically, they fell into four cultural periods, one for the work of each year of a four-year course. From a disciplinary point of view, they were classified into three groups: one designed to teach the arts of reading, understanding, and criticism; one primarily literary and linguistic; one mathematical and scientific.

[15] *Ibid.*, pp. 61, 74. Also see Hutchins, *No Friendly Voice, op. cit.*, chapter on "The Outlook for Public Education."

[16] Hutchins, *Education for Freedom, op. cit.*, p. 60.

This plan, according to Stringfellow Barr, represented a restoration of the liberal arts to American education; a return to the *trivium* and *quadrivium* of the medieval university, when education, in his words, "was concerned, and solely concerned, with cultivating through discipline the intellectual powers of young men." Also, as described by Barr in the *Magazine Digest* of November, 1943, the mastery of these arts carried with it alluring prospects: "The man who has learned to practice these arts successfully," he wrote, "can 'concentrate' on anything, can 'apply himself' to anything, can quickly learn any specialty, any profession, any business. That man can deliberate, can make practical decisions by other means than tossing a coin, can understand his failures, can recognize his obligations as well as his opportunities. He is in short what an earlier generation eloquently termed 'an educated man.'"

Critics have not hesitated to point out that the terms "liberal arts" and "the trivium and quadrivium," as used by Hutchins, Barr and others of the Education for Freedom group, are used loosely. To a student familiar with the trivium and quadrivium, say these critics, the hundred great books of the St. John's curriculum will come as a surprise, since they bear little resemblance to the original. Being mindful of this, Mark Van Doren suggested that the trivium and the quadrivium should be reinterpreted to mean, in the one case, the discipline of reading, writing, and thinking (trivium), and, in the other, mathematics and science. In other words, the liberal arts are to be considered flexible and variable in substance.

Perhaps this is as it should be since, as a matter of fact, both the subject matter and the methods of the seven liberal arts have undergone change in the course of the centuries. But, continue the critics, what does this imply with respect to the "one valid content of education" and the relation of this content to the social order? Once the principle of relativity is applied to the substance and the procedures of the trivium and the quadrivium, may we not reach another conclusion as well, one these reformers are eager to deny—that educational values do not reside as such in any arbitrary subject matter, but originate rather out of the interplay of the individual student with materials and methods relevant and appropriate to his abilities, interests, and needs! And thus we have an observation fatal to the dictum that provisions for individual differences have relevance only to method, none to content.

CRITICISM OF PUBLIC EDUCATION
HITS A STRIDENT NOTE

Neither Hutchins' criticisms nor the experimental curriculum at St. John's College succeeded in modifying substantially the conventional curricula of either school or college. But this is not to say the efforts of the Education for Freedom group bore no fruit. On the contrary, they undoubtedly cleared a path for the more violent and irresponsible attacks upon public schools by self-styled patriotic organizations of the late 1940's and the 1950's, as well as the indictments of influential groups of intellectuals—publicists, journalists, college professors, devotees of the liberal arts—who had become convinced that the "new education" was in process of weakening the intellectual and moral fiber of American youth.

To be sure, there is no valid reason for identifying Hutchins' charge that American schools were busily engaged in subverting the intellectual development of young people with the assertion in one of Allan Zoll's pamphlets, entitled, *They Want Your Child*, to the effect that our schools "were founded to preserve the American form of government and the American institutions of freedom and individual liberty. It can safely be asserted that 90 per cent of the texts and teachers in our schools today are in considerable measure subversive of these basic American principles." [17] Nevertheless, many a layman failed to recognize the difference between these two types of "subversion." This confusion of mind was rendered easier by the criticisms of the schools by educational "experts" who professed to demonstrate from firsthand knowledge that progressive education—with its introduction of new courses of study (such as the "Core Curriculum"), substitution of new organizations of subject matter for old (the "social studies" for history, economics, and civics), and new methods of classroom procedure with their emphasis upon group relationships—constituted a sinister plot to mould young people into pliant tools of an alien philosophy. Moreover, it was not difficult to find "experts" of this frame of mind, eager and willing to substantiate these charges.

One example will suffice. In an article entitled "The Initiators of Opera-

---

[17] Published by the National Council for American Education, one of a number of organizations in the 1950's engaged in the "investigation" of communism in the schools and the publication and distribution of pamphlets based on these "investigations." Other pamphlets distributed by Allan Zoll's organization included *Progressive Education Increases Delinquency, How Red Are the Schools?* and *Private Schools: The Solution to America's Educational Problem.*

tion Socialism," a Dr. Felix Witmer, once an instructor in a well-known teacher training institution, asked his readers to observe that "as the years went by and your children passed through the grades, you may have noticed a change going on. Subject matter, teaching methods, types of study, everything changed. If you put two and two together, you realized that the emphasis shifted from the individual to the group." Primary responsibility for these changes, Witmer ascribed "to a small group of educators who had gravitated toward Columbia Teachers College" and who, in the course of some twenty years, had "turned thousands and thousands of teachers into missionaries of the collectivistic, i.e., socialistic creed." It was these "thousands of converts" who were responsible for the changes described.[18]

More fundamental was the indictment of contemporary educators by Walter Lippmann, since it bore directly upon the principles of a democratic society and provided a philosophic foundation for a "new conservatism." In an address delivered before the Phi Beta Kappa Society in 1941, Lippmann put forth the following theses:

1. That during the past forty or fifty years those responsible for education have progressively removed from the curriculum of studies the Western culture which produced the modern democratic state;

2. That the schools and colleges have, therefore, been sending out into the world men who no longer understand the creative principles of the society in which they live;

3. That deprived of their cultural tradition, the newly educated Western men no longer possess in the form and substance and spirit, the ideas, the premises, the rationale, the logic, the method, the values of the deposited wisdom which are the genius of the development of the Western civilization;

4. That the prevailing education is destined if it continues, to destroy Western civilization and is in fact destroying it.[19]

[18] See the *National Republic*, June, 1953, p. 13. For a summary and an appraisal of criticisms of the schools in this period, see Harold Alberty and others, *Let's Look at Our Schools* (Columbus, Ohio: Ohio State University, 1951); Ernest Melby and Morton Pruner, *Freedom and Public Education* (New York: Frederick A. Praeger, 1953); C. Winfield Scott and Clyde M. Hill, *Education Under Criticism* (Englewood Cliffs, N.J.: Prentice-Hall, 1954).

[19] Walter Lippmann, "Education vs. Civilization," *The American Scholar*, Spring, 1941, pp. 184-193.

With the publication of *The Public Philosophy* in 1955, it became clear that Lippmann considers the failures of contemporary education but one manifestation of a more general "malady" with which the western democracies have been afflicted since the French Revolution. This malady has its roots in the "Jacobin heresy," inherited from the French Revolution. As stated by Rousseau in his *Émile* (1762), this assumes that man is "a being naturally loving justice and order; that there is not any original perversity in the human heart, and that the first sentiments of nature are always right." It is thus not in man's nature to go astray. His inherited faculties are good; the evil faculties are acquired; that is, his nature is corrupted by the established institutions of society.

In government this faith in the common man and the uncorrupted social will has led to a "functional derangement between the mass of the people and government," to the "devitalization of the executive power" through its subordination to the legislature, and to a too sensitive response of the latter to mass opinion. In education it has resulted in the cult of the child and the conviction, as Froebel put it in Section 8 of *The Education of Man* (1826), that "the still young being, even though as yet unconsciously like a product of nature, precisely and surely wills that which is best for himself."

On these assumptions, asserts Lippmann, educators have concluded that "The best education for democracy will be one which trains, disciplines, and teaches least." Since the necessary faculties are inborn, "they are more likely to be perverted by too much culture than to wither for the lack of it," and the curriculum "can be emptied of all the studies and the disciplines which relate to faith and to morals." These are conclusions our schools seem to have taken literally! [20]

What is Lippmann's remedy for this "democratic malady"? In government, if we are to arrest the decline of the western democracies and the present trend toward totalitarianism, we must return to the doctrine of natural law and the philosophic assumptions of an "objective moral order," rationally known, and consisting of principles universally binding upon all men. That is, we must return to a concept of government *for* the people, by leaders whom the people elect and with whom they align themselves, but whom they may not dominate. Similarly, it becomes the responsibility of the schools to reintroduce the materials of an education that

[20] Walter Lippmann, *The Public Philosophy* (Boston: Little, Brown & Co., 1955), pp. 73-78.

will transmit "the moral system" and the "universal laws of the rational order."

More specifically, we must (1) reject the Jacobin fallacy to the effect that the natural impulses are inherently right and the false notion of mind and reason as a process or a function of adjustment, as a balancing of one set of desires and wants against others in order to attain certain satisfactions; and (2) return, instead, to a valid concept of reason as a faculty of the mind "which represents society within the human psyche," by means of which men may recognize and employ in the solution of their problems "the principles of a universal order on which all reasonable men" are agreed. To accomplish these goals, however, it is necessary to bring back into the schools the classical studies of the nineteenth century, for these studies alone provide the essential content and discipline of an education.

Bereft of this content and this discipline, contends Lippmann, "The school cannot look upon society as a brotherhood arising out of a conviction that men are made in a common image. The teacher has no subject matter that even pretends to deal with the elementary and universal issues of human destiny. The graduate of the modern school knows only by accident and by hearsay whatever wisdom mankind has come to in regard to the nature of men and their destiny." [21]

BASIC EDUCATION VS. EDUCATION FOR ADJUSTMENT

The 1950's also witnessed a revival of interest on the part of instructors in colleges of liberal arts in the teaching of their subjects in elementary and secondary schools. The phrase "revival of interest" is used advisedly. Prior to 1900, the content of subjects taught in secondary schools tended to reflect the interests of advanced students in each field, and textbooks were written with these interests in mind. But with the rapid expansion of the school population in the first decades of the twentieth century and the diminishing proportion of the secondary school population which was preparing for college, considerations other than preparation for college

[21] Lippmann, *The American Scholar, op. cit.* For an examination of the philosophic underpinning of the "new conservatism," with its return to the doctrine of natural law, of "right reason" as a faculty, and of a realm of "essences" that yield self-evident principles of morality, see Morton White, *Social Thought in America* (Boston: Beacon Press, 1957), pp. 264-288, Also see Sidney Hook's book review of Clinton Rossiter and James Lare (eds.), *The Essential Lippmann: A Political Philosophy for Liberal Democracy* (New York: Random House, 1963), in the Book Review Section of *The New York Times*, July 14, 1963.

began to control the selection and organization of subject matter.[22] As one example, "community civics" was introduced as a means of acquainting the children of immigrants and of recent migrants from rural to urban areas with the agencies and institutions and problems of the community, in contrast with an exclusively political emphasis of the traditional course in civics. A second is the statement of no less an authority than Professor Jerrold R. Zacharias of the Massachusetts Institute of Technology to the effect that until a few years ago the professional scholar in science "has simply turned his back on the problem" of science instruction in secondary schools, and, "in many of the sciences he continues to do so." [23]

Parallel with this withdrawal of college teachers from firsthand concern with the problems of instruction in the lower schools and the development of professional schools of education, there came about a lack of mutual confidence and respect on the part of the faculties of education and the faculties of liberal arts. "Faculties of liberal arts colleges," writes Lindley J. Stiles, Dean of the School of Education, University of Wisconsin, "have placed a dunce cap on the educationist, partly to rationalize their own failure to take an interest in preparing teachers. Too often they treat programs of teacher education with disdain, if not contempt. Only the fact that a certain percentage of their students desires to qualify for teaching has kept interest in teacher education alive in many such institutions." [24]

Perhaps in retrospect a measure of credit should be given Professor Arthur Bestor of the University of Illinois for bringing about a renewed interest on the part of scholars in the colleges of the liberal arts in the problems of secondary education. Writing in 1953 as a historian (but with little evidence of that objectivity of judgment and strict devotion to accuracy which marks the seasoned judgment of the historian), Bestor undertook to show that changes in the curriculum of the schools since early in the century have resulted directly from the influence of an "educational directorate," consisting of the faculties of schools of education, superin-

[22] Contrast, for example, the assumptions underlying the recommendations of the Report of the Committee of Ten on Secondary School Studies (1893) with the implications of the Cardinal Principles of Secondary Education (1918) not only for the organization of the school but, as well, for the content of subjects taught.

[23] Jerrold R. Zacharias, "The Age of Science," in Eli Ginzberg, *The Nation's Children*, a volume prepared for the 1960 White House Conference on Children and Youth (New York: Columbia University Press, 1960), p. 112.

[24] Lindley J. Stiles, "The Role of Liberal Arts Colleges in Teacher Education," *The Educational Forum*, January, 1964, p. 171.

tendents and principals of public schools, and "bureaucrats" in state departments of education and the United States Office of Education.

"On every hand," Bestor asserted, "there is evidence of the debasement which the teaching profession is undergoing at the hands of the interlocking directorate of professional educators." So powerful is this directorate in its control over the preparation of teachers that able teachers who "oppose the anti-intellectual trend that is so obvious today" are powerless to do anything about it. "Across the educational world today stretches an iron curtain which the professional educationists are busily fashioning. Behind it, in slave-labor camps, are the classroom teachers, whose only hope of rescue is from without. . . . American intellectual life is threatened because the first twelve years of formal schooling in the United States are being put more and more completely under the policy-making control of a new breed of educator who has no real place in it—who does not respect and is not respected by the world of scientists, scholars, and professionals." [25]

Bestor's assertion that professional educationists have taken over the training of teachers and corrupted the curriculum has been echoed by the Council for Basic Education, which describes itself as a "lay-oriented group devoted to the maintenance of quality in American education." [26] For example, Mortimer Smith, in *A Citizen's Manual for Public Schools,* asserts that since 1900 "a new breed of schoolmasters" has taken over control of the schools. For the most part, this new breed is "a product of a pedagogical, rather than a humanistic training," favoring useful rather than "formative knowledge," and "animated by a humanitarianism that dictated that schools should provide social services as well as education, and by an equalitarianism that tended to deny excellence and ended in

[25] Arthur Bestor, *Educational Wastelands: The Retreat from Learning in Our Schools* (Urbana, Ill.: University of Illinois Press, 1953), pp. 120-121.

[26] The Council for Basic Education (725 Fifteenth Street, N.W., Washington, D.C.) publishes a monthly newsletter, the *CBE Bulletin, A Citizen Manual for Public Education,* and other material from time to time devoted "to the strengthening of basic education." It sponsored Admiral H. G. Rickover's book, *Swiss Schools and Ours: Why Theirs Are Better* (Boston: Little, Brown & Co., 1962). Its most comprehensive statement of position is contained in James D. Koerner (ed.), *The Case for Basic Education* (Boston: Little, Brown & Co., 1959). This volume includes an opening chapter by Clifton Fadiman on "The Case for Basic Education" and sixteen essays by scholars in as many subject matter fields, outlining what they believe a student should acquire from their specialties in twelve years of schooling. See also James D. Koerner, *The Miseducation of American Teachers* (Boston: Houghton Mifflin Co., 1963).

the doctrine that as far as students and subject matter are concerned, none are better or best, only different." But, above all, these educationists are "practical men of action," who, through "the consolidation of power" and "effective lobbying. . . . in the state legislatures," have succeeded in establishing professional criteria for entrance upon the profession of teaching and in substituting "life adjustment education" for the valid education our schools once provided.[27]

The evil effects of "life adjustment education" upon the schools as envisaged by these critics are many:

1. It has transformed the content of the purpose of subjects of study once considered basic for the training of the mind into subjects the contents of which are channeled in the direction of immediate life applications. Thus, courses in English that once emphasized grammar, rhetoric, and logic have eliminated rhetoric and logic and diluted grammar to the point at which there are no valid standards of usage; instead there are merely different levels of acceptance with which students may become acquainted in the "communications laboratory" while engaged in using the telephone, writing a letter, or participating in a panel discussion on radio or TV. For similar reasons, algebra and geometry give way to "consumer mathematics"; physics and chemistry, to "the finished words of science."[28]

2. Not only have traditional subjects been diluted by incorporating in them materials of superficial and transient value, recent years have also witnessed a proliferation of courses, nonvocational as well as vocational, with two reprehensible results. First, under an elective system, they function in the student's program as a camel's nose. (In 1949, for example, vocational and nonvocational subjects enrolled nearly as many students as mathematics, science, and foreign language combined.)[29] Secondly, the methods of teaching employed tend to center not upon the development of understanding but upon the "conditioning" of students in what Admiral Rickover terms "the minutiae of daily living."

[27] Mortimer Smith, *A Citizen's Manual for Public Schools: A Guide for School Board Members and Other Laymen* (Washington, D.C.: Council for Basic Education, 1959), pp. 34 ff.

[28] See John Keats, *Schools Without Scholars* (Boston: Houghton Mifflin Co., 1958), Chapter V.

[29] John F. Latimer, *What's Happened to Our Schools?* (Washington, D.C.: Public Affairs Press, 1958), pp. 120-121. Latimer also points out that in 1910 high schools offered 35 subjects, 27 of which were academic and 8 nonacademic. In 1949 they offered 141 subjects (in some 274 courses) of which 59 were academic and 82 nonacademic.

3. The "valid task of the school," the intellectual training of the young through the mastery of accepted subject matter, has become secondary to adjustment in areas social and civic. Social adjustment, moreover, is equated with complete "cooperation with the group" and the introverted personality with "suburban abnormality." Conformity to group pressures, the substitution of discipline by the group for correction of misbehavior at the hands of the teacher, pupil participation in lesson planning, and teacher "permissiveness" are being used to transform self-sufficient Americans into "organization men." [30]

4. Inherent in these trends, the critics insist, is an anti-intellectualism which discourages solid achievement and enables students to advance from year to year without adequate preparation. This indictment is repeatedly documented by tests given to recruits for the military and answers to questionnaires frequently addressed to high school and college students.

5. Finally, a primary source for these failures in education is the false philosophy of John Dewey!

THE PROGRAM OF BASIC EDUCATION

So much for what is wrong with contemporary education, as viewed by basic educationists. What of their positive program? It seems to be twofold: (1) return to the "valid curriculum" of the past; and (2) as advocated by Admiral Hyman Rickover, adopt a program similar to that of European schools.

The case for the first position is presented by Clifton Fadiman in an essay entitled "The Case for Basic Education," in a volume with that title.[31] Fadiman's proposal involves a return to the curriculum of the early years of the present century when the secondary school centered upon "master subjects" possessed of "generative power." These subjects, Fadiman assures us, are unique in that once learned they "enable the student to learn all other matters, whether trivial or complex, that cannot properly be the subject of elementary and secondary schooling." [32]

This assumption of a "generative power" peculiar to the "master subjects" should be identified neither with recent emphasis upon "structure"

[30] See William H. Whyte, *The Organization Man* (New York: Simon & Schuster, 1956), Chapter 28, on "The Organization Children," and Chapter 7, on "The Practical Curriculum."

[31] Koerner (ed.), *op. cit.*

[32] *Ibid.*, p. 6.

nor with the pedagogically different methods of thinking that students may acquire from work in fields as different as mathematics and science, literary analysis, and historical research. Educators who recognize the value of these disciplines realize also the importance of profiting from all that is known of the learning process and adapting both subject matter and method to the varying circumstances under which young people live and work.[33] The concept of "generative power," on the other hand, is used to justify the elimination not only of courses in life adjustment, but also new subject organizations drawn from the "master subjects" (as, for example, the social studies, general science, and general mathematics) in favor of a return to the subjects of study and the curriculum of the first two decades of the twentieth century.[34] This despite the fact that the problems with which advanced workers in the fields of science and social science are concerned today often cut across traditional boundary lines. One may sympathize with the insistence that the schools attempt to develop more consciously than they have in the past the intellectual disciplines peculiar to the broad fields of science, social studies, literature, mathematics, the arts, but this objective should not be confused with rigid adherence to the subject-matter divisions of the conventional curriculum of fifty years ago. Indeed, so to insist might well result in the exclusion of new concepts and materials within these general fields as new knowledge develops.

Relevant in this connection is a lecture delivered at the University of Southampton by the scientist Julian Huxley on the topic "Education and the Humanist Revolution." [35] Huxley draws attention to the present arti-

[33] Contrast, for example, Fadiman's statement on "The Case for Basic Education" with Arthur W. Foshay's "A Modest Proposal for the Improvement of Education" in *What are the Sources of the Curriculum? A Symposium* (Washington, D.C.: Association for Supervision and Curriculum Development, NEA, 1962).

[34] Observe, for example, the "basic subjects" recognized in *The Case for Basic Education*. The only electives discussed are art, music, philosophy, and speech. Evidently, home economics and the industrial arts lack "generative power."

It is interesting to observe that the high school students envisaged by the authors of this volume (all of whom, with one exception, are college professors) are in no way as varied in background or range of ability and interest as the high school population encountered by James B. Conant in his studies of the American high school. Indeed, there is little evidence of an awareness that these differences matter. As a result, we have an able and valuable discussion of each subject insofar, and insofar only, as it applies to the upper segment of the school population. The book, as other publications endorsed by the Council, evidently has in mind a curriculum of a one-track character.

[35] Julian Huxley, The Ninth Fawley Lecture, delivered on November 22, 1962. Reprinted in *The Plain View*, London, England, May, 1963.

ficial classification of the different sciences in education and urges educators to undertake the task of developing an "integrated curriculum" to replace the present "patchwork." He suggests a curriculum that will focus "on the pattern of man's relations with nature and the psychosocial process, instead of on separate aspects of nature like physics and botany, and on separate aspects and activities of man like literature and history." Different subjects in science, he continues, link up with and reinforce each other. "Physiology links up with chemistry and heredity, ecology with geography, soil science with agriculture and meteorology. The study of development leads on to biological evolution; evolution in turn links back to geology, astronomy, and cosmology. . . . To provide a "unitary pattern" is not easy, Huxley grants. It "will take much ingenuity and a great deal of good will. But it must be done, and I am sure it can be done."

ADMIRAL HYMAN G. RICKOVER
AND EDUCATIONAL REFORM

In *A Citizen's Manual for Public Schools,* Mortimer Smith states there are three attitudes toward the schools of today.[36] The first, that of educational associations, insists the schools of today are superior to those of the past. The second, represented by James B. Conant, assumes they can be improved by a little judicious rearranging and the spending of more money. The third, the viewpoint of Admiral Rickover, insists that drastic surgery is required. It is with this third position, states Smith, that he and the Council for Basic Education ally themselves.

A careful reading of Rickover's writings, however, reveals this identity of position to be more superficial than genuine. Rickover, for example, derives his recommendations for reform primarily from an engineer's analysis of conditions and trends of today and tomorrow. But basic education looks backward in both its theory and its recommendations for reform.

"Our schools," writes Rickover, "have done a fine job of making Americans out of motley groups of foreigners from all corners of the globe and doing it in record time. This job is finished. The schools must tackle a different job. They must concentrate in bringing the intellectual powers of each child to the highest possible level. Even the average child now needs almost as good an education as the middle-and-upper-class child used to

[36] Smith, *op. cit.,* p. viii.

get in the college-preparatory schools." [37] Basic educationists, in contrast, describe the period from 1900 to the present as one in which educators have neglected "the primary task of the school" and have permitted its "custodial and social adjustment functions" to take precedence over its "function as the transmitter of the accumulated knowledge and heritage of the race." [38]

Again, consider the sources from which Rickover derives his educational objectives, in contrast with those of basic education. Rickover looks to the stern realities of the present—to our rapidly vanishing natural resources, the "population expansion," the scientific revolution that "now engulfs us though not all of us are aware of this"—to realities which should impel Americans to develop to the utmost their human resources, including the minds of young people. Fadiman and the Council for Basic Education, as Robert Hutchins before them, are less impressed with change and the influence of contemporary trends upon the task of the school. Consequently, they insist that public education should revert to the curriculum of yesterday, which, according to Kimball and McClellan, was better designed to enable young people to escape from the surrounding culture than to contribute constructively to it.[39]

Finally, Rickover and the Council for Basic Education differ significantly in what they expect from the work of the lower schools. Rickover considers of first importance, in this age of technology, an education that centers upon flexibility and versatility of mind, upon competence to cope with rapid change. Consequently, he wishes students to be well-

[37] H. G. Rickover, *Education and Freedom* (New York: E. P. Dutton & Co., 1959), p. 31. See also Chapter 5, on "Energy Resources and Our Future." Rickover is evidently unmindful of the significance for education of the heavy migration from the underprivileged and undernourished sections of the United States, primarily rural, to the urban, industrial sections of the North and South. One wonders if he were more sensitive to conditions described by James B. Conant in *Slums and Suburbs* (New York: McGraw-Hill Book Co., 1961), whether he would not admit the complexities of the problems of education today and modify his insistence upon a one-track curriculum in order to salvage the ability and talent he recognizes to be all-important.

[38] Smith, *op. cit.*, p. 3.

[39] Solon T. Kimball and James E. McClellan, *Education and the New America* (New York: Random House, 1962). In Chapter 5, on "Progressive Education: The Transition from Agrarian to Industrial America," these authors picture progressive education as essentially a conservative movement in education. They consider it conservative in the sense that its leaders attempted to transform a school "typical of the nineteenth-century rural community" and serving "an agrarian-commercial town and country civilization" into an institution that would perform the positive function of transmitting "the deeper values of the American tradition to the new generations in their urban, industrial environment."

grounded in fundamental principles rather than in "factual know-how." In short, he would have the schools envisage as their final products technical experts of independent and creative minds who scorn the qualities valued by the "organization man." Mortimer Smith sounds a different note. Following his summary of the task of the elementary school (chiefly that of teaching the child to read and write, add, subtract, multiply, and divide with accuracy, to acquire the basic facts of the geography of his country and the world, a knowledge of elementary science, and, above all, to know "the difference between aimless mental activity and orderly thoughts"), he writes of the secondary school: "While the high school student is naturally capable of more judgment than a pupil in the elementary school and should be interested not only in the appearance of things but their significance as well, *the general principle holds here, too, that the school's task is primarily transmission of factual knowledge* in the basic subjects" (italics supplied).[40]

It is only when he turns from his analysis of revolutionary changes in contemporary American society to the implications of this analysis for the curriculum that Rickover, in a manner characteristically American, jumps from one extreme to another and accepts the program of basic education. Having convinced himself that the public school sacrifices the able in order to serve the average and the low in intelligence, he proposes a program keyed to the able. This program is essentially that of a one-track curriculum, consisting of the basic subjects of English (literature, composition, grammar), history, mathematics, science, and foreign language, with little provision for individual differences in ability or cultural background. "Those who do not have the mentality to master all of these subjects," he writes, "need the same kind of intellectual fare, only less of it." [41] The Admiral is not disturbed by the obvious indifference of his associates in the basic education movement to the implications for contemporary education of recent research in the psychology of learning and personality development and the obvious bearing of cultural factors upon the curriculum and methods of instruction.[42]

[40] Smith, *op. cit.*, pp. 6-7.
[41] Rickover, *Education and Freedom, op. cit.*, p. 154.
[42] See, for example, Clifton Fadiman's comments on the nature of the curriculum in Koerner (ed.), *op. cit.*, and Robert Hutchins' famous dictum to the effect that "The notion of educating a man to live in any particular time or place, to adjust him to any particular environment is ... foreign to a true conception of education." Observe also Rickover's complete misunderstanding of John Dewey in *Education and Freedom, op. cit.*, Chapter 8.

Rickover has attracted wide attention to his proposal that the essential features of European education be adopted here. Thus, in testimony before the House Appropriations Committee (released in September, 1962), he praised the English system on three counts: (1) for grouping pupils according to ability, (2) for concentrating on a thorough knowledge of important subjects rather than upon helping students to become socially well-adjusted, and (3) for early specialization.

It is interesting to observe, however, that this endorsement of the English system comes at a time when it is being subjected to severe criticism in England, not only by laymen but by representatives of the British Ministry of Education.[43]

JAMES B. CONANT, EMPIRICIST IN EDUCATIONAL REFORM

A more sympathetic and pragmatic approach to the problems of the American public school than any thus far reviewed is that of James B. Conant. Different also are his methods of determining what is needed in the way of reform. The approaches we have described tend to begin with an initial assumption of the nature of "valid education" against which they measure the achievements and failures of the schools of today. Conant, in contrast, confesses to a distrust of educational theory: "When someone writes or says that what we need today in the United States is to decide first what we mean by the word 'education,' a sense of distasteful weariness overtakes me. ... In such a mood, I am ready to define education as what goes on in schools and colleges. I am more inclined to examine the present and past practices of teachers than to attempt to deduce pedagogical concepts from a set of premises." [44]

We should not conclude from this statement, however, that there are no fundamental principles by means of which Conant attempts to appraise "what goes on in schools and colleges." Later in the same book, for example, he writes: "Talk about school problems which ignores the framework of society, or, by wishful thinking, replaces the real framework with an illusory one at the best is frivolous, at the worst is dangerous. The framework is in part legal, governmental, formal; in part it is extra-legal,

---

[43] See, for example, John Rosseli, "Where the Grass Is Greener: Some Reactions from a Britisher to Admiral Rickover's Comments on British Education," *NEA Journal*, December, 1962, pp. 40-42.

[44] Conant, *The Child, the Parent, and the State*, op. cit., pp. 1-2.

determined by local traditions, customs, by economic and social considerations, and, above all, by family attitudes." [45]

Basic, then, in Conant's procedure, is recognition of vital interplay between what he terms "the structure of American society," the dominant ideals and aspirations of its people, and the specific political, economic, and social environment in which these ideals operate. To him, "the notion of educating a man to live in any particular time or place" is *all*-important "to a valid concept of education."

Deeply rooted in American tradition and practice is the principle of state and local administration of schools. The system of administration permits a high degree of local autonomy in which school boards, subject only to general state regulations, employ teachers, approve curricula, adopt budgets, and the like under the watchful eye of the local community. From this flows considerable variation as between communities in curriculum and quality of education, in contrast with the centralized administration and uniform curricula common to many other countries.

Despite serious limitations in this system of local autonomy, limitations that have become most evident in recent years, with the cause of freedom at stake and competition with the communist bloc highlighting severe wastage of talent, Conant is convinced that adherence to the principle constitutes the best guarantee that the curriculum of each school will reflect the nature and the needs of its student population. In contrast with the pre-university schools of Europe and the secondary schools of the United States early in the century, the secondary school population of today is highly diversified.

The secondary schools now face the task of providing an adequate education for "all American youth" with an eye to communities as different, for example, as that of a suburban community with many well-to-do professional families and that of an underprivileged urban slum district with numerous families on relief or many recent impoverished migrants from rural areas. Obviously, the curricular offering for the majority of students in each of these schools will differ. In the suburban school, preparation for college will dominate. In the slum school, the larger number of students will combine their general education with courses that yield "marketable skills" upon graduation. But in neither school should the exceptional student or a minority group in terms of academic ability or vocational intent be lost sight of in educational planning. "In

[45] *Ibid.*, p. 65.

the average American community," writes Conant, "a good high school should offer a variety of elective programs, occupying about half the students' time; these should include a variety of courses designed to develop skills marketable on graduation (carpentry or auto mechanics for boys, stenography for girls, for example). For the academically talented there should be courses in physics, chemistry, twelfth-grade mathematics, and one or more foreign languages.[46] In order to offset the limitations of individual schools and school systems and to insure open opportunities for all students, Conant advocates cooperative arrangements between communities to permit a sharing of facilities and personnel. Thus only, he insists, may we avoid squandering "the most precious assets of the nation," the "potential talent of the next generation."

Other significant characteristics of American society (not unrelated to respect for local self-determination and recognition of individual differences as between people and their communities) are "low visibility" of class lines, social mobility, and acceptance of change. From these characteristics emerge as ideals equality of opportunity and social democracy.

Conant is too much of a realist, however, not to recognize the gap between an ideal and its realization in practice. But he is also sufficiently realistic to understand that, despite contrasts between creed and deed in our society, the concepts of equality of opportunity and commitment to social mobility are dynamic factors alike in the minds of educators and laymen concerned with educational reform. Loyalty to these ideals explains, in part, Conant's opposition to public assistance for nonpublic schools, as well as his preference for the comprehensive high school as against institutions that provide either an exclusively academic and general education or that minister primarily to vocational interests. Social democracy implies mutual respect and friendly understanding as between people of varying abilities and occupations, that is, "low visibility" of class lines. This mutual respect, Conant believes, is best promoted when young people of many kinds of talents and different life goals mingle together in the same school, and, within limits, within the same classroom. Although an advocate of a differentiated curriculum, Conant nevertheless would bring together students of all types in certain courses (a senior high school course in Problems of Democracy, for example) in the hope that

[46] Ibid., p. 37. For a detailed discussion of the curriculum of the secondary school in the light of differences between communities and individuals, see Conant, The American High School Today (New York: McGraw-Hill Book Co., 1959); and Slums and Suburbs, op. cit.

differences in background and points of view might enrich the experiences of all.

Finally, his concern for equality of opportunity and conditions that promote social mobility leads Conant, in contrast with basic educationists, to recognize the positive contributions of the "educational establishment" in giving shape to the secondary school of today. Thus, in discussing "A Quarrel Among Educators," he writes: "The emphasis on education for citizenship, on the socially unifying effects of the comprehensive high school, and on the public schools as instruments of democracy, the recognition of individual differences, and of the need for including practical courses in high school elective programs—all these characteristics, *which I applaud*, were the fruits of the labors of professors of education." [47]

Conant's recognition of the contributions of professors of education in recent years follows from his awareness of profound changes that have taken place in American society in the course of the past sixty years—changes to which many college professors have remained indifferent. "College professors of the liberal arts," he writes in *The Child, the Parent, and the State*, "often discuss school problems as though schools operate in the stratosphere—that is, in a social vacuum. To be sure, it is a convenient fiction to assume that a community has no interest in a school except as an institution for developing intellectual powers. If one needed an example to illustrate the insufficiency of such premises about education, what is happening south of the Mason-Dixon Line would provide a dramatic case." [48]

On the other hand, from his direct observation of schools throughout the country and his study of teacher education programs in some sixteen representative states, he is also convinced that educators, in their attempts to cope with change, have sadly neglected the academically talented student. Further, in their teacher education programs, they have both expanded unnecessarily strictly "educational courses" and excluded the potential contributions of scholars on liberal arts faculties from participation in the preparation of teachers.

Conant informs us that he first became aware of the limited vision of both the educationists and liberal arts professors when he assumed the presidency of Harvard University. Drawing upon his experience at Har-

[47] James B. Conant, *The Education of American Teachers* (New York: McGraw-Hill Book Co., 1963), p. 6.
[48] Conant, *The Child, the Parent, and the State, op. cit.*, pp. 64-65.

vard in bringing about a better understanding and cooperative relationship between the faculty of arts and sciences and the faculty of education in the preparation of teachers, he has since undertaken a similar task on a nationwide scale. His task is twofold, attempting (1) to offset several decades of indifference and outright misunderstanding on the part of liberal arts faculties with respect to the problems of public education, and to develop in them an appreciation of the role of professional training as well as "knowledge of subject matter" in the preparation of prospective teachers; and (2) to convince professors of education and others who comprise the "educational establishment" (professional organizations of administrators and teachers, state departments of education, officials of the National Education Association) of the importance of reducing the present number of required courses in education and increasing the contributions of scholars within the various subject matter fields in the preparation of teachers.

A further major concern of Conant's is practice teaching. He suggests that it be brought "under the direction of college and public school personnel in whom the state department has confidence and in a practice-teaching situation of which the state department approves..." together with a probationary period of employment under competent guidance.

The better to insure these developments and to encourage experimentation in teacher education, Conant would reduce the role of regional accrediting organizations to an advisory function, broaden representation upon their governing boards to include representatives of the scholarly disciplines and "informed representatives of the lay public," and lodge responsibility for the certification of teachers in the entire faculty—academic and professional—of individual colleges and universities that have entered into contract with state authorities to conduct state approved practice-teacher programs. As he states, "In view of the great diversity of opinions and practices to be found in leading institutions, I conclude that neither a state authority nor a voluntary accrediting agency is in a position to specify the amount of time to be devoted to either academic or educational courses. What is needed is on the one hand for the state to allow freedom for institutions to experiment, and on the other for the academic professors and professors of education in each institution to take joint responsibility for the reputation of their college or university in training of teachers." [49]

[49] Conant, *The Education of American Teachers, op. cit.*, p. 210.

Needless to say, this philanthropic effort to effect a "truce among educators" [50] has not resulted in the peaceful cooperation that Conant may have anticipated. Indeed, both the firm convictions and the long-established prerogatives of too many groups were held up to public view and found wanting in Conant's report to insure an enthusiastic reception of his suggestions.[51]

Few critics of American education have been privileged to speak under conditions more favorable for an assured hearing than James B. Conant. His prominence as educator and citizen, prior to turning his attention to the problems of public education, has provided him in advance with a receptive audience. Fortunate, too, has he been in securing the financial resources with which to enlist the services of a competent and professional staff to assist him in the gathering of data and the formulation of conclusions. Again, his announced determination to avoid abstract theory and to center directly upon past and present practices in education as a basis for suggested reform has appealed to large numbers of educators as well as to laymen who have viewed the theorist with misgivings, if not outright suspicion. Finally, in his studies of the secondary school, particularly, his methods have resulted in practical, middle-of-the-road recommendations of obvious plausibility—plausible, for the reason that they reflect what he and his staff have identified as the best in present practice.

Conant's is no mean achievement, when we consider the plural character of American school communities and the varied types of student bodies served by the school. Educators and laymen have every reason to be grateful for the sense of reality that pervades both his analysis of contemporary problems and his hardheaded suggestions for reform, in contrast with the oversimplified picture and easy generalizations put forth by many another critic of the schools. But the authority with which he speaks has its disadvantages. So impressed are many, they fail to observe that his recommendations seldom go beyond suggestions for administrative readjustments and program changes. (This, of course, is not true of Conant's recommendations for teacher education. Here he examines in some detail both the content of courses and the relative value of one subject as against another. What is said above implies particularly to the high school

---

[50] The title of an address delivered by Conant in 1944 at the 50th Anniversary of Teachers College, Columbia University.

[51] For two quite different reactions to Conant's report on *The Education of American Teachers*, see Stiles, *op. cit.*, and Harry S. Broudy, "Conant on the Education of Teachers," *The Educational Forum*, January, 1964.

curriculum.) Only by implication here and there do we find him facing the problem of subject matter in relation to differences in ability, interest, and environmental circumstance. Consequently, as some curriculum experts concerned with new organizations of subject matter have pointed out, Conant's recommendations tend to confirm the existing compartmentalization of subjects (physics, chemistry, biology, as separate subjects, for example, as against unified science courses) and to retard experimentalization with new organizations of subject matter in response to the interrelationships within broad fields characteristic of modern knowledge and the identifiable needs of students as individuals and groups.[52]

IN SUMMARY

Few contrasts are more striking than the attitudes of large numbers of Americans toward their public schools in the 1930's and in the two decades that followed. The 1930's were marked by a phenomenal increase in school enrollments and flexible adjustments in curricula in order to minister to the growing needs of young people for whom economic life no longer provided open opportunities. Indeed, in some respects, school and college served as much as a haven and a refuge for a "lost generation" as insurance for a new and attractive future.

The 1940's and 1950's witnessed a quite different attitude toward public education. Progressive education, with its emphasis upon experimentation, once welcomed, now encountered stubborn opposition and suspicion. A partial explanation for this reversal may be found in the fact of war, a hot war followed by a cold war of seemingly endless duration. War and the fear of war often generate a frame of mind and spirit unfavorable to experiment and creative thought.

In the wake of war came new demands upon the American people, demands that emphasized simultaneously the importance of conserving traditional values, the need to abandon long-established policies of isolation and relative indifference to the troubles of other peoples, and the assumption of positive leadership of the free world in opposition to strange ideologies and the conspiracies of totalitarian powers. Disillusionment, confusion of mind, and frustration of spirit accompanied these new developments, developments with which education in school and college

[52] See in this connection, Harold B. Alberty, *Public Education in the Sixties: Trends and Issues,* the Boyd H. Bode Memorial Lectures, 1962 (Columbus, Ohio: Ohio State University, 1963).

had obviously not prepared Americans to cope. For many Americans, long accustomed to view education as an open sesame to change, this failure of the schools to provide an answer to their problems, it was easy to conclude that the latter had played them false. What was once pride and confidence in public schools gave way to doubt and criticism—doubt in the efficacy of their work, doubt even in their integrity.

Criticism in this period, as we have seen, varied widely. One group, adopting demagogic and propagandistic methods, charged that educators had become victims of foreign ideologies and were engaged in attempts to subvert American youth to communistic and collectivistic ideas by means of new courses of study and group methods of instruction. A second, convinced that the schools were responsible for the failures of democracy, attributed these failures to the fact that school and college alike reflected in their work the least desirable characteristics of American society— materialism, scientism, shortsighted adjustment to the trivial demands of society—and were thus neglecting their essential task, the training of the mind. Only by concentrating upon the development of the intellect by means of materials drawn from the trivium and the quadrivium, insisted these critics, might the schools hope to educate for freedom.

In substantial agreement with this point of view was Walter Lippmann, who then, as he does today, attributed the failures of the western democracies in large measure to the fact that educators have substituted the "cult of the child," the "Jacobin fallacy," and an unprogrammed following of young people's interests for an earlier emphasis upon informing and disciplining man's rational nature by means of a curriculum that alone can transmit the "moral system" and the "universal laws of the natural order." While less philosophical in their basic premises than Lippmann, and less specific in their curricular recommendations than Hutchins and the Education for Freedom group, the basic educationists are in agreement with both their indictments of the schools and their conviction that reform in education calls for a return to the essentially one-track curriculum of the past.

Of the prominent critics of contemporary education, James B. Conant is unique in his willingness to build upon what the "best" schools are now doing. Nevertheless, as Richard Hofstadter points out,[53] the curriculum that Conant recommends as a minimum for "academically talented boys

[53] Richard Hofstadter, *Anti-intellectualism in American Life* (New York: Alfred A. Knopf, 1963), p. 330.

and girls" is strikingly similar to the recommendations of the Committee of Ten in 1893. That is to say, constructive as Conant's approach to educational reform is, it is conservative in that it lends his authority to the traditional subject matter organizations of the conventional curriculum and finds no place for new organizations, such as the "core curriculum," and new combinations of subjects, such as "general science" on the senior high school level as a substitute for the traditional divisions of subjects into chemistry, physics, biology, and the like.

Absent also in Conant's discussion of the American high school is any detailed consideration of factors in the contemporary world that carry a moral for education beyond the administrative arrangement of subjects in relation to academic ability and interest, cultural background, and environmental circumstance. Consequently, to the valuable contributions he has unquestionably made should be added a consideration of factors economic, social, and political—peculiar to today—that constitute a challenge to the school. It is to this challenge that we now turn.

SUGGESTED READING

Alberty, Harold B., and Alberty, Elsie J., *Reorganizing the High School Curriculum* (New York: The Macmillan Co., 3rd ed., 1962), Chapter I.

Broudy, Harry S., "Conant on the Education of Teachers," *The Educational Forum*, January, 1964, pp. 199-210.

Conant, James B., *The Child, the Parent, and the State* (Cambridge, Mass.: Harvard University Press, 1959), Chapters I-IV.

————, *The Education of American Teachers* (New York: McGraw-Hill Book Co., 1963), Chapter I.

————, *Shaping Educational Policy* (New York: McGraw-Hill Book Co., 1964), Chapters 1, 2, 5.

Hutchins, Robert M., *The Conflict in Education* (New York: Harper & Bros., 1953), Chapters I-IV.

Koerner, James D. (ed.), *The Case for Basic Education* (Boston: Little, Brown & Co., 1959), Chapter I.

Lippmann, Walter, *The Public Philosophy* (Boston: Little, Brown & Co., 1955), Chapters I, II, VII, VIII.

Rickover, H. G., *Education and Freedom* (New York: E. P. Dutton & Co., 1959), Chapters 1, 5, 8, 10.

Smith, Mortimer, *A Citizen's Manual for Public Schools: A Guide for School Board Members and Other Laymen* (Washington, D.C.: Council for Basic Education, 1959), Chapters, I, II.

CHAPTER 15
TODAY'S CHALLENGE
TO THE SCHOOLS

THE phrase "agonizing reappraisal," used so frequently in discussions of United States foreign policy in recent years, might be employed with equal relevance to describe the attitude of the American people toward their public schools in the 1950's. And the reasons for using the phrase would be similar. The instinct for survival aroused by the challenge of communism to the free world and represented in the phenomenal progress of Russia—industrially, scientifically, militarily—led many to compare education in the United States with that in Russia, and the conclusions reached were far from complimentary for the former. Still more basic was the growing awareness of profound changes under way in American society and in the relations of the people of the United States to other peoples of the world, for which the schools were failing adequately to prepare the young.

The first expressions of these concerns were those of fear and frustration, and, as we have seen, they were not too responsible or accurate indictments of failure. In the 1960's a more constructive attitude began to manifest itself, with attempts to identify factors of change and their implications for the schools. In this our final chapter, we should like to outline briefly the most significant of these latest developments.

WE HAVE BECOME A METROPOLITAN CIVILIZATION

First is the quickening pace with which a predominantly rural and small town civilization with its intimate community life has become a metropolitan, industrial, and scientific civilization. Today, for example, approximately 113,000,000 of our population of slightly over 180,000,000 is concentrated in 212 metropolitan areas. In 1960 the urban population of the United States stood at 70 percent of the total, "an increase of six percent over 1950, but the 28-million gain during this decade took place in urban centers and 97 percent in metropolitan areas." Rural families today number less than 10 percent of all families in the United States.[1] For this 10 percent, life, with its dependence upon science and the applications of science, has lost its onetime distinctiveness. No longer are the farms and rural communities safe retreats for the illiterate and the unskilled.

Life in the large metropolitan areas of today—in the family and the relations of the family to the outside world, the ways in which people earn their living and carry on their civic activities—differs significantly from life in the agricultural and small town economy of yesterday. As Kimball and McClellan point out, most young people today have to learn to live within two quite different cultural patterns—within the "nuclear family" (consisting of the insulated household of parents and siblings, relatives, and close friends) characterized by intimate personal relationships that minister to the basic needs of personality development and, eventually, in the impersonal and corporate society of business and industry, civic, cultural, and recreational associations. Only yesterday the individual lived and worked and discharged his responsibilities as a citizen in one and the same locality. Cities were aggregations of neighborhoods and the term "community" still referred to a geographical area in which one not only lived but also worked and joined with his neighbors in exercising the duties of a citizen. Frequent change in place of abode, characteristic of today, accentuated by ease of transportation and communication, have transformed life in urban as well as rural areas. The number of people who live and work in one and the same locality steadily decreases, and, with the absence of a sense of membership in a community, there evaporates the feeling of direct responsibility for the community's character. Yesterday the individual exercised his citizenship functions as an individual. Today he tends more and more to do so through

[1] Solon T. Kimball and James E. McClellan, *Education and the New America* (New York: Random House, 1962), p. 119. For a suggestive discussion of the changes in traditional ways of living and the values that have come with the emergence of a metropolitan-industrial civilization, see Chapters 6 and 7 of this volume. See also Max Lerner, *America as a Civilization* (New York: Simon & Schuster, 1957), Chapter III.

membership in a labor union, an employing association, a political party, or a civic organization in which his voice is merged with that of others.

In a chapter dealing with "The High School's Role in Adolescent Status Transition," Kitsuse and Cicourel write:

> In societies characterized by rapid social and cultural change, tradition provides few adult models for the young. The validity and relevance of the existing models are problematic, both as guides for adolescent conduct and as projections of the roles young people are expected to assume as adults. In such situations, the preparation of youth lacks the orientation of a clearly and confidently envisaged image of the society in which they are expected to take their place. Indeed, the fact that city parents rear their children under conditions of rapid social cultural change is the crux of urban youth problems.[2]

The possibilities of orientation programs in stimulating young people disadvantaged by slum life are being demonstrated in a number of large cities. The "Higher Horizons" project in New York, for example, has stimulated young people to improve their work in school and, in many instances, to go on to college, as a result of cultural enrichment. Work camp and community service programs with more privileged young people have given new meaning and understanding to the participants, which suggests the wisdom of broadening and extending the concept of laboratory experience in secondary education.

All of this implies a need for education that enables the young person to bridge the gap between his home and the complex world of adults in which he must eventually play a part, but for which neither home nor school prepares him adequately. It suggests, for example, on the secondary and college levels, that subjects of study be used to provide an orientation to life outside the school—economic, civic, cultural—that once could be taken for granted. It means an extension of the laboratory idea to subjects hitherto exclusively verbal and academic, so that young people may envisage each subject of the school as representative of adult interests outside the school. It enhances the importance of relating each young person through his interests to individuals and agencies within the com-

---

[2] John I. Kitsuse and Aaron V. Cicourel, "The High School's Role in Adolescent Status Transition," in B. J. Chandler, Lindley J. Stiles, and John I. Kitsuse (eds.), *Education in Urban Society* (New York: Dodd, Mead & Co., 1962), p. 72.

munity so as to dramatize the importance of these interests in his own personal development and to give significance to them through a firsthand realization of their public and social importance. Toward this end departments of government—such as a health department, a public library, an art museum—as well as private agencies of a social and civic character might be encouraged to add to their service functions those of education.

WE ARE NO LONGER A SELF-SUFFICIENT PEOPLE

A second factor with multiple implications for education today is the realization that we are no longer a self-sufficient people. Admiral Rickover has drawn dramatic attention to one important aspect of the present and the moral that follows for education—the rapidity with which the energy resources of the United States and the world are being depleted. Indeed, it is his anxiety with respect to the future (in the light of the present phenomenal increase in the world's population on the one hand and the impending exhaustion of conventional sources of energy on the other) that causes him to stress the critical necessity of improving the quality of education in school and college.[3] He concludes quite properly that unless the American people are willing to undergo the sacrifices necessary in order to provide their young people with the best possible education, the United States will lose its position as a great nation.

It is not surprising that Rickover, as scientist and engineer, should emphasize education in science and technology as a condition of our future material and cultural development. Relevant as this is, it is but one conclusion to be drawn, educationally, from the problems generated and rendered acute by our vanishing natural resources. These are problems which cannot be divorced from other factors that are bringing the American people into intimate contact with peoples of quite different cultural backgrounds: a new emphasis, for example, upon foreign languages as one means of acquiring a sympathetic insight into the life values, the habits, and the customs of other cultures and upon art, literature, and history, as well as geography and economics for similar reasons.

The United States is today the world's biggest market for the exports of other countries. We now consume about half of all the industrial raw

[3] See H. G. Rickover, *Education and Freedom* (New York: E. P. Dutton & Co., 1959), Chapters 5, 6, on "Energy Resources and Our Future" and "Investment in Human Resources."

material produced in the free world. Once a heavy exporter of raw materials, the United States now consumes about half of all the industrial raw materials produced in the free world. As James D. Calderwood has pointed out, the United States has ceased to export, and now imports instead, strategic materials such as lead, zinc, petroleum, and iron ore. In addition, we now import almost all of our tin, nickel, tungsten, asbestos, chrome, mercury, mica, and cobalt, as well as less well-known minerals. Calderwood also points out that Canada, Mexico, the Philippines, Peru, and Venezuela depend upon the United States to purchase each year one-half to two-thirds of their exports.[4] Taken together with other developments—the organization of the Common Market in Europe and its potential influence upon a United Europe of the future, the rapidity with which the colonial peoples of Asia and Africa have attained the status of independent nations, and the extent to which economic factors determine whether their future allegiance will be to the free or to the communist world—the impossibility of separating the economic from the political and the cultural is clear.

With incredible swiftness the American people have moved into a world of novel characteristics, a world of heterogeneous communities at home and plural cultures abroad. Neither in the local community nor in relations with foreign peoples of altogether different cultures do they enjoy their onetime independence. The domestic scene has been so transformed by ease of communication and transportation, together with economic changes, that men are called upon, more and more, to deal with individuals and groups whose values and interests often differ from their own. As a result, they are required to exercise a degree of sensitivity, imagination, and responsiveness to the habits, customs, and convictions of others far in excess of anything demanded of them in the past.

These new conditions carry a moral for virtually every subject in the curriculum. Scientists and mathematicians are already making attempts to introduce elementary and secondary school pupils to new ways of approaching these subjects and to new concepts in the light of contemporary research. Similar attempts should be undertaken by the social

[4] James D. Calderwood, "Resources Policies and International Relations," a paper read at a conference of persons engaged in resource-use education at Portland State College, Oregon, May, 1959, and published as *Resource-Use Education* (New York: Joint Council on Economic Education).

scientists (anthropologists, sociologists, historians, economists, even psychiatrists) in order to correct parochial and outdated conceptions of man and his institutions which now inhibit creative and constructive relations between people of different origins and cultural values.[5]

The American school assumes that it is preparing young people for participation in a democratic society. If it is to do so effectively, more than the revision and enrichment of subject matter is called for. Young people will have to be schooled in ways of thinking and living that enable them to live fruitfully with diversity.

Fortunately, we are not without suggestions concerning the kind of discipline to develop. On the home front, we can observe the evolution of new methods of thinking in the gradual substitution of collective bargaining between capital and labor for the method of decisions by combat or fighting it out. The gradual adoption of the group process in the deliberation of committees and commissions (long practiced in Quaker meetings and today employed even by an occasional committee of Congress!), constitutes another fertile field of application. For the classroom, this suggests replacing debate, and its rigid adherence to one partisan point of view, with a procedure that weighs principle against principle in the light of all relevant data, thus substituting a method sensitive to the responsibilities of a citizen in a world of plural interests for the traditional emphasis upon the preparation of partisan advocates and supersalesmen.[6]

SCIENCE AND THE "KNOWLEDGE EXPLOSION"

Phenomenal advances in science and the applications of science constitute a third formative influence in the education of young people today. The extent to which science affects vocational life is well illustrated by a statement of Ralph W. Tyler, Director of the Center for Advanced Study in the Behavioral Sciences at Stanford University. It is estimated, he said, that more than 50 percent of the occupations in which today's

[5] Lawrence K. Frank expands upon this point in his Burton Lecture delivered at Harvard in 1959, *The School as an Agent for Cultural Renewal* (Cambridge, Mass.: Harvard University Press, 1960).

[6] For a more extended discussion of methods of thinking relevant to a pluralistic society, see V. T. Thayer, *The Role of the School in American Society* (New York: Dodd, Mead & Co., 1960), Chapter 9, "Some Aspects of the Intellectual Task of the School." See also the discussion of Theodore Brameld's *Education for the Emerging Age*, Chapter 12 of the present volume.

college graduates will find employment did not exist when these young people were born! [7]

Tyler's statement refers to a development to which Sumner Slichter, the economist, called attention some years ago—the emergence of an "industry of discovery," by which Slichter meant research devoted to the discovery of new products and new areas of invention and expansion in industry. According to Slichter,[8] research of this type had become one of the most rapidly growing industries in the United States. In 1930, for example, industry spent $116 million in research and development; in 1940, $235 million; and in 1953, $1.5 billion. Ten years later James R. Killian, writing in the same magazine, reported that expenditures in the United States for scientific research and development had risen to $17 billion, or 3 percent of the gross national product! Of this total expenditure, according to Killian, $12.4 billion was being spent by government (with about 63 percent, however, going to industry under contract) and $5 billion by private industry. "Three quarters of all research and development in the United States," he wrote, "is performed in industrial laboratories."[9] In the light of this development it is understandable that Clark Kerr, President of the University of California, should compare the effects of the "knowledge industry" upon the second half of this century with that of the railroads upon the second half of the last century and the automobile upon the first half.[10]

The Lord giveth and the Lord taketh away! So it is with science and its offspring, automation, the product of scientific research and development. Not only is it increasingly necessary today to acquire an education prior to entering the labor market, but, in order to share in the advantages that flow from the "knowledge industry," continuous education and even reeducation and retraining become ever more imperative. To emphasize the importance of education today, the United States Department of Labor in 1960 published *Manpower: Challenge of the 1960's*. This pamphlet forecast employment opportunities as follows: Professional and Technical Workers, an increase of 41 percent; Proprietors and Managers,

[7] Quoted by Maurice B. Mitchell, President of Encyclopaedia Britannica, Inc., in a special supplement to *The New York Times* on "The Knowledge Explosion," Sunday, May 26, 1963.

[8] Sumner Slichter, "The Passing Keynesian Economics," *Atlantic Monthly*, November, 1957, pp. 141-146.

[9] James R. Killian, "The Crisis in Research," *Atlantic Monthly*, March, 1963, p. 69.

[10] Quoted and commented upon in an editorial in *The New York Times*, May 5, 1963.

22 percent increase; Clerical and Sales Workers, 25 percent increase; Semiskilled Workers, 18 percent increase; Unskilled Workers, zero percent increase; Farmers and Farm Workers, 17 percent decrease.

Schooling has long been recognized in American society as a means for bettering one's station in life, and, in that sense, its importance today merely accentuates a traditional value. What is novel is that the individual without education today is hopelessly lost. Novel also is the rapidity with which two trends in contemporary society have become accentuated: (1) the elimination of unskilled labor and the expansion of occupational opportunities for the broadly educated and highly trained, and (2) a rapid increase in the proportion of college graduates who proceed on to graduate school.

These trends were dramatically reflected in the employment situation in June, 1963. At one and the same time that the percentage of unemployment had increased slightly, and the press of the country was pointing to a high level of unemployment among high school students seeking jobs (approximately 18 percent in contrast with a national rate of 4 to 5 percent), Fred M. Hechinger of *The New York Times*, reported that college graduates were entering a "booming job market" with starting pay between 2 and 4 percent above that of the year before. "Science, engineering, accounting, and teaching," according to Hechinger, "dominate the job lists. Engineers, physical science, and mathematics graduates are in greatest demand." He also recorded a trend toward better opportunities for graduates of liberal arts colleges, other than in science and mathematics.[11]

Increased enrollments in graduate school also bear witness to these changes. For example, in the article referred to above, Hechinger reported that the University of Chicago anticipated from 65 to 80 percent of its graduating class in 1963 would go on to graduate school. New York University and the City College of New York reported a similar trend. And James B. Conant, in his *Slums and Suburbs*, informs us that more than half of the graduates of Harvard, Yale, and Princeton now go on to study in a professional or graduate school. Similar developments are evident in other institutions of high standing throughout the country.

These trends render tragic the condition of large numbers of young

[11] Fred M. Hechinger, "College Graduates Face a World of Good Jobs and Challenges," *New York Times*, June 9, 1963.

people who encounter little in their home environments or their community relations to accent the importance of schooling. Particularly deplorable are the situations of the children in impoverished families of rural background, whose parents are rapidly being displaced by modern agricultural methods, and of the offspring of a second and third generation of slum dwellers. Of the latter, Conant states, it is not uncommon for more than half of the boys between ages sixteen and twenty to be out of school and out of work.[12]

Uncertain also—if not tragic—is the future of the school dropout. "At the very time when jobs requiring higher educational attainments are increasing," write the authors of Education in Urban Society, "and the need for unskilled labor is decreasing, 7,500,000 youth are expected to drop out of school during the coming decade. Employers are demanding better-educated people; yet one out of every four new workers who joins (or attempts to join) the labor force in the next ten years is likely to have less than a high school education." [13]

Thus far we have emphasized the influence of science upon economic life. Of equal significance for education are the contributions of science to other areas of living, including man's conception of himself and the nature of the universe in which he lives. Not the least of the tasks of the school is to bring to young people an understanding of the manner in which the concepts of modern science are forcing a revision of what Lawrence Frank terms the "many obsolete, archaic concepts and assumptions, the long-accepted criteria of credibility, that are no longer valid." Frank believes this is particularly important in view of contemporary emphasis upon "crash" programs in science and mathematics, programs that are in danger of perpetuating anachronistic ideas and obsolete ways of thinking. He believes we both can and should "earnestly endeavor to acquaint all students, beginning with their first year in school, with contemporary scientific ideas and assumptions, helping them to understand that to live in the contemporary world, they need this orientation because our social order, as well as our individual living, is being transformed by scientific thinking and its applications in technology." [14]

[12] James B. Conant, Slums and Suburbs (New York: McGraw-Hill Book Co., 1961), Chapters I, II.
[13] Chandler, Stiles, and Kitsuse (eds.), op. cit., p. 16.
[14] Frank, op. cit., pp. 17-18.

MOBILITY OF POPULATION CREATES NEW PROBLEMS

When Admiral Rickover states that the task of assimilation in American education is past, he forgets the formidable problems confronting urban schools today in all sections of the country as a result of the migration from rural to urban centers. The children of these new arrivals are often severely handicapped not merely by inadequate formal education but also by lack of stimulation from parents. Unlike the immigrants of several generations ago, migrants from the South come from areas in which education above the minimum requirements of literacy frequently has little appeal. Upon their arrival in the city they commonly drift into slum areas, there to merge with others of little hope and ambition.

Between 1950 and 1960, the percentage of Negroes in the South fell from 60 to 52 per cent. In large measure, both Negro and white migrants from the South move from rural areas of meager educational facilities to urban centers. Arthur F. Cory of the California Teachers Association, writing in 1958, stated that the population of that state was increasing at the rate of more than 500,000 a year and was confronting California with the problem of staffing new schools "at the rate of one eighteen-classroom building per day, 365 days a year." He added that in many school districts the median IQ of twelfth graders declined eight to ten points in a period of two years, and communities, once upper-middle class, had quickly been transformed into low-cost housing tracts.[15] Similar problems confront other states. Chicago receives some 20,000 "functional illiterates" each year, and New York State now has the largest Negro population of any state in the Union.

To contend, under these circumstances, that the school's task is solely academic, and that it usurps the responsibilities of the home when it provides courses in home economics and facilities for guidance in areas of social and emotional development, is to forget that one of the traditional functions of the American school has been to serve as a supplementary institution. Far wiser is it to recognize with James Conant "that to a considerable degree what a school should do and can do is determined by the status and ambitions of the families being served"— [16] to which should be added, the school's obligation to the society it serves involves at times the attempt to better the attitudes of parents as well as children!

[15] Arthur F. Cory, "California Schools Do Educate," *Atlantic Monthly*, December, 1958, pp. 63-66.
[16] Conant, *op. cit.*, p. 1.

It would be a mistake, however, to assume that mobility of population, in its bearing upon education, applies only to the underprivileged and the disadvantaged. Rather is it a characteristic of Americans on all economic and cultural levels. "The man who leaves home," writes William H. Whyte, Jr., "is not the exception in American society but the key to it." And Whyte goes on to show that "the educational level is higher among migrants than nonmigrants, and the higher the educational level, the more intensive the migration." [17]

Mobility thus characterizes American society on all levels—economic, social, cultural. In all sections of the country, people are constantly on the move: from state to state, country to city, city to suburb, and (young people) from school to school. [18]

The effects of mobility upon those who move from place to place, and upon communities that receive the stranger, reaffirm the ancient principle that no man lives unto himself alone. The same applies to localities. Traditionally, education has been a state and local function with each governmental unit (town, city, county) free to exercise a high degree of self-determination with respect to the quality and the quantity of education it provides. So firmly established is this principle of state and local autonomy with respect to administration, finance, and curriculum that advocates of change have been as voices crying alone in the wilderness.

Today, however, these assumptions are being challenged. Within the states, the attempt to equalize educational opportunities (together with obvious differences in financial resources as between communities) is in process of modifying the concept of local autonomy and establishing units of financial support larger than those of administration. For much the same reason, educators and laymen alike are turning to the federal government for aid to education in the states, with insistence, however, upon

[17] William H. Whyte, Jr., *The Organization Man* (New York: Simon & Schuster, 1956), pp. 297-298. Whyte states that the records of long-distance movers indicate that "The greatest single group of their clients—between 40 and 50 per cent—is composed of corporation people. . . . If to this group are added government, Army and Navy people, and corporation people leaving one company for another, roughly three quarters of all moves are accounted for by members of large corporations."

[18] Although the city slum has come to resemble a stagnant pool from which it is difficult for young and old to escape, movement from tenement to tenement is common. As Conant writes in *Slums and Suburbs, op. cit.*, p. 18: "Often the composition of a school grade in such an area will alter so rapidly that a teacher will find at the end of a school year that she is teaching but few pupils who started with her in the fall." For an interesting discussion of the effects of mobility upon American culture, see Lerner, *op. cit.*, pp. 94-105.

the principle that this financial aid be dissassociated from federal control over educational policy.[19]

Pressure mounts, nevertheless, in favor of greater uniformity with respect to curricula and standards of achievement. To the demand of parents, on the move, that mobility not interfere with the educational progress of their children has been added, since the Russians launched their Sputnik I, popular recognition of the intimate connection between education and national security. It is the latter realization in large measure that has prompted both Congress and private foundations to subsidize research designed both to improve and to standardize instruction in elementary and secondary schools. Significant in this connection is the fact that scholars outside professional educational circles have shown an awakened interest in the teaching of their subjects in elementary and secondary schools, thus bridging a gap of long standing that has separated professional educators and scholars.

Collaboration between these two groups is most conspicuous today in the fields of science and mathematics. For example, Professor Jerrold R. Zacharias of the Massachusetts Institute of Technology has taken the lead in developing a new physics course for high schools, including textbook material, an elaborate teacher's guide of four volumes, a laboratory workbook, and films. Other groups are engaged in reorganizing the mathematics curriculum in elementary and secondary schools with emphasis upon original thought and discovery and upon the acquisition of concepts, in contrast with the mechanical learning of facts and processes. Cooperative projects of a similar nature are under way in the revision of high school biology, chemistry, and the social studies. More recently (June, 1963) the American Council of Learned Societies, the Council of Graduate Schools in the United States, and the United Chapters of Phi Beta Kappa established a Commission on the Humanities. The purpose of this Commission is to deal with questions of teaching as well as scholarship "at all levels from elementary school through post-graduate school."

Care will have to be exercised, however, not to leap from one extreme to another. Early in the century it was concluded that textbooks and courses of study reflected too exclusively the research interests of advanced students and too little the educational needs of young people of widely

---

[19] See Paul Mort and Donald H. Ross, *Principles of School Administration* (New York: McGraw-Hill Book Co., 2nd ed., 1957), pp. 281-283, for an elaboration of the thesis that units of finance and units of educational control should be distinguished.

different backgrounds and life goals. It was then that professional educators began to exercise a dominating influence upon the curriculum, often to the exclusion of scholars. Speaking as a scientist, Professor Zacharias condemns the scientist rather than the educator for this state of affairs. Unless the professional scientist is willing to participate in the details of planning courses of study, Zacharias asserts, we must "condemn ourselves to the situation that now exists; physics, chemistry, biology, and mathematics (and for all that, geography, history, and economics) as they are taught in the schools bear no relation whatsoever to physics, chemistry, biology, or mathematics (or geography, history, or economics) as they are practiced. They are irrelevant to the concerns or the environment of the student just as they are irrelevant to the concerns and the environment of the scholar." [20]

Today, as the need to improve the quality of education gains in recognition, there is danger of oversimplifying the task of curriculum construction. Indispensable as are the contributions of the subject matter specialist to the curriculum, it does not follow from the nature of his work that he is the most competent to determine what in his field is most relevant either to the growing needs of a young person at one age level as against another or to the unique circumstances of the environment. Consequently, unless the contributions of the scholar are supplemented by the equally important contributions of others—students of cultural trends, specialists in the learning process, and, by no means of least importance, teachers skilled in adapting materials and experiences to stages of development, different levels of ability, and conditions peculiar to the school community —much will be lost. As the educational commissions of the 1930's emphasized,[21] the purposes of education in a democracy are both general and special. Contemporary attention centers upon improving the quality of instruction in specific fields. But quality is plural! In order to bring subject matter up to date and to introduce young people to the structure and the discipline of a subject, it is not necessary to neglect other potential contributions. Indeed, the greater the extent to which each subject enlightens and informs young people in the basic relationships of living (personal, personal-social, social-civic, economic), the more vital will its

[20] Jerrold R. Zacharias, "The Age of Science," in Eli Ginzberg, *The Nation's Children,* a volume prepared for the 1960 White House Conference on Children and Youth (New York: Columbia University Press, 1960), p. 112.

[21] See Chapter 12 of this volume.

contributions be to an understanding of its structure and to disciplined ways of thinking.[22]

EQUALITY OF OPPORTUNITY GAINS NEW EMPHASIS AS AN IDEAL

There is pressing need to close the gap between ideal and reality with respect to equality of educational opportunity. One result of the Cold War and continuing competition with Russia has been to draw the attention of thoughtful Americans to the serious waste of talent in the United States.

James Conant has dramatized the inequalities of educational opportunities for youth that follow upon residence in a city slum in comparison with residence in the suburbs of a metropolitan area. Eli Ginzberg performs a similar service with respect to the untapped resources of talent in Negro youth.[23] The plight of large numbers of farm youth is rendered no less serious by virtue of the rapid decline of the farm population and the trek toward the cities in pursuit of better opportunities—economic, social, and cultural. Writing in *The New York Times* for September 29, 1963, Donald Janson states that only one-tenth of today's farm youth are destined for farm life. Unfortunately, however, these young people are attending rural schools that prepare them for no other future. As a result, unemployment of farm youth is 50 percent higher than that of urban youth. According to Janson, only a small proportion of farm youth go on to college. Their interests are in working with machines and tools, but they receive neither training in preparation for skilled and technical jobs nor competent vocational guidance.

Closely related is the problem of dropouts from elementary and secondary schools, totaling nearly 1,000,000 each year. While financial limitations account in part for the number of dropouts from high school, a major factor is also lack of motivation, responsibility for which is shared

[22] For a criticism of recent trends in curriculum organization and the tendency to center exclusively upon a "subject-centered curriculum," see Harold B. Alberty and Elsie J. Alberty, *Reorganizing the High School Curriculum* (New York: The Macmillan Co., 3rd ed., 1962), Chapter 5. See also their paper on "Utilizing Curriculum Sources in Education," in National Education Association, Association for Supervision and Curriculum Development, *What Are the Sources of the Curriculum? A Symposium* (Washington, D.C.: the Association, 1962), pp. 26-34. The Albertys deplore the gradual disappearance of the "core curriculum" as a supplement to special subjects. They believe there is a need and should be a place in the curriculum for a course that deals directly with problems confronting young people and that "cut across" fields such as science, social studies, the humanities, and the arts.

[23] Eli Ginzberg, *The Negro Potential* (New York: Columbia University Press, 1956).

by home and community as well as the school. Recent studies of slum children, Negro and white, reveal in vivid terms the manner in which the underprivileged child is denied the kinds of family experiences (commonplace for the middle-class child) which are indispensable for the mastery of the basic skills of schooling. In contrast with the child from a middle- or upper-class family, his formative years are spent in a nonverbal household, one that provides no reading and little conversation of a character to stimulate his imagination or acquaint him with the world about him. The adults with whom he associates speak in short and simple sentences and are incompetent (were they aware of the importance of so doing) to assist him in developing a sensitiveness to the correct sounds and uses of letters, syllables, words and sentences.

"The nonverbal atmosphere of the home," writes Charles E. Silberman, "also means that lower-class children have a limited perception of the world about them: they do not know that objects have names (table, wall, book), or that the same object may have several names (an apple is fruit, red, round, juicy). They also have very little concept of size or time." [24] Silberman proposes that the public school provide nursery school education for slum children at the age of three or four, of a type designed especially to meet their needs, in order to extend to them the beneficial results of recent experiment.

A nursery school open to the very young child and planned specifically to offset the disadvantages of slum life can do much to correct the inequalities of opportunity that weigh heavily upon underprivileged children. But these limitations do not end with the nursery school. They are merely accentuated as young people attempt to advance in school. Consequently, as a supplementary institution, the school in a slum area should function both as a settlement house and a school in the conventional sense, its staff consisting of men and women trained as social workers as well as teachers. Its program should embrace both parents and children. As a community center, it should provide opportunities and facilities for the discovery and development of interests in young and old, interests that reach into the home and tend to raise the cultural level of the community. Not least, it should be ably staffed for purposes of individual guidance and remedial instruction. Only thus will the phrase "equality of educational opportunity" take on a semblance of meaning.

The importance of salvaging talent in the interests of national defense

[24] Charles E. Silberman, "Give Slum Children a Chance: A Radical Proposal," *Harper's Magazine*, May, 1964, pp. 37-42.

and security, is one impelling reason for attempting to equalize educational opportunities. But it is only one. The 1960's have witnessed an awakening of conscience with respect to the effects upon young people of discrimination on the basis of group characteristics—upon a Mexican because he is a Mexican, an Indian because he is an Indian, a Jew for the reason that he is a Jew, and a Negro on similar grounds. With this awakening of conscience has also come the realization that discrimination ("second-class citizenship") is neither confined to any one section of the country nor uniform in pattern, although it does vary from an open and avowed character, as applied to the Negro in the South, to equally effective but more subtle and disguised forms in the North.

Along with this renewal of allegiance to the democratic principle that people are to be judged by what they demonstrate themselves to be ("By their fruits ye shall know them"!), rather than by their origins, has come the realization that equality in education does not spell identity of curriculum or procedure. This is evident from what has been said of education for children of the slums. It applies also to attempts to transform segregated schools into integrated institutions.

In the North, for example, well-meaning efforts to bring about immediate integration of previously segregated schools have led, at times, to serious differences between educators, sociologists, and psychologists, on the one hand, and ardent advocates of civil rights on the other. As the former see the problem, segregation results from housing and residential factors slow of remedy and over which school officials have no control. Consequently, they view the problem of the underprivileged Negro child as not unlike that of the underprivileged white child. For both they conclude the educational problem is to find ways and means of offsetting the injurious effects of cultural deprivation peculiar to their situation. Civil rights advocates, on the other hand, insist upon "integration now," even though this involves the merging of ill-prepared Negro children with children more advanced educationally as well as the sacrificing of the potential values of the neighborhood school.

This point of view has been forcefully presented by Inge Lederer Gibel.[25] The white wife of a Negro, Mrs. Gibel contends that the common practice in large cities of sectioning children on the basis of academic ability, a device that enables teachers to adapt their instruction to chil-

25 See Inge Lederer Gibel, "How Not to Integrate the Schools," *Harper's Magazine,* November, 1963, pp. 57-66.

dren of relatively similar academic needs, results in identifying the culturally deprived child as inferior in his own mind as well as in the minds of his schoolmates and thus defeats a major purpose of integration. She also insists a majority of parents of underprivileged children are more concerned with the improvement of their neighborhood schools than with integration brought about by the transporting of their children to unfamiliar surroundings. Mrs. Gibel is writing, of course, with the large city in mind, not of smaller communities in which segregation can be corrected without the disruption of the neighborhood pattern.

THE TASK OF THE SCHOOL IS PLURAL

From this hurried and partial survey of trends in American society it should be clear that formal education increases in importance daily and that the plight of the undereducated as well as the uneducated will become more serious with each passing decade. These facts are reflected in the substitution of the expression "functionally illiterate" for the term "illiterate." The illiterate was once an individual unable to read or to write. Today he is defined as one who has failed to receive more than a fifth-grade education. As automation continues to replace the worker, unskilled and skilled alike, the importance of education and training as a continuous process becomes ever more obvious.

For example, in his report to Congress on the problem of manpower (March 9, 1964), President Johnson called attention to the fact that two-thirds of the unemployed had received less than a high school education and that one out of every twelve workers with only an elementary school education was unemployed, as compared with but one out of every seventy college graduates. At the same time Secretary of Labor W. Willard Wirtz and other students of the unemployment problem were advocating raising the age of compulsory school attendance to eighteen as against the sixteen year cutoff now commonly in force. Thus a sizable proportion of unemployables would be removed from the labor market, and impetus would be given the development of technical institutes and training programs devoted to the preparation of young people for skilled occupations in which shortages of personnel exist.

Education and training thus serve the dual purpose of providing not only insurance against disaster but an open sesame to economic opportunity. John Gardner reminds us that as recently as 1930 learned treatises were being written warning Americans of an overproduction of the educated. Today, in contrast, the demand for highly trained people "is so great there is little likelihood of [their] unemployment"—provided their education has rendered them "capable of applying excellent fundamental training to a wide range of specific jobs." [26]

From these facts it does not follow, however, that the basic education-ists are correct in their advocacy of a one-track curriculum in the second-ary school. So to conclude would be to revert to the theory, long ago exploded, that all minds are essentially alike and will thrive on an identi-cal diet. It is also to ignore significant differences in school populations and communities served. It was after observing these differences, as they range from slum to suburb, together with their influence upon the young, that Conant was moved to express his impatience with both the critics and the defenders of public education who ignore the realities of school situ-ations and engage in "fruitless debate about philosophy, purposes, and the like." Rickover and others, it will be recalled, contend that for the school to concern itself with the students' problems of social and emotional de-velopment is to neglect its proper function—the intellectual training of the young. But this is to use the excesses and the errors of "education for ad-justment" as an excuse for ignoring the contributions of research in per-sonality development to education (to improved quality in education, if you will) and thus to throw out the baby with the bath water. It is also to ignore the increasing importance of qualities of personality in contemporary society at one and the same time that home and com-munity no longer function as they once did as an educational bridge lead-ing to adult society.[27]

As was suggested earlier, these facts carry a moral for the organization of subject matter and guidance programs. They also bear directly upon the administrative organization of the school and the way of life it fosters outside and inside the classroom. "Not only does the school shape the

[26] John Gardner, *Excellence: Can We Be Equal and Excellent Too?* (New York: Harper & Bros., 1961). See Chapter V, on "The Great Talent Hunt."

[27] Of interest in this connection are the data from a number of colleges, including Columbia and Harvard, which indicate that parallel with a noticeable increase in the proportion of intellectually superior students in these colleges, in the past ten years, there has resulted a sizable increase in the proportion of students who are plagued with serious emotional problems. Fred M. Hechinger, reviewing this situation in *The New York Times*, April 26, 1964, quotes the observation of a psychiatrist at Harvard to the effect that the traditional gap between intellectual and emotional maturity in late adolescence is getting wider and that "many of the most exceptional students are among the most immature." This hardly sanctions indifference in the lower schools to factors of emotional and social development.

development of young people," write Kitsuse and Cicourel, "it is the only agency that systematically assesses, records, and reports the progress adolescents make toward adulthood. Inasmuch as adolescents are excluded from equal participation in the social, economic, and political activities of the larger society, the school provides the only highway by which young people may make the journey to adulthood. As such, the school, particularly the high school, represents the only formally defined link between adolescent status and projected adult careers." [28] Kitsuse and Cicourel also sound a cautious note with respect to the use of conventional guidance programs in the best schools in the light of present-day pressures for achievement in academic fields—pressures that result from a meticulous monitoring of the student's progress and the adoption of remedial measures social and psychological. These pressures they believe sometimes result in disadvantages to healthy growth.

The concept of the school as a highway to adulthood carries implications for parent education and school-community relations as well as for the education of the young. For the latter, it implies an orientation to the economic, sociocivic, and cultural world of adults as well as guidance within the school program. It also raises grave questions regarding a contemporary trend in the administrative organization of schools in urban areas. This trend is to take on the characteristics of large-scale corporate organization with authority centered in a board of education which proceeds to delegate this authority—from superintendent to supervisory staff, to principals, until it finally reaches the classroom and the child in relation to his teacher. This system may have the outward form of efficient organization, but it fosters a conception of the acquisition of knowledge and skills in accordance with a fixed course of study as analogous to the production of goods in a factory. It thus renders difficult that warm and intimate relationship between student and teacher which is most essential for healthy growth and development.[29]

Kimball and McClellan believe that progressive education of some decades back was essentially conservative rather than radical in its basic objectives. In support of this position, they point to the rural and Protestant family origin of "the three major figures associated with the philos-

---

28 Kitsuse and Cicourel, in Chandler, Stiles, and Kitsuse (eds.), op. cit., p. 75.
29 See Kimball and McClellan, op. cit., Chapter 9, "The Corporate Society," for this criticism of the administrative organization of public education. See also John W. Poley, "Decentralization Within Urban School Systems," in Chandler, Stiles, and Kitsuse (eds.), op. cit., Chapter 8.

ophy of progressive education"—John Dewey, William Heard Kilpatrick, and Boyd H. Bode. These philosophers made their impact upon education as representatives "of the values of the agrarian tradition that were being threatened by the omnipresent cultural changes around them." And their contributions may be viewed as an attempt to provide through education "a basic outlook on the world that would enable the coming generations to use the new technological power to achieve the older values." [30] Whether or not we accept this thesis fully, it is clear that the major problems of education today—financial, administrative, curricular—reflect the growing pains of a society undergoing profound transformations at home and facing new and confusing responsibilities of relationships with other peoples in all corners of the globe.

Interdependence and interpenetration of interests at home and abroad thus characterize American society today in contrast with the independent and relatively insulated America of yesterday. These novel conditions are responsible for the reappraisal of purpose and activity on all levels of education. They have brought to the fore new problems in the relations of the federal government to education in the states. They render acute the need for a reexamination of conventional patterns of administrative organization, particularly in metropolitan areas. They call for experimentation in curriculum construction and new methods of instruction. In short, the future of education in the United States is a challenge to the stout of heart and clear of vision.

[30] Kimball and McClellan, *op. cit.*, pp. 97-98. See, particularly, Chapter 5, on "Progressive Education: The Transition from Agrarian to Industrial America."

SUGGESTED READING

Alberty, Harold B., *Public Education in the 1960's: Trends and Issues* (Columbus, Ohio: Bode Memorial Lecture, Ohio State University, 1962).

Alberty, Harold B., and Alberty, Elsie J., *Reorganizing the High School Curriculum* (New York: The Macmillan Co., 3rd ed., 1962), Chapter 1.

Chandler, B. J., Stiles, Lindley J., and Kitsuse, John I., *Education in Urban Society* (New York: Dodd, Mead & Co., 1962), Chapters 1, 4, 8-11, 16.

Frank, Lawrence K., *The School as an Agent for Cultural Renewal* (Cambridge, Mass.: Harvard University Press, 1960).

Gardner, John, *Excellence: Can We Be Equal and Excellent Too?* (New York: Harper & Bros., 1961), Chapters I, VI, X-XII.

Hook, Sidney, *Education for Modern Man: A New Perspective* (New York: Alfred A. Knopf, 1963), Chapter I.

Kimball, Solon T., and McClellan, James E., *Education and the New America* (New York: Random House, 1962), Chapters 2-6.

Lerner, Max, *America as a Civilization* (New York: Simon & Schuster, 1957), Chapters VII-VIII.

Venn, Grant, *Man, Education and Work* (Washington, D.C.: American Council on Education, 1964).

INDEX